TWENTIETH CENTURY VIEWS

The aim of this series is to present the best in contemporary critical opinion on major authors, providing a twentieth century perspective on their changing status in an era of profound revaluation.

Maynard Mack, *Series Editor*
Yale University

FAULKNER

FAULKNER

A COLLECTION OF CRITICAL ESSAYS

Edited by

Robert Penn Warren

Prentice-Hall, Inc. 

Englewood Cliffs, N. J.

To R. W. B. and Nancy Lewis

 Library of Congress Catalog Card Number 66-28113. Printed in the United States of America—C. P30820, C30821

Current printing (last number):
10 9 8 7 6 5 4 3 2

Contents

Introduction: Faulkner: Past and Future

by Robert Penn Warren

It was in the Spring of 1929 that John Gould Fletcher, on a visit to Oxford University, where I was a student, gave me a copy of *Soldiers' Pay*. I had been out of the South for a long time—in a sense, in flight from the South—and at least half of me was oriented toward Greenwich Village and the Left Bank and not toward the Cumberland Valley in Tennessee; but at the same time I was, I suppose, homesick, and was making my first serious attempt at fiction, fiction with a setting in the part of the South where I had grown up. As a novel, *Soldiers' Pay* is no better than it should be, but it made a profound and undefinable impression on me. Then came, in the order of my reading, *The Sound and the Fury, As I Lay Dying, Sanctuary,* and *These Thirteen.*

What happened to me was what happened to almost all the book-reading Southerners I knew. They found dramatized in Faulkner's work some truth about the South and their own Southernness that had been lying speechless in their experience. Even landscapes and objects took on a new depth of meaning, and the human face, stance, and gesture took on a new dignity.

If you, in spite of your own sometimes self-conscious and willed Southernness, had been alienated by the official Southern pieties, alibis, and daydreams, the novels of Faulkner told you that there was, if you looked a second time, an intense, tormented, and brutal, but dignified and sometimes noble, reality beyond whatever façade certain people tried to hypnotize you into seeing. With this fiction there was not only the thrill of encountering strong literature. There was the thrill of seeing how a life that you yourself observed and were part of might move into the dimension of art. There was, most personally, the thrill of discovering your own relation to time and place, to life as you were destined to live it.

Even the images of degradation and violence—by which Southern pride, as officially exemplified by the DAR and the Chamber of Commerce, was so often shocked—seemed added certification of the reality of the novels: a perverse and perhaps self-indulgent delight, which you yourself recognized, in the dark complications of Southern life, a reflexive response to an unidentified tension and a smouldering rage beneath the surface of Southern life. What, in other words, the fiction of Faulkner gave was a release into life, into the sense of a grand and disturbing meaningfulness beneath the crust of life, into a moral reality beneath the crust of history.

I am offering this local and personal testimony, because I want to indicate that the first, powerful impact of Faulkner's work was by an immediate intuition, not by the exegesis of critics. The great images—which the novels contain, and are—spoke in their own always enigmatic and often ambiguous terms, by an awakening of awareness, by a kind of life-shock, long before the exegeses were written.

This is not to disparage the work of criticism. It is, rather, to do it proper honor by saying that it refers to, and fulfills, a fundamental relation between life and art. It re-orders, refines, reinterprets, and corrects the burden of the original intuitions; it may even make new intuitions possible. Criticism may not only make more available the life-meaning of art—that is, may make clearer how the art it deals with may be read as significant for life. It may also make more available the art-meaning of life. And I may add that it is in this perspective that the non-Southern, even non-American, critics have done their greatest service, for, not knowing Southern life firsthand, they have sometimes been freer to regard the fiction as a refraction in art of a special way of life and not as a mere documentation of that way of life.

Let us look back to the place and time when Faulkner began to write.

In a profound way Faulkner resembles Robert Frost, and his relation to the South resembles that of Robert Frost to New England. Both men seem so deeply demanded by their moment in history, at the very end of their respective cultures, that, forgetting the matter of genius, one is tempted to say that the moment is the man, and the man a role created by the moment. Both Faulkner and Frost were firmly and intransigently rooted in Old America, the America which was liquidated by the First World War, and both were even more firmly and intransigently rooted in a particular locality and in the history of a locality. Both made a characteristic drama out of the locality and the history, and both—most importantly of all—created a role, a *persona,* a mask that defined a relation to the locality and the world beyond, and the mask gave the voice. Both, that is, knowing the shape and feel of life in a particular place and time, felt the story of man-in-nature and of man-in-community, and could, therefore, take the particular locality as a vantage point from which to criticize modernity for its defective view of man-in-nature and man-in-community. Last of all, in a paradoxical way, the appeal that both Faulkner and Frost have for the world of modernity stems from the fact that they represent something strange and lost—something that the modern world is deeply ambivalent about and therefore cannot quite ignore, no matter how much it would like to ignore it.

To return specifically to Faulkner: He was of the generation of World War I; but except for a brief period as a Royal Air Force cadet pilot in Canada, he missed the war, and this fact, if we may judge from his fiction, may have marked him, in its own way, more decisively than even combat could have done. He missed participating in the great communal effort that made the new United States. It is now hard for us to realize that in 1917, despite the adventure of 1898, the shadow of the events of 1861-65 was real, and there was concern that the South might not feel committed to the national effort; and if, in a sense, Belleau Wood and the Argonne finished the work of Appomattox, and confirmed the new United States, Faulkner had no hand in that work. It may also be significant that, in the general context of things, Faulkner's effort to participate in the war was in the Royal Air Force and not in that of the United States. In any case, these things, the fact that he enlisted in Canada and that he missed combat, may have emphasized his sense of "outsideness" vis-à-vis the new nation and its new boom—the sense of outsideness that must have been one of the factors that drove him to create a whole social order and a history to account for his outsideness; and on this matter of outsideness, we must bear firmly in mind that, though he knew, hated, and wrote of it, he was especially outside of the New South—the South that so desperately aspired to be like Kansas City or Cleveland, to be, in simple terms, rich.

Faulkner did not see the massive and benumbing violence of trench warfare, nor did he even see the human price exacted for the aristocratic individualism of the air. So some dreams remained intact. And some deep personal bias toward violence, some admiration of the crazy personal gesture (like that of the Bayard in *Sartoris* who gets himself killed going after anchovies on a dare from a captured Yankee officer), and an idealized version of the South's old war, could persist untarnished and uncriticized by grisly actuality. Untarnished and uncriticized, that is, until the logic of his imagination had done its work. It is hard to believe that a man as subtly aware as Faulkner of the depth of the human soul could have been unconscious of the possibilities in himself. And it is harder to believe that, in the complex chemistry of personality and of artistic creation, Percy Grimm, of *Light in August,* who has missed World War I and who lives in a dream of sadistic violence masked by military rigor, and Hightower, who, with his romantic dream of the Civil War, counterpoints him in that novel, are not projections—and purgations—of potentials in Faulkner himself.

The South which Faulkner had grown up in—particularly the rural South—was cut-off, inward-turning, backward-looking. It was a culture frozen in its virtues and vices, and even for the generation that grew up after World War I, that South offered an image of massive immobility in all ways, an image, if one was romantic, of the unchangeableness of the human condition, beautiful, sad, painful, tragic—sunlight slanting over a mellow autumn field, a field the more precious for the fact that its yield had been meagre.

Even if one had read enough history to know that things *do* change, that even the romantic image in the head was the result of prior changes, that the image of an elegiac autumn implied the prior image of a summer of violent energies, the image still persisted, as though the process of history had led to this stubbornly, and preciously, held vision of non-history.

Strangely, this elegiac vision in which energy was sublimated into poetry was coupled with another vision, a sort of antithetical vision, in which violence irrationally erupted through the autumn serenity to create the characteristic "Southern" drama. And in another way the vision of the South was paradoxical. The South, with its immobility, seemed the true challenge to youthful energy that always demands change, and at the same time it was, as I have indicated, the place where history *had* been, had already fulfilled itself, had died—and could be contemplated.

But this vision of non-history is only half the matter. The First World War had brought America into a shocking cultural collision with Europe. For the South, the shock in the period was even greater than for the North. The South, withdrawn and somnolent, came into collision not only with Europe but with the North and the new order there. It is true that in some ways the effects of World War I seemed more obvious in the North; for instance, the great Northern industrial and financial establishment was now out of debt and dominant in the world, with all the consequences which this entailed. But such changes in the North were changes, not so much of kind, as of degree. In the South, on the other hand, the changes, even if often concealed, were often more radical and dramatic; there were profound tensions, deep inner divisions of loyalties, new ambitions set against old pieties, new opportunities, new despairs, new moral problems, or rather, old problems which had never been articulated and confronted—all the things that stir a man, or a society, to utterance. The South, then, offered the classic situation of a world stung and stirred, by cultural shock, to create an art, in order to objectify and grasp the nature of its own inner drama.

The very style of this new utterance in the South is instructive. There was, of course, a strain of realism in the South, best exemplified in that period by Ellen Glasgow and T. S. Stribling, but this strain was not dominant. A variant of symbolism was often characteristic, as might be expected from the nearly irreconcilable tensions and the deep inwardness of the drama with which it dealt. Furthermore, as a fact to be associated with the tendency toward symbolism, Southern writing was often radical in method—more radical by and large, than the writing in other parts of the country. Its radicalism often had a European orientation, its ancestors in Dostoevsky, Conrad, Baudelaire, Proust, Joyce, and Yeats; and the Americans it found most compelling were usually those with a European bias—James Eliot, Pound, Hart Crane. If in the moment of cultural shock Southern writers were impelled to explore the traditional basis of their world, the language and techniques which many of them used for that exploration were antitraditional. This fact, in itself, implies the very spiritual tensions in the work; for a language and a technique are not mere instruments, they are gauges of attitude, instruments of evaluation and modes of discovery, and even against a man's will may modify what he makes of his own world. At the same time, as another point of tension, in contrast to the sophistication of technique, the folk tradition, especially folk humor, was very much alive for many Southern writers. We must recall, as the most obvious example, that Faulkner is a great humorist, in the line of Mark Twain, as well as a great technical virtuoso.

As a technican, Faulkner, except for his peers, Melville and James, is the most profound experimenter in the novel that America has produced. But the experiments were developed out of—that is, were not merely applied to—an anguishing research into the Southern past and the continuing implications of that past. We may remark, for instance, that the period when Faulkner developed his experiments is the period when his fundamental insights were achieved, when he pierced the crust of his traditional material, when he most deeply dramatized the key moral issues of Southern life. In that strange interfusion which seems to be characteristic of such a situation of cultural shock, the complexity of issues demanded the technique, but at the same time, the issues would not have been available, been visible in fact, without the technique. The cultural shock and the technical development go hand in hand.

The great period of Faulkner's achievement—from *The Sound and the Fury* to *The Hamlet*—overlaps, too, with the Depression and the time of the premonitory shadows of World War II, with another time, that is, of deep cultural shock. The tension and changes in this time were acute. This is not to say that Faulkner specifically took the Depression as a subject, but it is to say that the Depression accentuated the issues of time and change which Faulkner had already located as seminal for him. The sense of the unchangeableness of the human condition which had characterized the life of the rural South even after World War I, was now, suddenly, with the Depression, changed. Conversation turned to the question of what could be done to "change" things, even if for some people the desired change was, paradoxically enough, to change things back to their old unchangeableness; to escape, to phrase it another way, from *history-as-lived* back to *history-as-contemplated;* from *history-as-action* to *history-as-ritual.* But even to change back to unchangeableness would be a kind of change. There was, then, no way to avoid the notion of change; you had to take a bite, willy-nilly, of the apple from the mysterious tree that had sprung up in the Confederate garden.

We can, in fact, think of the poles of Faulkner's work as *history-as-action* and *history-as-ritual.* We may even see this polarity as related to another which he was so fond of—and so indefinite in the formulation of—the polarity of fact and truth. We may see it, too, in the drama of his outraged Platonism—outraged by the world and the flesh.

Faulkner began writing, of course, in the full tide of the Coolidge Boom, but the crash had long since come—in October 1929—by the time *l'affaire Faulkner* was presented to general attention with the publication, in 1931, of *Sanctuary.* Certainly, the assumptions and tone of Faulkner's work would have seemed irrelevant in the context of the Boom; in the context of the Depression they often seemed, not irrelevant, but inimical.

In the great objective world, in a context of human suffering, issues of the most profound social, political, and moral importance were being fought out, and it was only natural that practical men, if they happened to have read or have heard of Faulkner, should regard his work as merely a pathological vision happily distant from serious concerns—unless, of course, it could be used as evidence of the need for an enlarged PWA program or free shoes in that barefoot world. It was, as I have said, only natural that practical men, if they read Faulkner at all, should have read him in this spirit, and the fact is not significant.

What is, however, significant—and significant in a way far transcending the fate of the work of Faulkner—is that, by and large, the world of "impractical" men, of intellectuals, betrayed its trust by trying to be "practical," resigned its function of criticizing and interpreting the demands of the practical world, and often became a comic parody—comic because dealing with the shadow not the substance of power and action—of the world of practicality. What could not be converted in a mechanical, schematic, and immediate way into an accepted formula for social action was interpreted as "reactionary," "decadent," "gothic," "fascist," or merely "Southern."

All these elements were, in fact, in Faulkner's work. The work was certainly Southern to the bone, and it was easy to find elements in Southern life, and in Faulkner's work, which, taken in isolation, might suggest the word *fascist,* and all the rest. For instance, the delusions of a Gail Hightower might provide the compost for breeding fascism, and there was, thirty-odd years ago, as now, many a Percy Grimm in the South, a type not too unlike a certain kind of fascist bully-boy. But the mere presence, in isolation, is not what is important. What is important is the context, the dialectic, in which such elements appear. We have only to look at the role of Hightower in *Light in August,* or to remember that Faulkner prided himself on Percy Grimm as his invention of a Nazi Stormtrooper. Or we may set the distortions some critics made of the role of Negro characters in Faulkner's work over against the role Negroes actually play in the work. The fact that meaning is always a matter of relation should be clear to anyone—though it was not clear to certain well-intentioned men who had sacrificed their intelligence in the cause of what they regarded as virtue.

This is not to say that Faulkner was the victim of a conspiracy among card-carrying, or even fellow-traveling, book reviewers. A climate can be more lethal than a conspiracy, and the climate was that of para-Marxist neo-naturalism, with the doctrine of art-as-illustration—debates concerning which we can find embalmed, for example, in the proceedings of the American Writers' Congress. Since such "leftism" had become intellectually chic, the new attitudes were assimilated with no pain and little reflection by college professors, ladies' clubs, news-minded literary editors, and book reviewers who a few short years before might have attacked Faulkner merely because he was dirty and not very optimistic. In the new context, the combination of tragic intensity, ribald and rambunctious comedy, violence and pathology, Negro field hands and Mississippi aristocrats, old-fashioned rhetoric and new-fangled time shifts, symbolism and obscurity, amounted to outrage—and probably to fascism.

Even if *Sartoris, The Sound and the Fury,* and *As I Lay Dying* were commercial failures, a certain number of reviewers had recognized talent, but as the new decade took shape, the talent, even when recognized, was often recognized more grudgingly—or even with the sense that the presence of talent compounded the original outrage. This clearly was not a literature in tune with the New Deal, the new post office art, the new social conscience, the new Moscow trials, or the new anything. It was, simply, new: that is, created. And in some circles, at all times, for a thing to be truly created, is to be outrageous.[1]

[1] For the record, and for their honor, it must be pointed out that some of the critics most firmly grounded in, and best informed about, Marxism did not fall into the trap. For instance, that brilliant and seminal critic, Kenneth Burke, the whole thrust of whose work was counter to such bigotry, and who, in 1939, after war had begun, remarked in a letter to the present writer that one could still learn more about men "from tropes than from tropisms." And there is Malcolm Cowley, the differences in whose background and philosophical and political assumptions did not prevent the long struggle of imagination which led to his editing of *The Portable Faulkner.*

Some documentation of this struggle is to be found in the series of reviews (*Pylon, Absalom, Absalom!, The Wild Palms, The Hamlet, Go Down, Moses* which Cowley did in *The New Republic.* Cowley's main objection is repeated several times—that there is some sort of split in Faulkner, "a lack of proportion between stimulus and response," as he says of *Pylon,* and in other terms, about *Absalom, Absalom!,* which, he says, falls "short of the powerful mood it might have achieved." In fact, even as late as 1940, in reviewing *The Hamlet,* Cowley says that "one admires the author while feeling that most of his books are Gothic ruins, impressive only by moonlight." By 1942, however, in reviewing *Go Down, Moses,* he can say that "there is no other American writer who has been so consistently misrepresented by his critics, including myself." Then after an attack on the views of Maxwell Geismar and Granville Hicks, he says Faulkner is "after Hemingway and perhaps Dos Passos, the most considerable novelist of this generation."

The literary criticism of the Depression slipped without any grinding of gears into that of the War period. The literary criticism of the War period, stimulated by the War in Spain, antedated Pearl Harbor by several years. The atmosphere of war simply added a new element, and a new justification, to the attitudes of the Depression, and added to the list of writers to be taken by men of good will as irrelevant, or inimical, to social progress. As the shadow of war grew, critics more and more found reprehensible all literary work that emphasized lags between our professions of national faith and our performance. In fact, it sometimes seemed that, with the pressure of events, the rise of patriotism, and the exigencies of propaganda, it was less important to clean up our messes than to sweep them under the rug. If America was the temple, as well as the arsenal, of democracy, it should be presented, for the sake of a higher truth and by a higher law, in the most effective way possible, with *son et lumière*—appropriate music and strategically placed floodlights for tourists, who were to be admitted to the spectacle only after the vulgar, factual glare of day had been mercifully withdrawn.

In a way somewhat unfair to what he actually said, Archibald MacLeish's essay "The Irresponsibles" was generally taken as the prime statement of this attitude. But MacLeish did see and deplore a split between literature and what he regarded as political responsibility—an attitude which he put more precisely in another essay "Post-War Writers and Pre-War Readers" [2] where he specifically condemned Barbusse, Ford, Hemingway, Dos Passos, Remarque, and Aldington because "what they wrote, however noble it may have been as literature, however true to them as a summary of their personal experience, was disastrous as education for a generation which would be obliged to face the threat of fascism in its adult years." [3] Faulkner, of course, became—or rather, long before, had become—the most obvious target for this attitude; and the

[2] *The New Republic*, June 10, 1940.

[3] There was a kind of comic justice in the fact that MacLeish was occasionally tarred with his own brush. Oscar Cargill, in a book called *Intellectual America: Ideas on the March* (1941) did not forgive him, despite "The Irresponsibles," and pilloried him among those he calls the "Decadents"—a group including Eliot, Hart Crane, and Pound. Cargill admitted that it was "hard to find four other poets with equal importance, but went on to say that, "Like Naturalism, Decadence, has exerted an enfeebling influence on American character . . ." "The fall of France," he adds elsewhere, "was brought about in part (as Mr. MacLeish must realize) by decadent intellectualism."

This book, *Intellectual America*, is undoubtedly one of the curiosities of our (or any) literature. It also has a less morbid value as a reference book, in that it encyclopedically commemorates, in a naked and simple form, all the clichés of thought and expression of a decade. Mr. Cargill desperately wanted literature to serve the good of mankind, but having not the foggiest notion of what literature is, he couldn't easily figure out what good it might serve—not any good from the "Naturalists," nor the "Decadents," nor the "Primitivists," nor the "Intelligentsia," (with a sub-head for "Modern Cynicism") nor the "Freudians." Among those Polonian (and Procrustean) categories Faulkner is crammed among the "Primitivists."

notion that he was a liability for which American patriots should apologize, persisted even in the editorial in which the New York *Times* commented on the Nobel Prize:

> His [Faulkner's] field of vision is concentrated on a society that is too often vicious, depraved, decadent, corrupt. Americans must fervently hope that the award by a Swedish jury and the enormous vogue of Faulkner's works in Latin America and on the European Continent, especially in France, does not mean that foreigners admire him because he gives them the picture of American life they believe to be typical and true. There has been too much of that feeling lately, again especially in France. Incest and rape may be common pastimes in Faulkner's "Jefferson, Miss." but they are not elsewhere in the United States.

To return to the time of the coming of World War II, the notion that Faulkner's complicated techniques were somehow associated with reprehensible content anticipated a line of criticism brought to bear on Pound's poetry after his capture and imprisonment. Back in 1940, Percy Boynton had commented on such a connection in Faulkner's work by affirming that "the technique is simple and the content more lucid in those tales which have the greater normality," and becomes "more intricate and elusive in the tales of abnormality," and that "technique becomes a compensation for content as content sinks in the social scale." By this line of reasoning the prose of the famous corn cob scene would, of course, make that of *Finnegan's Wake* look like a selection from *The Bobbsey Twins*.[4]

Faulkner's trouble with the patriots was compounded by two other factors. First, he had no truck with any obvious programs for social salvation. Steinbeck and Caldwell, though they both showed abuses and degradation in American life, showed them with a diagnosis and the hint of a quick cure that was fashionable in the reviewing trade. Second, Faulkner was Southern. Of course, Wolfe was Southern too; but nobody ever took him for a fascist; he showed none of the dark ambivalences of Quentin Compson, off at Harvard, telling the story of Sutpen to the innocent Canadian. Furthermore, Wolfe hymned America in terms reminiscent of, it was said, Whitman.

A little later, with the War well started, *The Valley of Decision,* by Marcia Davenport, was widely hailed as a major contribution to literature and to the war effort. A little later still, *Strange Fruit,* by Lillian Smith, in the moment of a new conscience on the race question stimulated by the need for black factory hands and black troops and by A. Philip Randolph's March-on-Washington movement, was received with hosannahs by a chorus of critics led by Eleanor Roosevelt. By this time Faulk-

[4] In the section from *Love and Death in the American Novel,* by Irving Howe, which is quoted in this volume under "Notes and Comments," Irving Howe uses the same kind of argument about style in passages where Faulkner writes of characters of mixed Negro and white blood.

ner's most recent book, *Go Down, Moses,* which also had something to do with conscience and the race question, was forgotten, and by 1945 all seventeen of his books were out of print.

The great watershed for Faulkner's reputation in the United States is usually, and quite correctly, taken to be the publication of *The Portable Faulkner* in 1946. Several factors contributed to the effect of the *Portable.* First, Cowley's Introduction,[5] developing but substantially modifying a line of interpretation originally suggested, in 1939, by George Marion O'Donnell,[6] persuasively insisted on the significant coherence of Faulkner's work taken as a whole. Second, the selection itself was made with taste and cunning to support the thesis. Third, the fact that the reputation of Cowley himself as associated with the "left wing," as critic and as editor of *The New Republic* (in which *The Sound and the Fury* had been reviewed, though not by Cowley, under the head "Signifying Nothing"), gave a certain piquancy, and in some circles, an air of authority and respectability to his estimate of Faulkner. Fourth, the time was ripe.

By 1946 the climate had changed—if not for the better, at least for a difference. With Hitler dead in his bunker and the Duce hung by his heels at the filling station in Milan, and with the marriage of American liberalism and Joseph Stalin running on the rocks, a new kind of idiocy became fashionable and raced forward to fulfillment in Joe McCarthy; and Faulkner no longer served the old function of scapegoat of all work. He had survived—endured, in fact—and was part of the landscape, like a hill or a tree.

I do not know what force the college classrooms of the country exert in making or breaking literary reputations, but in the period of the late thirties and early forties, when professors of American literature and of the then new-fangled American Studies were often inclined to speak of Steinbeck's *In Dubious Battle* and of Howard Fast's *Citizen Tom Paine* in the tones of hushed reverence once reserved for the works of Sophocles, Faulkner had received short shrift. After the War, with the horde of returning GI's, the process backfired. As one GI put it to me, "I been robbed!" He reported that in the good university where he had pernoctated before the call to arms, his class in American literature had dedicated six weeks to *The Grapes of Wrath* and thirty minutes to Faulkner, thirty minutes being long enough to allow the professor to document from *A Rose for Emily,* the only work investigated, that Faulkner was a cryptofascist. Such young men immersed themselves in the work of Faulkner with ferocious attention. As far as I could determine, they had little of that kind of romantic disillusion that was reputed to have been common after World War I. They were motivated, rather, by a disgust

[5] P. 34.
[6] P. 23.

for simple, schematic, two-dimensional views of the world. Many of them had had, first-hand, a shocking acquaintance with the depths and paradoxes of experience, and now literary renderings that did not honor their experience were not for them. Furthermore, as a corollary, they, having been caught in the great dehumanizing machine of war, were forced to reflect on their own relation to the modern world, not in terms of political and social arrangements, but in terms of identity itself. That is, they found in the works of Faulkner and in the method of his works something that corresponded to, and validated, their own experience.

Returning GI's did not, however, exclusively constitute the new and expanding readership of Faulkner, though their view of the world may have had something in common with that of some nonmilitary citizens of the United States, or with that of the Japanese, French, and Italians, military and nonmilitary, who took his fiction to their hearts. It can, perhaps, be plausibly argued that Faulkner is one of the few contemporary fiction writers—perhaps the only American—whose work is to any considerable degree concerned with the central issues of our time, who really picks at the scab of our time, in the way that, in varying degrees of intensity and scale, Melville, Dostoevsky, Kafka, Conrad, Proust, Eliot, Yeats, and Camus, also do.

In thinking of such a question, we must remember that being topical and being central are two very different things. In the 1930s—as now—there were battalions of writers in the United States who programmatically tried to will themselves into tune with the Zeitgeist. The trouble was that, almost to a man, they confused the Zeitgeist with current newspaper headlines and lead reviews in the Sunday book sections. The Zeitgeist may speak through the headlines, just as it may speak through a new metric or a theory of corporate structure; but we cannot therefore assume that the headlines *are* the Zeitgeist. Rather, some writer who most obviously seems to be in tune with the Zeitgeist may be merely caught in a superficial eddy of history, which often, as Melville, in "The Conflict of Convictions," puts it, "spins against the way it drives." By the same token, the writer who seems alienated and withdrawn may appear, in the light of history, as central. For instance, at the moment when Milton, blind, defeated and obscure, was composing *Paradise Lost*, would anybody have thought him central?

Perhaps what the returning GI's found in Faulkner is what had drawn other readers, too. Perhaps the blind, blank, dehumanized and dehumanizing, depersonalized and depersonalizing modern war is the appropriate metaphor for our age—or for one aspect of our age—and paraphrasing Clausewitz, we may say that war is merely an extension of our kind of peace. In that case, we are all GI's, and any reader may come, in mufti, to Faulkner's work with the same built-in questions as the GI of 1946, seeking the same revelatory images of experience. Perhaps the images of violence, in which Faulkner's work abounds, are, to adapt a famous remark by Poe, not of the South but of the soul; and perhaps their Southernness has such a deep appeal because this order of violence, with the teasing charm of antiquity, is associated with the assertion of, or the quest for, selfhood, the discovery of a role, or the declaration of a value, in the context of anonymous violence or blankness. Perhaps all the images in Faulkner's work of the mystic marriage of the hunter and the hunted have a meaning more metaphysical than anthropological; and all the images of isolation, self-imposed by a wrong relation to nature or to history, or visited blindly on the individual, are to be taken as images of the doom that we all, increasingly in our time, must struggle against; and the images of Southern alienation are only images of Everyman facing one of the possibilities in his world. Perhaps we see in the agonies, longings, and nobilities of the unimportant people like Charlotte Rittenmeyer or the convict of *Wild Palms,* like Joe Christmas, like Ruby of *Sanctuary,* like Dilsey, or even like the idiot Snopes, some image of the meaningfulness of the individual effort and experience over against the machine of the world.

It is not only the implications of the objective dramatizations in Faulkner's work—character and situation—which have attracted readers. The sense of the work's being a subjective dramatization has been there too—the sense that the world created so powerfully represents a projection of an inner experience of the author somehow not too different from one the reader might know all too well. Faulkner has a remarkable ear for speech—either in dialogue or in the long narrative monologue, like that of Jason, for instance, or that of Ratliff in "Spotted Horses," the early version of the horse auction scene of *The Hamlet.* But generally Faulkner's narratives are sustained not by such reported, or ventriloquist, voices, but by a single dominant voice[7]—the highly personal style which, for better or worse, seems to be the index of the subjective drama, and which guarantees to the reader that the story is truly alive in the deepest way. As Albert Thibaudet says of Proust, the tide of his sentences carries with it as it advances the creative élan that gives it life; or as Monique Nathan puts it in her book about Faulkner, there is something "almost liturgical" in the function of his style. And we might add that, to take the Aristotelian terms, a novel of Faulkner combines the drama (or narrative) and the dithyramb, the latter being the personal medium in which the impersonal renderings of experience are sustained.

The mask-like, taciturn and withdrawn quality of Faulkner the man, and the impersonality of his fiction, compared, for example, with that of Wolfe, Hemingway, or Fitzgerald, seems, paradoxically, to attest to a deep, secret involvement, to the possibility of a revelation which the

[7] The transfer of the horse auction scene from Ratliff to the "voice" in the novel affords a beautiful case history of this point.

reader might wrest from the Delphic darkness. Malraux has hinted at this inner involvement, surmising that Faulkner would often imagine his scenes before imagining his characters, and that a work would not be for him "une histoire" the development of which would determine situation, but quite the contrary, springing from the encounter of faceless characters unknown to him, shrouded figures charged with possibility. If I read Malraux aright, he is implying that the germ of a work might lie in such an archetypal scene—a flash—in which all else, story and character, would be hidden; the scene being a living, intimate metaphor direct from the author's depth. There is some support for Malraux's surmise in the fact that *The Sound and the Fury,* according to Faulkner's testimony, developed from the vision of a little girl's muddy drawers, and *Light in August,* from the vision of "a young woman, pregnant, walking along a strange road." The relation of the author to such a vision is directly personal, springing unbidden, as I have said, from the depth; the vision like a poultice, draws the characters and the action out of him. To put it another way, the vision, in the first place, is only the projection of, and focus for, that subjective drama which, though distorted beyond all recognition, may become the story, the objective drama that will carry the mystic burden of the secret involvement from which it springs.

It would be misleading to imply that there is now a massive unanimity of praise for Faulkner's work. Over the years various kinds of attack have been mounted against it, but the most important line of adverse criticism now with us is that Faulkner is basically confused in thought and unclear in style. The best advertised exponents of this view appeared a number of years ago, one being Clifton Fadiman, in his review of *Absalom, Absalom!* in *The New Yorker* in 1936,[8] and the other being Alfred Kazin, whose *On Native Ground* appeared in 1942. Though Kazin recognized Faulkner's powers of invention, and stylistic and technical resourcefulness, he complained that Faulkner has "no primary and design-like conception of the South, that his admiration and acceptance and disgust operated together in his mind"; that "as a participant in the communal myth of the South's tradition and decline, Faulkner was curiously dull, furiously commonplace, and often meaningless, suggesting some ambiguous irresponsibility and exasperated sullenness of mind, some distant atrophy or indifference"; that his work does not "spring from a conscious and procreative criticism of society"; that there is a "gap between the deliberation of his effects, the intensity of his every conception, and the besetting and depressing looseness, the almost sick passivity, of his basic meaning and purpose"; and that his complicated technique "seems to spring from an obscure and profligate confusion, a manifest absence of purpose, rather than from an elaborate but coherent aim."

[8] Reprinted, in part, in the section "Notes and Comments," in this volume, p. 289.

In all fairness it should be said that in later years Kazin's attitude has mellowed greatly, a change of which I first became aware at a round table on Faulkner at Columbia University, provoked by the award of the Nobel Prize, where Kazin eloquently defended Faulkner's work against the old charge of being primarily a neurotic manifestation. Even so, though more willing, with the years, to recognize the importance of Faulkner's work and to be more lavish of compliments, Kazin is still distressed by what he terms Faulkner's "attempt to will his powerful material into a kind of harmony that it does not really possess." This remark appears in an excellent essay on *Light in August*,[9] which Kazin is willing to call "great" (the essay appearing as a book entitled *Twelve Original Essays on Great American Novels*), but which he says is "somewhat more furious in expression than meaningful in content." This essay does offer a brilliant and important treatment of Joe Christmas as the "incarnation of 'man,' "—but at the same time finds him "compelling rather than believable." So, here reappears, though in a more sympathetic and guarded form, the same objection that had appeared in *On Native Ground*: the objection that there is a gap between the talent ("compelling") and the meaning ("believable"), that the polarities and contradictions of the material have not been "really" put into "harmony."

There is no clear and objective way to settle this question, any more than there is to settle the similar question raised by E. M. Forster's charge, in *Abinger Harvest,* that Conrad "is misty in the middle as well as at the edges, that the secret casket contains a vapor rather than a jewel." In such cases, we usually come to a matter of temperament, training, and cast of mind. What many readers prize in Faulkner's work is often the fact of the polarities, contradictions, and inharmonious elements which they would take to be "really" inherent in life deeply regarded and which offer the creative spirit its most fruitful challenge—though the challenge is to a battle that can never be finally won. Kazin, however, would still seem to imply that the process of creation is much more deductive, that it should spring from an "elaborate but coherent aim," that good work should "spring from a conscious and procreative criticism of society . . . from some absolute knowledge."

Clearly, "absolute knowledge" is not what Faulkner's work springs from, or pretends to achieve. It springs from, shall we say, a need—not a program or even an intention or a criticism of society—to struggle with the painful incoherences and paradoxes of life, and with the contradictory and often unworthy impulses and feelings in the self, in order to achieve meaning; but to struggle, in the awareness that meaning, if achieved, will always rest in perilous balance, and that the great undergirding and overarching meaning of life is in the act of trying to create

[9] P. 147.

meaning through struggle. To a mind that is basically schematic, deductive, and rationalistic, with an appetite for "absolute knowledge," such a writer as Faulkner is bound to generate difficulties and severe discontents. But the service which a critic with such a cast of mind may do is important; he may set bounds to enthusiasms, may drive readers to define what kinds (if any) of resolution and unity have actually been achieved, may drive readers to try to determine how much of what they admire is actually there in a given work and how much is a projection of their own needs and prejudices.

But a critic, like a writer, must finally take the risk of his own formulations—this, despite the favorite delusion of all critics, who are after all human beings, that their formulations are somehow exempt from the vicissitudes of life which the novel or poem must endure. As a matter of fact, the moment a critic sets pen to paper, or finger to keyboard, the novel or poem itself becomes the silent and sleepless critic of the critic, and it is just possible that the split which Kazin sees between talent and achievement in Faulkner, between furious expression and meaningless content, indicates not so much a split in the thing criticized as in the critic—a split in the critic himself between a mind, with the laudable appetite for "absolute knowledge," and an artistic sensibility which allows for the sincere but troubling appreciation of "talent," "technique," and "effects," and for isolated instances of pathos and drama.

I have referred to Kazin because he puts the argument against Faulkner more fully and effectively than any other critic. But the argument is an old one. It had appeared, troublingly, in Cowley's early reviews. It had appeared in Wyndham Lewis' savage and funny essay, "The Moralist with a Corn-Cob," in his *Men Without Art* (1934). There Lewis has good sport at the expense of Faulkner's style, but finds little beyond the façade of "ill-selected words." The characters, he says, "are as heavily energized as the most energetic could wish," but they are "energized and worked-up to no purpose—all 'signifying nothing,' " and the "destiny" or "doom" behind Faulkner's fiction is merely a fraudulent device for operating the puppets. Sean O'Faolain, more than twenty years later, takes the same line—the style is inflated and inaccurate, is fustian, not the "artist's meaningful language" but the "demagogue's careless, rhetorical and often meaningless language," and all of this is an index to an "inward failure to focus clearly," to a lack of intelligence, to an inner "daemon" rather than a proper subject, to "ideals that he can vaguely feel but never express."

Somewhat more recently as an example of a somewhat different line of criticism, we may take an essay by Walter J. Slatoff, "The Edge of Order: The Pattern of Faulkner's Rhetoric," which maintains that Faulkner's "temperamental response rather than any theories of ideas and particular torments" are what the author "trusts to produce order in his art"—that the art represents an overabundance of oxymorons, contradictions, oppositions, polarities, which remain unresolved, that, in treating Isaac McCaslin, Faulkner has made "the choice which he can rarely resist, and which . . . seriously limits his stature, the choice not to choose." I have said that this line of criticisms, which in various forms not infrequently appears, is different from that of Lewis, Kazin, and O'Faolain: but it is different only in approach, for in the end it amounts to much the same thing, turgidity of style and inner meaninglessness, as temperament or obsession or daemon takes over the role of ideas, ideals, brains, intelligence, or "absolute knowledge."

I must refer to one more variant, and an important one, of the criticism that Faulkner's work lacks intelligence and meaning. This is the view that he has not been able to understand the nature of our age and therefore is not relevant for us who live in it. Faulkner, according to Norman Podhoretz,[10] who best exemplifies this line of attack, has entirely missed the Enlightenment, with its "qualities of reasonableness, moderation, compromise, tolerance, sober choice—in short, the anti-apocalyptic style of life brought into the modern world by the middle class." Faulkner "doesn't even hate" the middle class "accurately," his Jason being as much a creature of compulsion as Quentin, without "sober choice," etc. Having missed the Enlightenment and not understanding the middle class, Faulkner really lacks a sense of history, and therefore cannot record the real shock of change in modernity. For instance, what has the "Glory celebrated in Yoknapatawpha got to do with the Korean War[11] . . . a war uninspiring, nay meaningless, to the Yoknapatawpha mind, and thrilling only to children of the Enlightenment who understand its moral sublimity?" Faulkner has, in *A Fable* (and we are given to understand in his other works too) taken refuge in "Larger Considerations," and an apocalyptic view of life and literary style, because he fails to understand the real issues and values of modernity, including the sublimity of the Korean War.

Podhoretz's essay was prompted by *A Fable,* and I must say that I agree with him that this novel is, finally, a colossal failure and a colossal bore, and that it is as confused in conception as in execution. What I do not agree with is that it represents merely an extension of Faulkner's work. It may well be true—and I assume that it is true—that Faulkner intended *A Fable* to be an extension, and a generalization of the *meaning,* of his previous work, and to serve as a basis of exegesis for his work. And it is true that themes and ideas do come over from the past. But there is a difference, and a crucial one, between *A Fable* and the other work (with

[10] "William Faulkner and the Problem of War: His Fable of Faith," p. 243.
[11] The essay appeared in 1954.

the exception of *Intruder in the Dust,* of which I shall speak later). *A Fable* is abstractly conceived; it is an idea deductively worked out—and at critical moments, blurred out. By the very absoluteness of the failure, however, *A Fable* indicates, not so much the limit of, as the nature of, Faulkner's success. Faulkner, like Antaeus, could fight only with his feet on the ground—on home ground; he had to work toward meaning through the complexity and specificity of a literal world in which he knew his way about, as a man knows his way about his own house without thinking how he gets from one room to another; only in that world could he find the seminal images that would focus his deepest feelings into vision. And this process implies something about the kind of meaning, and kind of glory, he would assume possible in life; and remembering Podhoretz's remark that "lack of ideas is no virtue in a novelist," we may say that, be that as it may, an idea any novelist has that does not come with some tang of experience, some earth yet clinging to the roots, or at least one drop of blood dripping from it, has no virtue for a novelist. Ideas without the mark of their experiential origin can only, to use Eliot's word, "violate" the consciousness of such a novelist as Faulkner. In *A Fable,* an idea "violated" the consciousness of Faulkner.

Podhoretz ends his essay by wondering "whether the time will ever come again when a writer will be able to dismiss politics in favor of the Large Considerations without sounding like a chill echo from a dead world." Again I must register agreement with the critic, not with his generalization but with the implication that Faulkner is an a-political writer. It is really strange that in his vast panorama of society in a state where politics is the blood, bone, sinew, and passion of life, and the most popular sport, Faulkner has almost entirely omitted, not only a treatment of the subject, but references to it. It is easy to be contemptuous of politics anywhere, and especially easy in Jackson, Mississippi, but it is not easy to close one's eyes to the cosmic comedy enacted in that State House; and it is not easy to understand how Faulkner, with his genius for the absurd, even the tearfully absurd, could have rejected this subject. Unless, as may well have been the case, contempt overcame the comic sense. Furthermore, in *A Fable* and *Intruder in the Dust,* novels that do impinge on political realities, Faulkner seems to have little grasp of them. In *A Fable* the failure is at root one of tone—we don't know how we are to take his fable in relation to the "realities." In *Intruder in the Dust,* Faulkner, like many other Southerners, black and white, including the present writer at one time in his life, may have been beguiled by the hope that the South, on its own responsibility, might learn to deal with the Negro in justice and humanity. The fact was that such a hope, in the face of the political realities (as a reflex, perhaps, from economic and certain other realities), and with the lack of courageous and clear-headed leadership, was a fond delusion. On this point, Faulkner was as much out of touch with the political nature of his own world as Camus was with the *colons* of Algeria when he tried to address them.

More significant than that hope was, however, the idea, expressed by Gavin Stevens, of a cultural homogeneity of Negro Southerners and white Southerners that would prevail against the rest of society. The whole idea is foggy in the extreme, and is foggily expressed, but, as I read it, it implies that the shared experience of the races in the South, for all the bitterness and tension, has created a basis for reconciliation. Some Negroes, in fact, have held this view—or hope—and many whites. But this bond, whatever its force or meaning, which is referred to by Gavin Stevens, came from a rural, individualistic society, or from a town life which still carried its values over from such a society. What Gavin Stevens (and Faulkner, and many other Southerners, white and black) did not do was to take a look at the Negro slums in the great Northern cities, and see there the shape of the future in the South as the mechanization of farming, and other factors, drove, and drew, the Negro from the land, and, in fact, subtly but deeply changed the nature of the whites who remained on the land. Furthermore, an "homogeneity" would, in the world of practical affairs, come too late to have any effect—certainly too late to seal off Mississippi from Freedom Riders, workers for CORE, SNCC, and SCLC, to prevent the founding of the Freedom Democratic Party, or to halt U. S. marshals at the border.

Gavin Stevens was talking some twenty years ago, and had not had the benefit of instruction from this morning's newspaper. It is easy for us, with the newspaper in hand and with the grass green, to say that we heard that grass growing. We can see things that Gavin could not, or would not, see, and among those things is one that has a certain comedy about it. In the South even in the small Mississippi towns like Philadelphia, McComb, Canton, Grenada, Greenwood, and Oxford, it will probably be the middle-class business men, the group for whom Faulkner cherished no particular fondness, and who, in Oxford, were not particularly enthusiastic about closing their stores and offices for his funeral, who, not from moral virtue or any theory of homogeneity, but from stark self-interest, once the message gets through to them that "nigger-trouble" is bad for business, will take the lead in working out some sort of reasonably decent racial settlement.

Faulkner was a-political, and he was, as Podhoretz puts it, "out of touch with contemporary experience"—if by contemporary experience we mean experience at the level Podhoretz specifies. But this leaves us with some troubling questions. For one, if Faulkner, because he is a-political, is not relevant for us, why do we still read such a-political works as *Moby Dick, The Scarlet Letter, Madame Bovary, A la récherche du temps perdu,* and *The Portrait of a Lady*—or an outright anti-political work like Shakespeare's *Troilus and Cressida*?[12] Or do we read them merely from

[12] A case might be made out that the politics of Shakespeare's History Plays and

academic interest, plus the incidental pleasure of being able to say that they are not "relevant"? There is indeed a problem of relevance, of what makes a work of literature specially valuable for one age and not for another. Works are not arranged in a great museum in a Platonic outer space drenched evenly by the chill white light of Eternity, bearing placards to indicate category and value. They do have a relation to the continuing life process, a relation of enormous complexity, certainly of greater complexity than is hinted at in the essay now under discussion. In fact, the whole argument for "relevance" as put in this essay has, as Podhoretz says of the work of Hemingway, Faulkner, and Dos Passos, taken on "that slightly stilted archaic look" of an old photograph—and the archaic look, in this case, is that of the 1930s, when it was fashionable to assert that a wide assortment of writers, including Flaubert, Proust, Frost, and T. S. Eliot,[13] were not "relevant." But those writers have, somehow, survived, and we even have the comic fact that Faulkner, who in those days was often rejected as the most irrelevant of all, was passionately read in places as different as Tokyo and Paris for the simple reason that he was taken to have something to say to the modern soul. The fact is that man, though a political animal, is many other kinds of animal, too. He is, even, a human animal.

I do not accept the basic thrust of the argument of Lewis, Kazin, O'Faolain, Podhoretz *et al.*, but I do think that these critics point to what might be called the defects of Faulkner's virtues, and I think that their views help to locate and limit some of the critical problems appropriate to Faulkner's work; for always when a reputation is resurrected from the dead—and some twenty years ago, in America at least, Faulkner seemed to be consigned to the shades—there tends to be, among the faithful as well as the newly redeemed, especially among the latter, the notion that the final revelation is at hand. Now, not only in the South but elsewhere, there is, clearly, the atmosphere of a cult about Faulkner, as there was about Eliot in the dark days of the Marxist dispensation, or about Pound in the period of rehabilitation.

Something of this tone appears in a letter by Russell Roth in *Faulkner Studies*:[14] "I have the feeling that many critics—most of them, in fact—would prefer not to see that what he [Faulkner] has been driving at . . . what Faulkner says—is saying—cuts the feet out from under us; it flatly denies, or contradicts, or takes issue with most of our fundamental and

---

Roman plays is really nothing more than a facade, and that they, too, are basically anti-political.

[13] The game was carried so far that even a writer as definitely concerned with history and politics as Conrad, was said to be irrelevant; for instance, David Daiches, in *The Novel in the Modern World* said that Conrad was irrelevant because he was concerned only in the conflict of man against geography.

[14] Summer, 1952.

most dearly cherished assumptions regarding our relation as individuals, to the world." There is, of course, always—no matter how often we may deny it—some issue of the kind and degree of "belief" in relation to any work of literature. True, there is more than one spirit and one way in which such an issue may be resolved—or it may be argued, with some plausibility, that such an issue can never be finally resolved, that in one way or another we must believe in a work or reject it. And certainly all really new work of literature comes into the world with the promise of a new view of man and the world, with, in short, a new doctrine, stated or implicit. The new work, even though it may seem to be merely a new style, succeeds only because of the promise, usually secret, of some kind of redemption.

There is indeed a value, though not necessarily the final or overriding value, in such a promise; certainly there is a value in the fact—or in what I take to be the fact—that the issues implicit in Faulkner's work are deeply central to our time. But a cult does more than recognize such situations and values. A cult really denies the complexities of such a situation. It equates, quite simply, the doctrine with the value of the work, or if sophisticated, finds the values of style, for example, an implicit affirmation of doctrine, the emphasis here not being on the inner coherence of the work but on the doctrine which the style, and other technical elements, may be said to affirm. In other words, the present cult tends to repeat, in reverse, the old error of the 1930s, to make doctrine equal value.

The long period of exegesis in Faulkner criticism has contributed to the atmosphere of a cult. Exegesis delivers meaning from the cloudiness of text, and there is only one step from this fact to the conviction that the cloudiness was an aura of mana, a sacred cloudiness, and that those who have penetrated it are saved and set apart. And it is well to recall that the snobbery of the cult merges with the snobbery of the academy, and that the process of exegesis has contributed to the sense that only by the application of academic method and in the exfoliation of theses can the truth be found, be packaged, and be delivered for consumption. The very classrooms—sometimes the very same professors—which once granted a grudging half-hour to document Faulkner's social irrelevance or perhaps his fascism, have now set about the canonization.

By and large, the cultism and the academic snobbery were accidental, merely an unfortunate by-product of a necessary endeavor. For the exegesis was necessary. Only by exegesis—such attempts at general schemes as those pioneering essays by O'Donnell and Cowley or such attempts at exploring the logic of method and style as the essays by Aiken and Beck, or the later studies of individual books—could the charge be rebutted that the work of Faulkner was, at center, pernicious or meaningless, and that the complications of method and style were no more than incompetence or self-indulgence.

But the period of exegesis seems to be drawing to a close. I do not mean that new exegeses will not appear. They should appear, if we are not to see criticism puddle and harden into an orthodoxy. But other kinds of interest are beginning to be felt, and will, no doubt, be felt more urgently. For instance, though much has been written about Faulkner and the South, much is repetitious, and there is clearly need for further thinking about the writer and his world. Related to this but not to be identified with it, are the questions of Faulkner's own psychology—his own stance of temperament. Both of these lines of interest are primarily genetic, they have to do with the question of how the work came to exist; but if this kind of criticism is pursued with imagination and tact, it can lead to a new awareness of the work itself, with a fuller understanding of the work as that unity of an art-object and a life-manifestation.

The most immediate need, however, is a criticism that will undertake to discriminate values and methods among the individual items of the canon. Faulkner was a fecund, various, and restless artist, and he paid a price for his peculiar qualities; some of the work is so uneven and unsure, so blurred or pretentious, that it provides apt texts for the most virulent of his detractors. We need a criticism that will do something by way of sorting out the various strands and manifestations of Faulkner's work, and by way of evaluating them. Furthermore, an overall definition and evaluation of the achievement has not been seriously attempted.

Undoubtedly, as in the natural history of all literary reputations, Faulkner's work will enter a period of eclipse. Though man is, not merely a "political" animal, but a "human" one too, emphases do indeed shift, with the shift of time, from one aspect of his humanity to another, and his tastes and needs change; what appeals to some of us now will not appeal to another generation. But it is the obligation of criticism not merely to assert the taste and needs of one age, but to try to discriminate what values, if any, in a work may survive the merely accidental factors of taste and needs. Criticism is, in part, committed to the task of trying to build a bridge to the future. It is a hopeless task, certainly. It is, even, superfluous. A work itself is the only bridge possible, and that bridge may even lead the critic over into the future, where posterity may gather around to regard him, perhaps, as something as strange as the dodo or as blind as a fish drawn up from a stream in a cave.

In selecting essays from such a large body of criticism about a figure as many-faceted as Faulkner, one is forced to make omissions. For instance, there is no essay here about *The Hamlet,* certainly one of Faulkner's most powerful and important novels, and in fact, no essay about the rise of the tribe of Snopes. To approach the matter from the other side, there are a number of valuable or even important essays about topics here treated that I have omitted, for instance that by Lawrence Bowling on *The Sound and the Fury,* an essay which was an early and very influential contribution to the understanding of that key novel. But that omission is only one among my many causes for regret.

I wish to take this occasion to acknowledge some of my debts. The work of Frederick J. Hoffman and Olga Vickery in *Two Decades of Faulkner Criticism* and in *Three Decades of Faulkner Criticism* has been of enormous value to me. In a more personal way, I have reason to be grateful to Malcolm Cowley, R. W. B. Lewis, Cleanth Brooks, Michael Millgate, C. Vann Woodward, Maynard Mack, Henri Peyre, Orm Overland, and Jacqueline Merriam. I find pleasure now in remembering that fact.

Faulkner's Mythology

by George Marion O'Donnell

I

William Faulkner is really a traditional moralist, in the best sense. One principle holds together his [first] thirteen books of prose—including his new novel, *The Wild Palms*—giving his work unity and giving it, at times, the significance that belongs to great myth. That principle is the Southern social-economic-ethical tradition which Mr. Faulkner possesses naturally, as a part of his sensibility.

However, Mr. Faulkner is a traditional man in a modern South. All around him the antitraditional forces are at work, and he lives among evidences of their past activity. He could not fail to be aware of them. It is not strange, then, that his novels are, primarily, a series of related myths (or aspects of a single myth) built around the conflict between traditionalism and the antitraditional modern world in which it is immersed.

In a rearrangement of the novels, say for a collected edition, *The Unvanquished* might well stand first; for the action occurs earlier, historically, than in any other of the books, and it objectifies, in the essential terms of Mr. Faulkner's mythology, the central dramatic tension of his work. On one side of the conflict there are the Sartorises, recognizable human beings who act traditionally. Against them the invading Northern armies, and their diversified allies in the reconstruction era, wage open war, aiming to make the traditional actions of the Sartorises impossible.

The invaders are unable to cope with the Sartorises; but their invasion provides another antagonist with an occasion within which his special anti-Sartoris talent makes him singularly powerful. This antagonist is the landless poor-white horse trader, Ab Snopes; his special talent is his low cunning as an *entrepreneur*. He acts without regard for the legitimacy of his means; he has no ethical code. In the crisis brought about by the war, he is enabled to use a member of the Sartoris family for his own advantage because, for the first time, he can be useful to the Sartorises. Moreover, he is enabled to make this Sartoris (Mrs. Rosa Millard) betray

Reprinted with permission from *The Kenyon Review*, Vol. I, No. 3 (1939), pp. 285-299.

herself into an act of self-interest such as his, and to cause her death while using her as his tool.

The characters and the conflict are particular and credible. But they are also mythological. In Mr. Faulkner's mythology there are two kinds of characters; they are Sartorises or Snopeses, whatever the family names may be. And in the spiritual geography of Mr. Faulkner's work there are two worlds: the Sartoris world and the Snopes world. In all of his successful books, he is exploring the two worlds in detail, dramatizing the inevitable conflict between them.

It is a universal conflict. The Sartorises act traditionally; that is to say, they act always with an ethically responsible will. They represent vital morality, humanism. Being antitraditional, the Snopeses are immoral from the Sartoris point of view. But the Snopeses do not recognize this point of view; acting only for self-interest, they acknowledge no ethical duty. Really, then, they are amoral; they represent naturalism or animalism. And the Sartoris-Snopes conflict is fundamentally a struggle between humanism and naturalism.

As a universal conflict, it is important only philosophically. But it is important artistically, in this instance, because Mr. Faulkner has dramatized it convincingly in the terms of particular history and of actual life in his own part of the South—in the terms of his own tradition.

In *Sartoris,* which was published before *The Unvanquished* but which follows it in historical sequence, the conflict is between young Bayard Sartoris (the grandson of the Bayard Sartoris who was a youth in *The Unvanquished*) and the Snopes world of the 1920s. "General Johnston or General Forrest wouldn't have took a Snopes into his army at all," one of the characters says; but, significantly enough, one Flem Snopes has come, by way of local political usefulness, to be vice-president of old Bayard Sartoris' bank. Young Bayard's brother, John, has been killed in a war; but it is clear that it was a Snopes war and not a Sartoris war. Bayard himself is extremely conscious of his family's doom; he feels cheated because he did not die violently, in the tradition, like his brother; finally, he kills himself, taking up an airplane that he knows will crash.

The Snopes world has done more than oppose the Sartorises. It has weakened them internally (as it weakened Rosa Millard) in using them for its advantage; it has made them self-conscious, queer, psychologically tortured. Bayard Sartoris has something of the traditional instinct for noble and disinterested action, under a vital ethical code. But the strength is so warped internally by the psychological effects of the Snopes world upon it, and it is so alien to the habitual actions of that world, that it can only manifest itself in meaningless violence, ending in self-destruction.

The same pattern recurs, varied somewhat and handled in miniature, in the short story about the Sartorises—"There Was a Queen." Here the real conflict centers in Narcissa Benbow, the widow of young Bayard

Sartoris, who has given herself to a detective in order to recover from his possession a collection of obscene letters that one of the Snopeses had written to her anonymously and afterward stolen. The consciousness of Narcissa's deed kills the embodiment of the virile tradition, old Miss Jenny Sartoris (Mrs. DuPré). Narcissa's yielding to the detective is the result of the *formalization* of one aspect of her traditional morality—her pride—through the constant opposition of the Snopes world to it; this formalization allows the Snopes world to betray her into antitraditionalism by creating a situation in which she must make a formalized response. It is a highly significant tactic. For the moment a tradition begins to be formalized into a code, it commences to lose vitality; when it is entirely formalized, it is dead—it becomes pseudo-tradition.

As early as *Soldiers' Pay* (1926) the same theme is the basis for Mr. Faulkner's organization of experience; and it is the best possible indication of the urgency of the theme with him that it should be central in his first novel. Mahon, the old Episcopal clergyman, conscious of sin, tolerant of human weakness, is still unaware of the vital opponent to his formalized, and so impotent, tradition—the amorality with which history has surrounded him. Donald Mahon, his son, is brought home from the World War, dying; in him, the minister's code has faced antitraditional history. Because Donald is not dead, the conflict must continue; locally, it is between the preacher and Cecily Saunders (Donald's fiancée before he went to war) with her family and associates who are typical of the new Jazz Era. Obviously, Cecily's world of jazz and flappers and sleek-haired jelly-beans represents the same antitraditional historical movement that brought Flem Snopes into Bayard Sartoris' bank. The names and the settings are different; that is all.

In *The Sound and the Fury,* Quentin Compson represents all that is left of the Sartoris tradition. The rest of his family have either succumbed entirely to the Snopes world, like Jason Compson, or else have drugs to isolate them from it—Mr. Compson his fragments of philosophy, Uncle Maury his liquor, Mrs. Compson her religion and her invalidism, Benjy his idiocy. But Quentin's very body is "an empty hall echoing with sonorous defeated names." [1] His world is peopled with "baffled, outraged ghosts"; and although Quentin himself is "still too young to deserve yet to be a ghost," he is one of them. However, it is evident that Quentin's traditionalism is far gone in the direction of formalization, with its concomitant lack of vitality; he is psychologically kin to Bayard Sartoris and to Narcissa Benbow. When he discovers that his sister Candace has been giving herself to the town boys of Jefferson, Mississippi, and is pregnant, he attempts to change her situation by telling their father that he has committed incest with her. It is a key incident. Quentin is attempting to

[1] The quotations are from *Absalom, Absalom!,* the other novel in which Quentin appears; but they are necessary for an understanding of his function in *The Sound and the Fury.*

transform Candace's yielding to the amorality of the Snopes world into a sin, within the Sartoris morality; but the means he employs are more nearly pseudo-traditional and romantic than traditional; and he fails.

Quentin tells his father: "It was to isolate her out of the loud world so that it would have to flee us of necessity." Precisely. The loud world is the Snopes world, with which the Compson house has become thoroughly infected and to which it is subject. Quentin is really *striving toward the condition of tragedy* for his family; he is trying to transform meaningless degeneracy into significant doom. But because his moral code is no longer vital, he fails and ends in a kind of escapism, breaking his watch to put himself beyond time, finally killing himself to escape consciousness. Only he is aware of the real meaning of his struggle, which sets up the dramatic tension in *The Sound and the Fury*.

In a way, Quentin's struggle is Mr. Faulkner's own struggle as an artist. In *Sartoris,* Mr. Faulkner wrote of the name: "There is death in the sound of it, and a glamorous fatality." Sartoris—all that the name implies—is the tragic hero of his work; it is doomed, like any tragic hero. But the doom toward which the Sartoris world moves should be a noble one. In *Absalom, Absalom!,* although apparently with great difficulty, as if he were wrestling with the Snopes world all the while, Mr. Faulkner finally achieves the presentation of a kind of "glamorous fatality" for the Sartoris world—embodied in Thomas Sutpen and his house.

The book is really a summary of the whole career of the tradition—its rise, its fatal defects, its opponents, its decline, and its destruction. The action is of heroic proportions. The figures are larger than life; but, as Mr. T. S. Eliot has suggested of Tourneur's characters, they are all distorted to scale, so that the whole action has a self-subsistent reality. And the book ends with a ritualistic purgation of the doomed house, by fire, which is as nearly a genuine tragic scene as anything in modern fiction.

For the first time, Mr. Faulkner makes explicit here the contrast between traditional (Sartoris) man and modern (Snopes) man, dissociated into a sequence of animal functions, lacking in unity under essential morality. One of the characters says of traditional men:

> People too as we are, and victims too as we are, but victims of a different circumstance, simpler and therefore, integer for integer, larger, more heroic and the figures therefore more heroic too, not dwarfed and involved but distinct, uncomplex who had the gift of living once or dying once instead of being diffused and scattered creatures drawn blindly from a grab bag and assembled.

It was the world of these "diffused and scattered creatures" in which Quentin Compson lived; and it was the effort not to be "diffused and scattered"—to transform his own family's doom into the proportions of the world of Sutpen and Sartoris—that led to his death. But it is significant that it should be Quentin through whose gradual understanding the story of Sutpen is told, and that it should be Quentin who watches the final destruction of Sutpen's house. For Sutpen's tradition was defective, but it was not formalized as Quentin's was; and his story approaches tragedy.

As I Lay Dying stands a little apart from the rest of Mr. Faulkner's novels, but it is based upon the philosophical essence of his Sartoris-Snopes theme—the struggle between humanism and naturalism. The naïve hill folk who appear in the book are poor and ungraceful, certainly; they are of low mentality; sexually, they are almost animalistic. But when Anse Bundren promises his dying wife that he will bury her in Jefferson, he sets up for himself an ethical duty which he recognizes as such—though not in these terms. It is the fulfillment of this obligation, in spite of constant temptation to abandon it, and in spite of multiplied difficulties put in his way by nature itself, that makes up the action of the novel.

Fundamentally, *As I Lay Dying* is a legend; and the procession of ragged, depraved hillmen, carrying Addie Bundren's body through water and through fire to the cemetery in Jefferson, while people flee from the smell and buzzards circle overhead—this progress is not unlike that of the medieval soul toward redemption. The allegories of Alanus de Insulis and the visions of Sister Hildegard of Bingen would yield a good many parallels. On a less esoteric plane, however, the legend is more instructive for us. Because they are simpler in mind and live more remotely from the Snopes world than the younger Sartorises and Compsons, the Bundrens are able to carry a genuine act of traditional morality through to its end. They are infected with amorality; but it is the amorality of physical nature, not the artificial, self-interested amorality of the Snopeses. More heroism is possible among them than among the inhabitants of Jefferson.

II

So far I have been concerned mainly with exegesis, aiming to show how fundamental the Sartoris-Snopes conflict is in Mr. Faulkner's novels. To provide such exegesis of the six books that I have discussed, it is necessary to do violence to the fictions themselves, by abstraction. This is the significant point for criticism, because the necessity for abstraction is evidence that, in these six books, the theme is really informed in the fictions or myths.

The Sartorises and the Sutpens and the Compsons do not represent the tradition in its various degrees of vitality, as *x, y,* and *z* may represent a sequence of numbers in mathematics. They are people, in a certain way of life, at a particular time, confronted with real circumstances and with items of history. And their humanity (or their illusion of humanity, on a larger-than-life scale) is not limited, ultimately, by their archetypal significance. Moreover, in each book there is a dramatically credible fiction which remains particular and (sometimes with difficulty) coherent as action, even though the pattern is true, in a larger sense, as myth. In short, Mr. Faulkner's successful work has the same kind, though certainly not the same degree, of general meaning that is to be found in Dante's *Divina Commedia* or in the *Electra* of Sophocles. The only close parallel in American literature is the better work of Nathaniel Hawthorne, whom Mr. Faulkner resembles in a great many ways.

However, as I have suggested already, a literary and personal tension arises, for William Faulkner the artist, out of the same conflict that is central in his work. This tension sets up his crucial problem as an artist, and his failures result from it. Insofar as he can sustain his inherent tradition, he is enabled to project the central conflict in the valid terms of myth. However, as a Sartoris artist in a Snopes world, he is constantly subject to opposition that tends to force him into the same kind of reactionary formalization of tradition that betrayed Narcissa Benbow as a character. When, because of the opposition and his reaction to it, Mr. Faulkner writes as *formal* traditionalist rather than as *vital* traditionalist, he writes allegory. Allegory might be defined, indeed, as formalized—and therefore dead—myth.

Sanctuary, which is unfortunately the most widely known and misunderstood of Mr. Faulkner's novels, is a failure of this kind. In simple terms, the pattern of the allegory is something like this: Southern Womanhood Corrupted but Undefiled (Temple Drake), in the company of the Corrupted Tradition (Gowan Stevens, a professional Virginian), falls into the clutches of amoral Modernism (Popeye), which is itself impotent, but which with the aid of its strong ally Natural Lust ("Red") rapes Southern Womanhood unnaturally and then seduces her so satisfactorily that her corruption is total, and she becomes the tacit ally of Modernism. Meanwhile Pore White Trash (Godwin) has been accused of the crime which he, with the aid of the Naïve Faithful (Tawmmy), actually tried to prevent. The Formalized Tradition (Horace Benbow), perceiving the true state of affairs, tries vainly to defend Pore White Trash. However, Southern Womanhood is so hopelessly corrupted that she wilfully sees Pore White Trash convicted and lynched; she is then carried off by Wealth (Judge Drake) to meaningless escape in European luxury. Modernism, carrying in it from birth its own impotence and doom, submits with masochistic pleasure to its own destruction for the one crime that it has not yet committed—Revolutionary Destruction of Order (the murder of the Alabama policeman, for which the innocent Popeye is executed).

Here Mr. Faulkner's theme is forced into allegory, not projected as myth. In this sense, the book is a "cheap idea"—as Mr. Faulkner himself calls it in his preface to the Modern Library edition. Its defects are those of allegory in general. The characters are distorted, being more nearly grotesques than human beings, and they are not distorted to scale (Temple is only a type; Benbow is a recognizably human character, and so is Miss Reba, the keeper of the bawdy house); accordingly, the book lacks the "self-subsistent reality" which may be found in a work like *Absalom, Absalom!* It is powerful, and it contains some passages of bawdy folk humor that are of a high order of excellence, but it is fundamentally a caricature.

When *Light in August* appeared in England, an anonymous reviewer for *The Illustrated London News* suggested that it might be a parable of the struggle between good and evil. The notion is not entirely fanciful. But, more specifically, the book might be considered as an allegory based upon Mr. Faulkner's usual theme, with the clergyman, Hightower, standing for the Formalized Tradition. The simple-hearted Byron Bunch corresponds with the naïve traditionalist, Anse Bundren; Christmas, the mulatto, is a Snopes character, as is his partner, Lucas Burch, the seducer of Lena Grove. And the pregnant Lena might represent, vaguely, life itself, which Byron and Hightower are futilely attempting to protect from Lucas Burch and Christmas and their kind.

But the book is not so transparently allegorical as *Sanctuary*; indeed, it is a confused allegory in which realism is present as well. It fails, partly, because of this confusion, which never permits the two sides of the conflict really to join the issue. But it fails, even more clearly, because of the disproportionate emphasis upon Christmas—who ought to be the antagonist but who becomes, like Milton's Satan, the real protagonist in the novel.

This defines the second general type of failure in Mr. Faulkner's work: Mr. Faulkner is unable to sustain his traditionalism at all, and the forces of antitraditionalism become the protagonists.

The discussion reaches a dangerous point here. Since the time of Flaubert, at least, it has been customary to hold the view that one mark of a novelist's craft is his skill in creating all of his characters in the round and in maintaining an equal sympathy for all of them. However, it is not necessary to repudiate this view to suggest that there is a difference in kind between Flaubert's studies of human character in the behavior of the French bourgeois world and Mr. Faulkner's books, which are essentially myths, built around the conflict of two different worlds, to one of which Mr. Faulkner belongs as an artist, though he is of physical necessity a citizen of the other.

When one possesses traditional values of conduct, he has naturally a kind of hierarchy of sympathy, dependent upon the values, which makes him more or less sympathetic to characters in proportion as they are or are not traditional. Mr. Faulkner appears to maintain such a hierarchy in the greater part of his work; although he projects the characters of the Snopes world as clearly as he projects those of the Sartoris world, in his better books he is always seeing them and determining their proportionate stature from the Sartoris point of view.

But in *Light in August* the proportionate dramatic content of the characters is the reverse of the norm set up by the other books, and there is a corollary confusion of the whole scheme of traditional values. The Sartoris characters, like Hightower, are vague or typical; Christmas, the Snopes character, dominates sympathy, and his tortured amorality determines the ethical tone of the book. In proportion as Christmas becomes the protagonist, the Snopes world, with its total lack of values, seems to have supplanted the Sartoris values *within the artist himself,* although against his will. And the confused, malproportioned fiction, wavering between realism and allegory, seems to be the artistic issue of Mr. Faulkner's violent—but, in this case, unavailing—effort to maintain the Sartoris point of view in his work.

Mr. Faulkner never gives his whole consent to such a confusion of values. That he is not content to remain within the characters of his protagonists when they are antitraditional, but must go outside them for "purple passages," seems to be evidence of this fact. *Pylon* is a case in point. It is a study of the effect of machinery upon human beings; the aviators who people it are timeless and placeless; they stay drunk most of the time to aggravate their insensitiveness; they have oil in their veins instead of blood; flying is their obsession, and when they are not in the air they do not live at all. In short, they are artifacts of the Snopes world. Against the background of an airport opening and a Mardi gras carnival in a Southern city, they move like characters in an animated cartoon, performing incredible antics but never being alive. Unable to speak through them, Mr. Faulkner speaks about them, in an androgynous prose-poetry that is not to be found anywhere else in his work. *Pylon* is his most conspicuous failure; and his imperfect sympathy with, and his inability to control, the protagonists, who should be the antagonists, seem to account for the failure.

Mosquitoes fails for similar reasons. Here, however, the imperfect sympathy issues in satire—of the Snopes-world Bohemia that existed in the Vieux Carré section of New Orleans during the 1920s. Since this is Mr. Faulkner's second novel, and since it was written just after he had lived in the Vieux Carré himself, while he was still under thirty, it offers another clear indication of the centrality of his traditionalism. It shows how great is the distance separating him from many of his contemporaries, such as, let us say, Mr. Ernest Hemingway. For *Mosquitoes* makes it very plain that if Mr. Faulkner is of the "lost generation," it is only of the lost generation of Sartorises. But it shows, too, that Mr. Faulkner is not an Aldous Huxley and should not try to be one. He is primarily a mythmaker; and there can be no such thing as a satiric myth.

III

William Faulkner's latest novel, *The Wild Palms,* tells two entirely different stories, in alternating sections; but the stories are complementary in that they both derive from the conflict between humanism and naturalism.

For Harry, the young doctor, and Charlotte, his mistress, all humanistic morality is equated with the Snopes code of mere "respectability," into which morality has degenerated. Of that code, one of the characters says: "If Jesus returned today we would have to crucify him quick in our own defense, to justify and preserve the civilization we have worked and suffered and died . . . for two thousand years to create and perfect in man's own image." Charlotte and Harry are attempting to escape from the code into pure naturalism. Charlotte is natural, or amoral, Woman; with her, Harry becomes natural, amoral Man. They are constantly insisting upon the entirely physical nature of their love—and in no evasive terms. Their fear of any code amounts to an obsession: when they begin to feel as if they were married, living and working together in Chicago, they run off to a remote mining settlement in order to escape respectability. But Harry is conscious of doom: "So I am afraid. Because They [the forces of the code] are smart, shrewd, They will have to be; if They were to let us beat Them, it would be like unchecked murder and robbery. Of course we can't beat Them; we are doomed, of course. . . ." The fear is justified, for they are defeated by the very naturalism to which they have fled: Charlotte dies from the effects of an abortion that Harry attempts to perform on her.

The other story concerns a nameless convict, adrift in a small boat on the Mississippi River during the flood of 1927. Like Harry and Charlotte, the convict exists in a realm of unchecked natural forces; but unlike them, he has been put there against his will. With him in the skiff is a pregnant woman whom he has been sent to rescue. Like Anse Bundren, the convict is capable of genuine moral action; and his struggle with naturalism is based upon the ethical urge to return to his prison and to carry back the woman he has saved. When he is finally captured, he says: "Yonder's your boat and here's the woman"; with simple-minded tenacity, he has fulfilled his ethical obligation.

Technically, the book fails; only the complementary themes connect the two parts, and the connection is not strong enough for any sort of fictional unity. Indeed, it is a pity that the two parts are printed together; for the story of Charlotte and Harry is one of Mr. Faulkner's failures, whereas the story of the convict is one of his successes.

Charlotte and Harry, fleeing the Snopes world but fleeing all codes, too, are products of the antitraditional overbalancing in Mr. Faulkner which yielded *Pylon*. And the failure of their story derives, like the failure of that book, from the fact that in them the natural protagonist-antagonist schematism of Mr. Faulkner's myth is reversed. Sympathy must be given to them reluctantly, for though they are, as a matter of fact, running away from the Snopes world, they are running away from the Sartoris world, too; and, as Harry says, if they were to succeed, it would be like unchecked robbery and murder. In defense of one's own humanism, one must not yield entire sympathy to human beings who enter the realm of pure animalism.

But the story of the nameless convict is an heroic legend, similar to *As I Lay Dying*; it must be counted as one of Mr. Faulkner's definite achievements. Moreover, it has a quality of gusty humor (a sense of the outrageously grotesque heroic, related to the humor of the "tall tales" in folk literature) which is rarer in Mr. Faulkner's work but which is always impressive when it appears. It is to be found in some of the scenes of *Sanctuary*, notably in the gangster funeral and in the drunken "afternoon tea" of the middle-aged harlots at Miss Reba's house. It shows up in some of the short stories—"Spotted Horses," for example. And it appears in the scenes of the convicts alligator hunting in *The Wild Palms*. However, this quality does not destroy, but serves rather to strengthen, the heroic legend as a whole.

IV

William Faulkner's myth finds expression in work that is definitely romantic; when he comes near to tragedy, it is the tragedy of Webster. His art, like Webster's, is tortured. In form, each of his novels resembles a late-Elizabethan blank verse line, where the meter is strained, threatens to break, sometimes breaks, but is always exciting. He is an original craftsman, making his own solutions to his problems of form, often blundering, but occasionally striking upon an effect that no amount of studious craftsmanship could achieve. Consequently, like Dostoevsky, or like Miss Djuna Barnes in our own time, he is very special; and his work cannot be imitated except futilely, for he works within no general tradition of craft and hands on no tradition to his successors.

But Mr. Faulkner's difficulties of form derive, in part, from the struggle that he has to make to inform his material. The struggle is manifest, even in the prose itself. Discounting the results of plain carelessness in all of the books, the correlation between the fictions and the quality of the prose in Mr. Faulkner's books is instructive. It appears significant that *The Unvanquished* contains his least tortured and *Pylon* his most tortured prose.

He has worked to project in fiction the conflict between his inherent traditional values and the modern world; and the conflict has affected his fictional projection, so that all of his work is really a *striving toward* the condition of tragedy. He is the Quentin Compson or the Bayard Sartoris of modern fiction. He does not always fail; but when he does, his failure is like theirs—he ends in confused or meaningless violence. And for the same reasons: his heritage is theirs, and it is subject to the same opposition to which they are subject as characters. When he is partially successful, the result is tortured but major romantic art.

Now, in 1939, Mr. Faulkner's work may seem melodramatic. Melodrama differs from tragedy only in the amount of meaning that is subsistent in the pattern of events; and in our time the values of Mr. Faulkner's tradition are available to most men only historically, in the same way that, let us say, medieval values are available. The significance of the work as myth depends, then, upon the willingness of the reader to recover the meaning of the tradition—even historically.

Introduction to *The Portable Faulkner*

by Malcolm Cowley

I

Faulkner's mythical kingdom is a county in northern Mississippi, on the border between the sand hills covered with scrubby pine and the black earth of the river bottoms. Except for the storekeepers, mechanics, and professional men who live in Jefferson, the county seat, all the inhabitants are farmers or woodsmen. Except for a little lumber, their only product is baled cotton for the Memphis market. A few of them live in big plantation houses, the relics of another age, and more of them in substantial wooden farmhouses; but most of them are tenants, no better housed than slaves on good plantations before the Civil War. Yoknapatawpha County—"William Faulkner, sole owner and proprietor," as he inscribed on one of the maps he drew—has a population of 15,611 persons scattered over 2,400 square miles. It sometimes seems to me that every house or hovel has been described in one of Faulkner's novels; and that all the people of the imaginary county, black and white, townsmen, farmers, and housewives, have played their parts in one connected story.

He has so far written nine books wholly concerned with Yoknapatawpha County and its people, who also appear in parts of three others and in thirty or more uncollected stories. *Sartoris* was the first of the books to be published, in the spring of 1929; it is a romantic and partly unconvincing novel, but with many fine scenes in it, like the hero's visit to a family of independent pine-hill farmers; and it states most of the themes that the author would later develop at length. *The Sound and the Fury* was written before *Sartoris,* but wasn't published until six months later; it describes the fall of the Compson family, and it was the first of Faulkner's novels to be widely discussed. The books that followed, in the Yoknapatawpha series, are *As I Lay Dying* (1930), about the death and burial of Addie Bundren; *Sanctuary* (1931), always the most popular of his novels; *Light in August* (1932), in many ways the best; *Absalom, Absalom!* (1936) about Colonel Sutpen and his ambition to found a family; *The*

Unvanquished (1938), a book of interrelated stories about the Sartoris dynasty; *The Wild Palms* (1939), half of which deals with a convict from back in the pine hills; *The Hamlet* (1940), a novel about the Snopes clan; and *Go Down, Moses* (1942), in which Faulkner's theme is the Negroes. There are also many Yoknapatawpha stories in *These Thirteen* (1931) and *Dr. Martino* (1934), besides other stories privately printed (like "Miss Zilphia Gant") or published in magazines and still to be collected or used as episodes in novels.

Just as Balzac, who seems to have inspired the series, divided his *Comédie Humaine* into "Scenes of Parisian Life," "Scenes of Provincial Life," "Scenes of Private Life," so Faulkner might divide his work into a number of cycles: one about the planters and their descendants, one about the townspeople of Jefferson, one about the poor whites, one about the Indians (consisting of stories already written but never brought together), and one about the Negroes. Or again, if he adopted a division by families, there would be the Compson-Sartoris saga, the still unfinished Snopes saga, the McCaslin saga, dealing with the white and black descendants of Carothers McCaslin, and the Ratliff-Bundren saga, devoted to the backwoods farmers of Frenchman's Bend. All the cycles or sagas are closely interconnected; it is as if each new book was a chord or segment of a total situation always existing in the author's mind. Sometimes a short story is the sequel to an earlier novel. For example, we read in *Sartoris* that Byron Snopes stole a packet of letters from Narcissa Benbow; and in "There Was a Queen," a story published five years later, we learn how Narcissa got the letters back again. Sometimes, on the other hand, a novel contains the sequel to a story; and we discover from an incidental reference in *The Sound and the Fury* that the Negro woman whose terror of death was described in "That Evening Sun" had later been murdered by her husband, who left her body in a ditch for the vultures. Sometimes an episode has a more complicated history. Thus, in the first chapter of *Sanctuary,* we hear about the old Frenchman place, a ruined mansion near which the people of the neighborhood had been "digging with secret and sporadic optimism for gold which the builder was reputed to have buried somewhere about the place when Grant came through the country on his Vicksburg campaign." Later this digging for gold served as the subject of a story published in the *Saturday Evening Post*: "Lizards in Jamshyd's Courtyard." Still later the story was completely rewritten and became the last chapter of *The Hamlet.*

As one book leads into another, Faulkner sometimes falls into inconsistencies of detail. There is a sewing-machine agent named V. K. Suratt who appears in *Sartoris* and some of the later stories. By the time we reach *The Hamlet,* his name has changed to Ratliff, although his character remains the same (and his age, too, for all the twenty years that separate the backgrounds of the two novels). Henry Armstid is a likable figure in *As I Lay Dying* and *Light in August*; in *The Hamlet* he is mean and half-demented. His wife, whose character remains consistent, is called Lula in one book and Martha in another; in the third she is nameless. There is an Indian chief named Doom who appears in several stories; he starts as the father of Issetibeha and ends as his grandson. The mansion called Sutpen's Hundred was built of brick at the beginning of *Absalom, Absalom!* but at the end of the novel it is all wood and inflammable except for the chimneys. But these errors are comparatively few and inconsequential, considering the scope of Faulkner's series; and I should judge that most of them are afterthoughts rather than oversights.

All his books in the Yoknapatawpha saga are part of the same living pattern. It is this pattern, and not the printed volumes in which part of it is recorded, that is Faulkner's real achievement. Its existence helps to explain one feature of his work: that each novel, each long or short story, seems to reveal more than it states explicitly and to have a subject bigger than itself. All the separate works are like blocks of marble from the same quarry: they show the veins and faults of the mother rock. Or else—to use a rather strained figure—they are like wooden planks that were cut not from a log, but from a still living tree. The planks are planed and chiseled into their final shapes, but the tree itself heals over the wound and continues to grow. Faulkner is incapable of telling the same story twice without adding new details. In [*The Portable Faulkner*] I wanted to use part of *The Sound and the Fury,* the novel that deals with the fall of the Compson family. I thought that the last part of the book would be most effective as a separate episode, but still it depended too much on what had gone before. Faulkner offered to write a very brief introduction that would explain the relations of the characters. What he finally sent me [was] a genealogy of the Compsons from their first arrival in this country. Whereas the novel is confined to a period of eighteen years ending in 1928, the genealogy goes back to the battle of Culloden in 1745, and forward to the year 1945, when Jason, last of the Compson males, has sold the family mansion, and Sister Caddy has last been heard of as the mistress of a German general. The novel that Faulkner wrote about the Compsons had long ago been given its final shape; but the pattern or body of legend behind the novel—and behind all his other books—was still developing.

Although the pattern is presented in terms of a single Mississippi county, it can be extended to the Deep South as a whole; and Faulkner always seems conscious of its wider application. He might have been thinking of his own novels when he described the ledgers in the commissary of the McCaslin plantation in *Go Down, Moses.* They recorded, he said, "that slow trickle of molasses and meal and meat, of shoes and straw hats and overalls, of plowlines and collars and heelbolts and clevises, which returned each fall as cotton"—in a sense they were local and limited; but they were also "the continuation of that record which two hundred years had not been enough to complete and another hundred would not be enough to discharge; that chronicle which was a whole land in miniature, which multiplied and compounded was the entire South."

II

"Tell about the South," says Quentin Compson's roommate at Harvard, a Canadian named Shreve McCannon who is curious about the unknown region beyond the Ohio. "What's it like there?" he asks. "What do they do there? Why do they live there? Why do they live at all?" And Quentin, whose background is a little like that of Faulkner himself and who sometimes seems to speak for him—Quentin answers, "You can't understand it. You would have to be born there." Nevertheless, he tells a long and violent story that he regards as the essence of the Deep South, which is not so much a mere region as it is, in Quentin's mind, an incomplete and frustrated nation trying to relive its legendary past.

The story he tells—I am trying to summarize the plot of *Absalom, Absalom!*—is that of a mountain boy named Thomas Sutpen whose family drifted into the Virginia lowlands, where his father found odd jobs on a plantation. One day the father sent him with a message to the big house, but he was turned away at the door by a black man in livery. Puzzled and humiliated, the mountain boy was seized upon by the lifelong ambition to which he would afterward refer as "the design." He too would own a plantation with slaves and a liveried butler; he would build a mansion as big as any of those in the Tidewater; and he would have a son to inherit his wealth.

A dozen years later, Sutpen appeared in the frontier town of Jefferson, where he managed to obtain a hundred square miles of land from the Chickasaws. With the help of twenty wild Negroes from the jungle and a French architect, he set about building the largest house in northern Mississippi, using timbers from the forest and bricks that his Negroes molded and baked on the spot; it was as if his mansion, Sutpen's Hundred, had been literally torn from the soil. Only one man in Jefferson—he was Quentin's grandfather, General Compson—ever learned how and where Sutpen had acquired his slaves. He had shipped to Haiti from Virginia, worked as overseer on a sugar plantation and married the rich planter's daughter, who had borne him a son. Then, finding that his wife had Negro blood, he had simply put her away, with her child and her fortune, while keeping the twenty slaves as a sort of indemnity.

In Jefferson, Sutpen married again. This time his wife belonged to a pious family of the neighborhood, and she bore him two children, Henry and Judith. He became the biggest cotton planter in Yoknapatawpha County, and it seemed that his "design" had already been fulfilled. At this moment, however, Henry came home from the University of Mississippi with an older and worldlier new friend, Charles Bon, who was in reality Sutpen's son by his first marriage. Charles became engaged to Judith. Sutpen learned his identity and, without making a sign of recognition, ordered him from the house. Henry, who refused to believe that Charles was his half-brother, renounced his birthright and followed him to New Orleans. In 1861, all the male Sutpens went off to war, and all of them survived four years of fighting. Then, in the spring of 1865, Charles suddenly decided to marry Judith, even though he was certain by now that she was his half-sister. Henry rode beside him all the way back to Sutpen's Hundred, but tried to stop him at the gate, killed him when he insisted on going ahead with his plan, told Judith what he had done, and disappeared.

But Quentin's story of the Deep South does not end with the war. Colonel Sutpen came home, he says, to find his wife dead, his son a fugitive, his slaves dispersed (they had run away even before they were freed by the Union army), and most of his land about to be seized for debt. Still determined to carry out "the design," he did not even pause for breath before undertaking to restore his house and plantation to what they had been. The effort failed and Sutpen was reduced to keeping a crossroads store. Now in his sixties, he tried again to beget a son; but his wife's younger sister, Miss Rosa Coldfield, was outraged by his proposal ("Let's try it," he had said, "and if it's a boy we'll get married"); and later poor Milly Jones, with whom he had an affair, gave birth to a baby girl. At that Sutpen abandoned hope and provoked Milly's grandfather into killing him. Judith survived her father for a time, as did the half-caste son of Charles Bon by a New Orleans octoroon. After the death of these two by yellow fever, the great house was haunted rather than inhabited by an ancient mulatto woman, Sutpen's daughter by one of his slaves. The fugitive Henry Sutpen came home to die; the townspeople heard of his illness and sent an ambulance after him; but old Clytie thought they were arresting him for murder and set fire to Sutpen's Hundred. The only survival of the conflagration was Jim Bond, a half-witted creature who was Charles Bon's grandson.

"Now I want you to tell me just one thing more," Shreve McCannon says after hearing the story. "Why do you hate the South?"—"I don't hate it," Quentin says quickly, at once. "I dont hate it," he repeats, speaking for the author as well as himself. *I dont hate it,* he thinks, panting in the cold air, the iron New England dark; *I dont. I dont hate it! I dont hate it!*

The reader cannot help wondering why this somber and, at moments, plainly incredible story had so seized upon Quentin's mind that he trembled with excitement when telling it and felt it revealed the essence of the Deep South. It seems to belong in the realm of Gothic romances, with Sutpen's Hundred taking the place of the haunted castle on the Rhine, with Colonel Sutpen as Faust and Charles Bon as Manfred. Then slowly it dawns on you that most of the characters and incidents have a double meaning; that besides their place in the story, they also serve as symbols or metaphors with a general application. Sutpen's great design, the land he stole from the Indians, the French architect who built his house with the help of wild Negroes from the jungle, the woman of mixed blood whom he married and disowned, the unacknowledged son who ruined him, the poor white whom he wronged and who killed him in anger, the final destruction of the mansion like the downfall of a social order: all these might belong to a tragic fable of Southern history. With a little cleverness, the whole novel might be explained as a connected and logical allegory, but this, I think, would be going far beyond the author's intention. First of all, he was writing a story, and one that affected him deeply, but he was also brooding over a social situation. More or less unconsciously, the incidents in the story came to represent the forces and elements in the social situation, since the mind naturally works in terms of symbols and parallels. In Faulkner's case, this form of parallelism is not confined to *Absalom, Absalom!* It can be found in the whole fictional framework that he has been elaborating in novel after novel, until his work has become a myth or legend of the South.

I call it a legend because it is obviously no more intended as a historical account of the country south of the Ohio than *The Scarlet Letter* was intended as a history of Massachusetts or *Paradise Lost* as a factual description of the Fall. Briefly stated, the legend might run something like this: The Deep South was settled partly by aristocrats like the Sartoris clan and partly by new men like Colonel Sutpen. Both types of planters were determined to establish a lasting social order on the land they had seized from the Indians (that is, to leave sons behind them). They had the virtue of living single-mindedly by a fixed code; but there was also an inherent guilt in their "design," their way of life; it was slavery that put a curse on the land and brought about the Civil War. After the War was lost, partly as a result of their own mad heroism (for who else but men as brave as Jackson and Stuart could have frightened the Yankees into standing together and fighting back?), they tried to restore "the design" by other methods. But they no longer had the strength to achieve more than a partial success, even after they had freed their land from the carpetbaggers who followed the Northern armies. As time passed, moreover, the men of the old order found that they had Southern enemies too: they had to fight against a new exploiting class descended from the landless whites of slavery days. In this struggle between the clan of Sartoris and the unscrupulous tribe of Snopes, the Sartorises were defeated in advance by a traditional code that kept them from using the weapons of the enemy. As a price of victory, however, the Snopeses had to serve the mechanized civilization of the North, which was morally impotent in itself, but which, with the aid of its Southern retainers, ended by corrupting the Southern nation.

Faulkner's novels of contemporary Southern life continue the legend into a period that he regards as one of moral confusion and social decay. He is continually seeking in them for violent images to convey his sense of despair. *Sanctuary* is the most violent of all his novels; it is also the most popular and by no means the least important (in spite of Faulkner's comment that it was "a cheap idea . . . deliberately conceived to make money"). The story of Popeye and Temple Drake has more meaning than appears on a first hasty reading—the only reading that most of the critics have been willing to grant it. Popeye himself is one of several characters in Faulkner's novels who represent the mechanical civilization that has invaded and partly conquered the South. He is always described in mechanical terms: his eyes "looked like rubber knobs"; his face "just went awry, like the face of a wax doll set too near a hot fire and forgotten"; his tight suit and stiff hat were "all angles, like a modernistic lampshade"; and in general he had "that vicious depthless quality of stamped tin." Popeye was the son of a professional strikebreaker, from whom he had inherited syphilis, and the grandson of a pyromaniac. Like two other villains in Faulkner's novels, Joe Christmas and Januarius Jones, he had spent most of his childhood in an institution. He was the man "who made money and had nothing he could do with it, spend it for, since he knew that alcohol would kill him like poison, who had no friends and had never known a woman"—in other words, he was the compendium of all the hateful qualities that Faulkner assigns to finance capitalism. *Sanctuary* is not a connected allegory, as one critic explained it, but neither is it a mere accumulation of pointless horrors. It is an example of the Freudian method turned backward, being full of sexual nightmares that are in reality social symbols. It is somehow connected in the author's mind with what he regards as the rape and corruption of the South.

In all his novels dealing with the present, Faulkner makes it clear that the descendants of the old ruling caste have the wish but not the courage or the strength to prevent this new disaster. They are defeated by Popeye (like Horace Benbow), or they run away from him (like Gowan Stevens, who had gone to school at Virginia and learned to drink like a gentleman, but not to fight for his principles), or they are robbed and replaced in their positions of influence by the Snopeses (like old Bayard Sartoris, the president of the bank), or they drug themselves with eloquence and alcohol (like Quentin Compson's father), or they retire into the illusion of being inviolable Southern ladies (like Mrs. Compson, who says, "It can't be simply to flout and hurt me. Whoever God is, He would not permit that. I'm a lady"), or they dwell so much on the past that they are incapable of facing the present (like Reverend Hightower of *Light in August*), or they run from danger to danger (like young Bayard Sartoris) frantically seeking their own destruction. Faulkner's novels are full of well-meaning and even admirable persons, not only the grandsons of the cotton aristocracy, but also pine-hill farmers and storekeepers and sewing-machine agents and Negro cooks and sharecroppers; but they are almost all of them defeated by circumstances and they carry with them a sense of their own doom.

They also carry, whether heroes or villains, a curious sense of submission to their fate. "There is not one of Faulkner's characters," says André Gide in his dialogue on "The New American Novelists," "who, properly speaking, has a soul"; and I think he means that not one of them exercises the faculty of conscious choice between good and evil. They are haunted, obsessed, driven forward by some inner necessity. Like Miss Rosa Coldfield in *Absalom, Absalom!*, they exist in "that dream state in which you run without moving from a terror in which you cannot believe, toward a safety in which you have no faith." Or, like the slaves freed by General Sherman's army, in *The Unvanquished*, they blindly follow the roads toward any river, believing that it will be their Jordan:

> They were singing, walking along the road singing, not even looking to either side. The dust didn't even settle for two days, because all that night they still passed; we sat up listening to them, and the next morning every few yards along the road would be the old ones who couldn't keep up any more, sitting or lying down and even crawling along, calling to the others to help them; and the others—the young ones—not stopping, not even looking at them. "Going to Jordan," they told me. "Going to cross Jordan."

All Faulkner's characters, black and white, are a little like that. They dig for gold frenziedly after they have lost their hope of finding it (like Henry Armstid in *The Hamlet* and Lucas Beauchamp in *Go Down, Moses*); or they battle against and survive a Mississippi flood for the one privilege of returning to the state prison farm (like the tall convict in "Old Man"); or, a whole family together, they carry a body through flood and fire and corruption to bury it in the cemetery at Jefferson (like the Bundrens in *As I Lay Dying*); or they tramp the roads week after week in search of men who had promised but never intended to marry them (like Lena Grove, the pregnant woman of *Light in August*); or, pursued by a mob, they turn at the end to meet and accept death (like Joe Christmas in the same novel). Even when they seem to be guided by a conscious purpose, like Colonel Sutpen, it is not something they have chosen by an act of will, but something that has taken possession of them: Sutpen's great design was "not what he wanted to do but what he just had to do, had to do it whether he wanted to or not, because if he did not do it he knew that he could never live with himself for the rest of his life." In the same way, Faulkner himself writes not what he wants to, but what he just has to write whether he wants to or not.

III

He is not primarily a novelist: that is, his stories do not occur to him in book-length units of 70,000 to 150,000 words. Almost all his novels have some weakness in structure. Some of them combine two or more themes having little relation to each other, like *Light in August,* while others, like *The Hamlet,* tend to resolve themselves into a series of episodes resembling beads on a string. In *The Sound and the Fury,* which is superb as a whole, we can't be sure that the four sections of the novel are presented in the most effective order; at any rate, we can't fully understand and perhaps can't even read the first section until we have read the other three. *Absalom, Absalom!,* though pitched in too high a key, is structurally the soundest of all the novels in the Yoknapatawpha series; but even here the author's attention shifts halfway through the book from the principal theme of Colonel Sutpen's ambition to the secondary theme of incest and miscegenation.

Faulkner is best and most nearly himself either in long stories like "The Bear," in *Go Down, Moses,* and "Old Man," which was published as half of *The Wild Palms,* and "Spotted Horses," which was first printed separately, then greatly expanded and fitted into the loose framework of *The Hamlet*—or else in the Yoknapatawpha saga as a whole. That is, he is most effective in dealing with the total situation that is always present in his mind as a pattern of the South; or else in shorter units that can be conceived and written in a single burst of creative effort. It is by his best that we should judge him, like every other author; and Faulkner at his best—even sometimes at his worst—has a power, a richness of life, an intensity to be found in no other American novelist of our time. He has—once more I am quoting from Henry James's essay on Hawthorne —"the element of simple genius, the quality of imagination."

Moreover, he has a brooding love for the land where he was born and reared and where, unlike other writers of his generation, he has chosen to spend his life. It is ". . . this land, this South, for which God has done so much, with woods for game and streams for fish and deep rich soil for seed and lush springs to sprout it and long summers to mature it and serene falls to harvest it and short mild winters for men and animals." So far as Faulkner's country includes the Delta, it is also (in the words of old Ike McCaslin):

> This land which man has deswamped and denuded and derivered in two generations so that white men can own plantations and commute every night to Memphis and black men own plantations and ride in jim crow cars to Chicago and live in millionaires' mansions on Lake Shore Drive, where white men rent farms and live like niggers and niggers crop on shares and live like animals, where cotton is planted and grows man-tall

in the very cracks of the sidewalks, and usury and mortgage and bankruptcy and measureless wealth, Chinese and African and Aryan and Jew, all breed and spawn together.

Here are the two sides of Faulkner's feeling for the South: on the one side, an admiring and possessive love; on the other, a compulsive fear lest what he loves should be destroyed by the ignorance of its native serfs and the greed of traders and absentee landlords.

No other American writer takes such delight in the weather. He speaks in various novels of "the hot still pine-winey silence of the August afternoon"; of "the moonless September dust, the trees along the road not rising soaring as trees should but squatting like huge fowl"; of "the tranquil sunset of October mazy with windless wood-smoke"; of the "slow drizzle of November rain just above the ice point"; of "those windless Mississippi December days which are a sort of Indian summer's Indian summer"; of January and February when there is "no movement anywhere save the low constant smoke . . . and no sound save the chopping of axes and the lonely whistle of the daily trains." Spring in Faulkner's country is a hurried season, "all coming at once, pell mell and disordered, fruit and bloom and leaf, pied meadow and blossoming wood and the long fields shearing dark out of winter's slumber, to the shearing plow." Summer is dust-choked and blazing, and it lasts far into what should be autumn. "That's the one trouble with this country," he says in *As I Lay Dying*. "Everything, weather, all, hangs on too long. Like our rivers, our land: opaque, slow, violent; shaping and creating the life of man in its implacable and brooding image."

And Faulkner loves these people created in the image of the land. After a second reading of his novels, you continue to be impressed by his villains, Popeye and Jason and Joe Christmas and Flem Snopes; but this time you find more place in your memory for other figures standing a little in the background yet presented by the author with quiet affection: old ladies like Miss Jenny DuPré, with their sharp-tongued benevolence; shrewd but kindly bargainers like Ratliff, the sewing-machine agent, and Will Varner, with his cotton gin and general store; long-suffering farm wives like Mrs. Henry Armstid (whether her name is Lula or Martha); and backwoods patriarchs like Pappy MacCullum, with his six middle-aged but unmarried sons named after the generals of Lee's army. You remember the big plantation houses that collapse in flames as if a whole civilization were dying, but you also remember men in patched and faded but quite clean overalls sitting on the gallery—here in the North we should call it the porch—of a crossroads store that is covered with posters advertising soft drinks and patent medicines; and you remember the stories they tell while chewing tobacco until the suption is out of it. (Everything in their world is reduced to anecdote, and every anecdote is based on character.) You remember Quentin Compson not in his despairing moments, but riding with his father behind the dogs as they quarter a sedge-grown hillside after quail; and not listening to his father's story, but still knowing every word of it, because, as he thought to himself, "You had learned, absorbed it already without the medium of speech somehow from having been born and living beside it, with it, as children will and do: so that what your father was saying did not tell you anything so much as it struck, word by word, the resonant strings of remembering."

Faulkner's novels have the quality of being lived, absorbed, remembered rather than merely observed. And they have what is rare in the novels of our time, a warmth of family affection, brother for brother and sister, the father for his children—a love so warm and proud that it tries to shut out the rest of the world. Compared with that affection, married love is presented as something calculating, and illicit love as a consuming fire. And because the blood relationship is central in his novels, Faulkner finds it hard to create sympathetic characters between the ages of twenty and forty. He is better with children, Negro and white, and incomparably good with older people who preserve the standards that have come down to them "out of the old time, the old days."

In his later books, which have attracted so little attention that they seem to have gone unread, there is a quality not exactly new to Faulkner —it had appeared already in passages of *Sartoris* and *Sanctuary*—but now much stronger and no longer overshadowed by violence and horror. It is a sort of homely and sober-sided frontier humor that is seldom achieved in contemporary writing (except by Erskine Caldwell, another Southerner). The horse-trading episodes in *The Hamlet,* and especially the long story of the spotted ponies from Texas, might have been inspired by the Davy Crockett almanacs. "Old Man," the story of the convict who surmounted the greatest of all the Mississippi floods, might almost be a continuation of *Huckleberry Finn*. It is as if some older friend of Huck's had taken the raft and drifted on from Aunt Sally Phelps's farm into wilder adventures, described in a wilder style, among Chinese and Cajuns and bayous crawling with alligators. In a curious way, Faulkner combines two of the principal traditions in American letters: the tradition of psychological horror, often close to symbolism, that begins with Charles Brockden Brown, our first professional novelist, and extends through Poe, Melville, Henry James (in his later stories), Stephen Crane, and Hemingway; and the other tradition of frontier humor and realism, beginning with Augustus Longstreet's *Georgia Scenes* and having Mark Twain as its best example.

But the American author he most resembles is Hawthorne, for all their polar differences. They stand to each other as July to December, as heat to cold, as swamp to mountain, as the luxuriant to the meager but perfect, as planter to Puritan; and yet Hawthorne had much the same attitude toward New England that Faulkner has toward the South, together with a strong sense of regional particularity. The Civil War made

Hawthorne feel that "the North and the South were two distinct nations in opinions and habits, and had better not try to live under the same institutions." In the Spring of 1861, he wrote to his Bowdoin classmate Horatio Bridge, "We were never one people and never really had a country."—"New England," he said a little later, "is quite as large a lump of earth as my heart can really take in." But it was more than a lump of earth for him; it was a lump of history and a permanent state of consciousness. Like Faulkner in the South, he applied himself to creating its moral fables and elaborating its legends, which existed, as it were, in his solitary heart. Pacing the hillside behind his house in Concord, he listened for a voice; you might say that he lay in wait for it, passively but expectantly, like a hunter behind a rock; then, when it had spoken, he transcribed its words—more slowly and carefully than Faulkner, it is true; with more form and less fire, but with the same essential fidelity. If the voice was silent, he had nothing to write. "I have an instinct that I had better keep quiet," he said in a letter to his publisher. "Perhaps I shall have a new spirit of vigor if I wait quietly for it; perhaps not." Faulkner is another author who has to wait for the spirit and the voice. Essentially he is not a novelist, in the sense of not being a writer who sets out to observe actions and characters, then fits them into the architectural framework of a story. For all the weakness of his own poems, he is an epic or bardic poet in prose, a creator of myths that he weaves together into a legend of the South.

William Faulkner: The Novel as Form

by Conrad Aiken

The famous remark made to Macaulay—"Young man, the more I consider the less can I conceive where you picked up that style"—might with advantage have been saved for Mr. William Faulkner. For if one thing is more outstanding than another about Mr. Faulkner—some readers find it so outstanding, indeed, that they never get beyond it—it is the uncompromising and almost hypnotic zeal with which he insists upon having a style, and, especially of late, the very peculiar style which he insists upon having. Perhaps to that one should add that he insists *when he remembers*—he can write straightforwardly enough when he wants to; he does so often in the best of his short stories (and they are brilliant), often enough, too, in the novels. But that *style* is what he really wants to get back to; and get back to it he invariably does.

And what a style it is, to be sure! The exuberant and tropical luxuriance of sound which Jim Europe's jazz band used to exhale, like a jungle of rank creepers and ferocious blooms taking shape before one's eyes—magnificently and endlessly intervolved, glisteningly and ophidianly in motion, coil sliding over coil, and leaf and flower forever magically interchanging—was scarcely more bewildering, in its sheer inexhaustible fecundity, than Mr. Faulkner's style. Small wonder if even the most passionate of Mr. Faulkner's admirers—among whom the present writer honors himself by enlisting—must find, with each new novel, that the first fifty pages are always the hardest, that each time one must learn all over again *how* to read this strangely fluid and slippery and heavily mannered prose, and that one is even, like a kind of Laocoön, sometimes tempted to give it up.

Wrestle, for example, with two very short (for Mr. Faulkner!) sentences, taken from an early page of *Absalom, Absalom!*

> Meanwhile, as though in inverse ratio to the vanishing voice, the invoked ghost of the man whom she could neither forgive nor revenge herself upon

From *A Reviewer's ABC*, by Conrad Aiken, *A Reviewer's ABC* (New York: Meridian Books, 1958), pp. 200-207.

> began to assume a quality almost of solidity, permanence. Itself circumambient and enclosed by its effluvium of hell, its aura of unregeneration, it mused (mused, thought, seemed to possess sentience as if, though dispossessed of the peace—who was impervious anyhow to fatigue—which she declined to give it, it was still irrevocably outside the scope of her hurt or harm) with that quality peaceful and now harmless and not even very attentive—the ogreshape which, as Miss Coldfield's voice went on, resolved out of itself before Quentin's eyes the two half-ogre children, the three of them forming a shadowy background for the fourth one.

Well, it may be reasonably questioned whether, on page thirteen of a novel, that little cordite bolus of suppressed reference isn't a thumping aesthetic mistake. Returned to, when one has finished the book, it may be as simple as daylight; but encountered for the first time, and no matter how often reread, it guards its enigma with the stony impassivity of the Sphinx.

Or take again from the very first page of *The Wild Palms*—Mr. Faulkner's latest novel, and certainly one of his finest [novels]—this little specimen of "exposition":

> Because he had been born here, on this coast though not in this house but in the other, the residence in town, and had lived here all his life, including the four years at the State University's medical school and the two years as an intern in New Orleans where (a thick man even when young, with thick soft woman's hands, who should never have been a doctor at all, who even after the six more or less metropolitan years looked out from a provincial and insulated amazement at his classmates and fellows: the lean young men swaggering in the drill jackets on which—to him—they wore the myriad anonymous faces of the probationer nurses with a ruthless and assured braggadocio like decorations, like flower trophies) he had sickened for it.

What is one to say of that—or of a sentence only a little lower on the same page which runs for thirty-three lines? Is this, somehow perverted, the influence of the later Henry James—James the Old Pretender?

In short, Mr. Faulkner's style, though often brilliant and always interesting, is all too frequently downright bad; and it has inevitably offered an all-too-easy mark for the sharpshooting of such alert critics as Mr. Wyndham Lewis. But if it is easy enough to make fun of Mr. Faulkner's obsessions for particular words, or his indifference and violence to them, or the parrotlike mechanical mytacism (for it is really like a stammer) with which he will go on endlessly repeating such favorites as "myriad, sourceless, impalpable, outrageous, risible, profound," there is nevertheless something more to be said for his passion for overelaborate sentence structure.

Overelaborate they certainly are, baroque and involuted in the extreme, these sentences: trailing clauses, one after another, shadowily in apposition, or perhaps not even with so much connection as that; parenthesis after parenthesis, the parenthesis itself often containing one or more parentheses—they remind one of those brightly colored Chinese eggs of one's childhood, which when opened disclosed egg after egg, each smaller and subtler than the last. It is as if Mr. Faulkner, in a sort of hurried despair, had decided to try to tell us everything, absolutely everything, every last origin or source or quality or qualification, and every possible future or permutation as well, in one terrifically concentrated effort: each sentence to be, as it were, a microcosm. And it must be admitted that the practice is annoying and distracting.

It is annoying, at the end of a sentence, to find that one does not know in the least what was the subject of the verb that dangles *in vacuo*—it is distracting to have to go back and sort out the meaning, track down the structure from clause to clause, then only to find that after all it doesn't much matter, and that the obscurity was perhaps neither subtle nor important. And to the extent that one *is* annoyed and distracted, and *does* thus go back and work it out, it may be at once added that Mr. Faulkner has defeated his own ends. One has had, of course, to emerge from the stream, and to step away from it, in order properly to see it; and as Mr. Faulkner works precisely by a process of *immersion,* of hypnotizing his reader into *remaining immersed* in his stream, this occasional blunder produces irritation and failure.

Nevertheless, despite the blunders, and despite the bad habits and the willful bad writing (and willful it obviously is), the style as a whole is extraordinarily effective; the reader *does* remain immersed, *wants* to remain immersed, and it is interesting to look into the reasons for this. And at once, if one considers these queer sentences not simply by themselves, as monsters of grammar or awkwardness, but in their relation to the book as a whole, one sees a functional reason and necessity for their being as they are. They parallel in a curious and perhaps inevitable way, and not without aesthetic justification, the whole elaborate method of *deliberately withheld meaning,* of progressive and partial and delayed disclosure, which so often gives the characteristic shape to the novels themselves. It is a persistent offering of obstacles, a calculated system of screens and obtrusions, of confusions and ambiguous interpolations and delays, with one express purpose; and that purpose is simply to keep the form—and the idea—fluid and unfinished, still in motion, as it were, and unknown, until the dropping into place of the very last syllable.

What Mr. Faulkner is after, in a sense, is a *continuum.* He wants a medium without stops or pauses, a medium which is always *of the moment,* and of which the passage from moment to moment is as fluid and undetectable as in the life itself which he is purporting to give. It is all inside and underneath, or as seen from within and below; the reader must therefore be steadily *drawn in;* he must be powerfully and unremittingly hypnotized inward and downward to that image-stream; and this suggests, perhaps, a reason not only for the length and elaborateness of the sentence structure, but for the repetitiveness as well. The repetitiveness, and the steady iterative emphasis—like a kind of chanting or invocation—on certain relatively abstract words ("sonorous, latin, *vaguely* eloquent"), have the effect at last of producing, for Mr. Faulkner, a special language, a conglomerate of his own, which he uses with an astonishing virtuosity, and which, although in detailed analysis it may look shoddy, is actually for his purpose a life stream of almost miraculous adaptability. At the one extreme it is abstract, cerebral, time-and-space-obsessed, tortured and twisted, but nevertheless always with a living *pulse* in it; and at the other it can be as overwhelming in its simple vividness, its richness in the actual, as the flood scenes in *The Wild Palms.*

Obviously, such a style, especially when allied with such a *concern* for method, must make difficulties for the reader; and it must be admitted that Mr. Faulkner does little or nothing as a rule to make his highly complex "situation" easily available or perceptible. The reader must simply make up his mind to go to work, and in a sense to cooperate; his reward being that there *is* a situation to be given shape, a meaning to be extracted, and that half the fun is precisely in watching the queer, difficult, and often so laborious evolution of Mr. Faulkner's idea. And not so much idea, either, as form. For, like the great predecessor whom at least in this regard he so oddly resembles, Mr. Faulkner could say with Henry James that it is practically impossible to make any real distinction between theme and form. What immoderately delights him, alike in *Sanctuary, The Sound and the Fury, As I Lay Dying, Light in August, Pylon, Absalom, Absalom!,* and now again the *The Wild Palms,* and what sets him above—shall we say it firmly—all his American contemporaries, is his continuous preoccupation with the novel *as form,* his passionate concern with it, and a degree of success with it which would clearly have commanded the interest and respect of Henry James himself. The novel as revelation, the novel as slice-of-life, the novel as mere story, do not interest him: these he would say, like James again, "are the circumstances of the interest," but not the interest itself. The interest itself will be the use to which these circumstances are put, the degree to which they can be organized.

From this point of view, he is not in the least to be considered as a mere "Southern" writer: the "Southernness" of his scenes and characters is of little concern to him, just as little as the question whether they are pleasant or unpleasant, true or untrue. Verisimilitude—or, at any rate, *degree* of verisimilitude—he will cheerfully abandon, where necessary, if the compensating advantages of plan or tone are a sufficient inducement. The famous scene in *Sanctuary* of Miss Reba and Uncle Bud in which a "madam" and her cronies hold a wake for a dead gangster, while the small boy gets drunk, is quite false, taken out of its context; it is not endowed with the same *kind* of actuality which permeates the greater part of the book at all. Mr. Faulkner was cunning enough to see that a two-dimensional cartoon-like statement, at this juncture, would supply him with the effect of a chorus, and without in the least being perceived as a change in the temperature of truthfulness.

That particular kind of dilution, or adulteration, of verisimilitude was both practised and praised by James: as when he blandly admitted of *In the Cage* that his central character was "too ardent a focus of divination" to be quite credible. It was defensible simply because it made possible the coherence of the whole, and was itself absorbed back into the luminous texture. It was for him a device for organization, just as the careful cherishing of "viewpoint" was a device, whether simply or in counterpoint. Of Mr. Faulkner's devices, of this sort, aimed at the achievement of complex "form," the two most constant are the manipulation of viewpoint and the use of the flashback, or sudden shift of time-scene, forward or backward.

In *Sanctuary,* where the alternation of viewpoint is a little lawless, the complexity is given, perhaps a shade disingenuously, by violent shifts in time; a deliberate disarrangement of an otherwise straightforward story. Technically, there is no doubt that the novel, despite its fame, rattles a little; and Mr. Faulkner himself takes pains to disclaim it. But, even done with the left hand, it betrays a genius for form, quite apart from its wonderful virtuosity in other respects. *Light in August,* published a year after *Sanctuary,* repeats the same technique, that of a dislocation of time, and more elaborately; the time-shifts alternate with shifts in the viewpoint; and if the book is a failure it is perhaps because Mr. Faulkner's tendency to what is almost a hypertrophy of form is not here, as well as in the other novels, matched with the characters and the theme. Neither the person nor the story of Joe Christmas is seen fiercely enough—by its creator—to carry off that immense machinery of narrative; it would have needed another Popeye, or another Jiggs and Shumann, another Temple Drake, and for once Mr. Faulkner's inexhaustible inventiveness seems to have been at fault. Consequently what we see is an extraordinary power for form functioning relatively *in vacuo,* and existing only to sustain itself.

In the best of the novels, however—and it is difficult to choose between *The Sound and the Fury* and *The Wild Palms,* with *Absalom, Absalom!* a very close third—this tendency to hypertrophy of form has been sufficiently curbed; and it is interesting, too, to notice that in all these three (and in that remarkable *tour de force, As I Lay Dying,* as well), while there is still a considerable reliance on time-shift, the effect of richness and complexity is chiefly obtained by a very skillful fugue-like alternation of viewpoint. Fugue-like in *The Wild Palms*—and fugue-like especially, of course, in *As I Lay Dying,* where the shift is kaleidoscopically rapid, and where, despite an astonishing violence to plausibility (in the reflections, and *language* of reflection, of the characters), an effect of the utmost reality and immediateness is nevertheless produced. Fugue-like, again, in *Absalom, Absalom!,* where indeed one may say the form is really circular—there is no beginning and no ending properly speaking, and therefore no *logical* point of entrance: we must just submit, and follow the circling of the author's interest, which turns a light inward towards the center, but every moment from a new angle, a new point of view. The story unfolds, therefore, now in one color of light, now in another, with references backward and forward: those that refer forward being necessarily, for the moment, blind. What is complete in Mr. Faulkner's pattern, *a priori,* must nevertheless remain incomplete for us until the very last stone is in place; what is "real," therefore, at one stage of the unfolding, or from one point of view, turns out to be "unreal" from another; and we find that one among other things with which we are engaged is the fascinating sport of trying to separate truth from legend, watching the growth of legend from truth, and finally reaching the conclusion that the distinction is itself false.

Something of the same sort is true also of *The Sound and the Fury*—and this, with its massive four-part symphonic structure, is perhaps the most beautifully *wrought* of the whole series, and an indubitable masterpiece of what James loved to call the "fictive art." The joinery is flawless in its intricacy; it is a novelist's novel—a whole textbook on the craft of fiction in itself, comparable in its way to *What Maisie Knew* or *The Golden Bowl.*

But if it is important, for the moment, to emphasize Mr. Faulkner's genius for form, and his continued exploration of its possibilities, as against the usual concern with the violence and dreadfulness of his themes—though we might pause to remind carpers on this score of the fact that the best of Henry James is precisely that group of last novels which so completely concerned themselves with moral depravity—it is also well to keep in mind his genius for invention, whether of character or episode. The inventiveness is of the richest possible sort—a headlong and tumultuous abundance, an exuberant generosity and vitality, which makes most other contemporary fiction look very pale and chaste indeed. It is an unforgettable gallery of portraits, whether character or caricature, and all of them endowed with a violent and immediate vitality.

> He is at once [to quote once more from James] one of the most corrupt of writers and one of the most naïf, the most mechanical and pedantic, and the fullest of *bonhomie* and natural impulse. He is one of the finest of artists and one of the coarsest. Viewed in one way, his novels are ponderous, shapeless, overloaded; his touch is graceless, violent, barbarous. Viewed in another, his tales have more color, more composition, more grasp of the reader's attention than any others. [His] style would demand a chapter apart. It is the least simple style, probably, that was ever written; it bristles, it cracks, it swells and swaggers; but it is a perfect expression of the man's genius. Like his genius, it contains a certain quantity of everything, from immaculate gold to flagrant dross. He was a very bad writer, and yet un-

questionably he was a very great writer. We may say briefly, that in so far as his method was an instinct it was successful, and that in so far as it was a theory it was a failure. But both in instinct and in theory he had the aid of an immense force of conviction. His imagination warmed to its work so intensely that there was nothing his volition could not impose upon it. Hallucination settled upon him, and he believed anything that was necessary in the circumstances.

That passage, from Henry James's essay on Balzac, is almost word for word, with scarcely a reservation, applicable to Mr. Faulkner. All that is lacking is Balzac's greater *range* of understanding and tenderness, his greater freedom from special preoccupations. For this, one would hazard the guess that Mr. Faulkner has the gifts—and time is still before him.

William Faulkner's Style

by Warren Beck

No other contemporary American novelist of comparable stature has been as frequently or as severely criticized for his style as has William Faulkner. Yet he is a brilliantly original and versatile stylist. The condemnations of his way of writing have been in part just; all but the most idolatrous of Faulkner's admirers must have wished he had blotted a thousand infelicities. However, an enumeration of his faults in style would leave still unsaid the most important things about his style. There is need here for a reapportionment of negative and positive criticism.

It is true that the preponderant excellences of Faulkner's prose, when recognized, make his faults all the more conspicuous and irritating. And under criticism Faulkner has not only remained guilty of occasional carelessness, especially in sentence construction, but seems to have persisted in mannerisms. On the other hand, his progress as a stylist has been steady and rapid; his third novel, *Sartoris,* while still experimenting toward a technique, was a notable advance over his first two in style as well as in theme and narrative structure, and in his fourth novel, *The Sound and the Fury,* style is what it has continued to be in all his subsequent work, a significant factor, masterfully controlled. This growth has been made largely without the aid of appreciative criticism, and in the face of some misunderstanding and abuse of the most dynamic qualities in his writing. It is quite possible that Faulkner would have paid more attention to the critics' valid objections if these had not been so frequently interlarded with misconceptions of his stylistic method, or indeed complete insensitivity to it.

Repetition of words, for instance, has often seemed an obvious fault. At times, however, Faulkner's repetitions may be a not unjustifiable byproduct of his thematic composition. Some of his favorites in *Absalom, Absalom!*—not just Miss Rosa's "demon," which may be charged off to her own mania, nor "indolent" applied to Bon, but such recurrent terms as *effluvium, outrage, grim, indomitable, ruthless, fury, fatality*—seem to intend adumbration of the tale's whole significance and tone. Nor is the reiteration as frequent or as obvious here as in earlier books; perhaps

Reprinted with permission from *American Prefaces,* Vol. VI, No. 3, Spring, 1941, pp. 195-211.

Faulkner has been making an experiment over which he is increasingly gaining control.

Faulkner often piles up words in a way that brings the charge of prolixity. He has Wilbourne say of his life with Charlotte in Chicago,

> it was the mausoleum of love, it was the stinking catafalque of the dead corpse borne between the olfactoryless walking shapes of the immortal unsentient demanding ancient meat.

However, these word-series, while conspicuous at times, may have a place in a style as minutely analytical as Faulkner's. In their typical form they are not redundant, however elaborate, and sometimes their cumulative effect is undeniable—for example, the "long still hot weary dead September afternoon" when Quentin listens to Miss Rosa's story. Colonel Feinman, the wealthy exploiter of impecunious aviators, had as secretary "a young man, sleek, in horn rim glasses," who spoke "with a kind of silken insolence, like the pampered intelligent hateridden eunuchmountebank of an eastern despot," and here the amplification redounds to the significance of the whole scene. Quite often, too, these series of words, while seemingly extravagant, are a remarkably compressed rendering, as in the phrase "passionate tragic ephemeral loves of adolescence."

In fairness it must be noted too that Faulkner's later work never drops to the level of fantastic verbosity found in the thematic paragraph introducing his second novel, *Mosquitoes.* Nor does he any longer break the continuum of his narrative with rhapsodies like the notable description of the mule in *Sartoris,* a sort of cadenza obviously done out of exuberance. In the later books profuseness of language is always knit into the thematic structure. Thus the elaborate lyrical descriptions of the sunrise and of a spring rain in book three of *The Hamlet* furnish by their imagery and mood a sharp, artistically serviceable contrast to the perversion of the idiot Ike Snopes, and as such they deepen the melancholy perspective from which this episode is observed.

Faulkner's studied use of a full style and his sense of its place in the architectonics of an extended and affecting narrative is well displayed in the last chapters of *Light in August,* chapter nineteen closing with the first climax, Joe Christmas' death, poetically expressed; chapter twenty closing similarly in the second and more comprehensive climax of Hightower's final vision; and then chapter twenty-one, which completes the book, furnishing a modulation to detached calm through the simply prosaic, somewhat humorous account, by a new and neutral spokesman, of the exodus of Lena and Byron into Tennessee. Indeed, one of the best indexes to the degree of Faulkner's control of eloquence is in a comparison of the novels' conclusions—some of them in a full descriptive style, as in *Soldiers' Pay, Sartoris, Sanctuary,* and to a degree in *The Sound and the Fury* and *The Unvanquished;* more of the novels closing with a meaningful but plainly stated utterance or gesture of a character, as in *Mosquitoes, As I Lay Dying, Pylon, Absalom, Absalom!, The Wild Palms,* and *The Hamlet*—(the last that wonderful "Snopes turned his head and spat over the wagon wheel. He jerked the reins slightly. 'Come up,' he said.") This ratio suggests that while Faulkner does not avoid elaboration, neither is he its slave.

Faulkner's diction, charged and proliferate though it may be, usually displays a nice precision, and this is especially evident in its direct imagery. An example is in the glimpse of Cash, after he has worked all night in the rain, finishing his mother's coffin:

> In the lantern light his face is calm, musing; slowly he strokes his hands on his raincoated thighs in a gesture deliberate, final and composed.

Frequently, however, Faulkner proceeds in descriptive style beyond epithet and abstract definition to figurative language. Having written,

> It is just dawn, daylight: that gray and lonely suspension filled with the peaceful and tentative waking of birds.

he goes on in the next sentence to a simile:

> The air, inbreathed, is like spring water.

The novels abound in examples of his talent for imaginative comparisons; for instance, the hard-boiled flier Shumann, dressed up:

> He wore a new gray homburg hat, not raked like in the department store cuts but set square on the back of his head so that (not tall, with blue eyes in a square thin profoundly sober face) he looked out not from beneath it but from within it with open and fatal humorlessness, like an early Briton who has been assured that the Roman governor will not receive him unless he wear the borrowed centurion's helmet.

There is nothing unique, however, in Faulkner's use of direct and forceful diction or fine figurative image. What is most individual in his style is its persistent lyrical embroidery and coloring, in extended passages, of the narrative theme. In this sense Faulkner is one of the most subjective of writers, his brooding temperament constantly probing and interpreting his subject matter. Thus his full style is comprehensive in its intention. He may often be unfashionably rhapsodic, but he seldom falls into the preciosity that lingers over a passage for its own sweet sake. Definition of his story as a whole and the enhancement of its immediate appeals to the imagination are his constant aims.

The latest of Faulkner's novels [under consideration here] demonstrates the grasp he has developed upon all the devices of his style. *The Hamlet* is a sort of prose fantasia; the various episodes employ colloquial tall stories, poetic description, folk humor, deliberate reflective narration, swift cryptic drama, and even a grotesque allegory of Snopes in hell. Differing in tone from the elegiac brooding of *Light in August,* or the exasperated volubility of *Pylon,* the modulant intricacy and fusion of

Absalom, Absalom!, the tender directness of *The Unvanquished,* or the eloquent turbulence of *The Wild Palms, The Hamlet* seems an extravaganza improvised more freely in a more detached mood, the author apparently delighting in the realizations of varied subject matters through the flexibilities of his multiform style.

A number of passages in *The Hamlet* give precise indications of Faulkner's purpose as a stylist, inasmuch as they are reworkings of material released as short stories in magazines from four to nine years before the novel's publication. "Spotted Horses," which appeared in *Scribner's* for June 1931, contains in germ Flem Snopes' whole career in *The Hamlet.* The story is in first person; Ratliff is the reciter, but he is not quite the shrewd and benevolent spectator he becomes under the touches of Faulkner's own descriptions in the third-person narrative of the novel. The short story moves faster, of course, sketching the drama more broadly and making no pause for brooding lyrical interpretation. Faulkner's omniscient narration of the episode is almost twice as long as Ratliff's simple monologue, and rises to an altogether different plane of conception and diction. The contrast is almost like that between a ballad and a tone poem.

This difference, which certainly must indicate Faulkner's free and considered choice and his fundamental aesthetic inclination, can be defined by a comparison of parallel passages from the horse-auction scene, when the Texan tries to hold one of the animals and continue his salestalk. The Scribner short story, with Ratliff as first-person narrator, reads as follows:

> "Look it over," he says, with his heels dug too and that white pistol sticking outen his pocket and his neck swole up like a spreading adder's until you could just tell what he was saying, cussing the horse and talking to us all at once: "Look him over, the fiddle-headed son of fourteen fathers. Try him, buy him, you will get the best—" Then it was all dust again, and we couldn't see nothing but spotted hide and mane, and that ere Texas man's boot-heels like a couple of walnuts on two strings, and after a while that two-gallon hat come sailing out like a fat old hen crossing a fence. When the dust settled again, he was just getting outen the far fence corner, brushing himself off. He come and got his hat and brushed it off and come and clumb onto the gate post again.

In the novel the parallel passage has been recast in the third person thus:

> "Look him over boys," the Texan panted, turning his own suffused face and the protuberant glare of his eyes toward the fence. "Look him over quick. Them shoulders and—" He had relaxed for an instant apparently. The animal exploded again; again for an instant the Texan was free of the earth, though he was still talking: "—and legs you whoa I'll tear your face right look him over quick boys worth fifteen dollars of let me get a holt of who'll make me a bid whoa you blareyed jack rabbit, whoa!" They were moving now—a kaleidoscope of inextricable and incredible violence

> on the periphery of which the metal clasps of the Texan's suspenders sun-glinted in ceaseless orbit, with terrific slowness across the lot. Then the broad claycolored hat soared deliberately outward; an instant later the Texan followed it, though still on his feet, and the pony shot free in mad, stag-like bounds. The Texan picked up the hat and struck the dust from it against his leg, and returned to the fence and mounted the post again.

Obviously the difference is not only quantitative but qualitative. Instead of Ratliff's "that old two-gallon hat come sailing out like a fat old hen crossing a fence" there is Faulkner's "the broad claycolored hat soared deliberately outward"; Ratliff sees "that ere Texas man's boot-heels like a couple of walnuts on two strings," but Faulkner shows a "kaleidoscope of inextricable and incredible violence on the periphery of which the metal clasps of the Texan's suspenders sun-glinted in ceaseless orbit with terrific slowness across the lot." This latter represents the style Faulkner has chosen to develop; he can do the simpler and more objective narration, but when given such an opportunity as in the amalgamating of these magazine stories into a novel, he insists on transmuting the factual-objective into the descriptive-definitive colored by his imagination and elaborated by his resourcefulness in language.

In its typical exercise this style gives image only incidentally and exists primarily to enhance and sustain mood. Thus Wilbourne's first approach to the house where his meeting with Charlotte is to begin their passionate and disastrous love story is set in this key:

> . . . they entered: a court paved with the same soft, quietly rotting brick. There was a stagnant pool with a terra-cotta figure, a mass of lantana, the single palm, the thick rich leaves and the heavy white stars of the jasmine bush where light fell upon it through open French doors, the court balcony—overhung too on three sides, the walls of that same annealing brick lifting a rampart broken and nowhere level against the glare of the city on the low eternally overcast sky, and over all, brittle, dissonant and ephemeral, the spurious sophistication of the piano like symbols scrawled by adolescent boys upon an ancient decayed rodent-scavengered tomb.

The reporter's mood of anxious inquiry and the frustration which is thematic in *Pylon* are both represented as he telephones:

> Now he too heard only dead wirehum, as if the other end of it extended beyond atmosphere, into cold space; as though he listened now to the profound sound of infinity, of void itself filled with the cold unceasing murmur of aeonweary and unflagging stars.

This organic quality of Faulkner's style, sustaining through essentially poetic devices an orchestration of meaning, makes it impossible to judge him adequately by brief quotation. In the description of Temple's first hours in Madam Reba's brothel, for instance, the thematic recurrence from page to page to subjectively interpreted imagery builds up in a time continuum the mood of the girl's trance-like state of shock and also the larger fact of her isolation in the sordid. First,

> The drawn shades, cracked into a myriad pattern like old skin, blew faintly on the bright air, breathing into the room on waning surges the sound of Sabbath traffic, festive, steady, evanescent . . .

and then, three pages further,

> The shades blew steadily in the windows, with faint rasping sounds. Temple began to hear a clock. It sat on the mantel above a grate filled with fluted green paper. The clock was of flowered china, supported by four china nymphs. It had only one hand, scrolled and gilded, halfway between ten and eleven, lending to the otherwise blank face a quality of unequivocal assertion, as though it had nothing whatever to do with time . . .

and then, two pages further,

> In the window the cracked shade, yawning now and then with a faint rasp against the frame, let twilight into the room in fainting surges. From beneath the shade the smoke-colored twilight emerged in slow puffs like signal smoke from a blanket, thickening in the room. The china figures which supported the clock gleamed in hushed smooth flexions: knee, elbow, flank, arm and breast in attitudes of voluptuous lassitude. The glass face, become mirror-like, appeared to hold all reluctant light, holding in its tranquil depths a quiet gesture of moribund time, one-armed like a veteran from the wars. Half past ten o'clock. Temple lay in the bed, looking at the clock, thinking about half-past-ten-o'clock.

Yet side by side with this richly interpretative style there exists in almost all of Faulkner's work a realistic colloquialism, expressing lively dialogue that any playwright might envy, and even carrying over into sustained first-person narrative the flavor of regionalism and the idiosyncrasies of character. In the colloquial vein Faulkner's brilliance is unsurpassed in contemporary American fiction. He has fully mastered the central difficulty, to retain verisimilitude while subjecting the prolix and monotonous raw material of most natural speech to an artistic pruning and pointing up. *Sanctuary,* for an example, is full of excellent dialogue, sharply individualized. And Faulkner's latest book not only contains some of his most poetic writing but has one of his best talkers, Ratliff, both in extended anecdote in monologue and in dramatic conversations. Ratliff's reflective, humorous, humane, but skeptical nature, a triumph in characterization, is silhouetted largely out of his talk about the hamlet's affairs.

Faulkner also can weave colloquial bits into the matrix of a more literary passage, with the enlarging effect of a controlled dissonance. Thus Quentin imagines Henry Sutpen and Charles Bon, at the end of the war, Charles determined to marry Judith, Henry forbidding; and then into Quentin's elaboration of the scene breaks the voice of his father, continuing the story, giving its denouement in the words vulgarly uttered by Wash Jones:

> (It seemed to Quentin that he could actually see them. . . . They faced one another on the two gaunt horses, two men, young, not yet in the world, not yet breathed over long enough, to be old but with old eyes, with unkempt hair and faces gaunt and weathered as if cast by some spartan and even niggard hand from bronze, in worn and patched gray weathered now to the color of dead leaves, the one with the tarnished braid of an officer, the other plain of cuff, the pistol lying yet across the saddle bow unaimed, the two faces calm, the voices not even raised: *Dont you pass the shadow of this post, this branch, Charles;* and *I am going to pass it, Henry*)—and then Wash Jones sitting that saddleless mule before Miss Rosa's gate, shouting her name into the sunny and peaceful quiet of the street, saying, "Air you Rosie Coldfield? Then you better come on out yon. Henry has done shot that durn French feller. Kilt him dead as a beef."

Master of colloquialism in dramatic scene though he is, Faulkner sometimes lays aside this power in order to put into a character's mouth the fullest expression of the narrative's meaning. The mature Bayard Sartoris, looking back to Civil War times, telling the story of his boyhood and youth in *The Unvanquished,* opens what is Faulkner's most straightforward narrative, and his only novel related throughout by one character in the first person, in this strain:

> Behind the smokehouse that summer, Ringo and I had a living map. Although Vicksburg was just a handful of chips from the woodpile and the River a trench scraped into the packed earth with the point of a hoe, it (river, city, and terrain) lived, possessing even in miniature that ponderable though passive recalcitrance of topography which outweighs artillery, against which the most brilliant of victories and the most tragic of defeats are but the loud noises of a moment.

At times it seems as though the author, after having created an unsophisticated character, is elbowing him off the stage, as when the rustic Darl Bundren sees "the square squat shape of the coffin on the sawhorses like a cubistic bug," or as when in the short story, "All The Dead Pilots," the World War flier John Sartoris is characterized as having a vocabulary of "perhaps two hundred words" and then is made to say,

> . . . I knew that if I busted in and dragged him out and bashed his head off, I'd not only be cashiered, I'd be clinked for life for having infringed the articles of alliance by invading foreign property without warrant or something.

For the most part, however, the transcending of colloquial verisimilitude in the novels is a fairly controlled and consistent technique, the characters Faulkner most often endows with penetration and eloquence being his philosophical spectators. Undoubtedly his chief concern, though, is with a lyric encompassment of his narrative's whole meaning rather than with the reticences of objective dramatic representation.

Thus many of his characters speak with the tongues of themselves and of William Faulkner. As Quentin and his Harvard roommate Shreve evolve the reconstruction of Thomas Sutpen's story which constitutes the second half of *Absalom, Absalom!,* Quentin thinks when Shreve talks, "He sounds just like father," and later, when Quentin has the floor, Shreve interrupts with "Don't say it's just me that sounds like your old man," which certainly shows that Faulkner realizes what he is doing. Actually he does make some differences among these voices: Miss Rosa rambles and ejaculates with erratic spinsterish emotion, Mr. Compson is elaborately and sometimes parenthetically ironic, Quentin is most sensitively imaginative and melancholy, Shreve most detached and humorous. What they have in common is the scope and pitch of an almost lyrical style which Faulkner has arbitrarily fixed upon for an artistic instrument. The justification of all such practices is empirical; imaginative writing must not be judged by its minute correspondence to fact but by its total effect; and to object against Faulkner's style that men and women don't really talk in such long sentences, with so full a vocabulary so fancifully employed, is as narrowly dogmatic as was Sinclair Lewis, in *Main Street,* insisting that Sir Launcelot didn't actually speak in "honeyed pentameters."

Typical instances of Faulkner's endowing his characters with precise diction and fluency may show that on the whole it is not an unacceptable convention. Thus Wilbourne's full and finished sentence—

> We lived in an apartment that wasn't bohemian, it wasn't even a tabloid love-nest, it wasn't even in that part of town but in a neighborhood dedicated by both city ordinance and architecture to the second year of wedlock among the five-thousand-a-year bracket.

—though it is not stylistically rooted in his manner as characterized up to this point, is not inconsistent with his personality and sensibilities, and it does get on with the story. Equally acceptable is Ratliff's remark about the platitudinous family-fleeing I. O. Snopes,

> What's his name? that quick-fatherer, the Moses with his mouth full of mottoes and his coat-tail full of them already half-grown retroactive sons?

Its keen diction and nice rhythm are not essentially false to Ratliff, but only an idealization in language of the percipient, humorous sewing-machine salesman the reader already knows. The same is true of those tumbling floods of phrases, too prolonged for human breath to utter, with which the reporter in *Pylon* assaults the sympathies of editor Hagood; they are not so much a part of dialogue as an intense symbol of the pace of racing aviation and the reporter's frantic concern for his protégés among the fliers.

It is interesting to note that Faulkner's full style somewhat resembles older literary uses, such as the dramatic chorus, the prologue and epilogue, and the *dramatis personae* themselves in soliloquy and extended speech. The aim of any such device is not objective realism but revelation of theme, a revelation raised by the unstinted resourcefulness and power of its language to the highest ranges of imaginative outlook. No wonder that with such a purpose Faulkner often comes closer than is common in these times to Shakespeare's imperial and opulent use of words. If unfortunately his ambition has sometimes led Faulkner to perpetrate some rather clotted prose, perhaps these lapses may be judged charitably in the light of the great endeavor they but infrequently flaw.

More particularly Faulkner's full sentence structure springs from the elaborateness of his fancies ramifying in descriptive imagery. Thus editor Hagood, perpetually beset by small annoyances and chronically irritated by them, drops himself wearily into his roadster's low seat,

> . . . whereupon without sound or warning the golfbag struck him across the head and shoulder with an apparently calculated and lurking viciousness, emitting a series of dry clicks as though produced by the jaws of a beast domesticated though not tamed, half in fun and half in deadly seriousness, like a pet shark.

Another typical source of fullness in Faulkner's sentences is a tendency to musing speculation, sometimes proceeding to the statement of alternative suggestions. Thus Miss Rosa speaks of wearing garments left behind by the eloping aunt in "kindness or haste or oversight," that doing its bit in a sentence well over three hundred words long. Such characteristic theorizing may run to the length of this postscript to a description of Flem Snopes:

> . . . a thick squat soft man of no establishable age between twenty and thirty, with a broad still face containing a tight seam of mouth stained slightly at the corners with tobacco, and eyes the color of stagnant water, and projecting from among the other features in startling and sudden paradox, a tiny predatory nose like the beak of a small hawk. It was as though the original nose had been left off by the original designer or craftsman and the unfinished job taken over by someone of a radically different school or perhaps by some viciously maniacal humorist or perhaps by one who had only time to clap into the center of the face a frantic and desperate warning.

Even the most elaborate and esoteric of these speculations are not limited to third-person narrative; Faulkner's pervasive subjectivity injects such abstractions too, as well as extended imagery, into the reflections and speech of many of his characters, again most typically those who contemplate and interpret the action of the stories, who act as chorus or soliloquize. Here too the device proves itself in practice. When such characters brood over the events, painstakingly rehearsing details, piling one hypothesis upon another, their very tentativeness creates for the reader the clouded enigmatic perspective of reality itself. Thus Miss Rosa's account, with reinterpretation imposed upon memory, of Sutpen's driving in to church with his family:

> It was as though the sister whom I had never laid eyes on, who before I was born had vanished into the stronghold of an ogre or a djinn, was now to return through a dispensation of one day only, to the world which she had quitted, and I a child of three, waked early for the occasion, dressed and curled as if for Christmas, for an occasion more serious than Christmas even, since now and at last this ogre or djinn had agreed for the sake of the wife and the children to come to church, to permit them at least to approach the vicinity of salvation, to at least give Ellen one chance to struggle with him for those children's souls on a battleground where she could be supported not only by Heaven but by her own family and people of her own kind; yes, even for the moment submitting himself to redemption, or lacking that, at least chivalrous for the instant even though still unregenerate.

The foregoing examples, however, do not illustrate Faulkner's style at its most involved, as in this passage from Quentin's consciousness, while he listens to Miss Rosa's reconstruction of the Sutpen family history:

> It should have been later than it was; it should have been late, yet the yellow slashes of mote-palpitant sunlight were latticed no higher up the impalpable wall of gloom which separated them; the sun seemed hardly to have moved. It (the talking, the telling) seemed (to him, to Quentin) to partake of that logic- and reason-flouting quality of a dream which the sleeper knows must have occurred, stillborn and complete, in a second, yet the very quality upon which it must depend to move the dreamer (verisimilitude) to credulity—horror or pleasure or amazement—depends as completely upon a formal recognition of and acceptance of elapsed and yet-elapsing time as music or a printed tale.

By its parentheses and involution and fullness this last sentence illustrates that occasionally extreme eccentricity most often and most rightfully objected to in its author's style. At the same time this sentence may give a key to Faulkner's entire method and typify its artistic purposefulness—to create "that logic- and reason-flouting quality of a dream," yet to depend upon the recognized verisimilitude of "elapsed and yet-elapsing time." Such a product is not necessarily mere nightmare; it is often a real quality of experience at its greatest intensity and acuteness. In his most characteristic writing Faulkner is trying to render the transcendent life of the mind, the crowded composite of associative and analytical consciousness which expands the vibrant moment into the reaches of all time, simultaneously observing, remembering, interpreting, and modifying the object of its awareness. To this end the sentence as a rhetorical unit (however strained) is made to hold diverse yet related elements in a sort of saturated solution, which is perhaps the nearest that language as the instrument of fiction can come to the instantaneous complexities of consciousness itself. Faulkner really seems to be trying to give narrative prose another dimension.

To speak of Faulkner's fiction as dream-like (using Quentin's notion as a key) does not imply that his style is phantasmagoric, deranged, or incoherent. Dreams are not always delirium, and association, sometimes the supplanter of pattern, can also be its agent. The dreaming mind, while envisaging experience strangely, may find in that strangeness a fresh revelation, all the more profound in that the conventional and adventitious are pierced through. Similarly inhibitions and apathies must be transcended in any really imaginative inquiry, and thus do Faulkner's speculative characters ponder over the whole story, and project into cumulative drama its underlying significations. Behind all of them, of course, is their master-dreamer; Faulkner's own dominating temperament, constantly interpreting, is in the air of all these narratives, reverberant. Hence, no matter how psychological the story's material, Faulkner never falls into the mere enumeration which in much stream-of-consciousness writing dissolves all drama and reduces the narrative to a case history without the shaping framework of analysis, or even to an unmapped anachronistic chaos of raw consciousness. Faulkner is always a dynamic storyteller, never just a reporter of unorganized phenomena. His most drastic, most dream-like use of stream of consciousness, for instance, in *The Sound and the Fury,* is not only limited to the first two sections of the book, but it sketches a plot which in the lucid sections that follow gradually emerges clear-cut.

As clear-cut, at least, as Faulkner's stories can be. Here again is illustrated the close relation of his style to his whole point of view. If Faulkner's sentences sometimes soar and circle involved and prolonged, if his scenes become halls of mirrors repeating tableaux in a progressive magnification, if echoes multiply into the dissonance of infinite overtones, it is because the meanings his stories unfold are complex, mysterious, obscure, and incomplete. There is no absolute, no eternal pure white radiance in such presentations, but rather the stain of many colors, refracted and shifting in kaleidoscopic suspension, about the center of man's enigmatic behavior and fate, within the drastic orbit of mortality. Such being Faulkner's view of life, such is his style.

To this view the very rhythm of Faulkner's prose is nicely adjusted. It is not emphatic; rather it is a slow prolonged movement, nothing dashing, even at its fullest flood, but surging with an irresistible momentum. His effects insofar as they depend on prose rhythms are never staccato; they are cumulative rather than abrupt. Such a prose rhythm supplements the contributions of full vocabulary and lengthy sentence toward suspension rather than impact, and consequently toward deep realization rather than quick surprise. And the prolonged, even murmur of Faulkner's voice throughout his pages is an almost hypnotic induction into those detailed and darkly colored visions of life which drift across the horizons of his imagination like clouds—great yet vaporous, changing yet enduring, unearthly yet of common substance. It might be supposed that his occasionally crowded and circumlocutory style would destroy narrative pace and consequence. Actually this hovering of active imagination, while employing the sustained lyricism and solid abstraction which differentiate Faulkner from the objective realist, furnishes the epitome of drama. The whole aim is at perspective, through the multiple dimensions of experience, upon a subject in that suspension which allows reflection. The accomplishment is the gradual, sustained, and enriched revelation of meaning; in Faulkner's novels drama is of that highest form which awaits the unfolding of composite action, characterization, mood, and idea, through the medium of style.

Faulkner himself probably would admit the relative inadequacy of instrument to purpose, would agree with Mr. Compson in calling language "that meager and fragile thread by which the little surface corners and edges of men's secret and solitary lives may be joined for an instant." Faulkner perhaps has no greater faith in the word than have his contemporaries who have partially repudiated it, but instead of joining that somewhat paradoxical literary trend, he seems determined to exploit an imperfect device to the uttermost within the limits of artistic illusion. Thus, although in certain passages he has demonstrated his command of a simplified objective method, he has not made it his invariable device, nor does he allow its contemporary vogue to prevent his using words in the old-fashioned way for whatever they are worth, descriptively and definitively.

Faulkner's whole narrative method, as described, may seem to be a retrogression in technique. Two main tendencies in modern fiction have been toward a more and more material dramatic presentation, depending simply upon the naming of objects and acts and the reporting of speech, and on the other hand, toward an ostensibly complete and unbroken reproduction of the free flow of consciousness. These methods have produced books as radically different as *The Sun Also Rises* and *Ulysses,* yet they have elements in common. In both types the author attempts to conceal himself completely behind his materials, to give them the quality of integral phenomena, and in line with this purpose the style aims at pure reproduction, never allowing definition and interpretation from any detached point of view. These have been honest attempts, a great deal of fine craftsmanship has gone into them, and some of the products have been excellent in their kind. Yet at their most extreme these have been movements in the one direction toward bareness, impoverishment, and in the other toward incoherence. Confronted by the imperfections and confusions of the present scene, and made hyperskeptical by deference to scientific method, the writers who have attempted absolute objectivity (whether dramatic or psychological, whether in overt event or stream of association) have sometimes produced what looks like an anti-intellectual aesthetic of futility and inconsequence. So in another sense Faulkner's narrative technique, particularly as implemented by his full style, instead of being a retrogression may represent one kind of progression through the danger of impasse created by too great submission to vogues of photographic or psychographic reproduction.

Yet Faulkner's is not altogether a return to an older expressiveness, not a complete departure from the modern schools of Hemingway and Joyce. In his colloquial passages he is quite as objectively dramatic as the one, in his rehearsal of the fantasies of acute consciousness he follows the other—and it should be remembered that he is superlatively skillful at both, so that it cannot be said that he puts these objective methods aside because he cannot use them. Furthermore, Faulkner is fond of employing in extended passages one of the favorite modern means of objectivity in fiction, the first-person narrator, using the device toward its most honored modern purpose, the attainment of detached perspective and the creation of realistic illusion concerning large vistas of the story. In short, there is no method in modern fiction which Faulkner does not comprehend and use on occasion. Fundamentally Faulkner's only heterodoxy by present standards of style is his fullness, especially as it takes the form of descriptive eloquence or abstraction and definitiveness. What is stylistically most remarkable in his work is the synthesis he has effected between the subtleties of modern narrative techniques and the resources of language employed in the traditionally poetic or interpretative vein. That such a synthesis is feasible is demonstrated in the dynamic forms of his novels, and it may be prelude to significant new developments in the methods of fiction.

Faulkner or Theological Inversion

by Claude-Edmonde Magny

The French philosopher Alain wrote in his *Propos de Littérature*: "I am far from certain that beautiful works please the reader. Sometimes it seems they do just the opposite. They take hold of us even while we resist them. It may well be that admiration is not pleasure but a kind of attention. . . ." He applies these remarks to Balzac's novels, in which "the reader is neither soothed nor reassured; whether he is pleased or not is a matter of indifference; he may even be tempted to chastise an art devoid of all courtesy, by refusing it or by mocking it."

Among modern American novelists, Faulkner, in this respect, may be compared to Balzac. He cares just as little for the reader's opinion or approbation. Even more than Balzac, he is deliberately obscure, at times seems not to care if he wearies his victim, and is never more original or more inexorably true to himself than when he makes the fewest concessions and dares to be obscure or wearisome unashamedly. Such traits cannot be ascribed to technical immaturity, for they are found less in his early and rather simple works (*Mosquitoes, Soldiers' Pay*) than in the disconcerting ones (*Absalom, Absalom!, The Wild Palms*) which are of a later period. As with Balzac—during the forty-page description of Guérande which opens *Béatrix,* or when he resorts to melodrama in *l'Histoire des Treize*—the apparent narrative perverseness of Faulkner's stories seems justified and indeed inevitable as soon as the secret reasons for it are understood.

The most conspicuous peculiarities of Faulkner's art are: First, that he appears incapable of telling a story otherwise than by beginning at the end, tracing the course of time backward, as in the short story "Wash" or *Wild Palms* and especially in *Absalom,* where we have to work our way back through a hundred years and three generations. Secondly, that he needs to have two stories to tell at the same time, the stories being either juxtaposed as in *The Wild Palms* . . . or subtly interwoven . . . as in *Pylon*. . . . And finally, that Faulkner has an almost childish taste for riddles—as, for example, when he gives the same name, Quentin, to

Condensed from "Faulkner ou l'Inversion Theologique." From *L'Age du Roman américain,* by Claude-Edmonde Magny, trans. Jacqueline Merriam (Paris: Editions du Seuil, 1948), pp. 196–243.

both uncle and niece in *The Sound and the Fury,* or when he conceals to the very end the name of the reporter in *Pylon.* . . . Besides this, he often willfully avoids either *naming* a crucial event (such as the murder of Sutpen or the granddaughter of Wash Jones in "Wash") or informing us at all about decisive facts (the rape in *Sanctuary* or the Negro blood of Joe Christmas). The common reader is liable to get a headache and charge the novelist with coquetry and games.

Added to these narrative peculiarities are the purely stylistical ones: the lavish use of epithets ("the long still hot weary dead September afternoon . . ." in the second sentence of *Absalom*) and the immoderate length of sentences, laden with subordinate clauses, which bewilder and overwhelm the reader. (Proust is short-winded compared to Faulkner.) Take, for example, the six-page sentence of "The Bear" in *Go Down, Moses* which contains a two-page parenthesis to boot, or the long, confusing sentence in Caddy-Candace's biography in the appendix to *The Sound and the Fury,* supposedly written to clarify events occurring in the last part of the novel. . . . Like Mallarmé, Faulkner seems to have been stubbornly bent upon injecting a little more obscurity into a reality which appeared to him too orderly and not chaotic enough.

Time as Moloch

. . . Malcolm Cowley . . . suggested that Faulkner's scant concern for his eventual reader may be a question either of nervous diffidence or of his failure to realize that he had a public. He never seemed to care about the inaccurate information repeatedly published about his life or about the fate of his books, once he had completed them. . . . But this is only a partial explanation, for his works have become even more inaccessible with age and success. The narrative complexity of Faulkner's fiction cannot be dismissed as a lack of skill or as a mark of indifference to the reader. . . . It is closely bound up with the vision of the world he wishes to convey. . . .

As Jean-Paul Sartre and Jean Pouillon have shown, time in particular undergoes strange treatment in Faulkner's narrative. The story is continuously delayed by parentheses and interpolations. It unfolds backward, against the grain, instead of proceeding toward the future as one would normally expect. Each episode, wrapped in obscurity, sends the reader back to another one, equally obscure, which occurred twenty or thirty years before. Thus, in *Absalom, Absalom!,* one must eventually hear about events which took place years before in Haiti, in order to understand Sutpen's opposition to his daughter's marriage to his son's best friend. In *Light in August* we are abruptly taken back to a little boy's adventures in a children's home some thirty years previously, which explain the subsequent behavior of Christmas. Faulkner very often dismisses official chronology altogether: Quentin's act of breaking his watch has, as Sartre ingeniously explained, a symbolic value, as does the fact that Benjy, the idiot, cannot read time. Instead of the time of clocks, oriented toward the future and sucked in by it, Faulkner's is a frozen past which, like a Cyclopean wall, towers over the present minute and deprives it beforehand of any independent reality.

Sartre explained, in reference to *Sartoris,* that in his narrative Faulkner allows only events that have already taken place. And so it is in *The Sound and the Fury,* where all the action has taken place off-stage. The present is but a past future. Compared to the genuine past, it is powerless, colorless, and void. Even in the consciousness of the character who should, it seems, be living it, the present is completely screened out by earlier events. Only later does it appear, and almost always in the consciousness of another character. Having in its turn become a past, it has acquired the massive immutability of the past—like those young Chinese women who must wait to grow old before they become mothers-in-law and grandmothers, before they can reign over the household. . . . Unless events have taken place a long time ago, they have no genuine existence and cannot be registered by the characters' consciousness.

At certain moments, we seem to witness a sudden solidification of time as it congeals into a past and becomes isolated from the rest of duration: ". . . he would contemplate the inexplicable and fading fury of the past twenty-four hours circled back to itself and become whole and intact and objective and already vanishing slowly like the damp print of a lifted glass on a bar" (*Pylon*). It also happens that, to a particular character, a future event may seem to have already occurred, because it appears so inevitable. This is the case for Temple in *Sanctuary,* just before Popeye kills Red, her lover:

> He gave her the glass. She drank. When she set the glass down she realised that she was drunk. She believed that she had been drunk for some time. She thought that perhaps she had passed out and that it had already happened. She could hear herself saying I hope it has. I hope it has. Then she believed it had and she was overcome by a sense of bereavement and of physical desire.

At the most, a very brief passage might allow us to catch a rare glimpse of what a real event would be: a short pause within the inexorable plot of time where one moment overlaps another, like Gowan's automobile accident in the beginning of *Sanctuary*: "The engine ceased, though the lifted front wheel continued to spin idly, slowing." . . . It is a non-temporal present which seems to hover above the world for a fleeting moment before we relapse into the concrete universe of inflexible and consistent objects, which have no story. Only the past has this objective reality, because only through the past does a subjective and inconsistent event assume the solid existence of a thing.

Not only does the present not exist, it also can never be known. We never see it. We never see what happens while it is in the process of happening, but only when it is past. Only *fable* exists, that which is told, that which is made to be told. It alone is truthful. . . . The characters look obstinately at their past, are fascinated by it to the point of letting it devour them. They consent to this Moloch—or else their creator makes them consent. They are not, they were. Quentin goes to meet his suicide, Caddy her debauchery, Christmas his lynching, and Sutpen his death at the hands of Wash Jones. Temple refuses to leave the bootlegger's house when she still could have done it; the black woman, Nancy, seated by the fireside in her cabin, passively awaits her husband, Jesus, who will come to kill her. These people all want their lives to become destinies. They wallow in the tale of their ancestors' glories, spellbound with a strange hope in the midst of their despair, as they wait for the unpredictable and necessary catastrophe which is to seize them.

One can of course protest, as Sartre has done,* against such an alienation of man from his own freedom. One can also denounce Faulkner's vision of man and the world as arbitrary and partial, by showing that consciousness is more than just retrospection and reflection, that it is also a "project" turned toward the future as well as the past. . . . Faulkner's narrative technique is deceptive and insidious. Sartre is perhaps right in speaking of a kind of "dishonesty" whereby Faulkner tries to spread his own disease: the loss of any sense of the future, the absence of hope. He contends that Faulkner finds absurdity in life where he put it himself —not that life is not absurd, but that its absurdity is of a different nature. But the reason Sartre gives for this despair—namely, the present social conditions of life—is not very satisfying. It does not explain why such a joyless and unrepresentative image of the world should have been so willingly accepted. The world which *The Wild Palms* or *Light in August* describe is not simply a world where revolutions are no longer possible —no more than *The Castle* or *The Trial* are mythical transcriptions of the stifling bureaucracy under the Austro-Hungarian monarchy. We must admit that, beyond any optimism or appearance of truth, there is a certain *prestige* about the Faulknerian heroes and their destiny. And this poses the problem of the deeper meaning of literature and of its validity even when it so obviously cheats.

The Massacre of the Innocents

Any work of literature is to some degree an imposture, because it tries to make us accept as exclusively possible, and even as privileged, a certain point of view—generally a very strange and bewildering one. Faulkner's concept of time may be false, as Sartre declares, but its more profound

* See "On *The Sound and the Fury*: Time in the Work of Faulkner," reprinted below—Ed.

significance lies beyond the true and the false. It is almost religious—if the word may be used for a work apparently so profane—but a work which nevertheless comes from the land which produced the Negro spirituals. Do not the very title *Sanctuary* and the name Temple, of the girl who was violated, invite us to use such a term?

Malraux, in his famous preface to *Sanctuary,* had already spoken of Faulkner's art as "fascination," and Sartre, writing on *Sartoris,* as a "spell." Nowhere are those words more applicable than in *Absalom.* Even though at first the story is not particularly mysterious, the reader soon finds himself "possessed" by it, as are the two narrators, Quentin Compson and his Canadian friend, Shreve. The Canadian is fascinated by his initiation into what he thinks is the mystery of the "deep South," Quentin by the horror of incest—both the incest he knows exists between Judith and Charles Bon and the incest he imagines existed between himself and his sister Caddy—while we common readers are hypnotized by the motionless, frozen time which is gradually revealed to mortals as the only image of Eternity they will ever perceive.

Faulkner's family trees remind us of those long Biblical genealogies of the Old Testament or of those momentous sequences of names which climax, as in the beginning of the Gospel of St. Matthew, in one unique event, the birth of the Son of God: "Abraham begat Isaac; and Isaac begat Jacob; and Jacob begat Judas and his brethren. . . . And after they were brought to Babylon, Jechonias begat Salathiel. . . . And Jacob begat Joseph the husband of Mary, of whom was born Jesus, who is called Christ." The birth of Christ is an eternal event, since it had been announced from the beginning of time. And with this event the succession of historical moments which is Christ's genealogy becomes eternal as well. In short, the birth of Christ is the insertion of History into Eternity. Faulkner's novels, while secular, seem to be heralding Good Tidings: they keep us patient, as though by giving us gum to chew, while we wait for the Incarnation, whereby all promises will be fulfilled. Man, for want of Salvation, is for a while surrendered to Fatality; he is turned toward the past only because the future does not yet exist. The Temple in Jerusalem has been desecrated, the Sanctuary violated. Nothing real can happen until the supreme Event takes place, the one from which the years will be reckoned anew, starting from zero.

Faulkner's world is the world which precedes the Incarnation. It offers no hope, since Hope has not yet dawned. The Nativity is necessarily linked with the Massacre of the Innocents: Tommy is murdered, Goodwin burnt alive (*Sanctuary*), Christmas is lynched and Miss Burden strangled (*Light in August*), Benjy is castrated, Bayard Sartoris cast down like Icarus, Nancy devoured by vultures in the bottom of a ditch—and then those less pure victims such as Popeye, Sutpen, Quentin Compson, all afflicted with a punishment quite out of proportion with their deeds. . . .

The Violation of the Temple

One might think that looking for theological substructures to Faulkner's work is really stretching the point. Yet all critics have been struck by what they call his "Puritanism," his obvious repugnance for all that concerns the mystery of sex, as well as his deep-seated misogyny—a natural reaction in a world where the Immaculate Virgin did not come and restore order in the things Eve disrupted. Faulkner is explicitly referring to the Bible with his title *Absalom, Absalom!*—that is, to the Hebrew ritual of meditation upon the past. And how can the extravagant title, *Sanctuary,* be explained if it does not mean a continuous relation of sordid contemporary events to a sacred context. . . . *Sanctuary* has been characterized as the irruption of Greek tragedy into the detective novel. But it is even more the irruption of Biblical tragedy, of that drama where death is not the limit to cruelty.

It is therefore a *sacred* spell which Faulkner is trying to work on us. The devices used to achieve this magnetic effect are quite subtle. The most common one consists of making an observer of the drama reconstitute the order of events, so that soon he is no longer indifferent, but becomes implicated himself in these affairs which do not concern him. In *Sanctuary,* Horace Benbow becomes Goodwin's lawyer and involuntarily brings about his condemnation and his lynching. The anonymous reporter in *Pylon,* fascinated by the strange trio composed of Roger, Laverne, and the parachutist, ends up borrowing the money to buy the airplane in which Roger finds his death. In *Absalom,* Shreve and Quentin likewise become implicated and read their own tragic fates in those of the dead characters. The innocent fishermen by the Lake of Galilee, Thomas, Simon Peter, James, and Peter, had also, almost unwillingly, become the witnesses ("martyrs" in Greek means witnesses) of a tremendous Event. . . .

The "involved witness" in Faulknerian fiction prefigures the position of the reader himself. The reader can no more shake off the spell cast upon him than the characters themselves can cease being hypnotized by the contemplation of their fate. Thus attraction is mingled with horror; it is the kind of fascination the bird feels for the snake. One might say that in Faulkner's world sanctuaries assume their sacred character only through the profanation which despoils them forever. Temple's waiting in the bootlegger's house is prayer and contemplation as much as it is anguish. She might almost be preparing herself for a consecration: ". . . Tommy could hear a faint, steady chatter of the shucks inside the mattress where Temple lay, her hands crossed on her breast and her legs straight and close and decorous, like an effigy on an ancient tomb." In the prolonged instant which precedes the profanation, the sanctuary awaits the act of the ravisher which will sanctify it forever. Sartre, with his usual common sense, objects to such sorcery, which, he says, is neither plausible nor even conceivable. . . . But Faulkner has no pretensions of passing his narrations off for exact descriptions of everyday life. Nor is his world of spells any less *real* than the other one, for it accords perfectly with the very special structure of the universe he wants to present to us. . . .

Clear writing, according to the traditional rules of rhetoric, would be out of place in this universe, and quite inadequate for Faulkner's purpose. Heavy words and cumbersome adjectives are necessary to slow down and hamper the attempt at speech and communication. The characters and reader are supposed to flounder in them. . . . Adjectives do not describe any exterior reality; there are no adjectives in nature. They mark, rather, our grasp of things, of things as we recreate them, as we endow them with peculiarities which have meaning only in relation to us. Faulkner's sprawling sentences, loaded with modifiers, submerge and paralyze us; our consciousness becomes opaque and blind. But at the same time, they bestow an almost human life upon objects. While his people are transformed into objects, stubborn and inert, objects themselves, thanks to all his epithets, take on an animated, almost conscious existence. . . . *Pylon* is the most striking example of this reversal. It is a world in which airplanes are far more real than those who pilot them. The spectacle of an inhuman humanity, with fuel instead of blood in its veins, haunts Faulkner and his reader alike.

What is the necessity, the profound significance behind this magical interchange of beings and objects? . . . The concrete object and the temporal act cannot of themselves be described in a novel. But their human significance, the emotions which they unleash in the imaginary characters and in the author, may be conveyed to the reader by the use and abuse of epithets. Every great writer has his tools for operating witchcraft. As Malraux puts it, in his preface to *Sanctuary,* the tragic writer expresses what fascinates and torments him by projecting his fascination onto objects and forcing us, the readers, to share it. The sorcerer is only freed from his curse when he has succeeded in passing it on to others. The readers of Dostoevsky, Malraux, and Faulkner soon become their accomplices, and perhaps even their deputies. . . . Each novelist must thus invent his own means of capturing his readers and, thanks to those willing captives, of saving himself.

Literature as a Sacrifice of Substitution

The late Jean Prévost remarked, in his volume *La Création chez Stendhal,* that the very special charm of *La Chartreuse de Parme* is due to the speed with which it was written, in fifty-one days, all in one draught. The novelist who improvises "conceives as he writes and identifies with his characters at the same time, so that the rhythm of invention in him coincides with the rhythm of passion in his hero, and with the surge of sympathy in the reader." We can generalize this remark and say that a successful novel derives its power from the identification it achieves through the characters between the writer and his reader. Balzac achieves it through other means—through the intensity of his fictional vision—but the result is the same. . . . By means of the witchcraft these authors practise, the reader is compelled to perform this sacrifice of substitution which constitutes the very essence of literature; for without it, the work would be merely a succession of empty words on a sheet of paper. Herein lies the notion of the almost sacred function of art, which today has inherited the role once fulfilled mostly by religion.

How is this sacrifice of substitution consummated in Faulkner? The device mentioned above (of a witness who at first offers only the peculiar optics of the narrative, but who then becomes involved and engulfed in it) may be due in part to a scruple of artistic integrity: it might stem from the wish to show that a narrative is always somebody's narrative, and that an event only exists if it is perceived by a consciousness. This, however, is doubtful. Contrary to Henry James's "Peeping Tom" technique, the Witness in Faulkner does not long remain neutral or indifferent. This Mediator, whom the novelist places between the reader and himself, and with whom we identify, progressively introduces us into the very heart of Faulkner's personal universe, which might otherwise have remained incommunicable. . . . Since we find ourselves identifying with the Mediator, who finds himself identifying with the various characters, we are transformed not only into the individual characters, but rather into the total reality composed of all the characters as seen through the Mediator.

Faulkner first imparts to his characters his own obsession, the same mixture of horror and attraction with which the world in general inspires him. . . . Then he objectifies his fascination into a spectacle; he projects his emotion outside himself, supposing that it originated in what T. S. Eliot calls an "objective correlative." But this objective correlative (i.e., the plot and the structure of the narratives) is not enough to obtain the reader's participation in this same emotion. The Witnesses, the Mediators, have the job of communicating it to us through the contagion of their own experience. Similarly, in *La Chartreuse de Parme,* Stendhal is filled with fatherly tenderness and immense indulgence toward Fabrice, the son he never had. Through Mosca and la Sanseverina, he instills in us this admiring affection, to the point of concealing Fabrice's real mediocrity. But Faulkner has still other means besides epithets and Mediators for casting his spell over us.

Most of Faulkner's apparent perversities, the difficulties he seems to cultivate, may be explained by his ambition to obtain a total identification between himself and the reader. Again, let us take as an example the same name given to different people within the same narration. . . . Every time the author mentions the name "Quentin," he knows perfectly well which Quentin he means. But the reader, from whom an increase of attention and reflection is required in order to discriminate, is thereby forced to look behind the scenes to where the author is, where the creative vision is. We are forced to become his accomplices if we want to decipher his enigmas. He is not obscure out of scorn for us; he wants our complicity. He wants us to become, as it were, the authors of what we read. . . . Certain poets and modern critics proceed in a similar way, refusing to surrender their meaning too easily to us. It is as though the consumers of this cooperative literature are obliged to have been its producers and to have taken on their share of responsibility in the creation or re-creation of the work.

The goal of this kind of art is to transform a work into a snare that will catch the reader, that will involve his whole being as he tries to disentangle the knots. . . . It refuses merely to communicate a pre-existing meaning. It wants to entice the reader behind the words to a second, deeper, and hidden meaning. And this is the author's way of satisfying his secret ambition: to multiply himself indefinitely, to create somewhere in the world a theoretically unlimited number of beings like himself.

Faulkner's great achievement is to have brought under this demanding, Socratic discipline that notoriously lazy creature, the reader of fiction. . . . As a novelist, his major difficulty was to relay, by means of the narrative art, the idea that we live in an absurd world. Since any narrative, no matter how chaotic it is, inevitably rests upon temporal or causal relationships, it cannot avoid introducing too much order and clarity into the events it relates. The indispensable portion of darkness yields too much light, just as folly does reason. . . . Faulkner's recourse to an idiot or to a witness, who are as puzzled and uninformed as the reader, is an elegant solution. Balzac resorted to different devices—chronological disruptions . . . or sudden changes of tempo . . .—to produce a similar but more imposed effect. Faulkner is more subtle. . . . His spell is not cast directly, he merely leaves at our disposal the tools necessary for producing the desired effects—as one discreetly leaves a revolver within the reach of a condemned man so that he may conveniently do justice to himself. We ourselves come to wish the anguish expected from us. We lend ourselves to the novel to the point where we find in it only what we deposited. In short, we accept entire responsibility for the witchcraft practised upon us.

Faulkner and Balzac as Rivals of God the Father

A long familiarity with all of Faulkner's works is necessary in order to see through his mystification devices, and also to see these stories as successive parts of a single and great work. As in Balzac, one story fits into another, characters reappear, and multiple relationships are established between the different family dynasties . . . until finally we have before us a total work, a *total* world, which must have pre-existed in the mind of the author, but which remains obscured for the reader as long as he knows only one or two of its parts. We understand why, concentrating as he does on the universe which he carries within himself, the author forgets to realize that all is not as clear to the reader as it is to himself. . . . If Faulkner, like Balzac, so often seems to disregard us, it is more from distraction than from scorn, so busy are they managing, in their creative solitude, the complex network which binds their creatures.

Although the reader is annoyed at first, this creative indifference actually *impresses* upon him the massive stature of the work. The fictional monument strikes him as having existed before he approached it, even before its builder erected it. The reader is all the more fascinated because it does not flatter him or even demand his attention. It asks for nothing; it exists. Like the Civil War, to which it alludes without ever describing it, the work stands before us as a motionless image of eternity, as the exact opposite of that Time which presides over the spinning of the universe, so aptly defined by Plato in *Timaeus* as "a mobile image of eternity."

Faulkner's shorter novels, like Balzac's short stories, are microcosms; each of them (in *These Thirteen* or *Doctor Martino,* for example) reflects the whole of the work, as the Leibnitzian monad reflected the entire universe. . . . Each one is a piece of the same vast puzzle and cannot assume its full meaning until it is replaced in the whole.

There is thus a Faulknerian geography, as objective as the map of France in Balzac's *La Comédie Humaine,* and Malcolm Cowley has included it in his *Portable Faulkner.* . . . All his stories refer to the Yoknapatawpha Saga which is the name of the "Terra Faulkneriana," the new kingdom discovered and charted by the novelist. . . . Each story receives its extraordinary reality, its power of suggestion, from the literally "objective" existence of that county. This explains why Faulkner is capable of adding new details every time he retells the same story or why, each time he thinks back on one of his imaginary characters, he finds himself confronted with the whole of his vision, face to face as it were with the God he never ceased being.

Balzac too, with his famous trick of making his characters reappear or disappear from time to time, . . . enhances the credibility of the narration, intensifies the objectiveness of the characters' existence, and gives them this "third dimension" which we do not find again before Proust. . . . Calling back, at different moments in their existence, characters already familiar to us enables the novelist to combine a required precision with that sense of incompleteness, . . . indispensable for any description if it is to receive its full evocative powers. . . . Through their various reappearances, the characters gain a definite past which supposes still other pasts behind the events recounted. Their existence receives a mysterious, backward prolongation in time, with no visible limit.

This is precisely the situation in Faulkner's entire universe, which is more than a slice carved out of the flow of time. It is the memory of a race, of a country whose secret disease is the amnestic lack of roots and traditions. . . . Faulkner's work is like a vast autobiography, not of one isolated individual, but of a whole land, of a whole human group. And, as in all memoirs which appear true, there is a kind of natural "afflux," irresistible flow of the artesian well which sweeps away anything the author might have contrived or purposively intended. The author is invaded by what he reminisces—as in Proust or Henry James in the admirable autobiographical fragment which follows *Notes of a Son and Brother,* or as that tumultuous Mississippi which is the true hero of *The Wild Palms.* It is not the murky depths of an individual self, but a collective subconscious which is flushed to the surface. Its apparition into broad daylight is felt with the same irresistible giddiness which accompanies the exploration, by dreams or analysis, of our own past.

A writer, "possessed" to such a degree by what he wants to write, tries to say everything at once. His sentences, again as those of James and of Proust, become like a net cast upon a reality which is too rich. The reader finds himself entangled and enmeshed in the same situation as the author a moment earlier. Hence the obscurity of the opening chapters of *Sanctuary,* where the author endeavors to present all things at the same time as they are perceived by the various characters. . . . Faulkner's image is not so much that of an absurd world as it is that of a universe in which everything is given at the same time, in which all beings are first perceived together. In this sense the interior monologue of the idiot Benjy assumes a symbolic character. It restores for us the image of that synthetic universe of the "whole of feeling," to use F. H. Bradley's expression, in which reality has not yet been broken up into a multiplicity of appearances by the intervention of clear consciousness.

This synthetic ambition of Faulkner's art explains why plot and events predominate in his novels over character and men. Malraux suggested that Faulkner probably invented his scenes before he imagined his characters, that his characters, instead of determining a dramatic situation of tragic oppositions, were determined or imagined by this situation previously conceived. The conjecture seems justified. Maurice Coindreau tells us in his *Aspects du roman américain* that Faulkner first conceived *The Sound and the Fury* as the description of the reactions of a group of troubled children. . . . In Dos Passos also, and in O'Hara, we find the same kind of characters inexorably crushed and deprived of freedom by the mechanistic circumstances (economic, social, hereditary, and so on) of the plot. Faulkner's plot-machine is even more inflexible. . . . His heroes are not, as are others, defined by a complex of psychological, biographical, or social peculiarities which, taken together, secure their individuality. Their structure rests rather upon one atemporal and immutable act, often speculative or at least situated outside time, such as Christmas' Negro blood, the crime formerly committed by the old convict in *The Wild Palms,* or the vain cruelty of Popeye. . . . Faulkner's novels do not, like those of Stendhal and Balzac, increase our knowledge of man. They impart to us a vision of the world and that fascination which a certain image of eternity, of timelessness, holds for the human mind. . . .

Behind these beings, implacably riveted to the one thing that has determined them (Popeye to his physiological defects, Christmas to his childhood of shame and misery, the convict to his past crime, and so forth), looms what in them is timeless, changeless, and most real: the great eternal Act which constitutes them and which they can only contemplate if its image is projected into the past, even though it lies outside of time. Its equivalent for the South is the Civil War; for the North the landing of the Pilgrim Fathers; and for mankind that twin act which is the Creation and the Fall.

Like the Jews of the Old Testament or the Negroes of the Southern plantations, . . . Faulkner's characters have their faces turned backward as they ponder over a great, motionless Event weighing upon them. The Jews in the Psalms and Prophecies contemplate the captivity of Babylon; the Sartorises and the Compsons in Faulkner endlessly repeat the feats of the Civil War. It will not be otherwise for them until the Incarnation occurs, until that Event pierces Time and becomes ceaseless, for this will be the marriage of Time and Eternity.

It is not by chance that we have mentioned in relation to Faulkner the name of Balzac and of Proust, or that we have evoked the Old Testament. Faulkner's work, like Joyce's *Ulysses* and certain poems of T. S. Eliot, such as *The Wasteland,* . . . manifests that fairly common disease of the modern spirit, which consists of living in time before the birth of Christ—the disease which still characterizes the situation of the entire Jewish people today. . . . On account of this curse, Faulkner (like Joyce, like Balzac) assumes, almost unconsciously, a position toward his creatures which is traditionally that of God the Father. Dos Passos and Faulkner, the two most significant American writers of the era which precedes ours, find themselves curiously parallel to each other in the conception of time which secretly orders their work. Time in Dos Passos is the cosmic time which presides over the calendar, over the tides, over the waves of economic depression; it is the mobile image of eternity, the time of Plato's *Timaeus*. Faulkner's time is a motionless image of eternity, which he raises over his characters like a banner proclaiming "in hoc signo vinces"; their retrospection becomes a substitute for an impossible contemplation.

Time and Destiny in Faulkner

by Jean Pouillon

Few novels are more charged with destiny weighing heavily over them than those of Faulkner. We have the impression of characters irretrievably choked by fate, not only when we look back with some detachment through the development of the story, but at the very moment the events are being told. Reduced to an outline, Faulkner's stories are like many others: a contingent unfolding of events whose fatal aspect may simply be the illusion of those involved. That is why his plots never appear too easily as unified structures, as geometrical sequences of moments, events, and feelings. Much remains hidden from the reader, and it is this very obscurity of plot which weighs so much upon all that happens and exists. One of the purposes of Faulkner's apparently disordered narrative is to show that this sense of fatal oppression is not a device of cohesive narration, but that it subsists, and that by suggesting it the novelist is obeying the nature of things. It is easy to see how removed we are from the deductive novel and the novel of scenes. Such a form of destiny which abandons logic, which is never more conspicuous than in the utter absurdity of facts, can be considered as the petrification of contingency, but by no means as a transformation of contingency into necessity. We must therefore not look for the explanation of Faulknerian destiny in any supposedly deterministic time structure. Let us begin by seeing how time appears in his novels, then what consequences follow in the narrative (whose disorder is only apparent), and finally, how all this creates an impression of fatality.

Time

In reading *The Sound and the Fury,* whose first three chapters are interior monologues, we are immediately struck by the overlapping of present events and memories of past events. This is achieved in several unequally important ways. Most commonly, the past is evoked by the present; for example, Benjy remembers his sister Caddie when he hears

"Temps et Destinée chez Faulkner." From *Temps et Roman* by Jean Pouillon, trans. Jacqueline Merriam (Paris: Gallimard, 1946), pp. 238-60.

golf caddies mentioned. The reader is startled only by the abruptly subjective nature of the past and by the fact that he knows nothing about the character's life except what he learns from such evocations. Thus, through the persistence of past impressions, especially childhood impressions, Faulkner shows that the present is submerged in the past, that what is lived in the present is what was lived in the past. In this case, the past is not so much an evocation as it is a constant pressure upon the present, the pressure of what has been on what is.

Consciousness, therefore, is mostly memory. But not the kind of memory which attaches the present to a past known as past and no longer existing. For memory is so much a part of what actually exists that it does not know itself as memory, does not know itself as anything but the sense of reality. Since, however, memory cannot possibly be anything but the sense of the past, we must conclude—and this lies at the core of Faulkner—that it is the past which is real.

Quentin's monologue in *The Sound and the Fury* would be a typical illustration of this principle: while Quentin is fighting with another student, we read about a first fight he had with his sister's lover which took place several years previously, and this is what he is actually experiencing. In *Light in August* (which is not written as an interior monologue and thus proves that this time principle is not simply the result of a certain literary form) the chapter on Christmas' infancy begins as follows: "Memory believes before knowing remembers. Believes longer than recollects, longer than knowing even wonders. Knows remembers believes a corridor in a big long garbled cold echoing building. . . ."

The real, then, is the past, a past always there, always present. How is this to be understood? It is not enough to repeat the old adages—a man is what his past has made him, or, a man's actions today are determined by his actions yesterday. In these formulas the present does not lose its importance because of the past's primacy, for without the present there is nothing left to be determined. Before one thing can determine another, both must fully exist; an intra-temporal necessity must bind equally real moments. This of course does not explain Faulkner's works, where the past coexists with the present. It is a kind of lump in the present, which must not be chronologically unravelled, for then we would have a succession of relative pasts and presents. Faulknerian past is extra-temporal. The fact that an event slips into the past does not mean that it becomes pure memory labeled with a date, but that it sheds temporality, inasmuch as time is change and dispersion.

These ideas are difficult to express and not at all explicit in Faulkner. The past is not a temporal past, that which no longer is and can only be remembered. It is something here and now, present in the proper sense of the word. Inserted into time, the past *was* and is therefore past, but inasmuch as it subsists, it is present. This is why we can say it is extra-temporal—not, however, that it resides in a superior realm, because a timeless past accompanies each chronological present. It receives its significance from the present and at the same time incorporates the present into itself (the present becomes past, as Temple becomes the girl already raped whom we had just seen being raped). All this is certainly not supposed to constitute a theory on Faulkner. It only applies to his characters' manner of living, since time is nothing outside someone's consciousness of time. So when we say that present means past, that the past recaptures the present, we are speaking of the hero himself who feels bound to a past he cannot dismiss. This is when fate appears.

Having thus established the relationship between past and present, we have still to discover what part the future plays in Faulkner. The future does not seem to enter into a novel like *Light in August* or *Sanctuary*. In *Light in August* the end of the story, the murder, is already indicated at the beginning, so that the entire novel is but an exploration of the past. In *Sanctuary* there is indeed a progression of events, a very normal one in fact, and yet we are never given the impression that the various characters really have a future. They advance, but backward. They are not lured by a feat or fascinated by a certain type of behavior into which they madly throw themselves, as are Dostoevsky's heroes when they feel the call of destiny. Christmas has no concept of his future. Even though he vaguely knows he will kill, this murder is simply an advent of the past to which he adds nothing. He feels the meaninglessness of his performance even before he acts. The future can be compared to the present: we cannot say it is determined by the past since there is no reason why such and such a thing must happen. Anything might happen. But whatever does happen, the event immediately assumes the colors of the past without changing them in the slightest, just as each one of Reverend Hightower's sermons reflects his grandfather's function. The idea remains the same: the past is not so much what determines the present and the future as it is the sole reality. Being the past, it is untouchable, and that is why it is also destiny.

The past, therefore, not only was but is and will be; it is the unfolding of destiny. Note, though, that this development is not rendered either necessary or imperious. It little matters what happens, since Faulknerian destiny does not depend on the realization of a particular contingent event. The course destiny chooses is in a sense superfluous, for we are not dealing with the kind of fatality which manifests itself in a dramatic progression of events, from which we cannot add or subtract a single one without changing its entire passage, for to do so would be like saying that someone has not fulfilled his destiny because of a premature death. In this case destiny is recognized as life's term, whereas in Faulkner destiny is at the source of life, or, as Malraux states it in his preface to *Sanctuary*, it is always the past, the irremediable past.

In order to clarify Faulkner's position it will be helpful to compare it to that of Proust. The notion of time in the works of these two authors offers some obvious points of similarity. For Proust, too, the past is a present reality and the fundamental dimension of time. Even the title of his novel announces that the present has no consistency and is not really a presence, that it only becomes real in a past which purifies it, in a past which must be recaptured. Does not Proust, on an intellectual level, resemble Quentin in *The Sound and the Fury,* this being who can live only in the past? One needs but remember those famous examples: the little madeleine, the two paving-stones, or better still, Marcel's decision to write *The Past Recaptured.*

But there are also many points of diversity, which are due to more than the very different worlds of these two men. The past is not the same thing for both of them. With Proust it is strictly individual, made up of personal habits and sensations. The adventure of the little cake dipped in the cup of tea applies only to him. With Faulkner, on the other hand, it is not only my past that emerges and adapts itself as best it can (for Proust, not too well) to an exterior present, it is everybody's past, the pasts of all his characters. Faulkner's people are real only in their pasts. They do not rethink their pasts, they simply live them, because if the past is to be rethought, as by Proust, it has to be distinct from a perfectly real present. Christmas lives his memories, whereas Proust relives them. Since chronological time exists for Proust, he must account for and explain the irregular moments of memory which tend to disintegrate it, whereas for Faulkner, chronology is nothing and the past is constantly present. Proust lives in two times, in chronological time and in recaptured time. His analysis is born in the confrontation of the two, when subjective reality interferes with objective reality. But since Faulkner refuses chronological time, he has nothing to analyze. Subjective reality absorbs everything and becomes fate, intensified by the annihilation of all opposition.

Consequences: Faulknerian Narration

Destruction of chronology is the most obvious result of this depreciation of present and future to the benefit of the past. No doubt other authors have proceeded in this way to achieve their desired effects, but with them it remains a literary device, irrespective of the characters' consciousness of their lives. Conrad's narratives, for example, may cross one another, but the lives evoked in each retain a chronological order. Not so with Faulkner. Without warning the reader, he places one moment into another and shuffles all habitual order because, according to him, lives are not lived chronologically. This is what the interior monologues try to make us understand.

Chronological order would ruin the past for two reasons. First of all, there would be but a succession of mutually exclusive "nows," valid in themselves alone and not in their identification with the past. The trees in *Light in August* seem to be telling this to Byron Burch: ". . . you are just the one that calls yourself Byron Burch, today, now, this minute. . . ." Secondly, chronology would chop up the past into fictitious pasts, presents, and futures. The past which Faulkner's heroes feel weighing upon them is a detemporalized unit. Whereas the present is fragmented, dispersed, and not really experienced, the past forms an undecomposable whole. The entire novel is but an attempt to make this known, but not, however, through some sort of administrative report. We reach this past through a succession of plunges. The order of the plunges is determined by the appearance of those characters who know a certain past of a person from the exterior or from hearsay and are thus able to relate it. In *Light in August* we learn of the circumstances of Christmas' birth only when Doc Hines and his wife step onto the scene. In *Sanctuary* we hear explicitly of Popeye's impotence and of Red's role when Miss Reba receives her friends after the funeral. It is not only Faulkner's concept of time that obliges him to narrate in this fashion, but also his vision of people and events.

One might accuse Faulkner of artifice, for we all know that in fact things do happen in a certain order, that this order is still real for whoever lives these things. This of course is quite true, but we will never understand Faulkner's point of view unless we distinguish between consciousness and knowledge. Faulkner places himself on the level of the former. Consciousness is inevitable, knowledge only a possibility. Since one does not necessarily attain knowledge, Faulkner can omit it without deforming human nature, especially in the kind of characters he chooses. Chronology, being a posterior organization of a life, belongs to the domain of knowledge. It is a kind of intellectual liberation from destiny; it assures us that the past is indeed past even if we feel its pressure on our present. Faulkner's heroes enjoy no such liberation, which is itself a free rather than necessary category of the human mind. All this goes to confirm what we said before: destiny in Faulkner is the opposite of a geometrical relationship between chronologically situated moments.

The second obvious consequence of his concept of time is his use of the past tense throughout the narration. Sometimes, however, we hear the actors and observers converse, we see them move. But these are, so to speak, only the preliminaries. As soon as the essential part of the scene approaches, the part which will be absorbed into the character's omnipresent past—as the rape with a corn cob in *Sanctuary*—rather than the unimportant remainder which will dissolve and be forever forgotten—at this point, then, there is a kind of jump ahead of the crucial moment, because this moment is never known except as past. Chapter XIII of *Sanctuary* offers a typical example of this procedure—a device perhaps, but more than that too, for the characters do not truly live their present until it has taken form in the past. Here is the murder of Tommy:

> . . . Popeye drew his hand from his coat pocket.
> To Temple, sitting in the cottonseed-hulls and the corn-cobs, the sound was no louder than the striking of a match: a short, minor sound *shutting down upon the scene, the instant, with a profound finality, completely isolating it*. . . .[1]

This is a simple example. Other very different novelists have treated rapid events, like a pistol shot, in the same manner; and that is why we chose the example, to show that there is nothing artificial in Faulkner's technique. He has merely emphasized and generalized the psychological reality of omission. After all, everything that takes place has passed as soon as it happens, and can therefore only be told as a recollection, even in direct narration.

The nature of Faulkner's vision converges here with his concept of time: he never "sees" the important events for he is "with" his heroes (he "sees" one "with" the other), with these heroes who see only their past. Let us make an unexpected comparison with French classical tragedy: here too thc tragic events are only related; we never see them happening. The tragic is what has been (or, to use one of Sartre's expressions, what "is been") and cannot be seen directly. If we find this principle in two forms as different as Racine's theater and Faulkner's novel, it must be of a fairly general nature.

The Meaning of Destiny

We have already established that destiny, as it appears in all of these novels, must not be likened to temporal determinism, to a supposedly necessary chronological succession, for to be of such a nature, the past would have to retain in itself an ordered progression of presents and the present would have to be allowed its own reality, since destiny would not be complete without it. In the case of Faulkner, we have seen that the past is a whole receiving nothing from the present, that the very presence of the past disqualifies the present as such, and therefore eliminates or at least upsets chronological relationships. Even the most remote past affects the present, not through any series of temporally arranged causes, but by its immediate presence. Having been, it is. Its action, therefore, is not logical but psychological. Christmas is not *determined* by his past, he *is* his past. Again, it is in consciousness that we must seek his feeling of being dominated by destiny, and not in a particular time structure abstracted from what fills it. Faulkner's people are not "blind puppets of Fate" as Coindreau erroneously names them in his preface to *Light in August*. Faulkner's is undoubtedly "a world where man exists as a crushed being" as Malraux writes in his preface to *Sanctuary*,

[1] My italics—J.P.

but the pressure comes from within, not from without. Faulkner's man crushes himself more than he is crushed.

If this is true, if destiny is in fact an inner force, and if Christmas is dominated by himself more than by things, the hero must constantly feel fate's affirmation.

The feeling of inner fatality is expressed very clearly in the account of Christmas' attempt to escape in *Light in August*: "But there was too much running with him, stride for stride with him. Not pursuers: but himself: years, acts, deeds omitted and committed, keeping pace with him stride for stride. . . ." When we say that the hero feels his destiny from within himself, we of course do not mean that he *knows* it. Faulkner places himself on the level of his heroes' immediate consciousness of themselves and of things, not on the level of their knowledge of them. They feel in some way responsible for their fate since they have a vague foreboding of what is going to happen to them. Think, for example, of the episode in *Light in August* where MacEachern went to surprise Joe at a dance without even knowing where the dance was being held. He was pushed to it by an inner force. Faulkner does not define this force; he is only interested in marking its inner or psychological nature. Besides, were he to define it, he would have to rise to the level of knowledge, and this is precisely what he has forbidden himself to do. Consciousness without knowledge of destiny means that the heroes sense what awaits them without knowing it distinctly. They are not surprised by what happens because they at least know that no future can deliver them from their past. This is evident in the way they act. Faulkner always tries to give us the impression that they already know what one normally would not be able to foresee: ". . . as though she already knew what I was going to tell her . . ." (*Light in August*).

Since they have a dim but constant awareness of the destiny they bear, it is quite normal that Faulkner should reveal this consciousness by using interior monologues and by placing himself "with" his characters. There is an important connection between this manifestation of destiny, his conception of time, and his way of regarding his characters, which it will be necessary to clarify if we are to understand the psychological significance of destiny. We sense perfectly well, without knowing exactly why, that Dos Passos' manner would not suit Faulkner. Perhaps it is because Faulkner makes his characters appear in their own present and implies the reality and importance of this present. But why should the classical type of psychological analysis, where the author is "behind" his heroes, be equally ill-suited? Analysis presupposes, of course, an author and reader superior to the characters, on the level of omniscient reflection, and this again Faulkner refuses. But why?

We could analyze the feeling of destiny from such a vantage point—in fact, that is what we have just done, abstractly. But then we reduce consciousness to an illusion: we take a hero who believes he is a plaything of fate, we examine this belief from above, and in doing so, we transcend the feeling of oppressiveness which is the very nature of fate. Fate would thereby lose all reality except as a subjective impression. Perhaps it is nothing more. But Faulkner has no intention of presenting his reader with a theory of fatality. Rather, he wants to communicate to us those very impressions that strangle his characters, and to do this, the reader must not be entitled to privileged knowledge, he must not understand the characters any more than they understand themselves—it is the error of many novelists to imagine that an impression is strengthened when it is justified. Thus Faulkner, and, as a result, his reader stay "with" the hero.

Faulkner might have been confronted with an antinomy, because in certain cases there is no opposition between feeling and knowing. Perhaps there is even a mutual reinforcement—this certainly was Proust's idea. But then one must choose: destiny dissolves as soon as it is understood, as soon as it has been reduced to psychological causes which bear no relation to what one thinks destiny is while subjected to it. Destiny is real only while it is endured—that is to say, while it is not known but only felt. Proust chose to know, or rather he chose to go from experiencing to knowing, from pure enjoyment of the past to an intellectual understanding of it. For him, recapturing time meant understanding it just as much as reliving it. Past time—that is, time which was lost the moment it was lived—dissolves as such when it has been recaptured and analyzed. Experience is reduced to causes in a kind of Spinozian liberation, and time loses its mysterious fatality. The example of Proust proves what we were saying: understanding destiny is its undoing.

On *The Sound and the Fury*: Time in the Work of Faulkner

by Jean-Paul Sartre

The first thing that strikes one in reading *The Sound and the Fury* is its technical oddity. Why has Faulkner broken up the time of his story and scrambled the pieces? Why is the first window that opens out on this fictional world the consciousness of an idiot? The reader is tempted to look for guidemarks and to re-establish the chronology for himself:

> Jason and Caroline Compson have had three sons and a daughter. The daughter, Caddy, has given herself to Dalton Ames and become pregnant by him. Forced to get hold of a husband quickly . . .

Here the reader stops, for he realizes he is telling another story. Faulkner did not first conceive this orderly plot so as to shuffle it afterward like a pack of cards; he could not tell it in any other way. In the classical novel, action involves a central complication—for example, the murder of old Karamazov or the meeting of Edouard and Bernard in *The Coiners*. But we look in vain for such a complication in *The Sound and the Fury*. Is it the castration of Benjy or Caddy's wretched amorous adventure or Quentin's suicide or Jason's hatred of his niece? As soon as we begin to look at any episode, it opens up to reveal behind it other episodes, all the other episodes. Nothing happens; the story does not unfold; we discover it under each word, like an obscene and obstructing presence, more or less condensed, depending upon the particular case. It would be a mistake to regard these irregularities as gratuitous exercises in virtuosity. A fictional technique always relates back to the novelist's metaphysics. The critic's task is to define the latter before evaluating the former. Now, it is immediately obvious that Faulkner's metaphysics is a metaphysics of time.

Man's misfortune lies in his being time-bound.

> . . . a man is the sum of his misfortunes. One day you'd think misfortune would get tired, but then time is your misfortune. . . .

From *Literary and Philosophical Essays* by Jean-Paul Sartre, trans. Annette Michelson (London: Rider & Co., 1955), pp. 79-87.

Such is the real subject of the book. And if the technique Faulkner has adopted seems at first a negation of temporality, the reason is that we confuse temporality with chronology. It was man who invented dates and clocks.

> Constant speculation regarding the position of mechanical hands on an arbitrary dial which is a sympton of mind-function. Excrement Father said like sweating.

In order to arrive at real time, we must abandon this invented measure which is not a measure of anything.

> . . . time is dead as long as it is being clicked off by little wheels; only when the clock stops does time come to life.

Thus, Quentin's gesture of breaking his watch has a symbolic value; it gives us access to a time without clocks. The time of Benjy, the idiot, who does not know how to tell time, is also clockless.

What is thereupon revealed to us is the present, and not the ideal limit whose place is neatly marked out between past and future. Faulkner's present is essentially catastrophic. It is the event which creeps up on us like a thief, huge, unthinkable—which creeps up on us and then disappears. Beyond this present time there is nothing, since the future does not exist. The present rises up from sources unknown to us and drives away another present; it is forever beginning anew. "And . . . and . . . and then." Like Dos Passos, but much more discreetly, Faulkner makes an accretion of his narrative. The actions themselves, even when seen by those who perform them, burst and scatter on entering the present.

> I went to the dresser and took up the watch with the face still down. I tapped the crystal on the dresser and caught the fragments of glass in my hand and put them into the ashtray and twisted the hands off and put them in the tray. The watch ticked on.

The other aspect of this present is what I shall call a sinking in. I use this expression, for want of a better one, to indicate a kind of motionless movement of this formless monster. In Faulkner's work, there is never any progression, never anything which comes from the future. The present has not first been a future possibility, as when my friend, after having been *he for whom I am waiting,* finally appears. No, to be present means to appear without any reason and to sink in. This sinking in is not an abstract view. It is within things themselves that Faulkner perceives it and tries to make it felt.

> The train swung around the curve, the engine puffing with short, heavy blasts, and they passed smoothly from sight that way, with that quality of shabby and timeless patience, of static serenity. . . .

And again,

> Beneath the sag of the buggy the hooves neatly rapid like motions of a lady doing embroidery, *diminishing without progress*[1] like a figure on a treadmill being drawn rapidly off-stage.

It seems as though Faulkner has laid hold of a frozen speed at the very heart of things; he is grazed by congealed spurts that wane and dwindle without moving.

This fleeting and unimaginable immobility can, however, be arrested and pondered. Quentin can say, "I broke my watch," but when he says it, his gesture is *past*. The past is named and related; it can, to a certain extent, be fixed by concepts or recognized by the heart. We pointed out [elsewhere,][2] in connection with *Sartoris,* that Faulkner always showed events when they were already over. In *The Sound and the Fury* everything has already happened. It is this that enables us to understand that strange remark by one of the heroes, *"Fui. Non sum."* In this sense, too, Faulkner is able to make man a sum total without a future: "The sum of his climactic experiences," "The sum of his misfortunes," "The sum of what have you." At every moment, one draws a line, since the present is nothing but a chaotic din, a future that is past. Faulkner's vision of the world can be compared to that of a man sitting in an open car and looking backward. At every moment, formless shadows, flickerings, faint tremblings and patches of light rise up on either side of him, and only afterward, when he has a little perspective, do they become trees and men and cars.

The past takes on a sort of super-reality; its contours are hard and clear, unchangeable. The present, nameless and fleeting, is helpless before it. It is full of gaps, and, through these gaps, things of the past, fixed, motionless, and silent as judges or glances, come to invade it. Faulkner's monologues remind one of airplane trips full of air-pockets. At each pocket, the hero's consciousness "sinks back into the past" and rises only to sink back again. The present is not; it becomes. Everything *was.* In *Sartoris,* the past was called "the stories" because it was a matter of family memories that had been constructed, because Faulkner had not yet found his technique.

In *The Sound and the Fury* he is more individual and more undecided. But it is so strong an obsession that he is sometimes apt to disguise the present, and the present moves along in the shadow, like an underground river, and reappears only when it itself is past. When Quentin insults Bland,[3] he is not even aware of doing so; he is reliving his dispute with

[1] The author's italics.

[2] See *Literary and Philosophical Essays*—Ed.

[3] Compare the dialogue with Bland inserted into the middle of the dialogue with Ames: "Did you ever have a sister?" etc., and the inextricable confusion of the two fights.

Dalton Ames. And when Bland punches his nose, this brawl is covered over and hidden by Quentin's past brawl with Ames. Later on, Shreve relates how Bland hit Quentin; he relates this scene because it has become a story, but while it was unfolding in the present, it was only a furtive movement, covered over by veils. Someone once told me about an old monitor who had grown senile. His memory had stopped like a broken watch; it had been arrested at his fortieth year. He was sixty, but didn't know it. His last memory was that of a schoolyard and his daily walk around it. Thus, he interpreted his present in terms of his past and walked about his table, convinced that he was watching students during recreation.

Faulkner's characters are like that, only worse, for their past, which is in order, does not assume chronological order. It is, in actual fact, a matter of emotional constellations. Around a few central themes (Caddy's pregnancy, Benjy's castration, Quentin's suicide) gravitate innumerable silent masses. Whence the absurdity of the chronology of "the assertive and contradictory assurance" of the clock. The order of the past is the order of the heart. It would be wrong to think that when the present is past it becomes our closest memory. Its metamorphosis can cause it to sink to the bottom of our memory, just as it can leave it floating on the surface. Only its own density and the dramatic meaning of our life can determine at what level it will remain.

Such is the nature of Faulkner's time. Isn't there something familiar about it? This unspeakable present, leaking at every seam, these sudden invasions of the past, this emotional order, the opposite of the voluntary and intellectual order that is chronological but lacking in reality, these memories, these monstrous and discontinuous obsessions, these intermittences of the heart—are not these reminiscent of the lost and recaptured time of Marcel Proust? I am not unaware of the differences between the two; I know, for instance, that for Proust salvation lies in time itself, in the full reappearance of the past. For Faulkner, on the contrary, the past is never lost, unfortunately; it is always there, it is an obsession. One escapes from the temporal world only through mystic ecstasies. A mystic is always a man who wishes to forget something, his self or, more often, language or objective representations. For Faulkner, time must be forgotten.

> Quentin, I give you the mausoleum of all hope and desire; it's rather excruciatingly apt that you will use it to gain the reductio ad absurdum of all human experience which can fit your individual needs no better than it fitted his or his father's. I give it to you not that you may remember time, *but that you might forget it now and then for a moment* and not spend all your breath trying to conquer it. Because no battle is ever won he said. They are not even fought. The field only reveals to man his own folly and despair, and victory is an illusion of philosophers and fools.

It is because he has forgotten time that the hunted Negro in *Light in August* suddenly achieves his strange and horrible happiness.

> It's not when you realize that nothing can help you—religion, pride, anything—it's when you realize that you don't need any aid.

But for Faulkner, as for Proust, time is, above all, *that which separates.* One recalls the astonishment of the Proustian heroes who can no longer enter into their past loves, of those lovers depicted in *Les Plaisirs et Les Jours,* clutching their passions, afraid they will pass, and knowing they will. We find the same anguish in Faulkner.

> . . . people cannot do anything very dreadful at all, they cannot even remember tomorrow what seemed dreadful today . . .

and

> . . . a love or a sorrow is a bond purchased without design and which matures willynilly and is recalled without warning to be replaced by whatever issue the gods happen to be floating at the time. . . .

To tell the truth, Proust's fictional technique *should have been* Faulkner's. It was the logical conclusion of his metaphysics. But Faulkner is a lost man, and it is because he feels lost that he takes risks and pursues his thought to its uttermost consequences. Proust is a Frenchman and a classicist. The French lose themselves only a little at a time and always manage to find themselves again. Eloquence, intellectuality, and a liking for clear ideas were responsible for Proust's retaining at least the semblance of chronology.

The basic reason for this relationship is to be found in a very general literary phenomenon. Most of the great contemporary authors, Proust, Joyce, Dos Passos, Faulkner, Gide, and Virginia Woolf have tried, each in his own way, to distort time. Some of them have deprived it of its past and future in order to reduce it to the pure intuition of the instant; others, like Dos Passos, have made of it a dead and closed memory. Proust and Faulkner have simply decapitated it. They have deprived it of its future—that is, its dimension of deeds and freedom. Proust's heroes never undertake anything. They do, of course, make plans, but their plans remain stuck to them and cannot be projected like a bridge beyond the present. They are daydreams that are put to flight by reality. The Albertine who appears is not the one we were expecting, and the expectation was merely a slight, inconsequential hesitation, limited to the moment only. As to Faulkner's heroes, they never look ahead. They face backward as the car carries them along. The coming suicide which casts its shadow over Quentin's last day is not a human possibility; not for a second does Quentin envisage the possibility of *not* killing himself. This suicide is an immobile wall, a *thing* which he approaches backward, and which he neither wants to nor can conceive.

> . . . you seem to regard it merely as an experience that will whiten your hair overnight so to speak without altering your appearance at all. . . .

It is not an *undertaking,* but a fatality. In losing its element of possibility it ceases to exist in the future. It is already present, and Faulkner's entire art aims at suggesting to us that Quentin's monologues and his last walk *are already* his suicide. This, I think, explains the following curious paradox: Quentin thinks of his last day in the past, like someone who is remembering. But in that case, since the hero's last thoughts coincide approximately with the bursting of his memory and its annihilation, who is remembering? The inevitable reply is that the novelist's skill consists in the choice of the present moment from which he narrates the past. And Faulkner, like Salacrou in *L'Inconnu d'Arras,* has chosen the infinitesimal instant of death. Thus, when Quentin's memory begins to unravel its recollections ("Through the wall I heard Shreve's bed-springs and then his slippers on the floor hishing. I got up . . .") *he is already dead.* All this artistry and, to speak frankly, all this illusion are meant, then, merely as substitutions for the intuition of the future lacking in the author himself. This explains everything, particularly the irrationality of time; since the present is the unexpected, the formless can be determined only by an excess of memories. We now also understand why duration is "man's characteristic misfortune." If the future has reality, time withdraws us from the past and brings us nearer to the future; but if you do away with the future, time is no longer that which separates, that which cuts the present off from itself. "You cannot bear to think that someday it will no longer hurt you like this." Man spends his life struggling against time, and time, like an acid, eats away at man, eats him away from himself and prevents him from fulfilling his human character. Everything is absurd. "Life is a tale told by an idiot, full of sound and fury, signifying nothing."

But is man's time without a future? I can understand that the nail's time, or the clod's, or the atom's is a perpetual present. But is man a thinking nail? If you begin by plunging him into universal time, the time of planets and nebulae, of tertiary flexures and animal species, as into a bath of sulphuric acid, then the question is settled. However, a consciousness buffeted so from one instant to another ought, *first of all,* to be a consciousness and then, *afterward,* to be temporal; does anyone believe that time can come to it from the outside? Consciousness can "exist within time" only on condition that it become time as a result of the very movement by which it becomes consciousness. It must become "temporalized," as Heidegger says. We can no longer arrest man at each present and define him as "the sum of what he has." The nature of consciousness implies, on the contrary, that it project itself into the future. We can understand what it is only through what it will be. It is determined in its present being by its own possibilities. This is what Heidegger calls "the silent force of the possible." You will not recognize within yourself Faulkner's man, a creature bereft of possibilities and explicable only in terms of what he has been. Try to pin down your consciousness and probe it. You will see that it is hollow. In it you will find only the future.

I do not even speak of your plans and expectations. But the very gesture that you catch in passing has meaning for you only if you project its fulfilment out of it, out of yourself, into the not-yet. This very cup, with its bottom that you do not see—that you might see, that is, at the end of a movement you have not yet made—this white sheet of paper, whose underside is hidden (but you could turn over the sheet), and all the stable and bulky objects that surround us display their most immediate and densest qualities in the future. Man is not the sum of what he has, but the totality of what he does not yet have, of what he might have. And if we steep ourselves thus in the future, is not the formless brutality of the present thereby attenuated? The single event does not spring on us like a thief, since it is, by nature, a Having-been-future. And if a historian wishes to explain the past, must he not first seek out its future? I am afraid that the absurdity that Faulkner finds in a human life is one that he himself has put there. Not that life is not absurd, but there is another kind of absurdity.

Why have Faulkner and so many other writers chosen this particular absurdity which is so un-novelistic and so untrue? I think we should have to look for the reason in the social conditions of our present life. Faulkner's despair seems to me to precede his metaphysics. For him, as for all of us, the future is closed. Everything we see and experience impels us to say, "This can't last." And yet change is not even conceivable, except in the form of a cataclysm. We are living in a time of impossible revolutions, and Faulkner uses his extraordinary art to describe our suffocation and a world dying of old age. I like his art, but I do not believe in his metaphysics. A closed future is still a future. "Even if human reality has nothing more 'before' it, even if 'its account is closed,' its being is still determined by this 'self-anticipation.' The loss of all hope, for example, does not deprive human reality of its possibilities; it is simply a way of *being* toward these same possibilities." [4]

[4] Heidegger, *Zein und Zeit.*

The Sound and the Fury

by Michael Millgate

Perhaps the single most arresting fact about the manuscript of *The Sound and the Fury* is that the first page bears the undeleted title "Twilight."[1] Clearly the title was no more than tentative: it may, indeed, have been the title of the original short story from which the novel grew, and it is worth noting in this respect its closeness to "That Evening Sun Go Down," the quotation from W. C. Handy's "St. Louis Blues" used as the title of another story of the Compson children on its first publication. But it is interesting to speculate whether the title was intended to apply to the one section or to the work as a whole and on its possible breadth of reference in either case. As a title for the first section alone, "Twilight" would presumably refer to the half-world of Benjy himself, held in a state of timeless suspension between the light and the dark, comprehension and incomprehension, between the human and the animal. As a title for the whole book, the word immediately suggests the decay of the Compson family caught at the moment when the dimmed glory of its eminent past is about to fade into ultimate extinction.

In Quentin's section, in particular, twilight, as a condition of light and a moment in time, takes on very considerable importance. In his most agonizing recollections of Caddy, he sees her at twilight, sitting in the cleansing waters of the branch and surrounded by the scent of honeysuckle, and these three elements of the scene—the twilight, the water, and the honeysuckle—take on an obsessive significance for Quentin himself and operate as recurrent symbols throughout this section of the novel. As water is associated with cleansing, redemption, peace, and death, and the honeysuckle with warm Southern nights and Caddy's passionate sexuality, so twilight, "that quality of light as if time really had stopped for a while" (pp. 209-10),[2] becomes inextricably confused in Quentin's mind with the scents of water and of honeysuckle until "the whole thing came to symbolise night and unrest" (p. 211). Quentin continues:

From *The Achievement of William Faulkner* by Michael Millgate (New York: Random House, 1966), pp. 94-111.

[1] Alderman Library, University of Virginia.

[2] All page references are to the first edition (New York, Jonathan Cape and Harrison Smith, 1929).

> I seemed to be lying neither asleep nor awake looking down a long corridor of grey halflight where all stable things had become shadowy paradoxical all I had done shadows all I had felt suffered taking visible form antic and perverse mocking without relevance inherent themselves with the denial of the significance they should have affirmed thinking I was I was not who was not was not who. (p. 211)

This passage would seem to be central to the meaning both of the particular section and of the book as a whole. There has just been a momentary anticipation of Quentin's carefully planned final release through death by water—traveling back into Cambridge he becomes aware of "the road going on under the twilight, into twilight and the sense of water peaceful and swift beyond" (p. 210)—and we realize that Quentin himself is at this moment not merely midway between sanity and madness but precisely poised between waking and sleeping, between life and death.[3] His world has become in fact "shadowy paradoxical"—we have just seen his actual fight with Gerald Bland overlaid in his consciousness by his remembered fight with Dalton Ames—and, for all the apparent orderliness of his actions, hc has finally lost his sense of personal identity ("thinking I was I was not who was not was not who"). The passage, in this respect, seems also to relate directly to the passage in *Macbeth* from which Faulkner took his final title for the book, and specifically to its descriptions of life as "a walking shadow," a tale "signifying nothing."

The phrase about "all stable things" becoming "shadowy paradoxical" aptly defines the hallucinatory world of the Quentin section, but it is also relevant to the treatment of "Fact," of "truth," throughout the novel. Like *Absalom, Absalom!, The Sound and the Fury* is in part concerned with the elusiveness, the multivalence, of truth, or at least with man's persistent and perhaps necessary tendency to make of truth a personal thing: each man, apprehending some fragment of the truth, seizes upon that fragment as though it were the whole truth and elaborates it into a total vision of the world, rigidly exclusive and hence utterly fallacious. This forms an essential part of the conception which Faulkner dramatized through the interior monologues of the first three sections of *The Sound and the Fury,* and the novel might thus be considered as in some sense a development, much richer than anything of which Anderson himself was capable, of the "theory of the grotesque" propounded at the beginning of *Winesburg, Ohio*:

> The old man had listed hundreds of the truths in his book. . . . There was the truth of virginity and the truth of passion, the truth of wealth and of poverty, of thrift and of profligacy, of carelessness and abandon. Hundreds and hundreds were the truths and they were all beautiful.
>
> And then the people came along. Each as he appeared snatched up one

[3] See *A Green Bough,* Poem X, entitled "Twilight" on its first publication in *Contempo,* I (February 1, 1932), 1.

> of the truths and some who were quite strong snatched up a dozen of them.
> It was the truths that made the people grotesques. The old man had quite an elaborate theory concerning the matter. It was his notion that the moment one of the people took one of the truths to himself, called it his truth, and tried to live his life by it, he became a grotesque and the truth he embraced became a falsehood.[4]

Faulkner admired *Winesburg, Ohio,* and there is a discernible similarity between Anderson's conception of Winesburg and Faulkner's creation of Jefferson, the town which he had begun somewhat painstakingly to lay out in *Sartoris* and which in *The Sound and the Fury* is for the first time integrated into the structure and action of the novel. In 1925 Faulkner especially praised *Winesburg, Ohio* for its "ground of fecund earth and corn in the green spring and the slow, full hot summer and the rigorous masculine winter that hurts it not, but makes it stronger";[5] he praised it, that is to say, for just that recurrent evocation of the land and the moving seasons which he himself achieved in *Soldiers' Pay* and *Sartoris* and which is also present, though less persistently and much less obviously, in *The Sound and the Fury*. Some of the time-levels in the Benjy section can be identified by their allusions to the cold, the rain, and so on, while Quentin, in his section, is intensely aware, with the heightened sensitivity of a man about to die, of the countryside through which he walks:

> In the orchard the bees sounded like a wind getting up, a sound caught by a spell just under crescendo and sustained. The lane went along the wall, arched over, shattered with bloom, dissolving into trees. Sunlight slanted into it, sparse and eager. Yellow butterflies flickered along the shade like flecks of sun. (p. 151)

. . . It was at the Nagano Seminar in 1955 that Faulkner gave his fullest account of how *The Sound and the Fury* came to be written:

> That began as a short story, it was a story without plot, of some children being sent away from the house during the grandmother's funeral. They were too young to be told what was going on and they saw things only incidentally to the childish games they were playing, which was the lugubrious matter of removing the corpse from the house, etc., and then the idea struck me to see how much more I could have got out of the idea of the blind, self-centeredness of innocence, typified by children, if one of those children had been truly innocent, that is, an idiot. So the idiot was born and then I became interested in the relationship of the idiot to the world that he was in but would never be able to cope with and just where could he get the tenderness, the help, to shield him in his innocence. I mean "innocence" in the sense that God had stricken him blind at birth,

[4] Sherwood Anderson, *Winesburg, Ohio* (New York, 1919), pp. 4-5.

[5] Faulkner's *Dallas Morning News* article on Anderson, in *Princeton University Library Chronicle*, XVIII (Spring 1957), 90.

that is, mindless at birth, there was nothing he could ever do about it. And so the character of his sister began to emerge, then the brother, who, that Jason (who to me represented complete evil. He's the most vicious character in my opinion I ever thought of), then he appeared. Then it needs the protagonist, someone to tell the story, so Quentin appeared. By that time I found out I couldn't possibly tell that in a short story. And so I told the idiot's experience of that day, and that was incomprehensible, even I could not have told what was going on then, so I had to write another chapter. Then I decided to let Quentin tell his version of that same day, or that same occasion, so he told it. Then there had to be the counterpoint, which was the other brother, Jason. By that time it was completely confusing. I knew that it was not anywhere near finished and then I had to write another section from the outside with an outsider, which was the writer, to tell what had happened on that particular day. And that's how that book grew. That is, I wrote that same story four times. None of them were right, but I had anguished so much that I could not throw any of it away and start over, so I printed it in the four sections. That was not a deliberate *tour de force* at all, the book just grew that way.[6]

A number of points here demand discussion. In the first place, there is a good deal of evidence to support Faulkner's statement that the novel began as a short story. Maurice Coindreau recalls Faulkner telling him:

"Ce roman, à l'origine, ne devait être qu'une nouvelle, me dit, un jour, William Faulkner. J'avais songé qu'il serait intéressant d'imaginer les pensées d'un groupe d'enfants, le jour de l'enterrement de leur grand'mère dont on leur a caché la mort, leur curiosité devant l'agitation de la maison, leurs efforts pour percer le mystère, les suppositions qui leur viennent à l'esprit."

["Originally this novel was to be only a story," William Faulkner told me one day. "I thought it would be interesting to imagine the thoughts of a group of children on the day of the burial of their grandmother whose death had been concealed from them, their curiosity about the excitement in the house, their efforts to penetrate the mystery, the ideas which came to their minds."] [7]

It was to be a story, therefore, similar in conception to "That Evening Sun," in which the Compson children are again placed in a situation whose adult significance they do not fully comprehend; Faulkner published the story in March 1931, and he had written it at the very latest by October 1930.[8] With this in mind we can quite readily disentangle from the opening section of *The Sound and the Fury,* where they occur in chronological and logical sequence, the sometimes quite widely separated fragments of a short story, "without plot," describing the experiences of the Compson children on the night of their grandmother's

[6] Robert A. Jelliffe, ed., *Faulkner at Nagano* (Tokyo, 1962), pp. 103-5.

[7] Maurice Coindreau, Preface to *Le bruit et la fureur* (Paris, 1949), p. 7.

[8] James B. Meriwether, *The Literary Career of William Faulkner: A Bibliographical Study* (Princeton, 1961), p. 175.

funeral; it is in the course of this material, moreover, that we first meet the image of Caddy's muddy drawers—seen from below as she clambers up the tree outside the Compson house in order to see what is happening inside—which, on other occasions, Faulkner spoke of as the basic image from which the whole book originated.

The pattern established by Faulkner's disposition of the novel's four sections can be viewed in a number of different ways, and they have been seen, for example, as exemplifying different levels of consciousness, different modes of apprehension or cognition, contrasted states of innocence and experience; M. Coindreau speaks of them as four movements of a symphony.[9] All these elements are present, and there is an over-all movement outward from Benjy's intensely private world to the fully public and social world of the fourth section. The pattern, however, is not solely progressive: despite the superficial affinities between the first and second sections on the one hand and the third and fourth sections on the other, the most fundamental relationships would seem to be those between the first and last sections, which offer a high degree of objectivity, and between the second and third, which are both intensely subjective. Benjy is a first-person narrator, as are Quentin and Jason, but his observations do not pass through an intelligence which is capable of ordering, and hence distorting, them; he reports the events of which he is a spectator, and even those in which he is himself a participator, with a camera-like fidelity. His view of Caddy, it is true, is highly personal, but we infer this view from the scenes which his camera-mind records; Benjy does not himself interpret this or other situations and events; still less does he attempt to impose a distorted interpretation upon the reader, as, in effect, do Quentin and Jason. Nor does he himself judge people, although he becomes the instrument by which the other characters are judged, their behavior toward him serving as a touchstone of their humanity.

Faulkner seems to have worked gradually toward the convention of pure objectivity which he follows in the Benjy section, and it is interesting to see the trend of his revisions, between manuscript and published work, to the well known scene in which Benjy burns his hand. The incident begins in the manuscript as follows:

> "Ow, mammy," Luster said. "Ow, mammy." I put my hand out to the firedoor.
>
> "Dont let him!" Dilsey said, "Catch him back." My hand jerked back and I put it in my mouth, and Dilsey caught me. I could still hear the clock between the times when my voice was going. Dilsey reached back and hit Luster on the head.
>
> "Git that soda," she said. She took my hand out of my mouth. My voice went louder then. I tried to put it back, but Dilsey held it. She sprinkled soda on it. "Look in the pantry . . ."[10]

[9] Coindreau, *op. cit.*, pp. 9-12.

[10] Manuscript, Alderman Library, p. 26.

The published text reads as follows:

> "Ow, mammy." Luster said. "Ow, mammy."
>
> I put my hand out to where the fire had been.
>
> "Catch him." Dilsey said. "Catch him back."
>
> My hand jerked back and I put it in my mouth and Dilsey caught me. I could still hear the clock between my voice. Dilsey reached back and hit Luster on the head. My voice was going loud every time.
>
> "Get that soda." Dilsey said. She took my hand out of my mouth. My voice went louder then and my hand tried to go back to my mouth, but Dilsey held it. My voice went loud. She sprinkled soda on my hand.
>
> "Look in the pantry . . ." (p. 72)

. . . Some of the revisions are more substantial . . . and it will be useful to look more closely at the changes made between the manuscript of the novel and the bound carbon typescript, both now in the Alderman Library. Several of the discrepancies between these two versions reveal Faulkner working toward what was to prove at once an elaboration and a simplification of his technique in the opening section of the book. Thus the first page of the manuscript lacks all the references to Luster's hunting in the grass for his lost quarter and to the fact that the day is Benjy's birthday which appear in the typescript and on pages 1 and 2 of the published text, and in the manuscript version as a whole there is an almost total absence of material relating to Luster's search for the quarter, to his desire to go to the show, to Benjy's birthday, or to Benjy's age. Faulkner presumably realized before or during the process of reworking the first section that the allusions to Benjy's birthday and, still more, to Luster's search for the missing quarter, could be made to serve as a kind of motif or signal of present time in the section and thus assist the reader in keeping his bearings among the shifting and merging time-planes. . . .

In both manuscript and typescript Faulkner had indicated by means of underlining that he wished the breaks in time sequence within the Benjy section to be suggested by changes back and forth between roman and italic type: it seems not to have been his intention that all such breaks should be accompanied by a type change, but rather that occasional italicization should alert the reader to the kind of process going on in Benjy's mind. In his admirable article on the textual history of the novel, James B. Meriwether has shown that when Faulkner received the galley proofs from Cape and Smith he found that considerable editorial changes had been made in the first section, apparently by his friend and literary agent, Ben Wasson, whom Cape and Smith had recently appointed as an assistant editor. In particular, the device of italicization had been abandoned and replaced by the insertion of breaks in the text (i.e., wider spaces between lines) at points where breaks in the time sequence occurred.[11] Wasson had presumably defended his action on the

[11] James B. Meriwether, "Notes on the Textual History of *The Sound and the Fury*," *Papers of the Bibliographical Society of America*, LVI (1962), 294-99.

grounds that italicization permitted the differentiation of only two dates, whereas at least four distinct times were actually involved. Faulkner replied, rejecting these arguments and explaining why he had restored the italics as they had appeared in his typescript and even added a few more in order to avoid obscurity; his letter, forcefully phrased, reveals beyond all question the absolute self-confidence and intellectual clarity with which he regarded the finished novel and the technical experimentation which it embodied:

> I received the proof. It seemed pretty tough to me, so I corrected it as written, adding a few more italics where the original seemed obscure on second reading. Your reason for the change, i.e., that with italics only 2 different dates were indicated I do not think sound for 2 reasons. First, I do not see that the use of breaks clarifies it any more; Second, there are more than 4 dates involved. The ones I recall off-hand are: Damuddy dies. Benjy is 3. (2) His name is changed. He is 5. (3) Caddy's wedding. He is 14. (4) He tries to rape a young girl and is castrated. 15. (5) Quentin's death. (6) His father's death. (7) A visit to the cemetary [sic] at 18. (7) [sic] The day of the anecdote, he is 33. These are just a few I recall, so your reason explodes itself.
>
> But the main reason is, a break indicates an objective change in tempo, while the objective picture here should be a continuous whole, since the thought transference is subjective; i.e., in Ben's mind and not in the reader's eye. I think italics are necessary to establish for the reader Benjy's confusion; that unbroken-surfaced confusion of an idiot which is outwardly a dynamic and logical coherence. To gain this, by using breaks it will be necessary to write an induction for each transference. I wish publishing was advanced enough to use colored ink for such, as I argued with you and Hal [Harrison Smith] in the speak-easy that day. But the form in which you now have it is pretty tough. It presents a most dull and poorly articulated picture to my eye. If something must be done, it were better to re-write this whole section objectively, like the 4th section. I think it is rotten, as it is. But if you won't have it so, I'll just have to save the idea until publishing grows up to it. Anyway, change all the italics. You overlooked one of them. Also, the parts written in italics will all have to be punctuated again. You'd better see to that, since you're all for coherence. And dont make any more additions to the script, bud. I know you mean well, but so do I. I effaced the 2 or 3 you made.[12]

. . . In reworking the manuscript version of the second section Faulkner made for more extensive additions and revisions than in the preceding section. This becomes immediately clear from a comparison between the opening paragraph of the manuscript and the corresponding passage in the published book. The manuscript reads:

> The shadow of the sash fell across the curtains between 7 and 8 oclock, and then I was hearing the watch. again, But I didn't and I lay there look-

[12] A.l.s., Faulkner to Wasson, n.d., in Massey Collection, Alderman Library.

ing at the sinister bar across the rosy and motionless curtains, listening to the watch. Hearing it, that is. I dont suppose anybody deliberately listens to a watch or a clock. You dont have to. You can be oblivious to the sound for a long while, then in a second of ticking it can create in the mind unbroken the long diminishing parade of time you did not hear. Where up the long and lonely arrowing of light rays you might see Jesus walking, like. The true Son of Man: he had no sister. Nazarene and Roman and Virginian, they had no sister one minute she was
Beyond the wall Shreve's bedsprings complained thinly, . . .[13]

Here for comparison, are the opening paragraphs of section two in the published book:

When the shadow of the sash appeared on the curtains it was between seven and eight oclock and then I was in time again, hearing the watch. It was Grandfather's and when Father gave it to me he said, Quentin, I give you the mausoleum of all hope and desire; it's rather excrutiating-ly apt that you will use it to gain the reducto absurdum of all human experience which can fit your individual needs no better than it fitted his or his father's. I give it to you not that you may remember time, but that you might forget it now and then for a moment and not spend all your breath trying to conquer it. Because no battle is ever won he said. They are not even fought. The field only reveals to man his own folly and despair, and victory is an illusion of philosophers and fools.

It was propped against the collar box and I lay listening to it. Hearing it, that is. I dont suppose anybody ever deliberately listens to a watch or a clock. You dont have to. You can be oblivious to the sound for a long while, then in a second of ticking it can create in the mind unbroken the long diminishing parade of time you didn't hear. Like Father said down the long and lonely light-rays you might see Jesus walking, like. And the good Saint Francis that said Little Sister Death, that never had a sister.

Through the wall I heard Shreve's bed-springs . . . (pp. 93-94)

Faulkner's alterations achieve certain improvements in phrasing and elaborate the insistence on time, but perhaps the most interesting of the new elements are the references to Mr. Compson. Throughout the section, as revised in the carbon typescript and the published book, Quentin's mind runs on his father almost as much as it does on Caddy. Quentin is, of course, very much like his father in many ways, and in his obsession with family tradition and honor it is understandable that he should refer to his father, the head of the family, as a transmitter of that tradition and as a source of authority and advice. The irony of this situation, however, and a major cause of Quentin's tragedy, is that just as his mother has failed him as a source of love so his father fails him utterly in all his roles of progenitor, confessor, and counselor. He has become, indeed, Quentin's principal enemy, his cold and even cynical logic persistently undermining the very basis of all those idealistic concepts to which

[13] Manuscript, Alderman Library, p. 34 (reproduced as Fig. 10 of *The Literary Career of William Faulkner*).

Quentin so passionately holds. Throughout the section there is a battle in progress between Quentin's romantic idealism and Mr. Compson's somewhat cynical realism, a battle which is not finally resolved in *The Sound and the Fury* and which is resumed on an even larger scale in *Absalom, Absalom!* Indeed, if we are to understand that the discussion between Quentin and his father at the end of the section is purely a figment of Quentin's imagination and never actually took place, then it has to be said that in *The Sound and the Fury* the battle is never properly joined—as, according to Mr. Compson himself, no battle ever is—and that it is, rather, a series of skirmishes in which Quentin suffers a progressive erosion of his position and a steady depletion of his reserves. Father and son are, in any case, too much alike in their fondness for words, for abstractions, and in choosing to evade life—the one in drink, the other in suicide—rather than actively confront it.

Whenever Quentin acts, his concern is for the act's significance as a gesture rather than for its practical efficacy. He seeks pertinaciously for occasions to fight in defence of his sister's honor, knowing in advance that he will be beaten, and concerned in retrospect only that he has performed the act in its ritualistic and symbolic aspects. It is the fight with Gerald Bland which reveals most clearly the degree to which Quentin's obsessions have divorced him from actuality since throughout the struggle it is the remembered fight with Dalton Ames which remains for Quentin the superior reality. Throughout a whole day of quite extraordinary incident—with two fights, an arrest, a court hearing, much movement, and many encounters—Quentin's mind remains preoccupied with the past. It is almost as though Faulkner were playing on the idea that a drowning man sees his whole life pass before him, and we come to realize that this last day of Quentin's is a kind of suspended moment before death.

Quentin's own obsession with time derives primarily from his recognition of it as the dimension in which change occurs and in which Caddy's actions have efficacy and significance. His search is for a means of arresting time at a moment of achieved perfection, a moment when he and Caddy could be eternally together in the simplicity of their childhood relationship; his idea of announcing that he and Caddy had committed incest was, paradoxically, a scheme for regaining lost innocence:

> it was to isolate her out of the loud world so that it would have to flee us of necessity and then the sound of it would be as though it had never been . . . if I could tell you we did it would have been so and then the others wouldnt be so and then the world would roar away . . . (p. 220)

The similarity between this conception and the image of motion in stasis which haunted Faulkner throughout his life, especially as embodied in Keats' "Ode to a Grecian Urn," suggests—as do the echoes of Joyce—that Quentin is in some measure a version of the artist, or at least the aesthete, as hero. But Quentin's conception is artificial, rigid, life-denying: as Mr. Compson observes, "Purity is a negative state and therefore contrary to nature. It's nature is hurting you not Caddy . . ." (p. 143) The inadequacy of Quentin's position is exposed in terms of Caddy and her vitality and humanity. In the Benjy section we recognize Caddy as the principal sustainer of such family unity as survives: we glimpse her as the liveliest spirit among the children and their natural leader, as the protector and comforter of Benjy, and even as the pacifier of her mother, and it is highly significant for us as well as for Benjy that she is persistently associated with such elemental things as the fire, the pasture, the smell of trees, and sleep. . . .

Caddy finds an outlet from family repression in sexual activity, but she is also both a principle and a symbol of social disruption. Her assertion of individuality is much less positive and urgent than that of such a character as Ursula Brangwen in D. H. Lawrence's *The Rainbow;* even so, she is brought, like Ursula, to break with traditional patterns and, in so doing, to demonstrate just how moribund those patterns have become, how irrelevant both to modern conditions and to the needs of the human psyche. It is possible to feel, however, that although Caddy is the core of the book she is not herself a wholly successful creation. Faulkner often spoke of Caddy, outside the novel, with an intensely passionate devotion: "To me she was the beautiful one," he said at the University of Virginia, "she was my heart's darling. That's what I wrote the book about and I used the tools which seemed to me the proper tools to try to tell, try to draw the picture of Caddy." [14] The original image of the little girl with the muddy drawers grew into the rich and complex conception of Caddy, beautiful and tragic both as child and as woman, but although this conception is already present in the first section of the novel it is evoked, necessarily, in somewhat fragmentary fashion, as we glimpse Caddy in various family situations, as we sense how much she means to Benjy, as we come to associate her, through Benjy, with images of brightness, comfort, and loss. In the second section Caddy is more clearly visible, and there are passages of remembered dialogue as revealing of Caddy's character as of Quentin's, but the world of Quentin's section is so unstable, so hallucinatory, that the figure of Caddy, like so much else, is enveloped in uncertainty. In Jason's section Caddy's agony is most movingly evoked, but only briefly so, while in the final section of the book she is no more than a memory.

It was an essential element in Faulkner's over-all conception of the novel that Caddy never be seen directly but only through the eyes of her three brothers, each with his own self-centered demands to make upon

[14] Frederick L. Gwynn and Joseph L. Blotner, eds., *Faulkner in the University: Class Conferences at the Univerity of Virginia 1957-1958* (Charlottesville, 1959), p. 6.

her, each with his own limitations and obsessions. Asked at Virginia why he did not give a section to Caddy herself, Faulkner replied that it seemed more "passionate" to do it through her brothers, and one is reminded of his remarks at Nagano about the beauty of description by understatement and indirection: "Remember, all Tolstoy said about Anna Karenina was that she was beautiful and could see in the dark like a cat. That's all he ever said to describe her. And every man has a different idea of what's beautiful. And it's best to take the gesture, the shadow of the branch, and let the mind create the tree." [15] It certainly seems likely that to have made Caddy a "voice" in the novel would have diminished her importance as a central, focal figure. As the book stands, however, Caddy emerges incompletely from the first two sections, and in the last two attention shifts progressively from her to her daughter, Quentin. The different limitation in the viewpoints of Benjy, Quentin, and Jason makes unavoidable the shadowiness, the imprecision, of Caddy's presentation: because the mind of each is so closed upon its own obsessions it is scarcely true to speak of their interior monologues as throwing light upon Caddy from a variety of angles; it is rather as though a series of photographs in differing focus were superimposed one upon the other, blurring all clarity of outline or detail. The novel revolves upon Caddy, but Caddy herself escapes satisfactory definition, and her daughter's tragedy, simply because it is more directly presented, is in some ways more moving.

It is characteristic that Jason should be the only member of the Compson family who is able to cope with the practical and social implications of Caddy's defection. Where Mrs. Compson can only moistly complain, Benjy bellow his incomprehending grief, Quentin commit suicide, Jason can adjust himself to the situation and turn it to his own advantage and profit. Jason—the one Compson who was capable of meeting Snopes on his own ground, as Faulkner wrote to Malcolm Cowley[16]—becomes in this way the representative of the new commercial South, and his section strikes a specifically contemporary note in its evocation of the petty businessman, with Jason himself appearing, in this role, as a typical figure, sharing the fundamental characteristics of a legion of other small businessmen in North and South alike. It is perhaps for this reason that Jason's seems much the least "Southern" of the sections. If it also seems the most readily detachable section—it was the one which Faulkner first suggested for inclusion in *The Portable Faulkner*[17]—that is a measure of the degree to which Jason's singleminded and ruthless pursuit of material self-interest serves to isolate him not only from his family but from the community as a whole. . . . His contempt for the town is only exceeded by his contempt for his own family, its history, and its pretensions:

[15] *Faulkner at Nagano*, p. 72.
[16] T.l.s., Faulkner to Cowley, n.d., Yale University Library.
[17] *Ibid.*

> Blood, I says, governors and generals. It's a damn good thing we never had any kings and presidents; we'd all be down there at Jackson chasing butterflies. (p. 286)

Since Jason's instincts are commercial and materialistic, they are also antirural and antitraditional: his is a willed deracination from the community in which he continues to live. As we have seen, however, it is this very materialism and deracination which makes Jason the one male Compson with any practical competence.

The progression from Benjy's section through Quentin's to Jason's is accompanied by an increasing sense of social reality: Benjy is remote in his idiocy and innocence, Quentin moves from the isolation of his half-mad idealism into the total withdrawal of suicide, but Jason is wholly in the world, acutely sensitive to social values, swimming with the contemporary commercial current. The action of the novel is thus presented increasingly in terms of social, economic, and political perspectives; it is Jason who first refers, however ironically, to the family's more distinguished past, and it is not until the last section of the novel that we are first given an image of the Compson house in all its decrepitude. To interpret *The Sound and the Fury* simply as a socio-economic study of the decline of a Southern family is obviously inadequate; what can be said is that this is one of the novel's many aspects, and one which becomes increasingly important as the book proceeds. It seems possible that Faulkner felt that he had created the social context of the action in insufficient detail, that the book did not clearly evoke the patterns of manners and customs within which his characters moved: the Compson "Appendix" he wrote for *The Portable Faulkner* is devoted partly to clarifying the meaning of the novel at certain points but primarily to the elaboration of the Compsons' family history and to the further definition of their place in the social and economic life of Jefferson. It is in the Appendix, too, that we find the abundantly particularized description of the farmers' supply store which Jason now owns and which Miss Melissa Meek valiantly enters,

> striding on through that gloomy cavern which only men ever entered—a cavern cluttered and walled and stalagmite-hung with plows and discs and loops of tracechain and singletrees and mule collars and sidemeat and cheap shoes and horse linament and flour and molasses . . .[18]

It must be admitted that each of the first three sections of *The Sound and the Fury* has about it some suggestion of the *tour de force:* the Quentin section seems a deliberate exercise in the Joycean mode, while the Jason section raises to the level of art the self-revelatory interior monologue of the unimaginative man which Sinclair Lewis had developed

[18] Malcolm Cowley, ed., *The Portable Faulkner* (New York, 1946), pp. 745-46.

in *Babbitt* and *The Man Who Knew Coolidge,* published in 1922 and 1928 respectively. The Benjy section seems to have been more exclusively Faulkner's invention, a deliberate attempt to extend the boundaries of the novel beyond the point to which Joyce had already pushed them. Yet Faulkner never regarded the book as a *tour de force;* unlike *As I Lay Dying, The Sound and the Fury* was a book which took him a long time and much agony to write, and his adoption in the final section of the point of view of the omniscient author seems to have been forced upon him not by the demands of a deliberate design but by the more immediate pressures stemming from an urgent need for self-expression.

In various accounts of the writing of *The Sound and the Fury* Faulkner says that having failed in three attempts to tell the story, to rid himself of the "dream," he had tried in the final section to pull the whole novel together, retelling the central story more directly and clearly. In fact, the section contributes relatively little to our understanding of the narrative events touched upon in earlier sections; in a radically different way. Simply by giving us for the first time detailed physical descriptions of Dilsey, Benjy, Jason, and Mrs. Compson, Faulkner—playing on some of the most fundamental of human responses to storytelling—effectively modifies our feelings toward them. Simply by recreating in such detail the routine of Dilsey's day, evoking the qualities demanded in performing such duties in a household such as that of the Compsons', Faulkner allows her to emerge for the first time both as a fully drawn character and as a powerful positive presence. When the action shifts to Jason and his vain pursuit of Quentin we notice that many of his experiences have something in common with Quentin's experiences during the last day of his life—there are, for example, the journeyings back and forth, the moments of violence, the unsatisfactory brushes with the representatives of the law—and we come finally to recognize that, for all the differences between them, both brothers display a similar obsessiveness and fundamental irrationality. . . .

It is . . . tempting, in the final section, to see in the immensely positive figure of Dilsey, and the importance given to her, a certain over-all reassurance and even serenity; but although the section does contain positives which to some extent offset the negations of the previous sections, it would be too much to say that the novel closes on a note of unqualified affirmation. Dilsey "endures," but her endurance is tested not in acts of spectacular heroism but in her submission to the tedious, trivial . . . and wilfully inconsiderate demands made upon her by the Compson family. . . . The Easter Sunday service in the Negro church is immensely moving, an apotheosis of simplicity, innocence, and love, with Dilsey and Benjy as the central figures:

> In the midst of the voices and the hands Ben sat, rapt in his sweet blue gaze. Dilsey sat bolt upright beside, crying rigidly and quietly in the annealment and the blood of the remembered Lamb. (pp. 370-71)

But the moment passes; the sense of human communion rapidly dissolves as they move into the world of "white folks" (p. 371) and return to the Compson house, described now for the first time and seen as a symbol of decay:

> They reached the gate and entered. Immediately Ben began to whimper again, and for a while all of them looked up the drive at the square, paintless house with its rotting portico. (p. 372)

It is clear, however, that Faulkner does not intend any simple moral division between the Negroes and their white employers. Luster in particular has been less impressed by the service than by the performance on the musical saw he had witnessed the previous night, and in his treatment of Benjy he displays a streak of mischievous cruelty. Dilsey tries to comfort Ben, but she is forced to rely upon the treacherous Luster to take him to the cemetery and it is with a note of pathetic resignation that she says, "I does de bes I kin" (p. 396). On the final pages of the novel it is pride, the sin which has been the downfall of the Compson family, which induces Luster to drive to the left at the monument instead of to the right, and if the final restoration of Benjy's sense of order seems at first to offer a positive conclusion to the novel we must also remember that the order thus invoked is one purely of habit, entirely lacking in inherent justification, and that it is restored by Jason, whose concern is not with humanity or morality or justice but only with social appearances. As so often in this novel, such meaning as at first sight the incidents appear to possess proves on closer inspection to dissolve into uncertainty and paradox.

In Shakespeare's play, Macbeth's "sound and fury" soliloquy is spoken as death approaches, and by the end of Faulkner's novel the doom of the Compson family seems about to be finally accomplished. In *Macbeth* the forces of good, embodied in Malcolm and Macduff, are gathering strength and it is perhaps characteristic of the desperate mood of *The Sound and the Fury* that the forces of good are not so readily identifiable, nor seen as ultimately triumphant. Yet in *Macbeth* the forces of good are external to Macbeth and Lady Macbeth, whereas in *The Sound and the Fury* some of the elements making for life do appear within the Compson family group, most notably in Dilsey but also in Caddy and her daughter. It is Quentin who gives Luster the quarter he so desires, it is Quentin who struggles in the last section to maintain at least some semblance of family harmony and order but who finally breaks down under Jason's verbal torture, and it is perhaps to be taken as a sign of hope—especially in view of the resurrection images which some critics have perceived in the description of her empty room—that Quentin finally makes good her escape and that, unlike her mother, she leaves no hostage behind. In the Compson genealogy Faulkner speaks of Quentin in pessimistic terms, yet the suggestion that Faulkner wanted to write a novel about Quentin after her departure from Jefferson[19] at least indicates that he felt the Compsons were not yet finished with, that there was more to be said—or perhaps only more to be suffered.

[19] Robert Linscott, "Faulkner Without Fanfare," *Esquire*, LX (July 1963), 38.

Mirror Analogues in *The Sound and the Fury*

by Lawrance Thompson

The concept of holding a mirror up to nature suggests an attractive but thorny path across the history of ideas, because that trope has lent itself to so many conflicting usages and interpretations. Yet the persistent allusions to mirrors in *The Sound and the Fury* would seem to invite the reader to notice that Faulkner has adapted the ancient literary mirror device and mirror principle to his own peculiar purposes, as a means of reflecting various kinds of correspondences, antitheses, parallelisms, analogues—even as a means of illuminating certain thematic concerns which are implicit throughout the total action. At the risk of oversimplifying Faulkner's elaborately developed meanings, I propose to present in ascending order of significance a few mirror allusions and mirror devices, in the hope that such a progression may increase our awareness of certain basic meanings.

Perhaps the first hint or foreshadowing occurs when the idiot Ben touches a place on a wall where a mirror used to be. During the late afternoon of Ben's thirty-third birthday his Negro guardian, Luster, leads him into this experience:

> We went to the library. Luster turned on the light. The windows went black, and the dark tall place on the wall came and I went and touched it. It was like a door, only it wasn't a door.
>
> The fire came behind me and I went to the fire and sat on the floor, holding the slipper. The fire went higher. It went onto the cushion in Mother's chair.

Although each of those images in that passage has important associations for Ben, this initial allusion to "the dark tall place on the wall" must strike the first reader as being mysterious, even meaningless, except that the tantalizing phrase does have the effect of creating a tension of interest, a focus of attention, which sharpens the response of the reader to later pertinent passages. For example, the superficial tension is com-

Reprinted with permission from *English Institute Essays, 1952* (New York: Columbia University Press, 1953), pp. 83-106.

pletely resolved when Jason subsequently gives his recollection of a similar situation, and views it from a decidedly different angle.

> I went on into the living room. I couldn't hear anything from upstairs. I opened the paper. After awhile Ben and Luster came in. Ben went to the dark place on the wall where the mirror used to be, rubbing his hands on it and slobbering and moaning. Luster begun punching at the fire.
> "What're you doing?" I says. "We dont need any fire tonight."
> "I trying to keep him quiet," he says.

Even this superficial clarification does not help us to understand the significance to Ben of that "dark place on the wall where the mirror used to be" before some of the furnishings were sold. But through Ben's stream-of-consciousness associations evoked by that "dark place" and that fire, Faulkner proceeds to develop a gradually revealing series of analogues, involving Ben and his sister Caddy and his mother at about the time he had been repudiated by his family through the act of changing his name from Maury to Benjamin. Two brief passages may be quoted to suggest the still enigmatic allusions to mirrors.

> Versh set me down and we went into Mother's room. There was a fire. It was rising and falling on the walls. There was another fire in the mirror.

Next, and again by association, Ben is reminded of Caddy. " 'Come and tell Mother goodnight.' Caddy said. We went to the bed. The fire went out of the mirror."

The specific meaning of that final sentence is obvious: as Ben's angle of vision changed, he could no longer see the reflection of fire in the mirror. But the immediate context suggests a symbolic value for that sentence: as Ben turns from Caddy to his mother he suffers a sense of loss which may be symbolized by the disappearance of the reflected fire. His next associational memory dramatizes several reasons why Ben may well have suffered a sense of loss whenever he turned from Caddy to his mother.

> *I could see the fire in the mirror too. Caddy lifted me again.*
> "Come on, now." she said. "Then you can come back to the fire. Hush now."
> . . . "Bring him here." Mother said. "He's too big for you to carry." . . .
> "He's not too heavy." Caddy said. "I can carry him."
> "Well, I dont want him carried, then." Mother said. "A five year old child. No, no. Not in my lap. Let him stand up."
> "If you'll hold him, he'll stop." Caddy said. "Hush." she said. "You can go right back. Here. Here's your cushion. See."
> "Dont, Candace." Mother said.
> "Let him look at it and he'll be quiet." Caddy said. "Hold up just a minute while I slip it out. There, Benjy. Look."
> I looked at it and hushed.

"You humour him too much." Mother said. "You and your father both. You dont realise that I am the one who has to pay for it. . . ."

"You dont need to bother with him." Caddy said. "I like to take care of him. Dont I, Benjy."

"Candace." Mother said. "I told you not to call him that. . . . Benjamin." she said. "Take that cushion away, Candace."

"He'll cry." Caddy said.

"Take that cushion away, like I told you." Mother said. "He must learn to mind."

The cushion went away.

"Hush, Benjy." Caddy said.

"You go over there and sit down." Mother said. "Benjamin." She held my face to hers.

"Stop that." she said. "Stop it."

But I didn't stop and Mother caught me in her arms and began to cry, and I cried. Then the cushion came back and Caddy held it above Mother's head. She drew Mother back in the chair and Mother lay crying against the red and yellow cushion.

"Hush, Mother." Caddy said. "You go upstairs and lay down, so you can be sick. I'll go get Dilsey." She led me to the fire and I looked at the bright, smooth shapes. I could hear the fire and the roof. . . .

You can look at the fire and the mirror and the cushion too, Caddy said.

In that little dramatic action is ample evidence that Caddy, motivated by her compassion for her younger brother, has eagerly given Ben the kind of motherly attention previously denied to him because of his own mother's inadequacies. Tenderly, solicitously, Caddy has discovered ways of appealing to Ben's limited responses, to satisfy his instinctive and unreasoning hunger for orderliness, peacefulness, serenity. The fire, the red-yellow cushion, the smooth satin slipper are only a few of the objects used by Caddy to provide him with values which are positive to him because they are somehow sustaining. Then Caddy has also taught Ben the pleasure of multiplying these positive values through their reflections in the mirror. Because she has heightened his awareness of all those symmetrical visions of "bright, smooth shapes" which comfort him, it might be said that Caddy herself has become for Ben a kind of mirror of all his positive values, framed in love: her love for him and his love for her.

Ben's seemingly chaotic reverie in Part One of *The Sound and the Fury* is so contrived by Faulkner as to focus attention, not merely on fragments of the entire Compson story, but particularly on Ben's all-absorbing love for the Caddy who was and (like the mirror) is now gone. Her presence was Ben's joy; her absence his grief; her possible return his hope. The arrangement of these fragments in Part One enables Faulkner to withhold conclusive information as to how it happened that the finely sensitive and mothering child Caddy has so completely disappeared. The reader's tension of interest concerning that question is gradually resolved through various later uses of mirror analogues which disclose related aspects of Faulkner's complex theme.

Throughout *The Sound and the Fury* Faulkner employs the convention of using some of his characters to serve as mirrors of other characters: mirrors set at different angles so that they provide contrasting angles of vision. For example, we have already had occasion to observe two contrasting images of Ben: the image reflected in the articulated consciousness of Caddy, as differing from the image reflected in the articulated consciousness of Mrs. Compson. Although various characters in the narrative reflect various images of Ben, all these images may be reduced to two roughly antithetical categories: most of the characters view Ben as a disgrace, a menace, or at least as a slobbering idiot. By contrast, those who genuinely love Ben (particularly Caddy and the Negro servant Dilsey) insist that Ben has certain particular and extraordinary powers of perception. As Roskus phrases it, "He know lot more than folks thinks." Repeatedly Ben is represented has having the instinctive and intuitive power to differentiate between objects or actions which are life-encouraging and others which are life-injuring, and these are used by Faulkner to symbolize the antithesis between good and evil. In this limited sense, then, Ben serves as a kind of moral mirror, in which the members of his own family may contemplate reflections of their own potentialities, their own moral strengths and weaknesses. Most of them naturally refuse to acknowledge this power in Ben because they do not wish to see themselves in any light other than that of self-justification.

Appropriately, Caddy is represented as having the greatest sensitivity to her brother's power of serving as a kind of moral mirror, and her sensitivity is heightened by her unselfish love for him. Faulkner develops this aspect of Ben's significance in four episodes which illuminate the progressive phases of Caddy's growth. When she is old enough to be interested in adolescent courtship, she discovers that Ben's unreasoning reaction against the smell of perfume gives her a sense of guilt and prompts her to wash herself clean—a primitive ritual repeatedly correlated with Ben's potential for serving as moral agent and moral conscience in his family. Later, when Ben escapes from the house one night, to find Caddy and Charlie kissing in the swing on the lawn, Caddy leaves Charlie, ostensibly to quiet Ben, but also because Ben has again evoked in her a sense of guilt.

> We ran out into the moonlight, toward the kitchen. . . . Caddy and I ran. We ran up the kitchen steps, onto the porch, and Caddy knelt down in the dark and held me. I could hear her and feel her chest. "I wont." she said. "I wont anymore, ever. Benjy. Benjy." Then she was crying, and I cried, and we held each other. "Hush." she said. "Hush. I wont anymore."

> So I hushed and Caddy took the kitchen soap and washed her mouth at the sink, hard.

The third time when Ben is represented as a moral mirror occurs as Caddy returns home immediately after her first complete sexual experience. In that scene Faulkner correlates two implicit analogues which complement each other: first, the analogue of Ben as a moral mirror; secondly, the analogue between simple physical vision and conscious moral vision, suggested by the persistent recurrence of the word "eyes" and the cognate words, "looking" and "seeing," as Ben again evokes in Caddy a deeper sense of guilt.

> Caddy came to the door and stood there, looking at Father and Mother. Her eyes flew at me, and away. I began to cry. It went loud and I got up. Caddy came in and stood with her back to the wall, looking at me. I went toward her, crying, and she shrank against the wall and I saw her eyes and I cried louder and pulled at her dress. She put her hands out but I pulled at her dress. Her eyes ran. . . . We were in the hall, Caddy was still looking at me. Her hand was against her mouth and I saw her eyes and I cried. We went up the stairs. She stopped again, against the wall, looking at me and I cried and she went on and I came on, crying, and she shrank against the wall looking at me. She opened the door to her room, but I pulled at her dress and we went to the bathroom and she stood against the door, looking at me. Then she put her arm across her face and I pushed at her, crying.

Each of these three closely related episodes (involving Ben as moral mirror and also involving the symbolic and penitent ritual of washing away guilt with water) is associated in Ben's recollection with his ultimate reaction, at the time of Caddy's fake wedding, where the sense of guilt was ironically washed away with champagne until the celebration was terminated by Ben's unreasoning and bellowing protest. This fourth episode represents the end of the period in Ben's life when Caddy had been able to help him by bringing relative order out of his relatively chaotic experience, and the end of the period when Ben had served as moral mirror for Caddy. Notice that these two endings are obliquely suggested by reiterative mirror imagery in Quentin's recollection of that incident which broke up the wedding celebration.

> She ran right out of the mirror, out of the banked scent. Roses. Roses. . . . Only she was running already when I heard it. In the mirror she was running before I knew what it was. That quick, her train caught up over her arm she ran out of the mirror like a cloud, her veil swirling in long glints her heels brittle and fast clutching her dress onto her shoulder with the other hand, running out of the mirror the smells roses roses the voice that breathed o'er Eden. Then she was across the porch I couldn't hear her heels then in the moonlight like a cloud, the floating shadow of the veil running across the grass, into the bellowing.

Caddy goes away after the fake wedding ceremony, leaving a double image of herself as reflected in the consciousness of her family. The reader's initial image of Caddy has been that reflected repeatedly in the consciousness of Ben: the sensitive and mothering Caddy whose love for Ben evoked his love for her and gave meaning to his life. That image remains. Antithetically, the second image of Caddy is that soon reflected (with only minor variations) in the consciousness of Mrs. Compson, Quentin, and Jason: the image of the member of the family whose fall from innocence is said to have brought a peculiar disgrace on the entire family; a disgrace considered equal to, or even greater than, that of Ben's idiocy. Gradually, however, the reader appreciates that Mrs. Compson, Quentin, and Jason, each motivated by different kinds of need for self-justification, have first made a scapegoat of Ben and have then made a scapegoat of Caddy, so that they may heap on these two scapegoats the ultimate blame for the disintegration within the Compson family. Although this suggests one further aspect of Faulkner's complex theme, further elaboration of this central meaning may be postponed until we have considered other varieties of mirror analogues.

In Part Two of *The Sound and the Fury* Faulkner gradually suggests antithetical contrasts between Ben's preoccupation with mirrors and Quentin's preoccupation with mirrors. At one point in his reverie Quentin makes this sequence of observations.

> I could smell the curves of the river beyond the dusk and I saw the last light supine and tranquil upon the tideflats like pieces of broken mirror. . . . Benjamin the child of. How he used to sit before that mirror. Refuge unfailing in which conflict [was] tempered silenced reconciled.

Quentin is (if we may borrow a phrase which Faulkner affords to Quentin himself) "a sort of obverse reflection" of Ben. By contrast with Ben's instinctive response to objects used to symbolize positive values in human experience, Quentin serves to dramatize a consciously willed and obsessive love for negative values which are life-injuring, life-destroying, and which, in turn, are nicely symbolized by his elaborately planned act of suicide by drowning. Throughout *The Sound and the Fury* a recurrent motif, suggested by the title itself, is the traditional convention of conflict between order-producing forces and chaos-producing forces in human experience, here represented in part by the gradual drift of the Compson family from remembered dignity and order toward disgrace and chaos. Quentin is represented as one whose disordering self-love motivates not only his masochistic delight in creating inner chaos but also his erotic lust for his own death. Structurally, then, the juxtaposition of Ben's thirty-third birthday against Quentin's death day accentuates the contrasting life-visions symbolized by Ben (who is ironically the shame of the Compsons) and by Quentin (who is ironically the pride of the Compsons). The two brief passages which constitute, respectively, the end of Ben's day and the beginning of Quentin's day may be quoted to suggest, once again, Faulkner's fondness for the technical principle of antithesis, here used to illuminate obliquely the basic ways in which these two brothers serve as obverse reflections of each other. Ben's day ends with these words:

> Caddy held me and I could hear us all, and the darkness, and sometimes I could smell. And then I could see the windows, where the trees were buzzing. Then the dark began to go in smooth, bright shapes, like it always does, even when Caddy says that I have been asleep.

There, implicitly, recurs the thematic suggestion that Ben, with the aid of Caddy, has developed the ability to find within himself the power to convert even darkness into a pattern of meaningful and soothing symmetry, serenity, order: "refuge unfailing, in which conflict [was] tempered silenced reconciled," as Quentin phrased it. By contrast, Quentin begins his day with an irritated resentment of sunlight and with an insistence on finding within himself the power to convert even the life-giving value of sunlight into a reminder of time. After the manner of his father, Quentin has already endowed time with ugly and chaotic significance: "When the shadow of the sash appeared on the curtains it was between seven and eight o'clock and then I was in time again, hearing the watch."

For immediate purposes the pivotal image there is "shadow," an image subsequently enriched by Faulkner to represent Quentin's *alter ego,* his own reflected image of himself, developed by Quentin as an elaborate mirror analogue. Quentin's reasoning, obliquely suggested by his numerous references to his own mirror analogue, may be paraphrased briefly. To achieve his willed act of self-destruction, he is aware that he must cope with that other side of self which is represented by his physical being or body, which intuitively or instinctively clings to life while resisting the death-will of his mind. To insult and belittle that resisting other-self (the body), Quentin identifies his body with his sun-cast shadow. Because the sun is repeatedly represented as creating the shadow of his body, this shadow might be considered poetically as the body's tribute to the life-giving power of the sun. But this is exactly the kind of tribute which Quentin wishes to deny. His inverted attitude toward the instinctive life-wish of his body is nicely reflected in the following poetic sentence, so rich in suggested extensions of meanings: "There was a clock, high up in the sun, and I thought about how when you don't want to do a thing, your body will try to trick you into doing it, sort of unawares."

At first glance, this echo of the traditional body-versus-spirit antithesis suggests Quentin's warped Calvinistic Presbyterian heritage. On reconsideration, it becomes obvious that the thing which Quentin does not want to do is to live; that which his body tries to do is to resist Quentin's obsessive and erotic lust for death. Consequently Quentin perversely views the body's natural death-resistance as the body's attempt to "trick" him. This inverted concept evokes his further conviction that he must counter-attack that body-impulse by managing somehow to subdue and "trick" his shadow. Four very brief utterances of Quentin's may be quoted here to demonstrate the ironically enriching effects achieved by Faulkner in permitting this shadow-reflection of Quentin's body to represent Quentin's other-self opponent.

> [1] I stepped into the sunlight, finding my shadow again.
> [2] Trampling my shadow's bones into the concrete with hard heels. . . .
> [3] The car stopped. I got off, into the middle of my shadow . . . trampling my shadow into the dust.
> [4] The wall went into shadow, and then my shadow, I had tricked it again.

Obviously, Quentin's ultimate tricking of his "shadow" must be the destruction of his body in the planned act of suicide by drowning. In developing the double significance of this act (as being desired by the will and as being not desired by the body), Faulkner makes pertinent use of Quentin's initial experience on a bridge over the Charles River, where he stands contemplating his own shadow mirrored on the surface of the water below.

> The shadow of the bridge, the tiers of railings, my shadow leaning flat upon the water, so easily had I tricked it that it would not quit me. At least fifty feet it was, and if I only had something to blot it into the water, holding it until it drowned, the shadow of the package like two shoes wrapped up lying on the water. Niggers say a drowned man's shadow was watching for him in the water all the time. . . . I leaned on the railing, watching my shadow, how I had tricked it. I moved along the rail, but my suit was dark too and I could wipe my hands, watching my shadow, how I had tricked it.

Later, from another bridge, Quentin blindly contemplates another symbolic shadow: the trout, instinctively fulfilling its potentialities as it swims against the destructive element in which it has its being.

> I could not see the bottom, but I could see a long way into the motion of the water before the eye gave out, and then I saw a shadow hanging like a fat arrow stemming into the current. Mayflies skimmed in and out of the shadow of the bridge just above the surface. . . . The arrow increased without motion, then in a quick swirl the trout lipped a fly beneath the surface. . . . The fading vortex drifted away down stream and then I saw the arrow again, nose into the current, wavering delicately to the motion of the water above which the Mayflies slanted and poised. . . . Three boys with fishing poles came onto the bridge and we leaned on the rail and looked down at the trout. They knew the fish. He was a neighborhood character. . . . "We dont try to catch him anymore," he said. "We just watch Boston folks that come out and try."

That little parable or implicit mirror of meaning, wasted on Quentin, helps to correlate several different aspects of Faulkner's steadily developing emphasis on the value of certain kinds of instinctive response in human experience. There is even a suggested analogy between the instinctive action of the trout and the instinctive action of the sea gull which Quentin also blindly contemplates: each in its own discrete element instinctively uses the current or stream of its own element to achieve poise, even as the Mayflies do. Consider these two quotations in their relation to each other.

> . . . rushing away under the poised gull and all things rushing.
> . . . the arrow again, nose into the current, wavering delicately to the motion of the water above which the Mayflies slanted and poised.

Quentin's element is time, and instead of building on his own innate and instinctive potentialities for achieving poise against the motion of "all things rushing," he is represented as having deliberately chosen to pervert and destroy those potentialities. The trout, the gull, the Mayflies, along with Ben, make available to the reader the kinds of metaphorical "mirrors" of meaning which Quentin refuses to understand. By contrast with Ben, Quentin has a tendency to use all mirrors (literal or figurative) to multiply negative values, particularly those disordered and chaotic values symbolized by the reflection of his own death-obsessed face. On the evening of his death day, as he continues his chaotically systematic ritual of death courtship, Quentin momentarily finds in a window of a trolley car a mirror of things broken: "The lights were on in the car, so while we ran behind trees I couldn't see anything except my own face and a woman across the aisle with a hat sitting right on top of her head, with a broken feather in it."

Having established that mirror-image of the trolley car window, Faulkner subsequently develops extensions of meaning from it. Quentin, after returning to his dormitory room to clean himself up for death, stands before a conventional mirror, brushing his hair, troubled at the thought that Shreve, his roommate, may return in time to spoil his plans. Or perhaps, he thinks, Shreve may be coming into town on a trolley, just as Quentin is again going out on another trolley, and if so their faces will be momentarily juxtaposed and separated only by the two windows and the space between. The elliptical passage containing hints of these thoughts is of particular interest here, because it suggests a basic mirror principle—namely, Quentin's use of phrases which have only a superficial value for him, but a far deeper thematic suggestion for the reader. Here is the passage.

> While I was brushing my hair the half hour went. But there was until the three quarters anyway, except supposing seeing on the rushing darkness only his own face no broken feather unless two of them but not two like

> that going to Boston the same night then my face his face for an instant across the crashing when out of the darkness two lighted windows in rigid fleeing crash gone his face and mine just as I see saw did I see.

The potentials of meaning which go far beyond Quentin's immediate meaning there may be passed over to let us concentrate particularly on that striking phrase, less applicable to Shreve than to the total action of Quentin: "seeing on the rushing darkness only his own face." That again strongly suggests not only the conflict between Quentin's two opposed consciences but also the total contrast between Quentin's uses of mirrors and Ben's uses of mirrors.

Faulkner's most elaborately contrived mirror analogue, in the presentation of Quentin's death day, stands out as technically different from any mirror analogue we have yet considered. It is a figurative or symbolic mirroring of the meaning of a past action in a present action: the parallelism between the way Quentin plays big brother to the little Italian girl and the way Quentin previously played big brother to Caddy. Another kind of "broken mirror" effect is achieved by scattering through the entire episode involving the Italian girl evoked fragments of memories concerning earlier and related episodes involving Quentin and Caddy. This twofold sequence of analogous actions is much too long to be analyzed here. Yet it deserves to be mentioned as an extremely important example of a mirror analogue, in which Faulkner at least suggests that Caddy's love for her younger brother Ben and for her older brother Quentin was soiled, stained, and perverted by Quentin's self-love until Caddy, trying to keep up with her brother, got into trouble. To a large degree, Quentin is represented as having been personally responsible for the change which occurred in the character of Caddy. Yet, even as Quentin rejects as ridiculous the charge of the Italian brother, "You steela my sister," so he also rejects and ignores even the suggestions made by his own conscious or subconscious associations that he was, indeed, in some way responsible for what happened to Caddy. In this immediate context there is a highly ironic significance in the fact that Caddy should have chosen to name her daughter Quentin, even though her brother was not physically the father of her child.

Faulkner seems to have saved two oblique and "gathering" metaphors or symbolic actions for use in the concluding pages of *The Sound and the Fury,* and in this context it may be permissible to consider those two actions as mirror analogues, figuratively speaking. The first of these occurs in the episode involving Dilsey and Ben at the Easter service in the Negro church, and Faulkner begins it by making technical use, once again, of two contrasting or antithetical attitudes toward one person, namely, the monkey-faced preacher, who undergoes a metamorphosis, as he loses himself in the meaning of an action symbolizing self-sacrificial love:

> And the congregation seemed to watch with its own eyes while the voice consumed him, until he was nothing and they were nothing and there was not even a voice but instead their hearts were speaking to one another in chanting measures beyond the need for words, so that when he came to rest against the reading desk, his monkey face lifted and his whole attitude that of a serene, tortured crucifix that transcended its shabbiness and insignificance and made of it no moment, a long expulsion of breath rose from them.

Faulkner would seem to be dramatizing in that symbolic action a key aspect of his central theme, always pivoting, as it does, on various possible meanings for the single word "love." For that reason the responses of Dilsey and Ben to that action are pertinent.

> Dilsey sat bolt upright, her hand on Ben's knee. The tears slid down her fallen cheeks, in and out of the myriad coruscations of immolation and abnegation and time. . . . In the midst of the voices and the hands Ben sat, rapt in his sweet blue gaze. Dilsey sat bolt upright beside, crying rigidly and quietly in the annealment and the blood of the remembered Lamb.

The second of these gathering metaphors also illuminates and accentuates the implicit thematic antithesis between two kinds of vision. This time the extensions of meaning are ironically suggested through Luster's saucy analogy between how he does something and "how quality does it." While entertaining Ben by taking him for his customary ride to the cemetery on Easter Sunday, Luster decides to show off, for the benefit of some loitering Negroes. He merely proposes a simple violation of a simple law when he says, "Les show dem niggers how quality does it, Benjy." Instead of driving around the monument in the accustomed way, he starts Queenie the wrong way. Ben, instinctively feeling the difference between right and wrong even in such a trivial situation, begins to bellow and continues until the minor chaos of that situation (ironically corrected by Jason, out of mere embarrassment) has given way to the ritual of orderly return. So the total action of the narrative ends with the implicit and symbolic reiteration of the part Ben has played throughout, in terms of the antithesis between the human power to create chaos and the human power to create order.

> Queenie moved again, her feet began to clop-clop, steadily again, and at once Ben hushed. Luster looked quickly back over his shoulder, then he drove on. The broken flower drooped over Ben's fist, and his eyes were empty and blue and serene again, as cornice and façade flowed smoothly once more, from left to right; post and tree, window and doorway, and signboard, each in its ordered place.

Faulkner's choice of title deserves to be viewed figuratively as suggesting one further kind of mirror analogue, because the attitude of Macbeth, as dramatized in the familiar fifth-act soliloquy, nicely reflects an important element in the attitudes of Faulkner's three major protagonists of chaos, Mrs. Compson, Quentin, and Jason. All of these characters have this much in common: each is intent on self-pitying self-justification. All are certain that they have become victimized by circumstances beyond their control, and all of them project outward on life their own inner chaos, which has its roots in a perversion of love, through self-love. Similarly, in the fifth act, Macbeth is represented as refusing to recognize that he has been in any way to blame, or responsible, for what has happened to him. Instead, he also projects his own inner chaos outward, self-justifyingly, to make a scapegoat of the whole world, even of time, and to view life itself as a walking "shadow." Now consider the ironies of situation implicit in that passage which Faulkner's title suggests as a pertinent mirror of the attitudes not only of Quentin and Jason but also of Mr. and Mrs. Compson.

> Tomorrow, and tomorrow, and tomorrow,
> Creeps in this petty pace from day to day,
> To the last syllable of recorded time.
> And all our yesterdays have lighted fools
> The way to dusty death. Out, out, brief candle!
> Life's but a walking shadow, a poor player
> That struts and frets his hour upon the stage,
> And then is heard no more. It is a tale
> Told by an idiot, full of sound and fury,
> Signifying nothing.

Finally, the meaning of Faulkner's total structure may be suggested by one last mirror analogue. As narrator, he would seem to be intent on achieving a high degree of detachment by arranging his four separate parts in such a way that they do not tell a story in the conventional sense. Faulkner neither invites nor permits the reader to look directly at the total cause-and-effect sequence of events, as such. Instead, each of the four parts provides a different aspect, a different view, a different angle of vision, a different reflection of some parts of the story. Each of these four structural units, thus contiguous, hinged, set at a different angle from the others, might be called analogous to those hinged and contiguous haberdashery mirrors which permit us to contemplate the immediate picture reflected in any single one of those mirrors, and then to contemplate secondary or subordinate pictures which are reflections of reflections in each of the separate mirrors.

In Faulkner's four structural mirrors (the four parts), the first picture (or pictures) may be said to be provided through Ben's reflecting angle of vision. Although the reader's initial impression of Ben's reverie may, indeed, provide a sense that the tale is told by an idiot, signifying nothing, the ultimate impression is that Ben's angle of vision concentrates our attention symbolically on certain basic and primitive powers of perception, available even to an idiot; powers of perception which enable even a severely handicapped individual to create, from his own experience and with the aid of his instincts and intuitions, some forms of order which can give positive values to human experience.

Structurally, the second set of pictures is provided through Quentin's reflecting angle of vision. This time, although the reader's early impression of Quentin's reverie may provide a preliminary sense of a highly sensitive and Hamlet-like character, who views himself as intent on holding up to nature his own idealistic mirror, the ultimate impression is that Quentin's angle of vision reflects, by contrast with Ben's, several important aspects of the negative or obverse side of Faulkner's theme. Psychologically unbalanced by his own inner and outer conflicts, Quentin is represented as being partly responsible not only for what has happened to himself but also for what has happened to some other members of his family. He has permitted his warped and warping ego to invert exactly those basic and primitive and positive values symbolized by that which Ben instinctively and intuitively cherished.

The third set of images is provided by Jason's reflecting angle of vision, and even though Jason sees himself as the only sane Compson, the reader quickly becomes convinced that Jason's sadistic scale of values is more nearly analogous to the values of Iago than to those of the almost Hamlet-like Quentin. The irony of the total situation involving Jason culminates in a ridiculously fine burlesque of poetic justice when Faulkner permits Jason's golden fleece of Caddy to be avenged by Caddy's daughter's golden fleece of Jason. Even as Caddy's brother Quentin has somehow been at least partially responsible for the moral degeneration of Caddy, so Jason is represented as being at least partially responsible for the moral degeneration of Caddy's daughter.

The fourth set of images is provided through Dilsey's reflecting angle of vision. Implicitly and symbolically there is an analogous relationship between Dilsey's emphasis on certain basic, primary, positive values throughout and Ben's intuitive sense of values. Thus, the positive angles of vision, mirrored by Ben and Dilsey most sharply in the first and fourth structural parts of *The Sound and the Fury,* may be considered literally and symbolically as bracketing and containing the two negative angles of vision mirrored by Quentin and Jason in the second and third parts. Taken in this sense, the structural arrangement of these four hinged mirrors serves to heighten the reader's awareness of Faulkner's major thematic antithesis between the chaos-producing effects of self-love and the order-producing effects of compassionate and self-sacrificial love in human experience.

William Faulkner

by Günter Blöcker

"The only way to avoid the abyss is to descend into it, to measure and sound it out."

—Cesare Pavese: *Il Mestiere di Vivere*

In 1929, almost ten years after the second part of Proust's *Recherche* had received the Goncourt Prize and fragments of *Ulysses* had been released to a wide public in the American periodical *Little Review*, in the same year which saw both Hemingway's *A Farewell to Arms* and Thomas Wolfe's *Look Homeward, Angel*, William Faulkner published his novel *The Sound and the Fury*. . . .

Faulkner had already written some verse and several novels, but with *The Sound and the Fury* he begins to become a concern of the century. Here, establishing his concept of mythical time and employing his strange experience of it for the first time, he outstrips both Proust and Joyce. He does not laboriously reconstruct lost time in order to capture and preserve it as Proust does, trying to outwit it in a rational manner so typically French. Nor does he recreate time through an intense act of will as does Joyce, who enlarges intellectual consciousness and stretches it to its limit. Faulkner destroys time and throws it out of working order. We witness this in a symbolic act when Quentin Compson rips off the hands from his watch and so wrecks the tyranny of its dial. To be sure, the ticking of the clockwork continues and time passes as before, but at least man's consciousness is no longer subjected to the arbitrary action of a mechanical hand. The consciousness cannot be completely free until the sweet ticking of those little wheels that man devised for his own bondage stops, too. Only then can we enter authentic time, for, as Faulkner tells us: "Clocks slay time. Time is dead as long as it is being clicked off by little wheels; only when the clock stops does time come to life."

And then we can enter Faulkner's work, in a time without clocks, in the true rather than the construed time. Hence the mingling of streams of consciousness, the mutilation and entangling of the thinking process;

Condensed from "William Faulkner." From *Die Neuen Wirklichkeiten* by Günter Blöcker, trans. Jacqueline Merriam (Berlin: Argon Verlag, 1958), pp. 112-23.

hence, too, the apparent formlessness of his novels, this thicket of sentences, this mountain range of words, this bankless river bed through which the primitive stream of his narrative moves. Faulkner's people live in archaic time, in the primordial; they live in mythical space—since "back" always means "down" as well. And because the mythical, lying far ahead of the transforming grip of human arbitration, is the authentic, the writer without time becomes the poet of Being. He alone has access to the realms of the unfalsified, which is also the indistinct, the pre-individual. Thus, the alleged facelessness of many of Faulkner's characters: in the various family chronicles, where he tells the history of the southern United States in perpetual offshoots and digressions, it often happens that the single characters—at first anyway—do not appear as individuals with clearly defined personalities and physiognomies, but rather as voices, as sound-emitting raw material. It is like a vast whisper, a primeval groan, a rudimentary stammer in which the human, before taking form, is literally ex-pressed. Of this, too, *The Sound and the Fury* is at once the first and the extreme example. By presenting events right from the start through the vision of an imbecile—Benjamin Compson opens the dismal round of interior monologues which takes us sinuously through the novel's landscape—Faulkner manifests his intent: to seek out the original substance of man, his very being before it takes form. He deemed it more effective, as he later explains, to tell the story of someone who "knows only what happens to him, but not why it happens." More effective, indeed, because it allows us to penetrate Faulkner's notion of man more deeply and with greater surprise. The whimpering, blubbering, and bellowing of the harmless, good-natured idiot give the book not only its gruesome background music, but also its purifying significance. What we hear is the accusation of the unawoken creature against himself and the ill-bred world. In the face of the innate corruption of the human fiber (the "Compsonistic vulgarity"!), the curse of being, the original sin of existing, is thrust the paralyzing premonition of crude, undrawn forces of love.

As his contemporaries and immediate predecessors, Faulkner believed the domain of the individual, and with it the conventional concept of time as set by the individual consciousness, to have been thoroughly surveyed and already totally exhausted. This double insufficiency is felt with remarkable accord and spontaneity in our times whenever great literature is being produced. But what distinguishes Faulkner from Proust, Joyce, Virginia Woolf, Thomas Mann, Ezra Pound, and T. S. Eliot is that he does not experiment with time. He does not even acknowledge it. Time in the traditional sense simply does not exist for him. While with each of the others there remains the knowledge and even the coquetry of a bold venture, Faulkner has the thoughtlessness and the impact of naivety. . . .

Faulkner never experimented with the novel's form; he simply dismissed it. He imposes himself through force, virility, and the natural fury of his vision. He is the truly male talent of modern literature. Against Proust's painfully relished artistic exercise, Joyce's burrowing intellectuality, Thomas Mann's bourgeois understanding of art, or Ezra Pound's constructive mimicry of forms, Faulkner opposes the uncultivated as creative power. He does not need to penetrate the realm of myth through an effort of culture; he is at home in it. He does not have to first unlock the elemental zone of consciousness; he belongs to it. His force lies on the other side of skimpy reason, his measure defies measures, and his clarity is in the obscure. . . . With him, dreaming and composing are one. The solution he offers us is not to be found in an application of some allegorical transfer pictures. It lies in the fact that he allows us to dream with him, wild and transported, despairing and consoling, shaken by fear and blessed by hope. . . .

As far as Faulkner is concerned, this means that the mythical creates its own categories, its own language—in short, that the mythical *is* its own language. The mythical point of view excludes any separation of the two; there is no within and without, no here and there, but only an entirety. Faulkner's digressive, violent lyricism is the resonance of that primitive, unhewn rock of humanity. Images and visions flow into one another, the fantastic mingles with the real, the abstract feeds on the blood of things, the senses fraternize in their joint sovereignty over the world, and objects assume personality. A railway train sweeps wailing through the solitary landscape like a mourning spirit; memories become a peaceful corridor peopled with kind and nameless faces and voices; the taste and scent of the forgotten can never fade from the palate of consciousness. Lena Grove, the big simpleton of *Light in August* (1932), waits at the edge of the road for a mule team which advances on dream hooves, plodding along in a cloud of drowsiness; its slow approach weaves into the reveries of the pregnant woman who, with unshakable trust, travels through two states to find the father of her child, always in "identical and anonymous and deliberate wagons as though through a succession of creakwheeled and limpeared avatars, like something moving forever and without progress across an urn." . . .

This is neither the language of a poet nor that of a novelist. It is a total language which seizes the core of reality. It is the language of complete and authentic realism, enveloping all of reality, rather than that academic realism which mistakes the material, tangible surface of things for the things themselves. The obstinate persistence of this misconception makes it necessary to defend the great innovators against the charge that their renunciation of traditional means implies an inability to use them. Just as Picasso, when he thinks fit, can paint in the manner of Lenbach (Portrait of the Mother!), so can Faulkner "recount" in the conventional sense of the word—only incomparably much better than the so-called realists. He proves this very drastically in *The Sound and the Fury* with a stroke of surprise that even recalls Picasso. Although at the outset it seems that Faulkner intends, as a matter of principle, to substitute the narrative law of description and fixed characterization with his own law of a resounding raw material and a music of the subconscious, he suddenly recants in the last chapter. Four times the story heaves to a start with a kind of tremendous effort. Yet only when it rebegins for the fourth time does the narrator intercede to recapitulate the story for itself, a story which until now had been presented solely through the minds of its actors. The technique of interior monologues is replaced by a precise, external realism. The author evokes the outer appearance of things with superb approximation; current reality glows unexpectedly in colors a mere copyist of nature could never find because he sees only the smaller side of the world. A blossoming pear tree; a black staircase with its splash of light from a grey window; an old, unshapen Negro woman clutching a hotwater bottle "by the neck like a dead hen"—how alive these things are! . . .

With unjustified diffidence, Faulkner explains the strange technique of his novel as the result of a shortcoming. Supposedly he tries to tell the story from different points of view because he thinks he has not yet told it right. But, in fact, with this technique he has reached a realism more total than that of Joyce or anybody else before him. Even the realistic final chapter, which—according to the author's dissatisfied self-commentary—is meant to "fill the gaps," is by no means an artistic resignation. His purpose is to resume the whole nightmare and recast it once more in a visible form. And so once more we must pass through the abyss, this time with a seeing eye, for until now we had only groped our way through. The essence, not only of this book but of the Faulknerian narrative as a whole, lies in this double journey through Hell—namely, that we can overcome our fear not by avoiding it but by facing up to it.

With this we touch one of the most delicate points in Faulkner criticism. A French critic, obviously an enraged adherent of today's popular welfare-aesthetics, says in regard to Faulkner: "It is good but what is it good for?" Jean-Paul Sartre, in a revealing essay (revealing of himself) has likewise tried to show that Faulkner has no conception of the future and that his is an art of despair pointing to the collapse of a decrepit world. All this, unfortunately, is a language totally foreign to its subject. The mythical claims no grasp of the future because it excludes it, just as it excludes the notion of past and present. Nor does it have to deliberately take into account the notion of utility since it deals with primitive data, with destiny, and since each encounter with fate affects any responsive creature with a cleansing, awakening force which surpasses all utilities. Faulkner's novels share this quality with Greek tragedy.

One of the reasons for such distorted judgment of Faulkner stems from the fact that he is quite often thought of as the "epic poet of the

South." . . . If Faulkner really had only written the tragic tale of the southern states, the trembling saga of the South's curse, would he have caused such vast vibrations? His "provincialism," like Tolstoy's, is universal. In a geographically limited section of reality he has borne the full intensity of existence. While he appears to be telling the story of his home town, he is telling the story of the world. . . .

Everyone participates individually in the fate of all, deep down through the shafts of time. This again is mythical consciousness, living myth, archaic present. Man is made responsible not only for the single deeds he himself commits but for everything committed since his beginnings. Hence the continual descent into the shadows of the primordial, into the fear which is the beginning of all human recording, and, at the same time, the beginning of every purification. It is this same spirit that spoke—this time as a direct appeal—when Faulkner, at the end of 1950, accepted the Nobel Prize in a speech that came as a shock to many: "He [today's writer] must teach himself that the basest of all things is to be afraid, and teaching himself that, forget it forever, leaving no room in his workshop for anything but the old verities and truths of the heart, the old universal truths lacking which any story is ephemeral and doomed—love and honor and pity and pride and compassion and sacrifice. Until he does so, he labors under a curse."

Crime and Punishment: *Sanctuary*

by Olga Vickery

Sanctuary and *Requiem for a Nun* are related by more than continuity of plot and character, for the latter is not so much a sequel as a restatement and commentary on some of the ideas which were overshadowed by the bizarre and exaggerated brutality of the events in the former. Actually both books are concerned with violence, though in *Requiem for a Nun* it takes the form of a completed act which is talked about while in *Sanctuary* it is part of the developing action, provoking an immediate and often unformulated response. In both, violence is stressed not for its sensationalism but because it has the curious power to initiate two parallel and contradictory modes of response, one social and conventional, the other distinctively personal and exploratory. Thus it both confirms and disorders familiar patterns of thought and action, and in so doing, it forces a re-evaluation of self and society, together with a subsequent readjustment of one to the other. In short, violence administers a shock not only to the nervous system but to the moral intelligence as well.

In both books an act of murder signals an exploration of crime and punishment in its social, moral, and legal aspects. Justice with its attendant problems of guilt and innocence, responsibility and punishment is probed from various points of view. Temple's rape is merely a prelude to Tommy's murder which in turn starts Horace on his quest for justice. The concluding scene in which Horace discovers that justice and law have scarcely a nodding acquaintance echoes the opening scene of *Requiem for a Nun* in which Nancy's punishment is determined by the law whose jurisdiction she has already transcended. Through Gavin Stevens, the concern with the legal aspects of the situation, the terminal point of *Sanctuary,* is quickly subordinated to a preoccupation with divine justice which, in the last analysis, is simply human justice aware of its own divinity. The prose interchapters recount chronologically the history of Yoknapatawpha while exploring the process by which justice has become abstracted and conceptualized, housed in and symbolized by a courthouse, a jail, and a "gilded dome." At this point justice ceases to be a living reality in the heart of man and becomes a set of laws and precedents of

Reprinted by permission from *The Novels of William Faulkner: A Critical Interpretation* (Baton Rouge, Louisiana: Louisiana State University Press, 1959), Chap. 3.

the kind that defeat Benbow. Thus, *Sanctuary* and the two parts of *Requiem for a Nun* explore the same problem but by radically different approaches and techniques.

Lacking the historical perspective of *Requiem for a Nun, Sanctuary* is concerned not with the manner in which concepts of law and justice are established but with the way in which they function at one particular time and place. The result is a dramatic enactment of those ideas which are presented discursively in the later book. Temple's rape and Tommy's murder invoke certain social and legal rituals of justice which are more interested in completing the pattern of crime and punishment than in understanding its moral complexity. Violence is thus countered with violence whether in the form of a legally prescribed and exacted death sentence or a lynching performed by an infuriated mob. It is the act of murder that is being punished and the final grotesque and ironic proof of this is that the wrong man dies, his death satisfying the ritual of justice even as it reveals its ultimate injustice. In the process, Goodwin's self-elected executioners break the law, kill an innocent man, and debase their own moral natures, all in the name of justice and morality.

Even as this pattern crystallizes, Horace Benbow is forced to reevaluate it in the light of his own growing knowledge about the murder and his moral sense. As a product of his culture and tradition, he begins by assuming that society is the repository of human values and that it will act humanely and rationally even though individuals within it may fail to do so. He ends by uttering some of the bitterest condemnations of Jefferson's moral complacency, hypocrisy, and heartlessness to be found in any of Faulkner's novels. Disillusioned by his society, he yet has faith in the power of truth and the unimpassioned due process of law, but he finds that the court too lends itself to the horrifying travesty of justice based on prejudice and emotional appeals. Even religion proves hollow as the church turns viciously on Ruby while God, whom Horace believed to be "a gentleman," remains genteelly indifferent to the subversion of His divine laws by human ones. What reduces Horace to a state of shock is the discovery not of evil but of the shoddy foundations of his vision of a moral and rational universe, supported and sustained by the institutions of the church, the state, and the law.

All the groups with which Horace comes in contact during his desperate effort to make truth and justice prevail fall short, though in different ways, of his harmonious vision. Jefferson's respect for law and social morality manifests itself in self-righteousness and unconscious hypocrisy while its preoccupation with social values leads to an indifference to personal values. Thus, Ruby is first branded a whore, an adulteress, and a murderess, and then harried from one shelter to another in the name of decency and respectability. Horace himself becomes the subject of gossip and condemnation simply because he refuses to accept the public judgment of her or to treat her inhumanely. In contrast to

Jefferson's concern with social morality, Goodwin and Ruby do realize certain personal values in their love for each other, in their child, and in their care for Tommy and the old blind man. Similarly, Miss Reba shows a very real if maudlin love for the departed Mr. Binford and is able to sympathize with Ruby whom she does not know. On the other hand, both Goodwin's and Miss Reba's households exist in defiance of law and the rules of society. Each group thus lacks some quality essential to Horace's ideal of man in society enacting his own moral nature.

Furthermore, each group, marked by its own distinctive attitude and code of behavior, is both exclusive and excluded. The result is an uneasy antagonism flaring into violence whenever a member of one group intrudes into another. This pattern of intrusion and consequent violence is presented in its mildest form by the town boys gathering outside the college to watch the dance. The students become louder and more self-assertive, while the town boys scrawl lewd remarks about coeds on lavatory walls and strew the road with broken glass. More central is the arrival of Popeye at the Old Frenchman place. Indifferent to personal and social values alike, and therefore as much an intruder at Goodwin's as he is at Miss Reba's, Popeye by his very presence is a source of latent violence over which Goodwin manages to maintain a precarious control until two more intruders, Temple and Gowan, introduce a new and explosive element into his house.

By attempting to impose their code on a group and in a situation where that code is not only meaningless but dangerous, Temple and Gowan generate the violence which overwhelms them. Gowan's adolescent conviction that the honor of a Virginia gentleman is measured by his ability to drink every man under the table determines his behavior both with the town boys and later at Goodwin's. For him, the social and moral criterion is simply one's capacity for liquor. He actually seems to believe that by outdrinking Van he can establish his own standards of behavior and hence his control of a situation long since out of hand. Appropriately, he can only judge the events in which he and Temple have become involved and his own responsibility for them in terms of that same sorry code. He thinks not of what might have happened to Temple but of her returning among people who know him to reveal that he has committed the "unforgivable sin"—not holding his liquor—which makes him forever an outcast in decent Virginia society. Gowan's abject despair over his folly and his hope that the extent of that folly will never be revealed indicate not so much his youth and stupidity, though that is also present, as his inability either to act or to think in any but the ways established by his group. His obsessive concern with social values has atrophied his every moral and human instinct. In him conformity has been carried to an extreme at once ludicrous and tragic.

While Gowan is completely dominated by the mores of the Virginia campus, Temple's attitude is ambivalent. Thus, although her degradation is greater, there is also within her a greater possibility of redemption. . . . Yet, like Gowan, she clings to her customs in the presence of an alien group. Temple can never quite rid herself of the unnatural flirtatiousness and the arch provocativeness which had served her well at Ole Miss because the young men also knew their role in the *pas de deux* of sexual teasing. The men at the Old Frenchman place, however, do not know the rules of her game and have no intention of permitting her to establish them. For them, the only relationship between a man and a woman is sexual; and crude and violent though it may be, it still possesses a vitality and forcefulness which at once repels and attracts Temple.

Caught between her longing for the safety of her own world and her desire to share in the "adventure" of this new one into which she has stumbled, Temple reaches a state of semi-hysteria. She attempts to persuade herself that the two worlds are identical, or if not, that hers has the power of control. . . . But her wish not to be protected reveals itself in the constant advance and retreat, provocation and cringing withdrawal, that mark her behavior throughout her stay at Goodwin's. She forces herself on the attention of all the men including Popeye whose callous aloofness is not easily invaded and whose sexual desires are certainly not easily aroused. Temple's provocativeness, like Gowan's cavalier use of the bottle, are natural or at least accepted forms of social behavior in their world. At Goodwin's they become grotesque in their inappropriateness and highly dangerous once they are translated into the language of the Old Frenchman place. The flirtatiousness is construed as an open invitation and the drunkenness as indifference to what may happen.

Time and again Temple is given the opportunity to leave; time and again Ruby warns her to be quiet, to stop running, to stop impressing her fear and desire on the men. But she persists, half-fascinated by the idea of her own rape and half-dreading the actual experience. She can never quite make up her mind to flee either at Goodwin's, the filling station, or Miss Reba's. It is not her fear of encountering greater evils or dangers but her fascination with the idea of violence that holds her immobile. For only by becoming the victim of violence can she participate in Ruby's world without losing her position in her own. Since she does not will her rape, but only passively suffers it, she is freed of responsibility for it, thus enabling her to preserve her social innocence no matter what physical or moral degradation she experiences. In Ruby's spare room, her fear almost forgotten in her excitement and anticipation, Temple goes through a self-conscious ritual of preparing for her victimization and self-sacrifice. She combs her hair, renews her makeup, glances at her watch repeatedly, and lies down to wait, "her hands crossed on her breast and her legs straight and close and decorous, like an effigy on an ancient tomb."

In Temple's later account of the night she spent "in comparative inviolation," the alternation between fear and desire is obvious. Her wish to evade the coming rape is expressed by her fantasies: her vision of herself as somehow physically sealed against contact, as dead, as a matronly schoolteacher, and finally as an old man with a long white beard. But this is balanced by her repeated cries of "Touch me! You're a coward if you dont." And at the very moment of her rape, Temple's scream is one of mingled protest and exultation: "Something is happening to me!" At last even the naïve and inexperienced Horace realizes that the self-confessed "victim" is "recounting the experience with actual pride, a sort of naïve and impersonal vanity."

At Miss Reba's Temple gives full scope to her inclinations while still playing the role of "victim-prisoner." The door which she carefully locks not only keeps Popeye out but herself within. Certainly when she desires to leave, neither the door nor the servant-wardress stands in her way. During her stay she becomes completely corrupted, not because she is kept in a whorehouse, not even because she has accepted a gangster for a bed-mate, but because her capacity for moral commitments and responsibilities has steadily declined since Frank's death until, in the underworld, it is wholly atrophied. She has absolutely no interest in Red, her lover, as a human being. At the moment of his greatest danger, her one thought is to obtain just one more second of sexual gratification; and later she does not regret or mourn his death but only that "it will never be again." In short, Temple eagerly abandons all the social values of her group without accepting the personal values which, however minimal, lend significance to the lives of Ruby and Goodwin.

Temple's excursion into the underworld is paralleled by Ruby's forced sojourn in Jefferson. With her practical common sense or suspiciousness, Ruby not only accepts but jealously guards the isolation of her world, "asking nothing of anyone except to be let alone; trying to make something out of her life." Hence, she furiously resents Temple, the intruder who threatens her security. But she is also aware that she herself is the intruder in Jefferson and calmly accepts its intolerance and cruelty. She moves without protest from the Benbow house to the Hotel to the lean-to shed room in ironic repetition of Temple's flight from room to room at Goodwin's. But even in the shack Ruby is not safe from Narcissa who feels that her world has been threatened by her brother's interest in a woman who is not his kind. Though Narcissa consistently reveals a complete indifference to the moral qualities of any act including her own, she is intensely concerned with the interpretation that may be placed on these acts by people she knows. As she carefully explains to Horace, "I dont care where else you go nor what you do. I dont care how many women you have nor who they are. But I cannot have my brother mixed up with a woman people are talking about." It is with and through Narcissa that Jefferson rises to protect public morality, to speak in defense of an "odorous and omnipotent sanctity" in the eyes of which Ruby and Goodwin are murderers, adulterers, and polluters of "the free Democratico-Protestant atmosphere of Yoknapatawpha county."

Narcissa is coolly indifferent to the methods she uses as long as they succeed in bringing her brother, who refuses to conform to Jefferson's preconceptions and prejudgments, back into the fold. She points out that while he has been babbling about truth, justice, and responsibility, he has succeeded in offending social decorum past the point of forgiveness by taking another man's wife and then abandoning her, and finally, by sheltering a "streetwalker," "a murderer's woman" in his apartment. She attempts to frighten him with public opinion, shame him by an appeal to the Benbow past and tradition, bribe him with an offer of a better criminal lawyer than he is for Goodwin's defense, and when all these fail, to disillusion him about Ruby's motives and her needs. Her final step is to deny even lip service to truth and justice: "I dont see that it makes any difference who did it. The question is, are you going to stay mixed up with it?" Horace, of course, refuses to be swayed; but while he is savoring his indignation and exploring the possibilities of action, Narcissa acts expediently and effectively to thwart justice with law and to return a humbled Horace to Belle.

Society, concerned with its own preservation, is thus as intolerant of the saint as of the sinner, of Horace as of Popeye. Strangely enough, there are certain startling similarities between these two morally antithetical figures. Both are primarily spectators rather than participants in life. Popeye's fear of nature, his terror when he senses the swooping owl, is matched by Horace's inability to remember the name of the bird whose call he hears and by his desire to escape from the rich fertility of the land. Moreover, Popeye's rapt and unnatural absorption in watching Temple and Red perform an act in which he can never share is echoed by Horace's painful exclusion from the grape arbor where Little Belle casually experiments with sex. Both are conscious of their isolation and attempt to break out of it, the one through violence, the other through fantasy and hallucination which are themselves a form of violence. Popeye's brutal act fuses with Horace's thoughts and culminates in the nightmare vision of the rape of a composite Temple-Little Belle.

The separation from the world of nature also implies a separation from the nature of man, characterized by a capacity for good and evil. Both Horace and Popeye are therefore incomplete human beings—figures symbolic of good and evil, unintegrated into the human world. Significantly, Popeye is seen only through his actions, violent, reflexive, destructive; in contrast, Horace is all thought, sensitivity, and perception but without the ability to act effectively. The difference between them, and it is, of course, an overwhelming one, is that the latter is isolated by his dream of moral perfection, the former by his total indifference to all moral values. Consequently, they represent two possible aberrations from the social norm represented by Jefferson as well as the two possible alternatives between which society itself must choose. For only by sharing Horace's dream while recognizing it as a dream can society re-examine its conduct and make it once more a living expression of man's aspirations.

Unlike Horace, who discovers the force of human relationships even as he is rejected and threatened with lynching by society, Popeye continues to live in complete and utter isolation. The hereditary syphilis and insanity stress his inability to make any kind of meaningful contact, either physical or social, with other people. From his birth he is alone and his survival depends on accentuating that aloneness. The doctor warns that "he will never be a man, properly speaking. With care, he will live some time longer." Only by eschewing life can Popeye prolong his existence, and only by affirming the reality of death can he, by implication, affirm that existence. His killing the various animals is more than precocious sadism: it is his attempt to gain a fleeting and illusory sense of life through the very act of destroying it. Oddly enough, the same motive is present in his attachment to his half-crazed mother. Since he is rejected by all the groups with which he comes in contact, she is his only link with the human world, the source and therefore the living proof of his own existence.

Into this sterile, circumscribed world of Popeye's, Temple introduces lust, herself desiring that violation of which she suspects Goodwin to be capable and which she later admires so greatly in Red. But all that Popeye can offer is the mechanical violence of a corncob—a horrifying but futile protest against both his impotence and his isolation. His vicarious participation in sex terminated by Temple's revolt, his murder of Red proven an empty gesture, he chooses death out of sheer boredom and the realization that, quite literally, he has never lived. Once having chosen death, he finds it unimportant whether it comes as punishment for killing Tommy, Red, and indirectly Goodwin, or for slaying a policeman in a town he has never visited. It is, after all, the last joke that life will ever play on him and he makes no effort to counter this final gambit.

In contrast to Popeye, Horace wills his own isolation. His desire to escape from Kinston is caused initially by his disillusionment in those relationships which give meaning to a man's life. Experience mocks the poetic ideal as marriage settles into the routine of fetching shrimp from the station and locking doors, and love becomes identified with the grape arbor frequented by a multitude of young men. Narcissa, the "still unravished bride of quietness," proves to be a stupid, self-centered, and shallow woman. And even the fragile beauty of the fairy Titania is tarnished by too much handling so that he sees in Little Belle's portrait "a face suddenly older in sin than he would ever be, a face more blurred than sweet, . . . eyes more secret than soft." The world of beauty, symbolized by the glassblowers' cave in *Sartoris,* has been completely destroyed.

But though the beauty he worshiped is denied by experience, Horace yet has faith in goodness. As he travels from Kinston to the Old Frenchman place, Jefferson, the campus of Ole Miss, and finally Miss Reba's whorehouse, that ideal too is put to the test of reality. For wherever he goes, he carries with him his vision of a world peopled by gentlemen and benevolently ordered by a God who may be "foolish at times, but at least He's a gentleman." As an ideal, his dream is a noble one; as a description of reality, it is hopelessly inadequate. The crudity of actual life and the intermingling of good and evil in the very texture of experience leave him bewildered and helpless. The very ideals which make him an unerring judge of his society render him incapable of fighting that society.

All of Horace's actions are thus marked by a curious bifocal vision. As he becomes actively involved in helping Goodwin and Ruby, he sees various events and relationships with increasing clarity. But this is dependent on his intuitive comprehension of certain complex situations and their moral quality. Consciously, he cannot help but see through the eyes of a forty-three year old gentleman lawyer, scholar, and poet. He consistently forces the material of his perceptions into a pattern of abstractions which reduce irrationality and complexity to a simple order. He is, in short, hampered by the same kind of innocence and naïve faith in reason that plagues Sutpen. Reason and his legal training mediate between Horace's responses and his actions with the result that he finds himself conducting a mock battle with a phantom opponent: armed with Truth, Honor, and Justice, he assails Evil. The battle of abstractions continues while beneath it the intensely human drama of experience is played out to its bitter conclusion.

The source of Horace's frustration is his discovery that his concepts of justice and honor have no coercive power or even influence over either experience or people. When driven to it, Narcissa is prepared to admit that the possibility of a miscarriage of justice is far less important than her position in Jefferson. Senator Snopes and Eustace Graham are concerned only with advancing themselves in the name of justice; both are willing to attribute justice to the side which pays most. Horace cannot even convince Ruby and Goodwin, who have the most to lose, of the importance of truth. Goodwin decides simply to take his chances with the law while Ruby prepares to pay Horace for undertaking Goodwin's defense in the only way she can. The final and complete subversion of Horace's ethical system comes when he sees the Jefferson mob, acting in the name of the very justice he has defended, kill Goodwin.

It is increasingly borne in upon Horace that he will have to stand

and act alone. Though for a while he is strengthened by a stubborn courage, he is, nevertheless, doomed to fail. Because he himself is unsure of his ability to take control of a situation, he still relies for support on words and phrases. He offers Goodwin the protection of "law, justice, civilization" against the concrete menace of Popeye's gun, and talks to Ruby about "a thing called obstructing justice" as a counterweight to her concern for her husband's safety. While he talks to Temple about the importance of truth and justice, Miss Reba cuts through his abstract verbiage with "They're going to hang him for something he never done. . . . And she wont have nuttin, nobody. And you with diamonds, and her with that poor little kid." The sharp contrast between his generalizations and Miss Reba's concrete statement of the human issues is underscored by Miss Jenny, who points out that his moral indignation and championing of the right is purely verbal and that he is spending his time making speeches instead of doing something. Horace's answer is to go off on another tirade in which he threatens to legislate evil out of existence: "I'm going to have a law passed making it obligatory upon everyone to shoot any man less than fifty years old that makes, buys, sells or thinks whisky." Presumably his statement is intended ironically, but even so it reveals his habit of thought: one additional law will finally either regenerate or frighten men into living in accordance with virtue, decency, and the moral law.

Even though Horace finds that justice no longer lives in the hearts of men, he still retains his faith in the power of truth—if only all the facts are made available, then innocence and guilt, the victim and the murderer will be unmasked. Truth must prove itself independent of and stronger than individual prejudices and distortions. With Ruby's unwilling help he learns of Temple's presence at the Old Frenchman place; with Snopes's information he tracks her down. With dawning horror he realizes, however, that victim though she may be, Temple is also the cause of her victimization. The responsibility for the rape and hence for Tommy's murder is as much Temple's who provoked it as it is Goodwin's who did not act to prevent it or Popeye's who actually committed it. Gowan Stevens is also involved in the guilt, and even Ruby, who anticipated it and yet walked away, is not without blame.

Horrified as he is by his discovery that good and evil do not live in separate compartments, Horace yet risks a final throw of the dice. He presents his facts to the judge and jury and waits confidently for the only possible verdict. In the courthouse, if [in] no other place, justice and truth must be living realities. Yet they are not—he is defeated, and not by deliberate, conscious evil but by self-interest and respectability. Horace's collapse is complete and inevitably so. For through most of his conversations with Ruby and Goodwin one refrain had been dominant, that of "Good God. What kind of people have you lived with?" To find that the evil he abhors is in his own backyard, in Narcissa, in his wife and her daughter, in Temple and her respected father-judge, is too much. The enormity of fighting it becomes the impossibility of even challenging it, and Horace who anticipated total victory submits to total defeat. He returns meekly to Belle and the routine of his life with her. Murmuring "Night is hard on old people. . . . Something should be done about it. A law," he appears to shrink, to lose stature as he stands alone, gazing at the fragments of the Grecian Urn in whose aesthetic and abstract image he had built his life.

The pathos of this scene arises from the fact that Horace's sanctuary, his imaginative world of moral and aesthetic perfection, has been violated and destroyed by his one excursion into the world of concrete experience. For it is only in the verbal universe, whether philosophic, legal, or poetic, that evil can be isolated as the antithesis of good. In experience evil is a necessary condition of existence which cannot be destroyed without destroying life itself. That Horace contemplates such a destruction, though only in fantasy, suggests that he is not yet ready to live in terms of his painfully acquired knowledge of the real world. Because of his search, the separation of justice and law, truth and belief, dream and reality is recognized; but the task of reuniting them, which is the necessary prerequisite to the salvation of man and his society, is beyond his powers.

William Faulkner's *Sanctuary*

by Lawrence S. Kubie, M.D.

Anyone familiar with the phantasies of the insane is continually encountering incidents in daily life which remind him hauntingly of the hospital. Such experiences are at first disturbing. Ultimately, however, they become reassuring, because they prove that there is nothing in the phantastic world of the insane which is completely alien to ordinary human nature, and that insanity and normality merge into each other by imperceptible gradations. The psychiatrist who is also a psychoanalyst is in hourly contact with this borderline between sickness and health, and finds himself therefore in a special position. Frequently in observing the successive stages in the transition from sickness to health, or occasionally from health to sickness, he has an opportunity to study strange patterns of phantasy, perplexing symbolic distortions, and surprising shifts of feeling which are hidden from the casual onlooker. All products of the human spirit become to him objects of study without prejudice, so that he brings to literature a clinical eye, seeking in its pages masked expressions of hope and desire, of frustration, anxiety, and anger, similar to those which appear in his patients.

For this search modern literature offers a fertile field. Because it attempts to portray that which is neurotic and defeated in human nature, it is closer to truth than the old romantic tradition which was content to picture only the aspirations of man. And because it seeks for the causes of these defeats within man's inner nature, it is sounder than that "realism" which explains all distress by the workings of chance and external events. Despite its honesty, however, one finds that there is much in this modern literature that is as confused as the neurosis itself. This literature sometimes repeats itself compulsively, just as the neurosis indulges in endless and compulsive repetitions. Sometimes it is exhibitionistic, and even though the exhibitionism of literature is subjected to the discipline of an artistic technique, it reminds one that the neurosis too is exhibitionistic. Therefore, even where the portrayal of problems is accurate, the pseudo-solution which is offered may be confusing and neurotic. This makes it worthwhile to try to penetrate below the surface of some of these modern writings, if only because of the confusion which their very power

Reprinted with permission from *Saturday Review of Literature,* Vol. XI, No. 14 (October 20, 1934), pp. 218, 224-226.

can create in the minds of readers. Is it not a fair challenge to art to demand that when it deals with the neurotic components of human nature it should understand its subject?

Of the authors of these books the psychoanalytic critic of literature knows nothing because he has no access to direct information about their lives. He does not even know to what extent they have been conscious or unconscious of the meaning of what they have written. He does not know whether their own lives share in the problems which their books reflect. It would be an impossible and an intolerable presumption for him to draw any conclusion about them as individuals. Nonetheless, he is free to discuss the unconscious meaning of the books in which these men have written of matters of which they show, at least, only a dim comprehension. Of these books William Faulkner's *Sanctuary* is a brilliant and most interesting example. . . .

So familiar are tales of horror in literature that we accept them without realizing how strange a phenomenon they are, or how difficult to explain. Furthermore, in recent years changes have appeared in the literature of horror, comparable in many ways to those which have occurred in the literature of sex. In a general way it may be said that in both categories there has been a gradual drift from a romantic point of view, first to one of ridicule, and then to a frantic and tortured striving after realism.

Some readers resent this horror literature intensely; some exult in it; and still others find in it merely a thrilling exercise in literary craftsmanship. About its artistic significance there is, therefore, much disagreement. It would seem impossible to resolve this disagreement without first understanding in some measure its psychological origins.

This literature is so abundant that to study it in detail would involve the psychoanalytic dissection of a great many books and stories, drawn from many stages of the world's cultural evolution. Within the limits of this study that is impossible; and so one turns instead to a single book which brings together all the converging streams which have contributed to the development of the current trend. Such a book is William Faulkner's *Sanctuary*. It is not the only book, nor even the best one necessarily. But it serves our purpose both because of the turbulent power of its imagery, the violent eruption of unconscious forces, and also for the practical reason that it has been widely read.

As a further justification for concentrating on one book, one may point to the analogy to what may occur in the psychoanalytic treatment of a patient. There it happens not infrequently that a series of dreams appears, scattered perhaps over many weeks or months, the first ones of which are benign and relatively unemotional, the successive dreams becoming increasingly distressing. The translation of the earlier dreams into terms of fundamental instinctual drives and conflicts is rarely possible on the basis of any material which the patient can produce. As the work goes on, however, even if one ventures upon no specific interpretations of the dreams, the significance of the series becomes clearer. More violent feelings are aroused; the imagery becomes more turbulent; instinctual drives come steadily closer to direct expression. The dream series may be thought of as "ripening"; and gradually the evolution reaches a point at which a dream comes to the surface which can be analyzed fruitfully, throwing light retrospectively upon the mysterious shadows of all its predecessors.

In the history of the literature of horror it is possible to recognize stages which are roughly similar to this. From a boy's tales of adventure, with their naïve, exultant triumphs over external dangers, to the deep and biological horrors of *Sanctuary,* a series could be traced. In this series it would become evident that this constant preoccupation with fear and horror has a direct bodily meaning. The more naïve and childlike presentations are all externalized adventure stories with dangerous situations. The more "realistic," adult, and "morbid" stories penetrate below this surface into the instinctual reservoirs out of which terror arises. There is a direct link between the frequent nightmares of childhood and the rarer but equally significant nightmares of adults, and an identical relation between the naïve melodrama of a simple frontier civilization and the sophisticated shocker of a "morbid" modern community.

The problem which faces us reaches to the roots of certain complex issues. In the first place, it raises the question of the genesis of anxiety; and in the second place, the even more perplexing issue of the paradoxical pleasurable utilization of horror (what is technically known as the "erotization of anxiety"). Indeed, it is this paradoxical and perverted utilization of anxiety for "pleasure" purposes, rather than the problem of the genesis of anxiety, which constitutes our immediate concern.

The outstanding feature of this ultra-sophisticated literature of biological horror is its increasingly frank reference to some form of genital injury. It is not necessary for this reason to assume that all anxiety is genital in its derivation. It is enough to recognize that there is an important interplay of all phantasies of mutilation and contamination between one instinctual battlefield and another, but that, since in normal life the genital normally assumes a position of dominance among the instincts, all manifestations of anxiety tend to become focused in this direction. Whatever the source, however, the outcome is that through all of the books in which horror plays so large a role, the ultimate manifestation of the major horror is through some form of genital injury.

One might expect to find that a great deal of this literature had been written by women, because so frequently in these tales the victims are women, and since in real life the chief form of genital injury of which both sexes are *consciously* fearful is always the fear of rape, and especially of the forcible defloration of a virgin. Surprisingly enough, however, one finds that it is not women who write of defloration and its terrors, but men. Since the state of terror, whatever its apparent nature may be, must have a personal core to start with, this suggests that there must be a basic fear in all men which merely uses the idea of rape as a less distressing substitute. Therefore, one examines the men in these tales of rape for evidence of the nature of this basic fear and finds that they tend to an extraordinary degree to be figures who are crippled either in a directly genital sense, or indirectly through some other form of bodily injury. This crippling produces a state of real or psychic impotence.

It is out of just this sense of impotence that there arises one of the most characteristic nightmares of childhood, one in which the child feels helpless in the presence of danger and either runs frantically hither and thither and never escapes, or else is unable to move at all (cf. Temple Drake in *Sanctuary*). Besides that, one may place the not infrequent obsessive phantasy of an adult who finds himself bound helplessly while bandits attack the woman he loves. In such a phantasy the bandits execute for the man that which his own fear of impotence makes impossible; but he is freed from the painful acknowledgment of his fear of impotence by making it appear to be the result of external interference and external agents (that is, the bandits who tie him up) rather than the result of his own internal incapacity. (This, as we shall see, takes place either in fearful anticipation or as a reality not once but repeatedly in *Sanctuary*.)

It is for this reason, primarily, that we take it to be no accident that the chief villain in the tale of *Sanctuary* is described as totally impotent. This was not a device chosen by chance out of many alternatives, merely to intensify the horror. It was an inevitable choice, because the whole significance of such horror phantasies is linked to the male's constant subterranean struggle with fears of impotence. We shall see, after the main features of the story have been outlined, how almost every element in it represents one of the many ways in which the male deals with this fear.

It should be clearly stated and clearly understood that we are implying nothing about the psychosexual life of the author of this book. Anxieties about potency exist in masked forms in every living male. But the ability to write such a book gives no indication that such fears have acquired any special or unusual intensity in the personal life of the book's creator. The artist's intuitive perceptions and representations of problems may at times depend upon his own problems, but they may also come from an intimate association with others who have dramatized the problem before his eyes. Therefore, we must say clearly that in writing about *Sanctuary* and the relationship of horror literature to fears of impotence, we are not in any personal sense writing about William Faulkner.

The story is in two parts. In the first a young college girl named Temple Drake is landed by her drunken escort, Gowan Stevens, in the hands of a group of moonshiners. Stevens abandons her there and, after many false alarms and episodes of terror, she is criminally assaulted by a member of the band named Popeye. Popeye is suspected of having some Negro blood. Also he is sexually impotent, and therefore must execute his purpose by indirect methods which are overwhelmingly brutal and revolting. Furthermore, just before the assault he shoots another member of the band, a kindly, feeble-minded fellow named Tommy, who is trying to protect Temple.

In the second half of the book Popeye has carried Temple off to a brothel in Memphis. Goodwin, the head of the moonshiners, is accused of both crimes and is convicted on the false testimony of Temple herself, despite the efforts of a lawyer named Horace Benbow. Finally the innocent Goodwin is burned by a lynching mob, Popeye is hanged by accident for a crime he did not commit, Temple is taken abroad by her father, and Horace Benbow, after a brief effort to live a free life, goes back into bondage to his wife and sister. This is the skeleton of the story.

The first part of the book is a troubled, and sometimes confused, nightmare, a nightmare which at moments is vivid and gripping, but which occasionally verges on slapstick and burlesque, with somersaults out of haylofts, rats that spring in the dark, dim figures that can be smelled in blackness, eyes that gleam in lightless corners, and so on. Yet all of this buffoonery is in subtle harmony with the sardonic and excruciating denouement. For it is the uttermost limits of sour irony that this impudent, tantalizing, and provocative young girl, who had played fast and loose with the men of her own world without ever giving them the gift she kept dangling in front of them, should escape the relatively honest erotic purposes of the healthy members of the band, only to taunt the impotent and tortured figure of Popeye into committing a criminal assault upon her by artificial means.

That Temple invited the assault with her provocative, if unconscious, exhibitionism, is unquestionable. Ruby Goodwin, the mate of the bootlegger, is made to say that if Temple had only stopped running around where they had to look at her all the time it would never have happened, but that Temple wouldn't stay any place—that "she just dashed out one door and in a minute she'd come in from another direction." Horace Benbow noted that Temple told her story with actual pride, "with a naive and impersonal vanity."

Furthermore, in the face of danger, Temple had a momentary hallucination that her body had changed into that of a boy. The rude awakening from this dream, and the shocking rediscovery of her unchanged anatomy gave rise to a secondary phantasy (one which is familiar enough to psychoanalysts in their study of illness, but rarely encountered in literature), in which there was a fusion of the ideas of rape, castration, and death (cf. the coffin phantasy). From that moment, Temple behaves as though she herself were dead, and the blind, dead instrument of revenge. But the subtle and confusing thing is that she destroys first not those who have hurt her, but those who have helped her. She kills the lover that

Popeye procures for her. She kills Goodwin, the bootlegger, by giving false testimony against him. She crushes the lawyer who tries to help. It is only indirectly and in the very end that her taunts help to drive Popeye himself into a virtual suicide.

In the story there is no effort to explain why she sacrifices Goodwin, the potent man, to the furies of the mob and saves Popeye, her impotent malefactor. Popeye's disguised presence in the courtroom can hardly account for it. But Temple has by this time become an almost automatic engine of destruction. Perhaps one may venture the speculation that this paradoxical and perverted impulse to revenge herself on those who have not harmed her, but who are essentially normal in their masculinity, fits the whole history of her defiant, rebellious, and provocative attitude toward boys and men. Her career seemed to shape itself out of her hate of her father and her four stalwart brothers. It is almost as though she said, "To be a woman is worse than death or the same as death. Therefore I will take my revenge upon all you men who are really men. I will excite your desires, but I will not satisfy them. I will laugh in the face of your yearnings. I will gloat over you and scorn you as you drink yourselves into impotence. And finally I will be the instrument of your actual bodily destruction."

One good and valiant, but again feeble figure—that of Horace Benbow—battles throughout the second part of the book. He is a well-intentioned but powerless lawyer. He was "given to much talk and not much else"; and he said of himself, "I lack courage—the machinery is all here, but it won't run." Poor Benbow could not even scrub a floor, much less the community whose need for a scrubbing he felt so acutely.

The story of Benbow, like the story of Goodwin, runs through the book as a contrast to the more essential tale of Popeye and Temple. In his forty odd years Benbow had gradually built up a weak, wide-eyed, but gallant impulse to tilt against the smug and hypocritical forces of society which his sister Narcissa represented. In defiance of convention he had married a woman who had had to seek a divorce in order to marry him; and again in defiance of convention he had now left her. In the face of the mounting hostility of the community toward Goodwin, Benbow tried desperately to save him from an unjust conviction. But he was not strong enough to achieve this, and in the end merely accelerated and expedited his death.

Here the tale is a dramatization of the impact between the forces of instinctual evil (which are represented as rising up out of the pits of the underworld through Popeye and Temple) and the forces of an evil and savage conscience, operating through the blind vengefulness of a misdirected mob. It represents graphically the struggle which in psychoanalytic shorthand is known as the struggle between the Id (the reservoir of instincts) and the Super-ego (the all but blind forces of a conscience whose operation is by no means always rational and clear). Between the two stands this weak and feeble effort at a realistic dealing with life, embodied in the figure of Benbow. He is the weak representative of the much-battered "Ego," that fragment of the personality which is so often ground to pieces in the battle.

Beneath it all one feels the incessant struggle of Benbow against his own impotence and powerlessness. He is unable to defy the women who cramp him on all sides. All adult women seem to thwart him, to manage his life, to force him into channels toward which he has a revulsion. To carry a box of shrimps once a week from the railroad station to his home for all the years of his marriage, loathing the smell of them, hating the drip of them, identifying himself with "the small stinking spots," which left a trail behind him on the sidewalk, constituted his picture of marriage. Far deeper than that lay his incestuous yearnings for his stepdaughter. These tie him up in horror phantasies in which he sees himself helplessly standing by while his stepdaughter, Little Belle, plays around with other men. In fact, it is this which finally drives him from home. And toward the end of the book he is stirred to a dim recognition of his own impulses when her picture is described "as leaving upon his eye a soft and fading aftermath of invitation and voluptuous promise." At this point he becomes nauseated actively, and soon thereafter, giving in to the social pressure which forces him back to the hated protection of his sister, he returns to his wife. In other words, as he becomes conscious of his intolerable and unacceptable impulses, he experiences a direct revulsion of feeling which causes him to be sick, whereupon he gives up his frantic and compulsive rebellion against society.

The only figures in the book who take life in the body with simple, earthy realism, who hate and murder or love and make love wholeheartedly and without reservation, are Goodwin, the moonshiner, and his mate Ruby. They alone do not think that "all girls are ugly except when they are dressed." They alone do not subscribe to the parable that "Adam paid no attention to Eve until she put on a fig-leaf." They alone are not moved to revulsions of feeling by excrement, by hunger, dirt, and bleeding, or by any of the other natural phenomena of the body's living. They alone have no fear of the body, be it male or female. They recognize Temple's impudent coquetry in the face of danger, her blind exhibitionism, her invitation of the final disaster. On her Ruby heaps withering scorn for "just playing at it"; yet she is jealous and fearful of Temple's presence because she knows that this tantalizing and provocative coquetry might in the end seduce Goodwin himself. Together they recognize the significance of that "high, delicate head," the "bold, painted mouth and soft chin," the "eyes blankly right and left looking, cool, predatory, and discreet." To them Temple is no innocent victim. They view her realistically. Perhaps that is why Goodwin must be killed, and Ruby cast out by the savage "conscience" of the community.

It may seem to some readers that the author's claim that the book "is a cheap idea, because it was deliberately conceived to make money" would invalidate any effort to study its contents seriously. This we cannot admit. The phantasy still remains as an expression of more forces than those which the author can consciously control. It is only when the nightmare becomes a little too garish, the horrors too gruesome with a touch of the slapstick, that one notes the tongue bulging in the author's cheek. Naïve youths who rent a room in a brothel thinking it is a boarding house, the incredible funeral of Red and its solemn, drunken sequel at Reba Rivers's afternoon "tea" party—all make one chuckle a bit—but for the rest the tale stands firmly on its own unconscious sources. We have suggested above that this literature represents the working out in phantasy of the problems of impotence in men, meaning by impotence a frailty in all spheres of instinctual striving. In the end, however, this impotence always is seen to have a direct relation to psychosexual potency. It is as though sophisticated and civilized man is conducting a constant struggle against a sense of impending impotence, a struggle which seems to have in it three direct objects of fear—a fear of women, a fear of other men, and a fear of the community and of society in general. All of these three fears are dramatized in this story.

Furthermore, when a man feels unable to achieve some goal toward which he is struggling, he can in his phantasy handle his sense of powerlessness in one of several ways. In the first place, he can people the whole world with other impotent figures, spreading his own sense of infirmity to include everyone, and thus reducing his feeling of painful humiliation. Thus we find in *Sanctuary* that every "respectable" man is in one way or another crippled, impotent, or silly. Only the Negro who is hung, and the moonshiner who is burned alive, and Red, the dance-hall boy who is shot, are potent. This is true not only of the major figures, such as Popeye and Benbow, but also of such minor figures as Cla'ence Snopes, or the lamed district attorney, or Gowan Stevens.

Or, secondly, he may comfort himself in dreams of the ultimate triumph of the weak over the strong, of the impotent over the potent. Thus, as we have seen, in every line of the book evil and weakness triumph over goodness and strength.

Or he can turn with his rage against the sources of his humiliation and imagine them overwhelmed with disaster. Consequently, all women are made to grovel before men, whether it be Reba Rivers who keeps the brothel; or Ruby Goodwin who, though triumphant and defiant toward others, is ready to lick the boots of her mate; or Narcissa, who is jilted and falls in love with fools like Gowan Stevens; or Temple Drake, whose lean and immature body exists in the book only to taunt and tantalize men with promises which are never fulfilled, until finally the fulfilling of the promise is taken out of her hands and worked upon her with savage and sardonic vengeance by the sinister figure of the impotent Popeye.

Or again the sufferer from a sense of impotence can turn with sour scorn against the whole structure of society, seeing in it nothing but its pettiest aspects, corroding it with irony, taunting it with the failure of every decent effort at restitution or punishment, mockingly embodying all aspirations in the spirit of hypocritical and waspish women like Narcissa.

By all these devices man tries to evade the acknowledgment of his own instinctual helplessness—yet none of those devices succeeds. Just so Popeye, with intolerable suffering, has to bring in a potent male to mate with the woman with whom he himself can have no successful relationship. Here again one sees the actual living out of the primitive horror-ridden phantasy that arises so frequently in the male who is struggling with impotence fears, the fantasy of being helpless and bound while someone else rapes the woman he loves—a fantasy which appears not only in the actual experiences of Popeye and Temple, but in the constant anxieties of Benbow about his stepdaughter Belle.

There remains for the poor male only one other way out, one which never works too successfully, but which is always tried—that is, an effort to ridicule and make fun of his own yearnings, and thus to make his own frustrations more bearable. This appears in the book only in the passages of sudden burlesque.

Yet despite all such devices, man cannot free himself from the terror and pain of impotence which break through in horror-ridden phantasies. And that is why, in the end, Popeye is so willing to escape, through the hangman's noose, the Tyranny of fears which reigns in his heart. It is Popeye who shrieks like a child at a swooping owl, who in a panic shoots a harmless old dog who has sniffed at his leg, who sucks his cigarettes rather than smoking them, who tries to buy with gifts the girl he cannot woo, who is possessive and jealous, who suffers and yearns and wants and whinnies and froths, and all of whose frustrated yearnings turn to hate. And it is Popeye's very figure which is concretely described in the story in words which make it a graphic representation of the phallus whose impotence is the root of the whole tragedy.

And so, at the last, one is left to wonder about the name. Why "Sanctuary" in a tale in which there is no right of sanctuary, where neither impotence nor potency, neither the life of the defiant rebel nor that of the acquiescent conformist, where neither the free play of instinctual expression nor the life which is dominated by a restricting conscience, provides one with any escape from an ultimate state of doom and disaster? Why "Sanctuary" in a tale in which no one triumphs and everyone fails? Where in such a horror-driven conception of living is "sanctuary" to be found? Perhaps it is not accidental that in the book the only figure who laughs is "Tommy, the feeb," the feeble-minded lad who sets himself to guard Temple and is shot for his pains. He suffers no unhappiness, but laughs even when his pet dog is shot, and undoubtedly would have chuckled over his own demise had he had time to do so. Perhaps here in this cloudy brain is the sanctuary which Faulkner had in mind. For the rest the term is a mockery which says, "There is no escape from anxiety, no escape from horror; therefore, let us make of horror a gay tune to dance to and chortle over; let us roll it under our tongues; let us whistle in the dark to prove that we are not afraid; and let us write books about it, tell our friends, and 'hope they will buy it, too.' "

The Stillness of *Light in August*

by Alfred Kazin

Light in August begins unforgettably with a pregnant young woman from Alabama sitting beside a road in Mississippi, her feet in a ditch, her shoes in her hand, watching a wagon that is mounting the hill toward her with a noise that carries for a half mile "across the hot still pine-winey silence of the August afternoon." She has been on the road for a month, riding in a long succession of farmwagons or walking the hot dusty roads with her shoes in her hand, trying to get to Jefferson. There, she firmly expects, she will find her lover working in a planing mill and ready to marry her, and there—that is, the big city—she will put her shoes on at last.

This opening chapter, so dry and loving in its pastoral humor, centering on the picture of Lena and her precious burden being carried in one wagon or another, by one farmer after another, to her hoped-for destination in a husband, ends sharply on the outskirts of Jefferson, from which she can see smoke going up from a burning house. It is the house of Joanna Burden, who has just been murdered by Joe Christmas. The images that have crowded us—the dust and heat of the unending road; the young woman continually amazed at how far a body can go; the serenity of her face, "calm as a stone, but not hard"; the "sharp and brittle crack and clatter" of identical and anonymous wagons "weathered and ungreased wood and metal"; the mules plodding in a steady and unflagging hypnosis; the drowsy heat of the afternoon; Lena's faded blue dress, her palm leaf fan, her small bundle in which she carries thirty-five cents in nickels and dimes, and the shoes that she takes off and carries in her hand as soon as she feels the dust of the road beneath her feet—all these, we soon discover, provide us with that foundation in the local and the provincial, the earth and the road which man must travel on it, against which are set images of fire and murder, of aimless wandering and of flight, embodied in the figure who soon enters the book and dominates it in his remorseless gray anonymity. Joe Christmas does not even have a name of his own, only a mocking label stuck on him at the orphanage where he was deposited one Christmas Eve. "Joe Christmas"

Reprinted with permission from *Twelve Original Essays on Great American Novels,* edited by Charles Shapiro (Detroit: Wayne State University Press, 1958), pp. 257-83.

is worse than any real name could be, for it indicates not only that he has no background, no roots, no name of his own, but that he is regarded as a *tabula rasa,* a white sheet of paper on which anyone can write out an identity for him and make him believe it.

It is the contrast of Lena Grove and Joe Christmas, of the country girl and the American wanderer, who is a stranger even to himself, the ultimate personification of modern loneliness, that frames the book—literally so, since Lena Grove begins and ends it, while Joe Christmas's agony and crucifixion are enacted as within a circle round which he runs in an effort to catch up with himself. When he finds that he cannot run out of this circle and stands still at last in order to die, the book comes back to Lena Grove and ends on her ritualistic procession up the road with her baby and Byron Bunch—Faulkner's version of the Holy Family. By the time we have finished *Light in August,* we have come to feel that the real greatness of Faulkner in this book (and indeed of his extraordinary compassion) lies in the amazing depth which he brings to this contrast of which American writers—particularly in the South—are so fond: between the natural and the urban, between Lena Grove's simplicity and the world in which Joe Christmas walks all city pavements with the same isolation and indifference, eats at the coldly smooth wooden counter, and is murdered. Faulkner even leads up to a strange and tortured fantasy of Joe Christmas as Lena Grove's still unnamed son. There is virtually an annunciation to Lena, in the moving last phase of the book when Lena, delivered of her child just as Joe Christmas is running for his life, hears Mrs. Hines, Christmas's grandmother, calling the baby "Joey"—he who is a "nigger" murderer, and whom Lena has never seen. The reader comes to this with a shock, only because of Faulkner's reckless, desperate eagerness to wrest all the possible implications from his material, to think it out interminably, since there is no end to all one's possible meditations round and round the human cycle. One of the conflicts of which the book is made—between life and anti-life, between the spirit of birth and the murderous abstractions and obsessions which drive most of the characters—is in Faulkner himself, in his attempt to will his painful material into a kind of harmony that it does not really possess.

But in any event, it is Lena who opens the book, Lena's world, Lena's patience, that set the ideal behind the book—that world of the permanent and the natural which Joe Christmas seeks all his life without knowing that he does, and seeking it, runs full tilt into the ground. "Light in August" is itself a country saying: light as a mare or cow is light after delivery.* And it is this world of Lena Grove from Doane's Mill—the tiny hamlet too small for any post-office list, though Lena, living in the backwoods, had not seen it until her parents died—with the sound of the wagon wheel taking her away from it, that becomes in the book not

* Faulkner's own explanation of the title is quite literal: a quality of the light in August.

merely a world that Faulkner celebrates, but a mythic source of strength. As indeed it is. For it is this intense sense of the earth, this superb registering of country sights and sounds as the stillness is broken by the creaking and lumbering wagon coming up the hill, that is the secret of Southern writing. In his attachment to the irretrievable, in his obstinate feeling for the earth, the good Southern writer makes so much writing in America seem as shallow as if it had been composed by a young instructor in English sitting in his study surrounded by manuals on the great novels. Albert Camus, talking appreciatively about Southern novelists, once remarked to a friend of mine that what he liked about their books was "the dust and the heat." And to the man from North Africa, with his memories of the blazing world described in *Noces,* that world into which Paris can never enter, Faulkner's sense of local color must be especially moving. But after all, it is this sense of place that is the great thing about American writing. It is the "mossy scabs of the worm fence, heap'd stones, elder, mullein and pokeweed" in *Song of Myself*; the landscape that in *Walden* seems always to be reflected in water; the strong native sense of the here and now that is the basis of Emerson's aesthetic; the edge of the world seen from Hemingway's Michigan woods; "reading the river" in *Life on the Mississippi* and *Huckleberry Finn*; the "snow, the real snow" seen only beyond Chicago that Scott Fitzgerald described so rapturously in his memories of Midwesterners in Eastern colleges going home for Christmas. And if we ask what is so remarkable about that sense of place which is, after all, essential to imaginative writing, the answer is that we Americans are in fact just the opposite of the homogeneous mass we are always trying to be, and that what distinguishes American writing is exactly the fact that we are strangers to each other and that each writer describes his own world to strangers living in the same land with himself.

Now of all parts of the United States the South is certainly the strangest to the others; it is, in fact—or used to be—a separate nation. And almost all the good Southern writers have this sense of local color to an extreme, for to the degree that the South is what it is because of its rural background, its "backwardness," its isolation, its comparatively homogeneous white population—to that degree does the American's need to value and venerate his own region or place as the only escape from American bigness, American smoothness, American abstractness, American slogans, the juggernaut of American progress, find (at least it used to find) its deepest expression in the South. Even poverty, which in America certainly is a disgrace, becomes in Southern writing a sign of the natural man (Huckleberry Finn) or the earth-mother (Lena Grove). And, as so often happens in Southern writing—for sensitive Southerners are likely to feel that they are lost in the modern industrial world and, in mourning their traditional homeland, to see the immediate world around them as damned—Faulkner's pictures of the impersonal modern world, the opposite of Lena's sacred grove, are lurid. As Lena is all fertility, so the others are all barrenness. Destruction, fire, obsession, inhumanity, anonymity, the "friction-smooth" wooden counter at which Joe Christmas eats, the hard cold eyes of Bobbie the prostitute and Mame the madam and Max the pimp—these against the images of locality (the farmers in their faded and patched but clean overalls) and of time (the wagon along the road and the "heel-gnawed porch" of the country store around which farmers sit). As soon as we get to Jefferson, we catch the typical dialectic of life and anti-life, the contrast of birth and destruction on which the book is built, in the fact that the slow patient rhythms of Lena, the wagon, the road, are immediately followed by the whine of the saw in the planing mill, the reiteration of *smooth*. The world is narrowing down to the contest between the good Christian laborer, Byron Bunch, the very essence of the common ordinary good man, and those who, like Lena's seducer, have either taken on a name which is not their own, "Brown," a name too conventional even to be *his* name, or who, like Joe Christmas, have no name to begin with.

This contrast is familiar enough in Southern opinion, and one can find the same horror of miscegenation, of uprooting, of the city man's anonymity, in any expression of Southern agrarianism. But Faulkner does not stop at the abstraction of the alien: he carries it on, he carries it out to astonishing lengths. And it is this intensity of conception that makes the portrait of Joe Christmas so compelling rather than believable, that makes him a source of wonder, of horror, yet above all of pity, rather than of pleasure in the creation of a real human being. For Joe Christmas remains, as he is born, an abstraction; from the moment he appears, "there was something definitely rootless about him, as though no town nor city was his, no street, no walls, no square of earth his home." He comes to work in the only clothes he has, a serge suit and a white shirt; and Byron Bunch, watching him, knows that Joe Christmas "carried his knowledge with him always as though it were a banner, with a quality ruthless, lonely, and almost proud." So from the moment Joe Christmas appears, he is seen as what others say about him, he is only a thought in other people's minds. More than this, he is looked at always from a distance, as if he were not quite human, which in many ways he is not.

We see Joe Christmas from a distance, and this distance is the actual space between him and his fellows. It is also the distance between the name "Joe Christmas," which is clownish, and the actual suffering of someone who has to live up to the non-humanity of his name, to the obsession (founded on hearsay, not on actual evidence) that his father had "some" Negro blood in him. Joe Christmas, then, is really "man" trying to discover the particular kind of man he is. He is an abstraction created by the racist mania of his grandfather, a former preacher whose tormented life is spent insisting that Negroes are guilty in the eyes of God and must serve white men. When his daughter ran away with a "Mexican" circus hand, Doc Hines not only killed the man, and after his daughter died in childbirth on Christmas Eve, left the baby on the steps of an orphanage, but later took a job as a janitor in the orphanage in order to make sure that his "nigger" grandson would never be allowed to contaminate anyone. This obsession about race goes hand in hand with a Calvinist obsession of the elect and of the hopeless sinfulness of others, an obsession which is found both in Joe Christmas's rigidly doctrinaire foster-father, Calvin McEachern, and in his future mistress, Joanna Burden, a descendant of New Hampshire Puritans who remains in the South though she is the sworn enemy of its ways. All these obsessions about purity and guilt are, Faulkner indicates, the remnants of an inhuman religion that has added bigotry and arrogance to the curse of slavery. They are the symbols of a church that has lost its spiritual function and that has been deserted by the Reverend Gail Hightower, who spends his days in endless reveries of the South's irretrievable glory. The obsessions are all summed up in the fate of Joe Christmas, who is trying to become *someone,* a human being, to find the integrity that is so ripely present in Lena Grove. Lena does not have to try; her symbol is the wheel on the road. Joe Christmas's is flight: flight on the same road, but flight toward himself, which he cannot reach, and away from hatred of himself, which he cannot escape. Only his pursuers catch up with him, to murder and to castrate him.

Joe Christmas is an abstraction seeking to become a human being. In the race-mad South, many a Negro—and Mexican and Jew—is turned into an abstraction. But this man is *born* an abstraction and is seeking to become a person. He is an orphan, brought up in a foundling home, who in earliest childhood is watched by his own grandfather as if he were a caged beast. He is then bribed by the dietitian, whom he has heard making love with the interne, as if he knew enough to betray her. He is adopted by a farmer who renames him, lectures him, starves him, beats him for not learning the catechism. He is robbed and beaten by the pimp of the prostitute with whom he has fallen in love. He is constantly treated by his Negrophile mistress, Joanna Burden, as if his own personality were of no account and is beseeched in her sexual transports as "Negro." And finally, after being starved, betrayed, flogged, beaten, pursued by bloodhounds, he is castrated. The essential picture behind Joe Christmas is his grandfather's carrying him to the orphanage and then from it in a savage parody of loving care. Joe Christmas is nothing but the man things are done to, the man who has no free will of his own, who is constantly seeking a moment of rest ("When have I ever eaten in peace?") and who looks for an identity by deliberately provoking responses that will let him be *someone,* if only as a white man among Negroes, or as someone calling himself a Negro in an effort to shock the white prostitute he has just slept with. His passivity, his ability to lend himself to situations and to people who will "carry" him for a while, is immense and pitiful.

Joe Christmas is the most solitary character in American fiction, the most extreme phase conceivable of American loneliness. He is never seen full face, but always as a silhouette, a dark shadow haunting others, a shadow upon the road he constantly runs—a foreshadowing of his crucifixion, which, so terrible and concentrated is his suffering, already haunts the lives of others like a black shadow. For, almost *because* he does not look it, he becomes the "Negro," or the thought of, the obsession with, Negroes in the minds of those who, looking at Joe Christmas, can think of nothing else. And Joanna Burden, whose abolitionist grandfather was murdered in the South, whose whole life has been an obstinate carrying on, deep inside Mississippi, of her family's coldly abstract espousal of Negroes, shows us how much of an abstraction Joe Christmas is when she makes love crying to him "Negro! Negro!" Whether the "Negro" represent the white man's guilt or the white man's fear, he is always a thought in the white's mind, and—in the South—an obsession. So Joanna Burden, who befriends him, and Doc Hines, who hates him, come to see in him the cause of guilt that is finally the image of guilt. "I thought," Joanna says to her lover,

> of all the children coming forever and ever into the world, white, with the black shadow already falling upon them before they drew breath. And I seemed to see the black shadow in the shape of a cross. And it seemed like the white babies were struggling, even before they drew breath, to escape from the shadow that was not only upon them but beneath them, too, flung out like their arms were flung out, as if they were nailed to the cross.

And she quotes her father:

> In order to rise, you must raise the shadow with you. But you can never lift it to your level. I see that now, which I did not see until I came down here. But escape it you cannot. The curse of the black race is God's curse. But the curse of the white race is the black man who will be forever God's chosen own because He once cursed Him.

The grounds of this obsession, then, can be a compassion for the Negro that is as profound as hatred, and equally removed from brotherhood. This compassion seems to me the essence of Faulkner's approach to Joe Christmas, and the triumph of the book is Faulkner's ability to keep his leading character a shadow, and yet to make us feel all his suffering. Compare Joe Christmas with the types of the Northerner, the city man, the "stranger" in Southern writing, to say nothing of the Negro, and you realize that where so many neo-orthodox Southern literary critics are hysterically fearful of the "stranger," Faulkner, by a tremendous and moving act of imagination, has found in Joe Christmas the incarnation of "man"—that is, of modern man, reduced entirely to his unsupported and inexplicable human feelings. There are no gods in Faulkner's world; there are only men—some entirely subject to circumstances, some protesting against them, and some even moved to change them. The hero of *A Fable* is of the last; Joe Christmas is of the first. He is human to us because of the experiences he undergoes, but his passivity is so great that he is finally a body castrated, a mere corpse on a dissection table—or someone whose body has been turned into the host, material for a ritual, so that his last agony will earn him the respect he never earned while he was alive. He is not, like the Christ of *A Fable,* a man who gives new meaning to life; like Benjy in *The Sound and the Fury,* he is an incarnation of human suffering, unable to speak—except in the tremendous action near the end of the book when he stops running from his pursuers and waits for them, and attains in this first moment of selfhood the martyrdom that ends it.

We see Joe Christmas always from a distance. This distance from ourselves to him seems to me the key to the book, for it explains why Joe exists for us principally as a man who is described, not seen. He is so far away that we cannot see him; he is reported to us. And this distance is filled with the stillness of a continuous meditation. *Light in August* tells a story of violence, but the book itself is curiously soundless, for it is full of people thinking to themselves about events past. As soon as Lena Grove arrives in Jefferson, at the end of the first chapter, the story of Joe Christmas comes to us through flashbacks, through talk by the other men at the planing mill, through a whole chapter of summary biography, Chapter VI, through rumors and gossip of the townspeople, and at the very end, when Joe Christmas's whole story is put together for us, by Gavin Stevens's telling a stranger about the grandparents. Almost everything we learn about Joe Christmas comes to us in the form of hearsay, accusation, the tortured memories of others; even his death is told as an incident in the life of his murderer, Percy Grimm. All these reports about the stranger sufficiently suggest his alienation. But in themselves they also create that stillness, that depth of meditation into which all the characters are plunged.

This meditation begins in Joe Christmas himself, who in his distance from other men is constantly trying to think himself back to life, and who, without knowing exactly how his ordeal began—and certainly not why—finds himself like a caged animal going over and over the same ground. We hear him talking to himself, and we follow his slow and puzzled efforts to understand the effect of his actions upon others. We see him as a child in the orphanage, eating the toothpaste, frightening the dietitian out of her wits because he is staring straight at her trying to understand what she is accusing him of. We watch him walking the path between his cabin and Joanna Burden's house for his meals, thinking out everything he finds between the four walls of her kitchen. Finally we watch him running, and thinking deliriously in his flight, until, in that magnificent and piercing scene near the end of his flight, he falls asleep as he runs. The pressure of thought, the torture of thought, is overwhelming—and useless—since Joe Christmas does not know who he is and so cannot locate the first cause of his misery. But still he thinks, he broods, he watches, he waits. And it is this brooding silence in him, fixed in attention over he knows not what, that explains why he is so often described in the book as looking like a man in prayer—even like a "monk." There is a strange and disturbing stillness about him that eases him, more swiftly than most men, into the stillness of non-being.

The stillness of the book has, of course, an immense reverberation within it. Describing Doc Hines, Faulkner notes about him "a quality of outworn violence like a scent, an odor," and the actual violence of Joe Christmas is always felt about him even when he sits rigidly still at counters like a man in prayer. When Joe's past history is run off in the rapid newsreel style of Dos Passos, one feels not only his personal insignificance, but the just leashed violence of American life of which Joe is, in his way, completely the creature:

> He stepped from the dark porch, into the moonlight, and with his bloody head and his empty stomach hot, savage, and courageous with whiskey, he entered the street which was to run for fifteen years.
>
> The whiskey died away in time and was renewed and died again, but the street ran on. From that night the thousand streets ran as one street, with imperceptible corners and changes of scene, broken by intervals of begged and stolen rides, on trains and trucks, and on country wagons with he at twenty and twenty-five and thirty sitting on the seat with his still, hard face and the clothes (even when soiled and worn) of a city man and the driver of the wagon not knowing who or what the passenger was and not daring to ask.

Yet it is a stillness of thought that generally pervades the book, in the form of enormous meditations by which Faulkner tries to lift his material into place. The stillness is interrupted by shooting, burning, beating, the barking of bloodhounds, and Percy Grimm's mutilation of Joe Christmas, which interrupts the pervading stillness like the sound which nails must make when they are driven into wood through human flesh. Yet, just behind this obvious figure of the Roman soldier torturing Christ, there is a pastoral world. As Irving Howe has noted, the arrangement of the book "resembles an early Renaissance painting—in the foreground a bleeding martyr, far to the rear a scene of bucolic peacefulness, with women quietly working in the fields." Despite its violence, *Light in August* is one of the few American novels that remind one of the humanized and tranquil landscape in European novels. Its stillness is rooted in the peaceful and timeless world which Lena Grove personifies and in which she has her being. It is the stillness of the personal darkness inside which Joe Christmas lives. But his stillness is also the sickly, after-dark silence of the Reverend Gail Hightower sitting in his study, with his stale clothes and stale thoughts, going over and over the tragedy of his life, his grandfather's "glorious" death, his wife's desertion and suicide—and finally and typically summing it all up into a stale round of human illusion and defeat. Faulkner wishes us to understand that Hightower finally cuts the gordian knot of his thoughts when he delivers Lena's baby and is struck down by Percy Grimm as he stands between him and Joe Christmas. But Hightower, whether brooding out upon the street or sitting behind the green lamp in his parlor when he receives Byron Bunch, his only visitor, enlarges the stillness, increases its weight, by personifying what is immediately present in the book and throughout Faulkner's novels—the Southern effort to explain, to justify, and through some consummation in violent physical action even to lighten the burden of this obsession with the past.

Hightower, by general consent, is one of the failures of the book: he is too vague, too drooping, too formless, in a word too much the creature of defeat and of obsession, to compel our interest or our belief. But this is so partly because Hightower is both a surrogate figure for Faulkner's meditations and a kind of scapegoat on whom Faulkner can discharge his exasperation with Southern nostalgia and the endless searching in the labyrinths of the past for the explanation of the Southern defeat and of the hold it keeps on the descendants of the Confederate aristocracy. Hightower is a failure because Faulkner both uses and parodies him. Because of the absurdly literal symbolism of his name, his constant watchful position behind the green lamp, his useless reveries, he is never on the same scale with the other characters, who are equally obsessed by the past, but who function on the plane of some positive action. Hightower not only lives by his thoughts, he has no life but his thoughts. We miss in him the lifelike element of violence (the only possible end to characters so entirely formed of reverie) that we find in Joanna Burden's degeneration, in Joe Christmas's hatred, in Percy Grimm's fanaticism, in Doc Hines's mania. Hightower, acting in various sections of the book as a foreground observer, brings to them not merely a stillness but a deadness which intervenes between us and the other characters. This shapeless, ghostly body of thought has its symbolic place in the mind of Hightower. For just as his life is over, and he has no function but to brood, so Faulkner has signified in Hightower that wholly retrospective, watchful-concern, not with the past but with their bondage to the past, that seems to be the essence of what Faulkner's characters are always thinking about.

Joe Christmas, Joanna Burden, Gail Hightower—each of these is the prisoner of his own history, and is trying to come to terms with this servitude in his own mind. None of them can ever lift themselves out of the labyrinth by taking thought. But in this effort to think man's life out of the circumstances that enclose it, Faulkner sees the condition of man. Man is engulfed in events that are always too much for him. Hightower, listening to Byron Bunch make plans for Lena's confinement, thinks: "It is because so much happens. Too much happens. That's it. Man performs, engenders, so much more than he can or should have to bear. That's how he finds out that he can bear anything. That's it. That's what is so terrible. That he can bear anything, anything." Endurance, as we know, is the key word in Faulkner's system of values. At least this was so up to *A Fable*. There, as Faulkner himself has told us, the highest value is represented not by the young Jewish pilot officer who says, "This is terrible. I refuse to accept it, even if I must refuse life to do so"; not by the old French quartermaster general who says, "This is terrible, but we can weep and bear it," but by the English battalion runner who says, "This is terrible, I'm going to do something about it." *Light in August* does not arrive at this step. Man never thinks of changing the world; it is all he can do to get a grip on it, to understand some part of what has happened to him and to endure all of it. Any release that occurs is a purely individual one, as when Hightower finally frees himself, in the one profoundly unselfish act of his life, by delivering Lena's baby. In the freshness of the early morning, after Lena has given birth, Hightower feels that he is in touch with the earth again—the symbol throughout the book of rightness, authenticity, peace. But the earth is not his life, as it is Lena Grove's. Man's highest aim in this book is to meet his destiny without everlasting self-concern. Yet this profoundly tragic cast to *Light in August,* so much like a Hardy novel in the implacable pattern that unrolls against a country background and the inarticulate stillness of its leading characters, is matched by Faulkner's ironic awareness that man, in his endless brooding over events, can never stop, that the event is nothing compared with the speculation that follows and in a sense replaces it. One of the most revealing phrases in Faulkner's rhetoric is: "not that"—it is not peace, not an end, that his people ever want. The violence may be "outworn," but it is the human passion. He describes his chorus, the townspeople, scurrying around Joanna Burden's house after her murder, looking "for someone to crucify":

> But there wasn't anybody. She had lived such a quiet life, attended so to her own affairs, that she bequeathed to the town in which she had been born and lived and died a foreigner, an outlander, a kind of heritage of astonishment and outrage, for which, even though she had supplied them at last with an emotional barbecue, a Roman holiday almost, they would never forgive her and let her be dead in peace and quiet. Not that. Peace is not that often. So they moiled and clotted, believing that the flames, the blood, the body that had died three years ago and had now just begun to live again, cried out for vengeance, not believing that the rapt infury of the flames and the immobility of the body were both affirmations of an attained bourne beyond the hurt and harm of man. Not that.

We can never let the event go, for that would mean an end to the human history that is lived in retrospection. Just as Faulkner's language is full of words, like "avatar" and "outrage," which are really private symbols left over from his unceasing meditation, and just as his style is formed from the fierce inner pressure of problems which give no solution, so the actual texture of *Light in August* suggests, in the tension and repetition of certain verbal motifs, that man can never quite say what the event originally meant, or what he is to think of it now. Language never quite comes up to the meaning of events. To adapt Faulkner's phrase, it is not that, or that. The townspeople exist in *Light in August,* as in so many Faulkner novels, to ask questions whose very function is to deny the possibility of an answer. Faulkner's grim, sarcastic asides show that he views language as in some basic sense unavailing. The astounding repetition of certain key phrases and verbal rhythms in his work signifies his return back and back on the question.

Call the event history, call it the Fall: man is forever engaged in meditating, not the past itself, for that would bring knowledge, but man's guilt, for that may bring freedom. Guilt, not history, is the nightmare from which all of Faulkner's deepest characters are trying to escape. The guilt arises from man's endless complicity in his own history, as when the innocent, gravely staring child that Joe Christmas was ate toothpaste and listened to the dietitian making love. Hightower is guilty because his sickly, foolish nostalgia for his grandfather's one day of glory made him unavailable to his own wife, who committed suicide; Joanna Burden feels so guilty that she has remained an alien in the Southern town in which she was born, accepting her isolation as the price of her identification both with her Abolitionist forebears, who were shot down in the South, and with the Negroes, on whom a curse must have been laid. Even Doc Hines and Percy Grimm murder in order to "clean" life of the stain that Negroes have put on it, for as the Negroes were cursed by God, so they have cursed life, and the maniac "saviors" of Southern racial purity have to save their hallowed country from contagion. But just as no one of them can really distinguish the hate they feel for others from self-accusation, so no one can say with whom guilt began, where the ultimate human crime was committed. The paths which lead back to the human past are endless through the human brain, and sitting at his study window after he has gained new self-respect by delivering Lena's baby and by standing up to Percy Grimm, the dying Hightower still ruminates, goes over and over the past, as "the final copper light of afternoon fades" and "the world hangs in a green suspension in color and texture like through colored glass." The everlasting reverie begins again, but now the wheel of life that brought Lena Grove to Jefferson begins to slow down, runs into sand, "the axle, the vehicle, the power which propels it not yet aware." These memories are endless and the style in which they are described is overcolored in a way that shows how static action often becomes in Faulkner's work, how much it serves as the raw material for reflection, which is why he can lavish so many Joycean compound words on objects which do not seem to move of their own accord, but to be rallying points in Faulkner's tortured concern with guilt.

Guilt is endless; in the labyrinths of the mind there is turning, but no deliverance. Like T. S. Eliot, Faulkner is a favorite today because he takes his stand on human guilt; this is the side of ourselves that we can recognize, and, curiously, stand by; for in this alone, as we feel, is the possibility of our freedom. When men feel so wretchedly small before their own past, they must be guilty. So runs the legend. This is the argument behind Faulkner's novels: of the God who made Yoknapatawpha County. In the beginning, life was free and good and natural; but something inexplicable, a curse, was put on it. Perhaps the curse is nothing more than man's effort to get the better of events that are "too much for us"; the evil lies in arrogance. Doc Hines hears God addressing him personally, ordering him to act for Him. Calvin McEachern, Joe Christmas's adopted father, starves and beats him because he cannot memorize portions of the catechism on order. "He asked that the child's stubborn heart be softened and that the sin of disobedience be forgiven him also, through the advocacy of the man whom he had flouted and disobeyed, requesting that the Almighty be as magnanimous as himself, and by and through and because of conscious grace." Even Joanna Burden tries to play God to her Negro charges. *Light in August* is one of the sharpest criticisms of Calvinism ever written, but unlike so many Southern writers on Puritanism, Faulkner knows that the same religion is found in Doc Hines and Joanna Burden. The guilt that is the mainstay of their faith is embodied in the assumption of excessive authority by fathers, lawgivers, teachers, ministers. Everyone wants to play God to the orphan Joe Christmas. In Faulkner's eyes, life is an ironic and tragic affair that is beyond human rule and misrule; but Calvinists like Doc Hines and Calvin McEachern, the children of Calvinists like Joanna Burden, even murdering, simon-pure "patriots" like Percy Grimm, take life in their hands, they dominate and they murder. Joe Christmas is their favorite pupil; he is the man "things are done to." His final ignominy comes when his mistress, Joanna Burden, regarding him in her new phase as a Negro charge to be "brought up," tells him that she wants him to go to school so that he can become a lawyer. And it is at this point that he breaks. It is this point that has always been the signature of the everlasting victim. Other men are the lawgivers; the law is passed out to him, through him, inflicted on him. And so finally he murders and dies, a pure victim, shot, castrated, treated like a thing. It is the final ignominy. But in the very unattainability of his suffering, in its expressibility, is the key to his healing power over others. For where life exists so much in the relation of master to man, of the elect to the sinner, the only possible consummation man can ever reach, for Joe Christmas as for Uncle Tom, is in the final consistency of his suffering, in a fate so extreme that it becomes a single human word which men can read. This is what Faulkner means in that exalted passage after Joe Christmas's immolation:

> . . . when they saw what Grimm was doing one of the men gave a choked cry and stumbled back into the wall and began to vomit. Then Grimm too sprang back, flinging behind him the bloody butcher knife. "Now you'll let white women alone, even in hell," he said. But the man on

> the floor had not moved. He just lay there, with his eyes open and empty of everything save consciousness, and with something, a shadow, about his mouth. For a long moment he looked up at them with peaceful and unfathomable and unbearable eyes. Then his face, body, all, seemed to collapse, to fall in upon itself, and from out the slashed garments about his hips and loins the pent black blood seemed to rush like a released breath. It seemed to rush out of his pale body like the rush of sparks from a rising rocket; upon that black blast the man seemed to rise soaring into their memories forever and ever. They are not to lose it, in whatever peaceful valleys, beside whatever placid and reassuring streams of old age, in the mirroring faces of whatever children they will contemplate old disasters and newer hopes. It will be there, musing, quiet, steadfast, not fading and not particularly threatful, but of itself alone serene, of itself alone triumphant.

Joe Christmas has attained the stillness that will finally allow us to see him. Of sufferings alone is he made, and in this sense, and in this sense alone, is he a figure whose condition is so total that he reminds us of Christ in the sense of Christ's integrality. That tortured and would-be Christian philosopher, Simone Weil, understood this when she found that *malheur,* affliction, could become so much in itself that she felt riven to the universe by bonds of pain. The arch-victim may not be a "martyr," as students of totalitarianism have noticed; but there is a kind of suffering in our time which is so extreme that it becomes an integral *fact* of the human condition. Father Zossima bowed down to Dmitri Karamazov because of all the affliction he would undergo. So marvelous is Faulkner's compassion, he can visualize in the man who was nothing but a victim the shadow thrown from the Cross of Christ, who was nothing, as it were, but Himself. Men are men because events are always "too much" for them; Joe Christmas became one with his life in that extreme moment when even he had no longer to search out the past. The figure on the Cross is the most tremendous interventive symbol in history; the castrated man on the floor has only one free power in his life—to stop running at last and to face his murderer. Faulkner intends no parody; he is moved by the likeness of totality to totality. But neither is he a Christian. There is no redemption; there is not even in *A Fable*—but there man has the courage to redeem circumstances by denying their fatality. In *Light in August* the past is not merely exigent, it is malicious, the spirit of pure bad luck, a godlike force that confronts man at every turn with everything he has been, and so seems to mock and to oppose him. This spirit is called "The Player": Lena's seducer, "Brown," still running away from her at the last, sends a Negro boy to the sheriff for the reward money he has earned in informing on Joe Christmas, but knows despairingly that he will never see the money.

> "He wont do it. He cant do it. I know he cant find him, cant get it, bring it back." He called no names, thought no names. It seemed to him

> now that they were all just shapes like chessmen—the negro, the sheriff, the money, all—unpredictable and without reason moved here and there by an Opponent who could read his moves before he made them and who created spontaneous rules which he and not the Opponent, must follow.

This is the Opponent that Joe Christmas decides finally not to elude again, the "Player" who moves Percy Grimm unerringly from position to position:

> He was beside the ditch now. He stopped, motionless in midstride. Above the blunt, cold rake of the automatic his face had that serene, unearthly luminousness of angels in church windows. He was moving again almost before he had stopped, with that lean, swift, blind obedience to whatever Player moved him on the Board. He ran to the ditch.

All things are fated; man is in any place because the Player moved him there. Our past sets up the positions into which we fall. This is why Joe Christmas's grandmother, Mrs. Hines, utters the most significant lines in the book when, at the end, she pitifully cries:

> I am not saying that he never did what they say he did. Ought not to suffer for it like he made them that loved and lost suffer. But if folks could maybe just let him for one day. Like it hadn't happened yet. Like the world never had anything against him yet. Then it could be like he had just went on a trip and grew man grown and come back. If it could be like that for just one day.

And it is in these terms that we come to understand why Joe Christmas, in running away from a past that he cannot escape, seems constantly to be looking back as he runs. Not only is no one free of his past; he even has, at the most critical moments, the sense of not moving at all, but of being silently lifted from position to position. It is because of this curious effect of immobility in Faulkner's characters as they run (as if they were held up in the air by wires) that Faulkner can lavish such idle poetic largesse upon them: can see in a Percy Grimm that "serene, unearthly luminousness of angels in church windows," and at various points throughout the book emphasized Joe Christmas's rigid likeness to a man in prayer. Even the countrymen in overalls move at one point "with almost the air of monks in a cloister." The reason is that all these characters are lost in contemplation as they are moved here and there by the Player. There is no free action for anyone; everyone is carried, as Lena Grove was carried to Jefferson in a whole succession of farmwagons, by the fate that was and so shall be.

Faulkner's world is grim—a world in which the past exerts an irresistible force, but against which there is no supernatural sanction, no redeeming belief. He believes in original sin, but not in divine love, and he is endlessly bemused by the human effort to read fate or to avoid it. The highest reach of his belief is the effort to become "a saint without God" (Albert Camus), but this is a point not yet tried for in *Light in*

August. Correspondingly, there is great power in his work, but little color, and *Light in August,* for all its brilliance, somehow wears the lackluster look of the year in which it was published, 1932. It is a grim book and the countryside described in it already has the pinched, rotted look that one sees in so many depression novels about the South. The greatest fault of the book is its overschematic, intellectualized past. Although Faulkner himself has lived more like Joe Christmas than like the Sartorises, he is socially far from the world of Joe Christmas and Lena Grove, and there are telltale signs in the novel that it is written *down*—for Faulkner, too much from his head down, and about people whom he tends to generalize and to overpraise, as if he saw them only as symbols rather than as entirely complex beings. And it is a simple fact that the opening of *Light in August* is so beautiful that nothing after quite comes up to it.

On the other hand, it is one of Faulkner's greatest books, and although it does not have the blazing directness of *The Sound and the Fury* (a book written more directly out of Faulkner's own experience), it has much of the creative audacity which is Faulkner's highest ideal in art. With this book, published in 1932, Faulkner completed a period of extraordinary fertility. He was only thirty-five; since 1929 he had published, in rapid order, *Sartoris, The Sound and the Fury, As I Lay Dying, Sanctuary,* and *Light in August.* It was a period of tremendous creative power. When he was recently in Japan, Faulkner said of this period:

> I think there's a period in a writer's life when he, well, simply for lack of any other word, is fertile and he just produces. Later on, his blood slows, his bones get a little more brittle, his muscles get a little stiff, he gets perhaps other interests, but I think there's one time in his life when he writes at the top of his talent plus his speed, too. Later the speed slows; the talent doesn't necessarily have to fade at the same time. But there's a time in his life, one matchless time, when they are matched completely. The speed, and the power and the talent, they're all there and then he is . . . "hot."

Light in August comes out of that "one matchless time." The only possible objection one can have to the book is the number of implications which Faulkner tries to bring out of his material—for just as the characters' own lives are "set" for them to mull over, so Faulkner constantly mulls over them, wringing a poetry that has grandeur, but also an intensity of contemplation that is sometimes more furious in expression than meaningful in content. If we see Faulkner's narrative method as essentially recollective, in the form of individual meditation over past events, we can recognize the advantage he has over most "naturalistic" writers and we understand why Faulkner refers to himself as a "poet." For what makes the portrait of Joe Christmas so astonishing is the energy of imagination lavished upon it, the consistency of texture that derives from the poet's sense that he has not only to *show,* in the modern realistic sense, but to *say*—that is, to tell a story which follows from his contemplation of the world, and which preserves in the nobility of its style and in the serene independence of its technique, the human victory over circumstances.

It is this that makes us hear Faulkner's own voice throughout the book, that allows him to pull off the tremendous feat of making us believe in a character who in many ways is not a human being at all—but struggling to become one. And this, after all, is the great problem of the novelist today. Joe Christmas is an incarnation not only of the "race problem" in America, but of the condition of man. More and more, not merely the American novel, but all serious contemporary novels, are concerned with men who are not real enough to themselves to be seriously in conflict with other men. Their conflicts, as we say, are "internal"; for they are seeking to become *someone*. Joe Christmas lives a life that is not only solitary but detached. He lives in society physically, but actually he is concerned only with the process of self-discovery, or of self-naming, even of self-legalization. This is a fate which, as we know, can be as arduous and deadly as that of the classic heroes. But in Joe Christmas's case, there is no conflict from positions of strength, no engagement between man and man—only the search of the "stranger," *l'étranger,* to become man.

Joe Christmas: The Hero in the Modern World

by John L. Longley, Jr.

I

"Aristotle has not defined pity and terror," said Stephen Dedalus. "I have. Pity is the feeling which arrests the mind in the presence of whatsoever is grave and constant in human sufferings and unites it with the human sufferer. Terror is the feeling which arrests the mind in the presence of whatsoever is grave and constant in human sufferings and unites it with the secret cause." Stephen's definition is appropriate, for different as he is from Joe Christmas, they are alike in being heroes who are distinctly modern and who must make their way in a cosmos that is violent, chaotic, and absurd.

Of course, not everyone will be willing to accept the word "tragic" in connection with the works of William Faulkner, or, indeed, with anything in the literature of this century. Some readers do not like his work at all and say so. Many have confessed that they find it difficult to understand. The objections will vary with the individual, but the major factors in the dissatisfaction are not at all difficult to discover. One factor is the "difficulty" of the style—the nonstop sentences and the obliqueness of presentation. In a very basic sense, the ultimate meaning of the book has not reached the reader. Another factor, of course, is hostility: hostility to Faulkner's region and/or his matter, or a simple quarrelsome disagreement with a view of life that is not the reader's own. And much of the hostility has been generated by bad criticism.

But I do not for a moment wish to suggest that Mr. Faulkner is primarily interested in writing tragedy to prescription. There is probably no writer living who cares less what the professors say of his work. And, as we know, tragedy ground out in conformity to a set prescription has almost without exception failed to become tragic. Tragedy is autochthonous and mantic, and set prescriptions for these conditions cannot be written;

Reprinted with permission from *The Tragic Mask* (Chapel Hill: The University of North Carolina Press), 1957 pp. 192-205. First published in *Virginia Quarterly Review*, Spring 1957.

they must be achieved in another way. One is reminded of Jane Harrison's admission: "Great things in literature, Greek plays for example, I most enjoy when behind their bright splendors I see moving darker and older shapes." It is this kind of infinitely extended suggestivity, the waking of universal echoes, that the better work of Faulkner so conspicuously has and the work of so many modern writers—for instance, Arthur Miller—so conspicuously lacks.

But even assuming Faulkner's possession of a tragic sensibility and granting him the ability to shape it into art, how can the very long jump to Joe Christmas as tragic hero be made? There are perhaps two possible approaches, and perhaps both of them should be used: to what extent is Christmas authentically tragic by traditional criteria, and to what extent can it be shown that he is tragic by some entirely modern, different set of criteria which apply? Vastly oversimplified, the modern protagonist should be one who is typical of the age and not so remote from typical human beings as to make emotional identification difficult for the spectator. In some highly symbolic fashion, the modern hero must typify the major myths and problems of our century. In a cosmos where all is chaos and all standards have disappeared, he will very likely be destroyed as a result of his failure to define himself correctly in relation to that cosmos. Lastly he must embody the perpetual human constants which are the property of any age. Bypassing for a moment the very interesting second possibility, let us examine Christmas in the light of traditional, classic tragic criteria. At first glance, this procedure appears unpromising.

Granting his acts of persistence, his arrogance and pride, how can Christmas be called noble? How can he be said to be illustrious in rank and fortune? Above all, how can a human so conditioned, so utterly predestined to violence and death ever be called free: free to choose and free to act or not act? It is my belief that this is precisely the point.

Aristotle awarded the palm for classic tragedy to the *Oedipus Tyrannos* of Sophocles. If this is not quite the same thing as saying that Oedipus is the most perfect example of the tragic protagonist, perhaps he will do for comparison. Everyone knows his tragic story, at least in outline, for it is one of the ironies of history that he has given his name to the folklore of psychology. In that same folklore, in the modern world, we give tacit agreement to the belief that human free will is all but impossible. In the Greek world, once the oracle had spoken, who was ever so hopelessly "predestined" as Oedipus?

But, as everyone also knows, that is not it at all. To vastly oversimplify, Oedipus becomes tragic only because he does strive against the prediction. Resolved to know, he goes to the oracle himself and hears with his own ears the dire prophecy repeated. He runs away. His hubris lies not in the running but in boasting that he has escaped and has become king of Thebes by his own strength and cunning. His confidence unbroken, he is convinced he can save Thebes again as he did before. He pronounces the curse on the unknown polluter of the city, and as the process of ferreting out the guilty one goes on, Oedipus' search becomes one of finding out his own identity. But even as the dark hints begin to accumulate, and Jocasta has guessed the truth, he boasts of his contempt for oracles and prophecy; his father is still alive and his mother is far away. He will trust only that godlike strength and cunning that has made him tyrannos—"first of men." As the flawlessly plotted action unfolds, there comes the crushing peripateia: all along he had been nearer home than he knew.

We could say that Oedipus' fault lies in trying to beat the rap. But again, everyone knows that his tragedy has to mean more than this; that this expenditure of human striving and achievement and suffering has to stand for something grave and constant in the eternal human condition. It is very true that his is the classical hubris, the sin of pride and arrogance and overconfidence in his own ability. But far more to our purpose, we can say it is a failure to achieve self-knowledge, a failure of self-definition. Oedipus was saddled with an incredibly horrible, inevitable future; he had not asked for it and had done nothing to deserve it; it was all "decided" before he was born. But he persists, and demands to know the truth. Bernard Knox has noted how in the original there is the constant cruelly ironic interrunning of "Oedipus" and "Oidi" ("swell," as with pride and arrogance) and "Oida" ("I know"), words that are all too often in Oedipus' mouth. At the beginning of the play there is too much that he does not know, and at the end there is too much that he does. It is in the interweaving of guilt and innocence, in the willing of his own actions against the pressure of his destiny, in the godlike insistence on knowing *who* he is, and in the crushing ruin that this knowledge brings him to, that the tragic glory of Oedipus lies.

Consider another hero. About his birth there is mystery also. He too is spirited away as an infant because dreadful things are whispered about him, and he too is brought up by foster-parents whom he leaves hurriedly for fear he may have killed his foster-father. In a very direct way, it can be said that his very begetting caused the death of his real father. He brings terrible shame, agony, and death to his real mother. After a great deal of wandering, he returns to that part of the world which, unknown to him, was the scene of his begetting and birth. Early in life he was given a free choice of two lines of conduct, one of which will remove him from all danger to himself. He persists in the other because it is necessary to the terms of his own definition of himself. He lives connubially with an older woman, who as a result of his drive toward self-definition dies a horrible death. The fearful rumors about him break out afresh. There is an old, mad visionary who claims to have special insight into the truth about him, and as a result, his fellowmen are convinced he is a ritual pollution in the community. Pursued by them, he is harried for days and is eventually sacrificed in a particularly horrible ritual murder. He was saddled with an incredibly horrible, inevitable curse; he had not asked for it and had done nothing to deserve it; it was all "decided" before he was born. The second hero is, of course, Joe Christmas.

II

If the fall of Oedipus comes as the direct result of his terribly mistaken idea of who he is and his insistence on finding out, then the death of Christmas is a result of his insistence that he already knows who he is and his persistence in the demand for the right to be himself, to live on the terms of his own self-definition. To state the paradox in another way, the classic tragic protagonist, such as Oedipus, Othello, Hamlet, or Macbeth, rejoices in an existence which allows him a superb scope of action in which to achieve self-realization, including knowledge, even though in this same drive toward self-fulfillment he destroys himself. The modern tragic protagonist, such as the heroes of a Dostoevsky, a Conrad, a Kafka, a Faulkner, a Hemingway, or a Warren, must use all his intelligence, his strength, his luck, merely to travel the tightrope between Cosmic Chaos on the one hand and Cosmic Absurdity on the other. He can trust in nothing, hope for nothing, and accept nothing at face value until he has tried it on the test of his own pulses. He may have heard of determinism, but does not believe in it; in the face of those joyous theories of self-exculpation formulated by present-day psychology and sociology which presumably give the individual the right to scream "It's not my fault! It's not my fault!" his preference is much nearer the dreadful freedom of the existentialist: since existence is prior to essence, the individual is totally free, and totally accountable for his own view of things, for with total freedom comes total responsibility.

In the case of Joe Christmas, Faulkner takes pains to make this freedom absolute. Here we must be blunt: previous critical opinion seems almost never to have been aware of that freedom. Partly because, one supposes, the term "conditioning" is now a household word, it was decided that Christmas is the helpless victim of his own conditioning. But surely it is obvious that the wellspring of all his actions is his refusal to surrender to that conditioning. The conditioning is well documented, but in the first mention of him his significant quality is his rootlessness, his freedom from the customary restraints of job, property, wife, children, and taxes. Straw hat on head and razor in pocket, he is ready for a journey of one mile or a thousand.

One of Faulkner's clearest strokes of genius is in leaving the question of Christmas's possible Negro blood unanswered. We, no one, will ever know if he has it or not. If he does have it, the percentage is very small, which not only adds to the irony, but leaves him free to "pass" if he chooses. Although various characters in the novel make statements, and very positive statements, about the matter, the author never commits himself. Christmas is putatively a Negro child at the orphanage largely through the efforts of Old Doc Hines, but he is adopted and brought up as a white child by the McEacherns. ("He dont look no more like a nigger than I do," says a white character.) This is probably the most crucial point in the book: Christmas is free to choose what he will be. Precisely as Oedipus, he must find out who and what he is. One remembers a scene in the orphanage: Old Doc Hines is recalling how the five-year-old Christmas has begun following the Negro yard-boy around:

> . . . until at last the nigger said, "What you watching me for boy?" and he said, "How come you are a nigger?" and the nigger said, "Who told you I am a nigger, you little white trash bastard?" and he says, "I aint a nigger," and the nigger says, "You are worse than that. You dont know what you are. And more than that, you wont never know. You'll live and you'll die, and you wont never know. . . ."

But he must know. As with his determination to keep his own name, and because he is free, he cannot let others tell him how and what to be. All his life people attempt to force him to be what they insist he must be: McEachern's beating him to inculcate worship of the Moloch-Jehovah; Mrs. McEachern's sickening attempts to make him as cringing as herself; Joanna Burden's final insistence that he "become a nigger." His method is active. In the fifteen years of wandering he tries life as a black man, living with Negroes, and as a white man attempting to live with whites. But ultimately he chooses to be neither—he will simply be himself. Until the very end, the community cannot decide for sure what he is; their deep distrust grows from his refusal to declare himself one *or* the other in a social pattern where this is the most important distinction of all. He will insist on his right to simply be; he has defined himself and has fought hard for the definition. The murder of Joanna Burden and his own death are the fruit of that insistence.

Granted he has freedom and choice, what about rank and fortune? The hero, like Oedipus and Macbeth, makes his own. Christmas's distinction lies in the strength of his proud, ruthless, arrogant, cold self-sufficiency, as rigid as that of a Richard or an Ahab, and more adequate to the strain placed upon it than Macbeth's. As with any modern hero, the simple fact that he is still alive may be as much good fortune as he can expect. It is more important for our purposes to prove he is typically human.

Part of the difficulty in understanding Christmas again lies in the form and structure of the novel. The sequence of telling is such that he is first seen as the utterly sinister alien, and is revealed early in the book as a brutal murderer. It is only as the flashbacks begin to unfold and we see him as a child and youth that we are made aware of his simple humanity. Presented for the most part at a distance, his inmost thoughts and feelings are not often enough open to us, but at rare intervals a momentary flash of insight will give a total revelation. We see the denial of love and belonging in the orphanage and the beatings by McEachern, and the effect of these is of course cumulative, but one of the revealing flashes comes when he hears that his name will be changed:

> "He will eat my bread and he will observe my religion," the stranger said. "Why should he not bear my name?"
>
> The child was not listening. He was not bothered. He did not especially care, anymore than if the man had said the day was hot when it was not hot. He didn't even bother to say to himself *My name aint McEachern. My Name is Christmas.* There was no need to bother about that yet. There was plenty of time.

We are shown the idyllic relationship with Bobbie, the stunted and no-longer young waitress who is a working prostitute in her spare time. His slipping away from the McEachern farm to be with her is part of his program of defiance, but it is truly, at least at the beginning, the adolescent's first tentative awe-struck discovery of the body of the beloved and all its possibilities. Again, just before the dawn of the day on which he will murder Joanna Burden, when the pressures that will compel either murder or complete surrender are building past endurance, he muses:

> . . . it seemed to him, sitting on the cot in the dark room, that he was hearing a myriad of sounds of no greater volume—voices, murmurs, whispers: of trees, darkness, earth; people: his own voice; other voices evocative of names and times and places—which he had been conscious of all his life, without knowing it, which were his life, thinking *God perhaps and me not knowing that too* He could see it like a printed sentence, fullborn and already dead *God loves me too* like the faded and weathered letters on a last years's billboard *God loves me too.*

His humanity and perhaps even his own completely tragic awareness of his situation are revealed in that incredible week in which we run with him while he eludes mobs, sheriff, deputies, Lucas, and bloodhounds. All that has gone before in the novel is brilliantly recapitulated as Christmas, still wrapped in the rags and tatters of his self-sufficiency and pride, works himself slowly away from the violence of the attack on the Negro church toward his tragic reconciliation with his fate, his acceptance of the price of the risk of the human condition. The incidents of his life which have "predestined" him toward the proud denial of his own humanity are echoed. Aware, as perhaps never before, of the simple joy of merely being alive and breathing, he watches another day begin:

> It is just dawn, daylight; that gray and lonely suspension filled with the tentative and peaceful waking of birds. The air, inbreathed, is like spring water. He breathes deep and slow, feeling with each breath himself diffuse in the neutral grayness, becoming one with loneliness and quiet that has never known fury or despair. "That was all I wanted," he thinks, in a quiet

what about earlier sexual experiences?

and slow amazement. "That was all, for thirty years. That didn't seem to be a whole lot to ask in thirty years."

Perhaps the right to live one's life is not too much to ask. But Christmas's dilemma is the truly tragic one. He is caught not between clear cut right and wrong, but between right and right. Rejected, feared, hated, he has sought and been proud of that rejection and fear; but pushed too far he has gone too far, and unable to reconcile conflicting responsibility, he has committed a brutal murder. Now he must accept responsibility for the freedom of choice he exercised in his actions and pay the price of that freedom. But, because he is truly tragic, he will not practice a mere lethargic passivity, and wait for the men with the dogs to come up and shoot him. He will actively seek his human reconciliation; his problem is how to begin to get back inside the human community. It is not easy; he has been isolated for too many years. He waits in the dawn for a farmhouse to come alive and the men to leave for the fields. Then he approaches the farm wife, who recognizes him, and he quietly, from a respectful distance, asks: "Can you tell me what day this is? I just want to know what day this is."

Even though the white woman sends him away, the symbolism is clear. He wants to begin again by re-accepting the limitations of one of the most human and communal inventions: time. The next step involves a basic human need and social ritual. Having violently rejected the offer of food on a number of symbolic occasions, he approaches a Negro cabin to ask for a meal.

> . . . He was sitting at a table, waiting, thinking of nothing in an emptiness, a silence filled with flight. Then there was food before him, appearing suddenly between long, limber black hands fleeing too in the act of setting down the dishes. It seemed to him that he could hear without hearing them wails of terror and distress quieter than sighs all about him, with the sounds of the chewing and the swallowing. "It was a cabin that time," he thought. "And they were afraid. Of their brother afraid."

This is not enough. Rejected and feared by Negroes as well as whites, he shaves himself carefully with the razor, the murder weapon, and strikes across country to Mottstown. Given a ride on a wagon by a Negro youth who does not know who he is, he reviews his life:

> . . . he is entering it again, the street which ran for thirty years. It had been a paved street, where going should be fast. It had made a circle and he is still inside of it. Though during the last seven days he has had no paved street, yet he has travelled farther than in all the thirty years before. And yet is still inside the circle. "And yet I have been farther in these seven days than in all the thirty years," he thinks. "But I have never got outside that circle. I have never broken out of the ring of what I have already done and cannot ever undo," he thinks quietly, sitting on the seat, with planted

> on the dashboard before him the shoes, the black shoes smelling of Negro: that mark on his ankles that gauge definite and ineradicable of the black tide creeping up his legs, moving from his feet upward as death moves.

One is tempted to abandon the story for the fascination of peeling back the layers of meaning in the symbol. At first, the obvious meaning seems brutal and shocking, but it must be recalled that for thirty centuries or so the black-white, light-dark, Apollonian-Dionysian, rational-irrational opposition has existed in Western civilization. If this were the only meaning, its use would be forgivable but little more. It should be remembered that Christmas gleefully exchanged his own shoes for these, worn by a Negro woman, to throw the bloodhounds off the scent. (At this stage Christmas, like Oedipus, is full of devices.) But there is another meaning, far more important. Now, completely alone, he is feared and rejected by black and white alike. Urged on by the frantic greed of Lucas Burch and the fanatic madness of Old Doc Hines, the white community considers him a Negro, hunts him as a Negro, and will lynch him as a Negro. Continuing to wear the shoes, he looks at that mark ". . . moving upward from his feet as death moves." No one has ever been able to compel him to choose, black or white; but now the murder is the result of that refusal. While choice of action remains (which may not be long), he will choose his means of reconciliation. Had he chosen sooner, or had he merely gone away as he was also free to do, Joanna Burden would not be dead and he would not be about to die. As surely as he sees the blackness (his acceptance of Negro status) creep up his body, as surely his body is sinking into the darkness, the extinction, of death. He walks quietly about the streets of Mottstown until he is captured.

At this point only the last of the tragedy remains to be played out. It may be felt that Christmas is unable to sustain his resolution, that his breaking away from the officers only to be shot and castrated by Percy Grimm is an artistic defect on the part of the writer. But Oedipus and Lear have moments toward the end when the old rage and arrogance blaze out; Antigone, St. Joan, Richard, all have moments when human fear of absolute extinction overwhelms human integrity. The moment is there for a conscious artistic purpose: to give us that ultimate awareness of pity and terror by reminding us that the protagonist is not a hollow tragic mask, but a living human being only a little less lucky than ourselves. And there is a further meaning: free to the end, Christmas has held onto his life until the proper moment has come to give it, the moment most filled with meaning.

As Gavin Stevens says, no one will ever know what Christmas hoped for from Hightower, but that it was the conflict in his blood that let him run but would not let him escape; that made him snatch up the pistol but would not let him kill Grimm with it. Stevens has his opinion of Christmas's origin, as do various others, but by this time it does not seem to matter. The meaning has taken on almost universal significance. It is the light-dark opposition that is in the blood of all of us; the savage pull between bright rationality and the instinctiveness and bestiality of the darkness that leads to irrationality and death.

Few scenes in modern literature have the speed and inevitable onward sweep of the chapter in which Percy Grimm pursues Christmas and kills him. Taken merely as the realistic evocation of a scene, the writing is superb: the shots, the shouting; the blind rushes and clotted confusion of the mob; the added detail of the fire siren, a characteristic sound of our time, screaming the rise and fall of its meaningless message; the early resolution of the pursuit into a personal contest between Christmas and Grimm. The rendition of Grimm as a type is as merciless as anything of the sort ever done. He is Faulkner's equivalent of the classic Nemesis or the Furies; machine-like, unerring, impersonal, mindless.

As the narrative continues, Christmas runs into Hightower's house still holding the pistol he has snatched up on the way. He could kill Grimm easily, but with nothing more to lose by an additional killing, he does not; this is his final gesture of human reconciliation. Grimm empties the magazine of the automatic into Christmas's body, but this is not all.

> When the others reached the kitchen they saw the table flung aside now and Grimm stooping over the body. When they approached to see what he was about, they saw that the man was not dead yet, and when they saw what Grimm was doing one of the men gave a choked cry and stumbled back into the wall and began to vomit. Then Grimm too sprang back, flinging behind him the bloody butcher knife. "Now you'll leave white women alone, even in hell," he said. But the man on the floor had not moved. He just lay there, with his eyes open and empty of everything but consciousness, and with something, a shadow, about his mouth. For a long moment he looked up at them with peaceful and unfathomable and unbearable eyes. Then his face, body, all, seemed to collapse, to fall in upon itself, and from out the slashed garments about his hips and loins the pent black blood seemed to rush like a released breath. It seemed to rush out of his pale body like the rush of sparks from a rising rocket; upon that black blast the man seemed to rise soaring into their memories forever and ever. They are not to lose it, in whatever peaceful valleys, beside whatever placid and reassuring streams of old age, in the mirroring faces of whatever children they will contemplate old disasters and newer hopes. It will be there, musing, quiet, steadfast, not fading and not particularly threatful, but of itself alone serene, of itself alone triumphant. Again from the town, deadened a little by the walls, the scream of the siren mounted toward its unbelievable crescendo, passing out of the realm of hearing.

They are not to lose it, nor, I think, are we. In Stephen Dedalus's terms, we feel pity and terror to a degree that is almost unbearable. No one knows why we feel these emotions, or even less why the tragic spectacle is so compelling. It may be that it is better that we don't know. Behind the stark shapes of Grimm and Christmas outlined against the blinding light of August we seem to see the darker shapes of human sacrifice and mutilation that go back beyond the earliest human history. Certainly, as Nietzsche claimed, the tragic emotions lurk in the dark, irrational part of the blood, and very likely the rational mind wants nothing to do with them. "Pity is the feeling which arrests the mind in the presence of whatsoever is grave and constant in human sufferings and unites it with the human sufferer." We feel with Joe Christmas because he is the modern Everyman. In a cosmos where the only constants are absurdity and instability, we have the right to expect anything except rationality. Any one of us could become the victim. His suffering far transcends the time and place and means Faulkner has used, and comes to stand for, everything that is grave and constant in the human condition.

"Terror is the feeling which arrests the mind in the presence of whatsoever is grave and constant in human sufferings and unites it with the secret cause." The union with the secret cause is almost as terrible as the suffering itself, because it gives a moment of true insight into ourselves. Part of this insight is perfectly symbolized in *Light in August* when the injured Hightower, in a scene that might have come straight out of Dostoevsky, is working himself toward complete self-knowledge. As the wheel of his memory turns on and on, he comes to realize that his own cold selfishness, his absorption in the Confederate grandfather, has caused his wife's disgrace and death. As the crowd of faces in his memory struggle to come into focus, one of them becomes the dead face of Christmas, but the focus is not clear; another face is struggling with that face, struggling to become clear and be recognized. Suddenly it emerges: it is the face of Percy Grimm; gunman, mutilator, avenging fury, lyncher extraordinary. Hightower never saw either of them before the lynching, but their terrible failure and terrible guilt are somehow the direct result of his own failure to live up to his humanity. Somewhere at the root of the secret cause of things as they are, we are all related; we are all involved. We are all responsible because we are all a part of mankind. So far as the rational mind goes, the union with the secret cause is a moment of awareness, of realizing that grave and constant human suffering is truly constant. Once we achieve this awareness, the acceptance of the tragic human situation, with all its absurdity and irrationality, becomes possible, and with the acceptance come the emotions of peace and tranquility.

Yet the union with the secret cause has another side, which is less commendable. This emotion, which we are not so willing to let swim up to conscious awareness, can be curtly put as "There but for the Grace of God. . . ." The hero has fallen, but we, for the moment at least, are safe. Let society pick its victims as it pleases, so long as the victim is not I. It is in just this area of playing upon our deep, instinctual fears and misgivings that Faulkner has succeeded in achieving favorable comparison with classic tragedy. It was impossible to put the Furies believably on the stage, but Faulkner found the perfect equivalent in the lynch mob, which in one way or another elicits a strong emotion in all of us, or better still, a mixed one. In an age where the very name of Oedipus has been explained away, tamed, and embalmed in the clinic, where almost no one can truly feel why Macbeth should think the murder of a king to be so much worse than any murder, and where no one believes in such an absurdity as an ancestral curse, the beholder is simply asked: "Did Joe Christmas inherit a curse?" Or rather, it is not necessary to ask, since we know. Faulkner has used the subconscious fear of mutilation and distrust of miscegenation that lurks in all of us, the love of and response to violence and death, the simultaneous love and hate of the loved one, to arouse these emotions or their equivalents in us. We love the violence and evil because we acquiesce in them. No doubt these emotions are despicable, but no doubt the emotions aroused by the spectacle of what Oedipus had done were despicable also. The doctor who tamed the legend of Oedipus and rechristened it a complex only found out very late what the Christian world had known all along: when there are guilt and filth in the human psyche, the only possible remedy is to cast them out.

III

This essay has dealt only with the analysis of Joe Christmas as a modern tragic protagonist. It has hardly mentioned the many other excellences of the novel *Light in August,* leaving completely out of consideration the tragic situations of Joanna Burden and Hightower, who are also classic examples of the tragedy of isolation, strongly complementing the situation of Christmas. This study does not bring up the very skillfully handled elements of humor or comic relief, nor even mention by name Lena Grove, who is Faulkner's equivalent of the Shakespearian norm of humanity. There is no mention of Byron Bunch, who is as surely a comic hero as Christmas is a tragic one. But they are not properly matter for the subject of this essay.

Tradition tells us that the Greeks demanded that each trilogy submitted in the great dramatic contests be accompanied by an outrageous and lewd satyr-play, which preferably would burlesque the very elements and events just presented as tragedy. Perhaps some such comic relief is essential. After the human emotions have endured all they can, after the catharsis, something has to sustain us until we can touch down on earth again. Perhaps this is the explanation of the bawdy, almost folksy humor of the Lena-Byron episode in the last chapter of *Light in August,* so often dismissed with bewilderment or anger as an artistic botch. The direct experience of pity and terror is a little like being caught up in a cyclone, or, to use another metaphor, like being at the heart of what goes on in a thermonuclear explosion. In contemplating the question "When will I be blown up?" the author of *Light in August* has always been willing to risk a small side bet on mankind. This risk and this faith are also a part of the tragic paradox. The Greeks knew, as did the Elizabethans after them, that once the mushroom cloud has blown away and the fallout has ceased to fall, there is always that continuing residue of humanity. It, as the author would no doubt say, will endure.

Past as Present: *Absalom, Absalom!*

by Hyatt Waggoner

Absalom, Absalom! has no close precedent, even in Faulkner's own works. Hindsight suggests now that much in modern fiction, and in modern opinion, should have prepared us for it, but it is not really surprising that most of the early reviewers were bewildered. Like *The Waste Land, Absalom* has many voices but no official, sanctioned Voice. The voices in it speak from many points of view, none of them removed from the criticism of irony. *Absalom* demonstrated once more Faulkner's artistic courage. . . .

The complications of the telling can be clarified somewhat if we think of the basic story—Sutpen, from his early youth through the death of his remaining son and half-Negro daughter—as having not one but several narrative frames. The telling of the story by Quentin to Shreve—and partly later by Shreve to Quentin—makes the frame which encloses all the others. But this telling and retelling is based on versions of the same story, or of parts of it, given to Quentin by Miss Rosa and father; and father's version is based in large part on a version given him by his father, who got it in part from Sutpen himself. Since in Quentin's version each of these people speaks in his own voice, often at great length and circumstantially, with unintended revelation of himself in the process, what we have in effect is a series of frames, one within the other, like the picture of a picture containing a picture, and so on.

The outer frame, the telling of the story within the present of the novel—not the present of the first chapter, which is a memory of a day some four months before—takes place in Quentin's college room at Harvard in January 1910. At first Quentin is alone, reliving in memory that afternoon in Miss Rosa's house and the later talk of Sutpen by his father. Then Shreve comes in and together they go over the story once more, with Shreve doing much of the talking, basing his version on what Quentin has already told him and using his imagination to fill the gaps.

Reprinted with permission from *William Faulkner: From Jefferson to the World* by Hyatt Waggoner (Lexington: University of Kentucky Press, 1959), pp. 148, 153-69.

When they come to Bon's part of the story they are in perfect agreement, though about Bon and his motives and character they know less than about anyone else. Finally they go to bed and Quentin relives in memory once more the evening with Miss Rosa at the Sutpen house of which he has already told Shreve. This Shreve-Quentin frame is the largest and most distant of the frames.

In the first chapter, then, we begin where memory intersects the past at a point very close to the present, with Quentin becoming actively involved in the story whose general outline he has known for as long as he can remember. Almost at once we move back into the more distant past with Miss Rosa, without however being allowed to forget the present (now already past) in which Quentin sits in the stifling room and listens. Then this frame, this telling, is replaced by a frame supplied by father's account of Sutpen and his speculations on the meaning of the letter he gives Quentin. Again we move back and forth between past and present —the present of the telling, which is already past by the time we are able to identify it. Then the absoluteness of this frame too is destroyed and we see father's telling of the story as only another version, and not without its distortions. Shreve and Quentin talking in their college dormitory room now supply the frame to replace Miss Rosa in her "office" and father on the gallery. Miss Rosa's inadequacy as interpreter—her bias—has been apparent all along, and now it becomes clear that some of father's interpretations and speculations too are unacceptable: ". . . neither Shreve nor Quentin believed that the visit affected Henry as Mr. Compson seemed to think. . . ." But on another matter, "maybe this was one place where your old man was right." As the frames are shifted and the implicit distortions discovered, we see the motive for the continual retelling. Each new version is a part of the search in which Quentin and Shreve involve the reader, the search for a truth beyond and behind distortion.

So the past has to be continually reinterpreted; and each reinterpretation becomes a part of the accumulating past; a part even of the past which it attempts to interpret. A knowledge of the end supplies the motive for the search for the beginning: the earliest part of the story—Sutpen's boyhood and young manhood before he came to Jefferson—is retold by Quentin, as his father had told him, in response to Shreve's reaction to Miss Rosa's completed story of the "demon." Perhaps the demon could be understood if we knew what made him as he was. So the telling circles in on the story from a different angle—Sutpen's own account, multiply filtered, of his past and his intentions. The motive for the retellings, the reinterpretations, each of which adds new facts as well as a new perspective and makes necessary a reinterpretation of the facts already known, is constant, and it supplies the organizing principle of the novel.

Shreve's role as interpretive listener and finally as partial narrator is crucial. By the time we discover his presence we are more than halfway through the book and we realize now that both Miss Rosa's telling and father's retelling are part of the past which Shreve and Quentin have rehearsed. Now a new frame, more distant from Sutpen, comes into focus. As father had been less intimately involved in the Sutpen story than Miss Rosa, so Shreve the Canadian is less involved than father. The movement is one of progressive disengagement, a moving outward from the center. Yet the parts of the story that Shreve retells are among the most vivid and circumstantial in the whole book. Shreve's imagination moves freely. His presence in the story makes possible the widest of the circling movements through which the subject is approached.

In one of his recapitulations, Shreve calls Sutpen, in a caricature of Miss Rosa's own words, "this Faustus, this demon, this Beelzebub . . . who appeared suddenly one Sunday with two pistols and twenty subsidiary demons," thus reducing Sutpen to ordinary size by his humorous exaggeration and offering an implicit comment on Miss Rosa's "demonizing." His humorous summary follows immediately after a recital calculated to make us feel the weight and at least the partial justice of Miss Rosa's terms. Shreve's presence in the book is one of the ways in which the tone is controlled.

Shreve puts Sutpen's whole story in another kind of perspective when he says, toward the end, " 'So he just wanted a grandson. . . . That was all he was after. Jesus, the South is fine, isn't it. It's better than the theater, isn't it. It's better than Ben Hur, isn't it.' " *Absalom* has been called Gothic and obsessive, but true Gothic cannot survive irony, and obsession does not admit criticism. Here the irony and the criticism are central. When Shreve speaks of "the money, the jack, that he (the demon) has voluntarily surrendered" his very language, even when he is not offering any explicit comment, provides a perspective that can come only with distance and that could not come from Quentin, who is part and product of what he is telling.

As Quentin and Shreve sit "in the now tomblike air,"

> the two of them creating between them, out of the rag-tag and bob-ends of old tales and talking, people who perhaps had never existed at all anywhere . . .

what emerges is substantially different from what would have emerged had there been no Shreve for Quentin to talk and listen to. In the context of the passage I have just quoted we don't know for sure that there *was* a dishonest lawyer who had private reasons for wanting Bon to come in contact with his father, Sutpen, much less that the reasons Shreve is giving for the posited lawyer's actions are the true ones. But we are ready now, prepared by the interchange between Quentin and Shreve, to speculate with them, to invent probable characters and fill in details to make the story, the given incomprehensible facts, plausible. This is one of the most extreme examples of the conjectural method of the whole search that Quentin and Shreve are engaged in; and it is made to seem natural [and] right because Shreve, who cannot be accused of excessive closeness to the material, offers the speculation.

In the last chapter Shreve's presence becomes decisive. He speaks for most readers when he says

> We don't live among defeated grandfathers and freed slaves . . . and bullets in the dining room table and such, to be always reminding us to never forget . . . a kind of entailed birthright father and son and father and son of never forgiving General Sherman. . . .

This would be a peculiar sort of comment for one of the two narrators to make at a climactic point if there were as little aesthetic distance in *Absalom* as some have said. In Shreve's definition of the difference between his own Canadian background and Quentin's Southern one there is an implied comment on Sutpen's story that Quentin would have been incapable of making. Not that Shreve is right and Quentin wrong, but that Shreve's is another, and clarifying, point of view. "You cant understand it," Quentin tells Shreve. "You would have to be born there." To which a comment Shreve makes later, on another matter, could serve as a partial reply: "The South. Jesus. No wonder you folks all outlive yourselves by years and years and years."

And it is Shreve who at the end offers the prediction that "the Jim Bonds are going to conquer the western hemisphere" and asks Quentin why he hates the South. Shreve adds distance, controlling irony, to a story that otherwise might be obsessive or too shrill. If his final question to Quentin is, perhaps, somewhat unprepared for, so that we may find the ironic effect a little forced at this point, nevertheless he discharges his crucial function in the story with wonderful economy. His point of view is not the final one because there is no final one explicitly stated anywhere in the book. There are only other points of view and the implications of the form of the whole.

In the absence of chronologically related plot as the controlling factor, the relations of points of view govern the order of the chapters. Chapter One is Miss Rosa's. Miss Rosa lives in the past, in the cherishing of her hatred and her frustration. Quentin is restive as he listens, not only because of the heat, and partly discounts what she tells him. Her view of the past is simple, moralistic, and, to Quentin, quite incredible. For her Sutpen was an evil man, satanic, with no redeeming qualities.

The next three chapters are Quentin's father's. His point of view is that of the interested but emotionally uninvolved rational observer. Unlike Miss Rosa, father is impressed by the mystery of human action and frequently confesses himself baffled in his search for understanding. If he is biased in any way it is slightly in Sutpen's favor, partly because the town condemned Sutpen and father is an iconoclast who has little respect for conventional opinion, partly because much of his information he got from his father, who was Sutpen's one friend in the community, the only one willing to defend him against outraged public opinion.

Chapter Five is Miss Rosa's again. We are now prepared for a verbatim report of a part of what she said to Quentin that afternoon. Miss Rosa, it is clearer now, not only hates Sutpen but judges him from a point of view not wholly distinct from his own. Sutpen's actions destroyed not only his "design"—his plan for his life, his purpose—but hers. She shares, it begins to appear, both his racial and his class prejudices, and she hates him chiefly because he destroyed for her that social eminence, respectability, and security which it was the aim of his design to secure for himself and his posterity. Yet though we recognize and allow for her obsessive hatred, we learn much from her account that we should not otherwise know, and we cannot entirely discount her judgment.

Chapter Six is Shreve's retelling of what Quentin has told him of what Quentin's father has told Quentin. Shreve keeps calling Miss Rosa "Aunt Rosa": he does not quite understand and he is not concerned to try to master the details of Southern kinship ties and class etiquette. He sees "this old dame," Miss Rosa, and her tale without any of Quentin's painfully mixed feelings, simply with astonishment verging on incredulity. The snow on Shreve's overcoat sleeve suggests the distance from which he views this tale which began for us in the "long still hot weary" afternoon when Quentin sat with Miss Rosa. And Shreve himself, with his ruddy vitality, contrasts sharply with the other narrators—with the passive Quentin and with Miss Rosa herself, whose very existence seems a mere "disturbance" of the dust of that "dead September afternoon."

Parts of Sutpen's story have been told and retold now from points of view both hostile and friendly or neutral, by narrators within his own culture, and again from a point of view entirely external. How did he view himself? What would be added to our knowledge of him and his motivations if we could share his own self-awareness? Chapter Seven gives us Sutpen's story, the first part of it largely in a paraphrase of his own statements and some of it in his own words, as he told it to Quentin's grandfather—and as grandfather told it to father and father told it to Quentin and Quentin told it to Shreve: there is no certainty even in *ipsissima verba,* no possibility of getting back to "the thing in itself" of Sutpen's consciousness.

Sutpen saw himself alternately in the role of innocence betrayed and the role of a man who had made some mistake in adding a row of figures. Grandfather does not question his self-evaluation, simply passes it on. We are given almost no reason and very little opportunity,

Sutpen's self-view

within the early part of this chapter, to question Sutpen or to step outside his frame of reference. The poor child who had been turned away from the door of the rich man's house conceived a design for his life calculated to put him in a position where he could never again be humiliated by anyone. Since he could see that the rewards in life went to the "courageous and shrewd" and since, though he felt sure he had courage, he had failed in his design, he must have made a mistake, a miscalculation somewhere. What could it be?

Toward the end of the chapter there is, not negative moral judgment and certainly not Miss Rosa's hatred of Sutpen, but a kind of neutral clarification of Sutpen's own story offered in the comments of Quentin prompted by the interruptions of Shreve. Quentin interprets the "design" as essentially "getting richer and richer" and the innocence as a kind of moral obtuseness:

> that innocence which believed that the ingredients of morality were like the ingredients of pie or cake and once you had measured them and balanced them and mixed them and put them into the oven it was all finished and nothing but pie or cake could come out.

Quentin's father, on whose report Quentin is drawing here, sees Sutpen as "fogbound by his own private embattlement of personal morality" but he seems to accept Sutpen's idea that his design was created solely for the "vindication" of "that little boy who approached that door fifty years ago and was turned away." He gives us Sutpen's climactic question to grandfather without indicating that he thinks we should have to redesign it to make it ask another question, with different assumptions in it, before we could answer it:

> You see, I had a design in my mind. Whether it was a good or a bad design is beside the point; the question is, Where did I make the mistake in it. . . .

Most of the material of this chapter comes ultimately from grandfather, who was not only Sutpen's "advocate" but the only one in Jefferson who knew about the past which had shaped him to be what he was. Since this report of Sutpen's history has the additional advantage, if "inside knowledge" is an advantage, of resting on Sutpen's own self-awareness, it constitutes an effective foil to the "demonizing" of Miss Rosa, through whom we first met Sutpen.

Chapter Eight is Bon's chapter, his story (and Henry's, but chiefly his) as interpreted sympathetically by Shreve and Quentin. Shreve is no longer amused, ironic. He has been drawn into the tale now: this is a part he can feel, thinks he can understand. And for the first time he and Quentin are in complete agreement in their interpretive reconstructions. It no longer matters who is speaking: each is capable of taking up where the other left off, completing the other's thought. This is the most direct and circumstantial segment of the whole tale. It might be called interpretation by immersion, or by empathy. It penetrates Bon's consciousness to discover his point of view, reporting his experiences in detail, complete with imaginary conversations for which there is no warrant in the literally known facts. In place of Miss Rosa's bald summaries of Sutpen's whole career, mingled with moral judgments, we have here a detailed "realistic" rendering of the qualitative aspects of a few of Bon's experiences. There is no certainty, of course, that Shreve and Quentin are right in the details of their reconstruction. They are biased, for one thing, being young like Bon and easily aroused to sympathy by the spectacle which the idea of him presents. And they are relatively uninformed, for another thing; there are some very crucial facts that they cannot know for sure, such as when Bon told Henry, if in fact he did tell him, that he was not only his half-brother but was part Negro. Yet the reader is led by the circumstantial solidity of this chapter to feel more certain that this sympathetic account of Bon is correct than he is of any other interpretation he has encountered so far in the book.

Chapter Nine presents what might be called a general perspective on the whole tale. We are beyond the uniquely biased views of those who were closest to Sutpen. Two things happen at this point. First, Quentin and Shreve come into the foreground of the picture explicitly as narrators. No longer merely voices speaking to us in the words of the past, chiefly through direct and indirect quotation, they now appear as preservers of a past which must in some degree be created in order to be preserved. We are told more of Quentin's immediate sensations than we have been told before. The afternoon in Miss Rosa's house when she talked to Quentin in the office seems far away, as though it were as remote in time as in space. Miss Rosa is dead, and we recall from her tale chiefly a sense of the "victorious dust" that her recital made Quentin think of at the time. All those able to speak from direct knowledge of Sutpen are now gone; all that remains is the mutual creative remembering of Quentin and Shreve.

The second thing that happens is that, as the appearance of objectivity evaporates, the "facts" come back into focus and we move out again from subjective to objective. We learn for the first time in this last chapter what Quentin experienced that night when he went with Miss Rosa to Sutpen's decaying mansion. Everything before this has been hearsay, rumor, conjecture, hypothesis, or, at best, biased accounts of matters of fact. Here we are in the presence of something that we know "really happened," the terrible culmination of the Sutpen story. We are in a position to understand and to respond emotionally and imaginatively. Quentin does not need to theorize, or even create an atmosphere. The bare, elliptical, subjective record, the fragmentary memory, of what happened that night is enough. Without what has preceded the record would be meaningless. We now see that Quentin had to prepare Shreve for this direct confrontation with the living past; that any literal-minded insistence on "sticking to the facts" would have made it impossible for these facts, the only ones connected with Sutpen that Quentin can be absolutely sure of from personal experience, to convey any meaning.

Though Quentin's meeting with Henry is the one thing in the novel which may conceivably justify a charge of pointless mystification—why are we not told what Quentin learns from Henry?—yet I think the bareness of this climactic episode suggests its own justification. This meeting was a confrontation with a flesh-and-blood ghost. Here is proof that the past is "real" (though not yet, for Quentin at the time, explicable). This is the shock that motivates the search for understanding. In giving us the incident only in the barest outline, Faulkner is following the Jamesian formula of making the reader imagine. By the time we come to the episode in the book we have plenty of material for the imagination to work with. We discover, better than if we were told, that the past is still alive, still with us, demanding to be understood.

We end, in this last chapter, sharing Quentin's and Shreve's certainty about just two other matters of the first importance: that Sutpen brought his destruction upon himself, and that Bon asked only for recognition. But the first of these certainties rests upon the second, and the second is itself "certain" only if we either decide to trust Quentin and Shreve to be right or if we have so far shared their imaginative adventure as to arrive with them at the same conclusion. It is, at any rate, beyond proof. The whole meaning of Sutpen's history hangs on this leap of the imagination.

If Shreve and Quentin are right in their sympathetic estimate of Bon, then the immediate cause of the tragic events that resulted in the failure of Sutpen's design was his refusal to recognize his part-Negro son. Bon, Shreve and Quentin both believe, would have given up Judith and gone away if he had had any sign at all from his father, even the most private and minimal acknowledgment of their relationship. Shreve and Quentin cannot be sure that they are right. If they are wrong and Bon was a conscienceless extortioner, then the failure of Sutpen's design was caused not by moral failure but, as he himself thought, by ignorance, by the simple fact of his not knowing when he married her that Bon's mother was part Negro.

The title of the book, with its Biblical allusion, supports the hypothesis of Shreve and Quentin. Sutpen would not say "My son" to Bon as David said it to Absalom even after Absalom's rebellion. And different as he was from his father, Henry acted in the end on the same racist principle, killing Bon finally to prevent not incest but miscegenation. One meaning of *Absalom,* then, is that when the Old South was faced with a choice it could not avoid, it chose to destroy itself rather than admit brotherhood across racial lines.

But the theme is broader and deeper than the race problem which serves as its vehicle and embodiment. Sutpen was a cold and ruthless man motivated by a driving ambition to be his own god. His intelligence and courage won him a measure of success, but his pride destroyed him. In Martin Buber's contemporary terminology, for Sutpen other people were objects to be manipulated, related to him in an "I-it" relation. He not only never achieves, he never once even approaches, an "I-Thou" relation. Sutpen was the new man, the post-Machiavellian man consciously living by power-knowledge alone, refusing to acknowledge the validity of principles that he cannot or will not live by and granting reality to nothing that cannot be known with abstract rational clarity. He lives by a calculated expediency.

Sutpen the rationalist and positivist would have agreed with a pronouncement in a recent book-length attack on the Christianity of Eliot and other modern writers, that "Progress for the whole human race would be, if not inevitable, at least highly probable, if a sufficient majority of people were trained to use their reasoning power on their general experience, as a scientist is trained to use his reasoning power on his special experience." [1] Sutpen of course was not so much interested in the progress of "the whole human race" as he was in the progress of Sutpen, but there the difference ends. When he came to grandfather to review his life he was concerned to discover not which of his actions had been morally right and which wrong but where he had made the mistake which kept them from being, as modern scienteers would say, "effective." "Whether it was a good or a bad design is beside the point." When he put away Bon's mother, his first wife, on discovering her taint of Negro blood, he did so, he told grandfather later, because he found her "unsuitable to his purpose"—that is, ineffective for the forwarding of his intelligently conceived plan. Later he could calculate no advantage to be gained by recognizing Bon as his son, and he was not one to be moved by the incalculable. There is point as well as humor in Shreve's characterization of him as Faustus. He is also related to Ahab and Ethan Brand.

The total form of the novel implies the ultimate reason for the failure of Sutpen's design. Considered as an integral symbol the form of *Absalom* says that reality is unknowable in Sutpen's way, by weighing, measuring, and calculating. It says that without an "unscientific" act of imagination and even of faith—like Shreve's and Quentin's faith in Bon—we cannot know the things which are most worth knowing. Naturally Sutpen failed in his design, and naturally he could not imagine where his error had been. His error had been ultimately, of course, in the moral sense, that he had always treated people as things. Even Bon falls into the same error when he tries to use Judith as a lever to move Sutpen [in order] to get recognition.

[1] Kathleen Nott, *The Emperor's Clothes* (Bloomington: Indiana University Press, 1955), p. 5.

Absalom also has implications about the nature and role of history that are worthy of further thought. Quentin's effort to understand Sutpen is an attempt to interpret all history, man's history. Quentin encounters two conflicting modes of interpretation, is satisfied by neither, and creates, with Shreve, a third that has some of the features of both.

Miss Rosa's interpretation epitomizes the traditional views with which Quentin has grown up. This "demonizing," this interpretation in terms of inflexible moral judgment, does not, to his mind, explain: the past remains incredible and unreal. Nor is he satisfied by his father's view that there is no meaning at all in history, that the only proper response is to call it a mystery that we are "not meant to understand." Father is as close to nihilism here as he was in *The Sound and the Fury*. Quentin is unable to choose between Miss Rosa's belief that Southern history was God's punishment of the South, and of herself in particular—precisely for *what* she is unable to imagine—and father's denial of any intelligibility.

The view that he and Shreve together work out has in common with these two views more than its tragic cast. Implicitly—and unlike Miss Rosa's and father's views, the final one in the book is wholly implicit—they find room for moral judgment: Sutpen's hubris, his narrow rationalism, his lack of love, all these are descriptions that imply the relevance of moral judgment. But Quentin and Shreve do not categorize Sutpen as simply a "bad" man: they know that to do so is to substitute judgment for explanation. With father they feel the mystery of human life, but they are not satisfied cynically to give up the effort to understand. The view in terms of which they operate is that of classical-Christian tragedy, at once Greek and Biblical: history contains both God's judgment and man's decision, both necessity and freedom, and it has sufficient intelligibility for our human purposes. But its meaning is neither given nor entirely withheld. It must be achieved, created by imagination and faith. Historical meaning is a construct.

Such a view of history contrasts sharply with Marxist and "scientific" theories of history, but it has much in common with the best historiography of the thirties and of our own time. It has in it something of the historical relativism of the school of Beard and Becker. Becker's presidential address to the American Historical Association in 1931 criticized simplistic notions of historical "fact." Robinson's "new history," more than a decade older than *Absalom,* had been an attack on "scientific" history. More recently, Herbert Butterfield's essays on the philosophy of history, in *History and Human Relations* and *Christianity and History,* are written in terms of assumptions perfectly consistent with those that are operative in *Absalom.* Oscar Handlin's recent *Chance or Destiny: Turning Points in American History* brilliantly displays the interpretive possibilities which a creative search like that of Quentin and

Shreve may offer. As a novel built from the clash of conflicting views of history, *Absalom* seems to me as relevant now as when it was written.

No doubt *Absalom* gets its chief effect as a novel from our sense that we are participating in its search for the truth. *Absalom* draws us in, makes us share its creative discovery, as few novels do. The lack of an authoritative voice puts a greater burden on us as readers than we may want to bear. Faulkner ran this risk when he wrote it. He has had to wait long for a just appreciation of its greatness. Few readers were ready for it in the thirties. But if we can and will bear our proper burden as readers we shall find the rewards correspondingly great.

Absalom is the novel not denying its status as fiction but positively enlarging and capitalizing upon it. It appropriately closes Faulkner's period of most rapid and successful productivity with a full-scale thematic exploration of what had been implied in all the major works so far: that fiction is neither lie nor document but a kind of knowledge which has no substitute and to which there is no unimaginative shortcut. Adding to this the implication that fiction is not unique in its dependence upon imagination and the necessary deviousness of its strategy, it suggests a view of life that Faulkner was to make increasingly explicit in later works.

History and the Sense of the Tragic: *Absalom, Absalom!*

by Cleanth Brooks

Absalom, Absalom!, in my opinion the greatest of Faulkner's novels, is probably the least well understood of all his books. The property of a great work, as T. S. Eliot remarked long ago, is to communicate before it is understood, and *Absalom, Absalom!* passes this test triumphantly. It has meant something very powerful and important to all sorts of people, and who is to say that, under the circumstances, this something was not the thing to be said to that particular reader? . . .

Harvey Breit's sympathetic introduction to the Modern Library edition provides a useful—because it is not an extreme—instance of the typical misreading that I have in mind. Mr. Breit writes:

> It is a terrible Gothic sequence of events, a brooding tragic fable. . . . Was it the "design" that had devoured Sutpen and prevented him from avowing the very thing that would have saved the design? Was it something in the South itself, in its social, political, moral, economic origins that was responsible for Sutpen and for all the subsequent tragedy? Quentin can make no judgment: Sutpen himself had possessed courage and innocence, and the same land had nourished men and women who had delicacy of feeling and capacity for love and gifts for life.

These are questions which the typical reader asks. Shreve, the outsider, implies them. But it is significant that Quentin does not ask them. The questions are begged by the very way in which they are asked, for, put in this way, the questions undercut the problem of tragedy (which is the problem that obsesses Quentin). They imply that there is a social "solution." And they misread Sutpen's character in relation to his society and in relation to himself.

It is the quality of Sutpen's innocence that we must understand if we are to understand the meaning of his tragedy, and if we confuse it with innocence as we ordinarily use the term or with even the typical American "innocence" possessed by, say, one of Henry James's young heiresses as

Condensed from *William Faulkner* by Cleanth Brooks (New Haven: Yale University Press, 1954), pp. 295-322.

she goes to confront the corruption of Europe, we shall remain in the dark. Sutpen will be for us, as he was for Miss Rosa, simply the "demon" —or, since we lack the justification of Miss Rosa's experience of personal horror, we shall simply appropriate the term from her as Shreve, in his half-awed, half-amused fashion, does.

Faulkner has been very careful to define Sutpen's innocence for us. "Sutpen's trouble," as Quentin's grandfather observed, "was innocence." And some pages later, Mr. Compson elaborates the point: "He believed that all that was necessary was courage and shrewdness and the one he knew he had and the other he believed he could learn if it were to be taught." It is this innocence about the nature of reality that persists, for Sutpen "believed that the ingredients of morality were like the ingredients of pie or cake and once you had measured them and balanced them and mixed them and put them into the oven it was all finished and nothing but pie or cake could come out." That is why Sutpen can ask Quentin's grandfather, in his innocence, not "Where did I do wrong" but "Where did I make the mistake . . . what did I do or misdo . . . whom or what injure by it to the extent which this would indicate? I had a design. To accomplish it I should require money, a house, a plantation, slaves, a family—incidentally of course, a wife. I set out to acquire these, asking no favor of any man."

This is an "innocence" with which most of us today ought to be acquainted. It is par excellence the innocence of modern man, though it has not, to be sure, been confined to modern times. One can find more than a trace of it in Sophocles' Oedipus, and it has its analogies with the rather brittle rationalism of Macbeth, though Macbeth tried to learn this innocence by an act of the will and proved to be a less than satisfactory pupil. But innocence of this sort can properly be claimed as a special characteristic of modern man, and one can claim further that it flourishes particularly in a secularized society.

The society into which Sutpen rides in 1833 is not a secularized society. That is not to say that the people are necessarily "good." They have their selfishness and cruelty and their snobbery, as men have always had them. Once Sutpen has acquired enough wealth and displayed enough force, the people of the community are willing to accept him. But they do not live by his code, nor do they share his innocent disregard of accepted values. Indeed, from the beginning they regard him with deep suspicion and some consternation. These suspicions are gradually mollified; there is a kind of acceptance; but as Quentin tells Shreve, Sutpen had only one friend, Quentin's grandfather, General Compson, and this in spite of the fact that the society of the lower South in the nineteenth century was rather fluid and that class lines were flexible. Men did rise in one generation from log cabins to great landed estates. But the past was important, blood was important, and Southern society thought of itself as traditional.

That Sutpen does remain outside the community comes out in all sorts of little ways. Mr. Compson describes his "florid, swaggering gesture" with the parenthetical remark: "yes, he was underbred. It showed like this always, your grandfather said, in all his formal contacts with people." . . . Yet though Sutpen's manners have been learned painfully, Sutpen has complete confidence in them. "He may have believed that your grandfather or Judge Benbow might have done it a little more effortlessly than he, but he would not have believed that anyone could have beat him in knowing when to do it and how."

Mr. Compson is not overrating the possession of mere manners. More is involved than Miss Rosa's opinion that Sutpen was no gentleman, for Sutpen's manners indicate his abstract approach to the whole matter of living. Sutpen would seize upon "the traditional" as a pure abstraction —which, of course, is to deny its very meaning. For him the tradition is not a way of life "handed down" or "transmitted" from the community, past and present, to the individual nurtured by it. It is an assortment of things to be possessed, not a manner of living that embodies certain values and determines men's conduct. The fetish objects are to be gained by sheer ruthless efficiency. (Sutpen even refers to "my schedule.") Thorstein Veblen would have understood Sutpen's relation to traditional culture. . . . The New York robber baron's acquiring a box at the opera did not usually spring from a love of music, and one is tempted to say that Sutpen's unwillingness to acknowledge Charles Bon as his son does not spring from any particular racial feeling. Indeed, Sutpen's whole attitude toward the Negro has to be reinspected if we are to understand his relation to the Southern community into which he comes.

It would seem that the prevailing relation between the races in Jefferson is simply one more of the culture traits which Sutpen takes from the plantation community into which he has come as a boy out of the mountains of western Virginia. Sutpen takes over the color bar almost without personal feeling. His attitude toward the Negro is further clarified by his attitude toward his other part-Negro child, Clytie.[1] Mr. Compson once casually lets fall the remark that Sutpen's other children "Henry and Judith had grown up with a negro half sister of their own." The context of Mr. Compson's remarks makes it perfectly plain that Henry and Judith were well aware that Clytie was indeed their half-sister, and that Clytie was allowed to grow up in the house with them. This fact in itself suggests a lack of the usual Southern feeling about Negroes. . . .

After Sutpen has returned from the war, Clytie sits in the same room with Judith and Rosa and Sutpen and listens each evening to the sound of Sutpen's voice. When Sutpen proposes to Rosa, he begins, " 'Judith, you and Clytie—' and ceased, still entering, then said, 'No, never mind. Rosa will not mind if you both hear it too, since we are short for time.' " Clytie is accepted naturally as part of the "we." She can be so accepted because acceptance on this level does not imperil Sutpen's "design." But

[1] For the Sutpen genealogy see below, Appendix III.

acceptance of Charles Bon, in Sutpen's opinion, would. For Sutpen the matter is really as simple as that. He does not hate his first wife or feel repugnance for her child. He does not hate just as he does not love. His passion is totally committed to the design. . . .

As for slavery, Sutpen does not confine himself to black chattel slavery. He ruthlessly bends anyone that he can to his will. The white French architect whom he brings into Yoknapatawpha County to build his house is as much a slave as any of his black servants: Sutpen hunts him down with dogs when he tries to escape.

The trait that most decisively sets Sutpen apart from his neighbors in this matter of race is his fighting with his slaves. Sutpen is accustomed to stripping to the waist and fighting it out with one of his slaves, not with rancor, one supposes, and not at all to punish the slave, but simply to keep fit—to prove to himself and incidentally to his slaves that he is the better man. Some of Sutpen's white neighbors come to watch the fights as they might come to watch a cockfight. But it is significant that they come as to something extraordinary, a show, an odd spectacle; they would not think of fighting with their own slaves. To Miss Rosa, Sutpen's sister-in-law, the ultimate horror is that Sutpen not only arranges the show but that he enters the ring himself and fights with no holds barred —not even eye-gouging.

Sutpen is not without morality or a certain code of honor. He is, according to his own lights, a just man. As he told Quentin's grandfather with reference to his rejection of his first wife:

> suffice that I . . . accepted [my wife] in good faith, with no reservations about myself, and I expected as much from [her parents]. I did not [demand credentials] as one of my obscure origin might have been expected to do. . . . I accepted them at their own valuation while insisting on my part upon explaining fully about myself and my progenitors: yet they deliberately withheld from me one fact which I have reason to know they were aware would have caused me to decline the entire matter.

But Sutpen, as he tells General Compson, "made no attempt to keep . . . that [property] which I might consider myself to have earned at the risk of my life . . . but on the contrary I declined and resigned all right and claim to this in order that I might repair whatever injustice I might be considered to have done [in abandoning my wife and child] by so providing for" them.

Moreover, Sutpen is careful to say nothing in disparagement of his first wife. Quentin's grandfather comments upon "that morality which would not permit him to malign or traduce the memory of his first wife, or at least the memory of the marriage even though he felt that he had been tricked by it." It is Sutpen's innocence to think that justice is enough—that there is no claim that cannot be satisfied by sufficient money payment. Quentin imagines his grandfather exclaiming to Sutpen: "What kind of abysmal and purblind innocence would that have been which someone told you to call virginity? what conscience to trade with which would have warranted you in the belief that you could have bought immunity from her for no other coin but justice?"

Sutpen thinks of himself as strictly just and he submits all of his faculties almost selflessly to the achievement of his design. His attitude toward his second wife conforms perfectly to this. Why does he choose her? For choose he does: he is not chosen—that is, involved with her through passion. The choice is calculated quite coldbloodedly (if, to our minds, naïvely and innocently). Ellen Coldfield is not the daughter of a planter. She does not possess great social prestige or beauty and she does not inherit wealth. But as the daughter of a steward in the Methodist church, she possesses in high degree the thing that Sutpen most obviously lacks—respectability. Mr. Compson sees the point very clearly. He describes Mr. Coldfield as "a man with a name for absolute and undeviating and even Puritan uprightness in a country and time of lawless opportunity, who neither drank nor gambled nor even hunted." For Sutpen, respectability is an abstraction like morality: you measure out so many cups of concentrated respectability to sweeten so many measures of disrespectability—"like the ingredients of pie or cake."

The choice of a father-in-law is, in fact, just as symbolically right: the two men resemble each other for all the appearance of antithetical differences. Mr. Coldfield is as definitely set off from the community as is Sutpen. With the coming of the Civil War, this rift widens to an absolute break. Mr. Coldfield denounces secession, closes his store, and finally nails himself up in the attic of his house, where he spends the last three years of his life. No more than Sutpen is he a coward; like Sutpen, too, his scheme of human conduct is abstract and mechanical. "Doubtless the only pleasure which he had ever had . . . was in [his money's] representation of a balance in whatever spiritual counting-house he believed would some day pay his sight drafts on self-denial and fortitude."

This last is Mr. Compson's surmise; but I see no reason to question it or to quarrel with the motive that Mr. Compson assigns for Coldfield's objection to the Civil War: "not so much to the idea of pouring out human blood and life, but at the idea of waste: of wearing out and eating up and shooting away material in any cause whatever." Mr. Coldfield is glad when he sees the country that he hates obviously drifting into a fatal war, for he regards the inevitable defeat of the South as the price it will pay for having erected its economic edifice "not on the rock of stern morality but on the shifting sands of opportunism and moral brigandage."

Some critics have been so unwary as to assume that this view of the Civil War is one that the author would enjoin upon the reader, but William Faulkner is neither so much of a Puritan nor so much of a materialist as is Mr. Coldfield. The truth of the matter is that Mr. Coldfield's morality is simply Sutpen's turned inside out. Faulkner may or may not have read Tawney's *Religion and the Rise of Capitalism;* but on the evidence of *Absalom, Absalom!* he would certainly have understood it.

Sutpen is further defined by his son, Charles Bon. Bon is a mirror image, a reversed shadow of his father. Like his father, he suddenly appears out of nowhere as a man of mystery: "a personage who in the remote Mississippi of that time must have appeared almost phoenix-like, fullsprung from no childhood, born of no woman and impervious to time." Like his father, Bon has an octoroon "wife," whom he is prepared to repudiate along with his child by her. Like his father, he stands beyond good and evil. But Bon is Byronic, rather than the go-getter, spent, rather than full of pushing vitality, sophisticated, rather than confidently naïve.

Sutpen is the secularized Puritan; Bon is the lapsed Roman Catholic. Whereas Sutpen is filled with a fresh and powerful energy, Bon is world-weary and tired. Bon is a fatalist, but Sutpen believes in sheer will: "anyone could look at him and say, *Given the occasion and the need, this man can and will do anything.*" Bon possesses too much knowledge; Sutpen on the other hand is "innocent." The one has gone beyond the distinction between good and evil; the other has scarcely arrived at that distinction. The father and the son define the extremes of the human world: one aberration corresponds to—and eventually destroys—the other. The reader is inclined to view Bon with sympathy as a person gravely wronged, and he probably agrees with Quentin's interpretation of Bon's character: that Bon finally put aside all ideas of revenge and asked for nothing more than a single hint of recognition of his sonship. Faulkner has certainly treated Bon with full dramatic sympathy—as he has Sutpen, for that matter. But our sympathy ought not to obscure for us Bon's resemblances to his father, or the complexity of his character. Unless we care to go beyond Quentin and Shreve in speculation, Charles Bon displays toward his octoroon mistress and their son something of the cool aloofness that his father displays toward him. If he is the instrument by which Sutpen's design is wrecked, his own irresponsibility (or at the least, his lack of concern for his own child) wrecks his child's life. We shall have to look to Judith to find responsible action and a real counter to Sutpen's ruthlessness.

These other children of Sutpen—Judith and Henry—reflect further light upon the character of Sutpen—upon his virtues and upon his prime defect. They represent a mixture of the qualities of Sutpen and Coldfield. Judith, it is made plain, has more of the confidence and boldness of her father; Henry, more of the conventionality and the scruples of his maternal grandfather. It is the boy Henry who vomits at the sight of his father, stripped to the waist in the ring with the black slave. Judith watches calmly. And it is Judith who urges the coachman to race the coach on the way to church.

Henry is, of the two, the more vulnerable. After Sutpen has forbidden marriage between Bon and Judith and during the long period in which Henry remains self-exiled with his friend Bon, he is the one tested to the limit by his father's puzzling silence and by his friend's fatalistic passivity. But he has some of his father's courage, and he has what his father does not have: love. At the last moment he kills, though he kills what he loves and apparently for love. It is the truly tragic dilemma. Faulkner has not chosen to put Henry's story in the forefront of the novel, but he has not needed to do so. For the sensitive reader the various baffles through which that act of decision reaches us do not muffle but, through their resonance, magnify the decisive act.

Henry's later course is, again, only implied. We know that in the end —his last four years—he reverted to the course of action of his grandfather Coldfield, and shut himself up in the house. But there is a difference. This is no act of abstract defiance and hate. Henry has assumed responsibility, has acted, has been willing to abide the consequences of that action, and now, forty years later, has come home to die.

If it is too much to call Henry's course of action renunciation and expiation, there is full justification for calling Judith's action just that. Judith has much of her father in her, but she is a woman, and she also has love. As Mr. Compson conjectures:

> And Judith: how else to explain her but this way? Surely Bon could not have corrupted her to fatalism in twelve days. . . . No: anything but a fatalist, who was the Sutpen with the ruthless Sutpen code of taking what it wanted provided it were strong enough. . . . [Judith said] *I love, I will accept no substitute; something has happened between him and my father; if my father was right, I will never see him again, if wrong he will come or send for me; if happy I can be I will, if suffer I must I can.*

It is Judith who invites Charles Bon's octoroon mistress to visit Bon's grave. It is Judith who, on his mother's death, sends to New Orleans for Bon's son and tries to rear him. Some years later she also tries to free him (as Quentin conjectures) by promising to take care of his Negro wife and child if he will go to the North to pass as white, and Quentin imagines her saying to him: "Call me Aunt Judith, Charles." But Quentin's conjectures aside, we know that Judith did take him into the house when he was stricken with yellow fever, and that she died nursing him. The acknowledgment of blood kinship is made; Sutpen's design is repudiated; the boy, even though he has the "taint" of Negro blood, is not turned away from the door.

Both Henry's action, the violent turning away from the door with a bullet, and Judith's, the holding open the door not merely to Bon, her fiancé, but literally to his part-Negro son, are human actions, as Sutpen's actions are not. Both involve renunciation, and both are motivated by love. The suffering of Henry and Judith is not meaningless, and their very capacity for suffering marks them as having transcended their father's radical and disabling defect. . . .

One must not alter the focus of the novel by making wisdom won through suffering the issue. But the consequences entailed upon Judith and Henry have to be mentioned if only to discourage a glib Gothicizing of the novel or forcing its meaning into an overshallow sociological interpretation.

Miss Rosa feels that the Coldfields are all cursed; and certainly the impact of Sutpen upon her personally is damning: she remains rigid with horror and hate for forty-three years. But it is Miss Rosa only who is damned. Judith is not damned; nor am I sure that Henry is. Judith and Henry are not caught in an uncomprehending stasis. There is development: they grow and learn at however terrible a price. . . .

Sutpen, as has been pointed out, never learns anything; he remains innocent to the end. As Quentin sees the character: when Charles Bon first comes to his door, Sutpen does not call it "retribution, no sins of the father come home to roost; not even calling it bad luck, but just a mistake . . . just an old mistake in fact which a man of courage and shrewdness . . . could still combat if he could only find out what the mistake had been." I have remarked that Sutpen's innocence is peculiarly the innocence of modern man. For like modern man, Sutpen does not believe in Jehovah. He does not believe in the goddess Tyche. He is not the victim of bad luck. He has simply made a "mistake." He "had been too successful," Mr. Compson tells Quentin; his "was that solitude of contempt and distrust which success brings to him who gained it because he was strong instead of merely lucky." . . . Sutpen resembles the modern American, whose character, as Arthur M. Schlesinger has put it, "is bottomed on the profound conviction that nothing in the world is beyond [his] power to accomplish." [2] Sutpen is a "planner" who works by blueprint and on a schedule. He is rationalistic and scientific, not traditional, not religious, not even superstitious.

We must be prepared to take such traits into account if we attempt to read the story of Sutpen's fall as a myth of the fall of the Old South. Unless we are content with some rather rough and ready analogies, the story of the fall of the house of Sutpen may prove less than parallel. The fall of the house of Compson as depicted in *The Sound and the Fury* is also sometimes regarded as a kind of exemplum of the fall of the old aristocratic order in the South, and perhaps in some sense it is. But the breakup of these two families comes from very different causes, and if we wish to use them to point a moral or illustrate a bit of social history, surely they point to different morals and illustrate different histories.

[2] "What Then Is the American, This New Man," *American Historical Review,* XLVIII (1943), 244.

Mr. Compson, whose father, General Compson, regarded Sutpen as a "little underbred," has failed through a kind of overrefinement. He has lost his grip on himself; he has ceased finally to believe in the values of the inherited tradition. He is a fatalist and something of an easy cynic. His vices are diametrically opposed to those of Thomas Sutpen, and so are his virtues. . . . Indeed, Sutpen is at some points more nearly allied to Flem than he is to the Compsons and the Sartorises. Like Flem, he is a new man with no concern for the past and has a boundless energy with which to carry out his aggressive plans.

Yet to couple Sutpen with Flem calls for an immediate qualification. Granting that both men subsist outside the community and in one way or another prey upon the community, Sutpen is by contrast a heroic and tragic figure. He achieves a kind of grandeur. Even the obsessed Miss Rosa sees him as great, not as petty and sordid. His innocence resembles that of Oedipus (who, like him, had been corrupted by success and who put his confidence in his own shrewdness). His courage resembles that of Macbeth, and like Macbeth he is "resolute to try the last." . . .

Up to this point we have been concerned with the character of Thomas Sutpen, especially in his relation to the claims of the family and the community. We have treated him as if he were a historical figure, but of course he is not. More than most characters in literature, Thomas Sutpen is an imaginative construct, a set of inferences—an hypothesis put forward to account for several peculiar events. For the novel *Absalom, Absalom!* does not merely tell the story of Thomas Sutpen, but dramatizes the process by which two young men of the twentieth century construct the character Thomas Sutpen. Fascinated by the few known events of his life and death, they try, through inference and conjecture and guesswork, to ascertain what manner of man he was. The novel, then, has to do not merely with the meaning of Sutpen's career but with the nature of historical truth and with the problem of how we can "know" the past. The importance of this latter theme determines the very special way in which the story of Sutpen is mediated to us through a series of partial disclosures, informed guesses, and constantly revised deductions and hypotheses.

Young Quentin Compson, just on the eve of leaving Mississippi for his first year at Harvard, is summoned by Miss Rosa Coldfield and made to listen to the story of her wicked brother-in-law, Thomas Sutpen. Sutpen had been a friend of Quentin's grandfather, General Compson, and as Quentin waits to drive Miss Rosa out to Sutpen's Hundred after dark, as she has requested, Quentin's father tells him what he knows about the Sutpen story.

Nobody had really understood the strange events that had occurred at Sutpen's Hundred—the quarrel between Thomas Sutpen and Henry, the disappearance of Henry with his friend Charles Bon, the forbidding of the marriage between Judith and Bon, and later, and most sensational of all, Henry's shooting of his friend Charles Bon at the very gates of Sutpen's Hundred in 1865. Mr. Compson makes a valiant effort to account for what happened. What evidently sticks in his mind is the fact that Charles Bon had an octoroon mistress in New Orleans. Presumably Judith had told General Compson or his wife about finding the octoroon's picture on Charles Bon's dead body. But in any case the visit, at Judith's invitation, of the woman to Charles Bon's grave would have impressed the whole relationship upon General Compson and upon his son, Mr. Compson. Mr. Compson thinks that it was the fact of the mistress that made Thomas Sutpen oppose Bon's marriage to his daughter, but that Henry was so deeply committed to his friend that he refused to believe what his father told him about Bon's mistress, chose to go away with Charles, and only at the very end, when Charles Bon was actually standing before his father's house, used the gun to prevent the match.

It is not a very plausible theory. For, though it could account for Sutpen's opposition to Bon, it hardly explains Henry's violent action, taken so late in the day. Mr. Compson does the best that he can with this aspect of the story and says: "[Henry] loved grieved and killed, still grieving and, I believe, still loving Bon, the man to whom he gave four years of probation, four years in which to renounce and dissolve the other marriage, knowing that the four years of hoping and waiting would be in vain." But Mr. Compson has to concede that, after all, "it's just incredible. It just does not explain. . . . Something is missing."

Quentin's other informant about the Sutpens is Miss Rosa Coldfield, Sutpen's sister-in-law. Miss Rosa clearly does not understand what happened. She exclaims that "Judith's marriage [was] forbidden without rhyme or reason," and her only theory for accounting for the murder is that Sutpen was a demon, and as a demon, dowered his children with a curse which made them destroy themselves. Even Judith evidently did not know why her marriage was forbidden nor did she know why her brother killed Charles Bon. After the murder and Henry's flight, Judith tells Mrs. Compson, the General's wife, that the war will soon be over now because "they [the Confederate soldiers] have begun to shoot one another." The remark indicates her bafflement as well as her despair.

By the time we have reached the end of section 5—that is, halfway through the book—we have been given most of the basic facts of the Sutpen story but no satisfactory interpretation of it. We know the story of Sutpen's life in the Mississippi community pretty much as the community itself knew it, but the events do not make sense. The second half of the book may be called an attempt at interpretation. When section 6 opens, we are in Quentin's room at Harvard and Quentin is reading a letter from his father telling about the death of Miss Rosa Coldfield. From this time on until past midnight, Quentin and Shreve discuss the story of Sutpen and make their own conjectures as to what actually happened. In this second half of the book there are, to be sure, further disclosures about Sutpen, especially with reference to his early life before he came to Mississippi. Sutpen, it turns out, had once told the story of his early life to General Compson, and his information had been passed on to Quentin through Mr. Compson. As Shreve and Quentin talk, Quentin feeds into the conversation from time to time more material from his father's and grandfather's memory of events, and one very brilliant scene which he himself remembers: how, hunting quail on a gray autumn day, he and his father came upon the graves in the Sutpen family graveyard and his father told him the touching story of Judith's later life. But as the last four sections of the book make plain, we are dealing with an intricate imaginative reconstruction of events leading up to the murder of Charles Bon—a plausible account of what may have happened, not what necessarily did happen.

If the reader reminds himself how little hard fact there is to go on—how much of the most important information about the motivation of the central characters comes late and is, at best, vague and ambiguous—he will appreciate how much of the story of Sutpen and especially of Sutpen's children has been spun out of the imaginations of Quentin and Shreve.

Absalom, Absalom! is, indeed, from one point of view a wonderful detective story—by far the best of Faulkner's several flirtations with this particular genre. It may also be considered to yield a nice instance of how the novelist works, for Shreve and Quentin both show a good deal of the insights of the novelist and his imaginative capacity for constructing plausible motivations around a few given facts. . . . Most important of all, however, *Absalom, Absalom!* is a persuasive commentary upon the thesis that much of "history" is really a kind of imaginative construction. The past always remains at some level a mystery, but if we are to hope to understand it in any wise, we must enter into it and project ourselves imaginatively into the attitudes and emotions of the historical figures. . . .

To note that the account of the Sutpens which Shreve and Quentin concoct is largely an imaginative construct is not to maintain that it is necessarily untrue. Their version of events is plausible, and the author himself—for whatever that may be worth—suggests that some of the scenes which they palpably invented were probably true: e.g., "the slight dowdy woman . . . whom Shreve and Quentin had . . . invented" and who was probably "true enough." But it is worth remarking that we do not "know," apart from the Quentin-Shreve semifictional process, many events which a casual reader assumes actually happened.

To provide some illustrations: Charles Bon's telling Henry "So it's the miscegenation, not the incest, which you cant bear" is a remark that rests upon no known fact. It is a conjecture, though a plausible one. Again, Bon's agonized waiting for his father to give him the merest hint of a father's recognition and Bon's comment that this was all that Sutpen needed to do to stop his courtship of Judith are both surmises made by Quentin and Shreve. So too is the scene in which the boys imagine the visit of Bon and Henry to New Orleans and hear Bon's mother's bitter question, "So she [Judith] has fallen in love with him," and listen to her harsh laughter as she looks at Henry. The wonderfully touching scene in which Judith asks Charles Bon's son to call her "Aunt Judith" is presumably an imaginative construction made by Quentin.

One ought to observe in passing that in allowing the boys to make their guesses about what went on, Faulkner plays perfectly fair. Some of their guesses have the clear ring of truth. They are obviously right. On the other hand, some are justified by the flimsiest possible reasoning. For example, notice Shreve's argument that it was Henry, not Bon, who was wounded at the battle of Shiloh.

One of the most important devices used in the novel is the placing of Shreve in it as a kind of sounding board and mouthpiece. By doing so, Faulkner has in effect acknowledged the attitude of the modern "liberal," twentieth century reader, who is basically rational, skeptical, without any special concern for history, and pretty well emancipated from the ties of family, race, or section. . . .

Shreve teases Quentin playfully and even affectionately, but it is not mere teasing. When Shreve strikes a pose and in his best theatrical manner assigns a dramatic speech to Wash, Faulkner, in one of his few intrusions as author, observes: "This was not flippancy. . . . It too was just that protective coloring of levity behind which the youthful shame of being moved hid itself." . . .

The last sections of the novel tell us a great deal about Shreve's and Quentin's differing attitudes toward history and of their own relation to history. Shreve has been genuinely moved by the story of Sutpen. For all of his teasing, he is concerned to understand, and late in the evening he says to Quentin: "Listen. I'm not trying to be funny, smart. I just want to understand it if I can and I dont know how to say it better. Because it's something my people haven't got." And though he cannot suppress his bantering tone in alluding to the Southern heritage—it is "a kind of entailed birthright . . . of never forgiving General Sherman, so that forevermore as long as your children's children produce children you wont be anything but a descendant of a long line of colonels killed in Pickett's charge"—Shreve's question is seriously put. What is it that Quentin as a Southerner has that Shreve does not have? It is a sense of the presence of the past, and with it, and through it, a personal access to a tragic vision. For the South has experienced defeat and guilt, and has an ingrained sense of the stubbornness of human error and of the complexity of history. The matter has been recently put very well in C. Vann Woodward's *The Burden of Southern History:* "The experience of evil and the experience of tragedy," he writes, "are parts of the Southern heritage that are as difficult to reconcile with the American legend of innocence and social felicity as the experience of poverty and defeat are to reconcile with the legends of abundance and success." [3]

In remarking on how little of hard fact one has to go on, we should bear in mind particularly the question of Bon's Negro blood and of his kinship to Henry. Quentin says flatly that "nobody ever did know if Bon ever knew Sutpen was his father or not." Did anyone ever know whether Bon knew that he was part Negro? In their reconstruction of the story, Shreve and Quentin assume that Bon was aware that he was Henry's part-Negro half-brother (though a few pages earlier Quentin and Shreve assume that Bon did not know that he had Negro blood). If in fact Bon did have Negro blood, how did Shreve and Quentin come by that knowledge? As we have seen, neither Judith nor Miss Rosa had any inkling of it. Nor did Mr. Compson. Early in the novel he refers to Bon's "sixteenth part negro son." Since Bon's mistress was an octoroon, his son could be one-sixteenth Negro only on the assumption that Charles Bon was of pure white blood—and this is evidently what Mr. Compson does assume. Mr. Compson, furthermore, knows nothing about Bon's kinship to Henry.

The conjectures made by Shreve and Quentin—even if taken merely as conjectures—render the story of Sutpen plausible. They make much more convincing sense of the story than Mr. Compson's notions were able to make. And that very fact suggests their probable truth. But are they more than plausible theories? Is there any real evidence to support the view that Bon was Sutpen's son by a part-Negro wife? There is, and the way in which this evidence is discovered constitutes another, and the most decisive, justification for regarding *Absalom, Absalom!* as a magnificent detective story. Precisely what was revealed and how it was revealed are worth a rather careful review.

In the course of his conversation with Quentin, Shreve objects that Mr. Compson "seems to have got an awful lot of delayed information awful quick, after having waited forty-five years." Quentin confirms the fact that his father *had* got delayed information—had got it from Quentin himself—had got it, indeed, the day after "we" (that is, Quentin and Miss Rosa) had gone out to Sutpen's Hundred. A little later, when Quentin tells Shreve of Sutpen's long conversation with General Compson about his "design" and about the "mistake" that Sutpen had made in trying to carry it out, Shreve asks Quentin whether General Compson had then really known what Sutpen was talking about. Quentin answers that General Compson had not known; and Shreve, pressing the point, makes Quentin admit that he himself "wouldn't have known what anybody was talking about" if he "hadn't been out there and seen Clytie." The secret of Bon's birth, then, was revealed to Quentin on that particular visit. Shreve's way of phrasing it implies that it was from Clytie that Quentin had got his information, but, as we shall see, it is unlikely that Clytie

[3] Baton Rouge: Louisiana State University Press, 1960, p. 21.

was Quentin's informant. In any case, when Shreve puts his question about seeing Clytie, he did not know that another person besides Clytie and her nephew was living at Sutpen's Hundred.

Miss Rosa has sensed that "something"—she does not say *someone*—was "living hidden in that house." When she and Quentin visit Sutpen's Hundred, her intuition is confirmed. The hidden something turns out to be Henry Sutpen, now come home to die. Presumably, it was from Henry Sutpen that Quentin learned the crucial facts. Or did he? Here again Faulkner may seem to the reader either teasingly reticent or, upon reflection, brilliantly skillful.

We know from the last section of the book that after Miss Rosa had come down from the upstairs room with her "eyes wide and unseeing like a sleepwalker's," Quentin felt compelled to go up to that room and see what was there. He does go, though Faulkner does not take us with him into the room. He descends the stairs, walks out of the house, overtakes Miss Rosa, and drives her home. Later that night, however, after he has returned to his own home and is lying sleepless, he cannot—even by clenching his eyelids—shut out his vision of the bed with its yellowed sheets and its yellowed pillow and the wasted yellow face lying upon it, a face with closed, "almost transparent eyelids." As Quentin tosses, unable to erase the picture from his eyes, we are vouchsafed one tiny scrap of his conversation with Henry, a conversation that amounts to no more than Quentin's question "And you are—?" and Henry's answer that he is indeed Henry Sutpen, that he has been there four years, and that he has come home to die. How extended was the conversation? How long did it last? Would Henry Sutpen have volunteered to a stranger his reason for having killed Charles Bon? Or would Quentin Compson, awed and aghast at what he saw, put such questions as these to the wasted figure upon the bed? We do not know and Faulkner—probably wisely—has not undertaken to reconstruct this interview for us. (It is possible, of course, that Henry did tell Miss Rosa why he had killed Bon and that Miss Rosa told Quentin in the course of their long ride back to Jefferson.)

At all events, the whole logic of *Absalom, Absalom!* argues that *only* through the presence of Henry in the house was it possible for Quentin —and through Quentin his father and Shreve and those of us who read the book—to be made privy to the dark secret that underlay the Sutpen tragedy.

At the end of the novel Shreve is able to shrug off the tragic implications and resume the tone of easy banter. His last comment abounds with the usual semi-sociological clichés: the Negroes "will bleach out again like the rabbits and the birds. . . . In a few thousand years, I who regard you will also have sprung from the loins of African kings." Though the spell of the story has been powerful enough to fire his imagination and involve all his sympathies, he is not personally committed, and we can see him drawing back from the tragic problem and becoming again the cheery, cynical, common-sense man of the present day. In the long perspective of history, how few issues really matter! The long perspective is antihistorical: make it long enough and any "sense of history" evaporates. Lengthen it further still and the human dimension itself evaporates.

From his stance of detachment, Shreve suddenly, and apropos of nothing, puts to Quentin the question "Why do you hate the South?" And Quentin's passionate denial that he hates it tells its own story of personal involvement and distress. The more naïve reader may insist on having an answer: "Well, does he hate it?" And the response would have to be, I suppose, another question: "Does Stephen Daedalus hate Dublin?" Or, addressing the question to Stephen's creator, "Did James Joyce hate Ireland?" The answer here would surely have to be yes and no. In any case, Joyce was so obsessed with Ireland and so deeply involved in it that he spent his life writing about it.

At this point, however, it may be more profitable to put a different question. What did the story of Sutpen mean to Quentin? Did it mean to him what it has apparently meant to most of the critics who have written on this novel—the story of the curse of slavery and how it involved Sutpen and his children in ruin? Surely this is to fit the story to a neat and oversimple formula. Slavery was an evil. But other slaveholders avoided Sutpen's kind of defeat and were exempt from his special kind of moral blindness.

What ought to be plain, in any event, is that it is Henry's part in the tragic tale that affects Quentin the most. Quentin had seen Henry with his own eyes and Henry's involvement in slavery was only indirect. Even Henry's dread of miscegenation was fearfully complicated with other issues, including the problem of incest. In view of what we learn of Quentin in *The Sound and the Fury,* the problem of incest would have fascinated him and made him peculiarly sensitive to Henry's torment. Aside from his personal problem, however, Sutpen's story had for Quentin a special meaning that it did not have for Shreve.

The story embodied the problem of evil and of the irrational: Henry was beset by conflicting claims; he was forced to make intolerably hard choices—between opposed goods or between conflicting evils. Had Henry cared much less for Bon, or else much less for Judith, he might have promoted the happiness of one without feeling that he was sacrificing that of the other. Or had he cared much less for either and much more for himself, he might have won a cool and rational detachment, a coign of vantage from which even objections to miscegenation and incest would appear to be irrational prejudices, and honor itself a quaint affectation whose saving was never worth the price of a bullet. Had Henry been not necessarily wiser, but simply more cynical or more gross or more selfish, there would have been no tragedy. . . . But Shreve is measurably closer to the skepticism and detachment that allow modern man to dismiss the irrational claims from which Quentin cannot free himself and which he honors to his own cost.

The reader of *Absalom, Absalom!* might well follow Quentin's example. If he must find in the story of the House of Sutpen something that has special pertinence to the tragic dilemmas of the South, the aspect of the story to stress is not the downfall of Thomas Sutpen, a man who is finally optimistic, rationalistic, and afflicted with elephantiasis of the will. Instead, he ought to attend to the story of Sutpen's children.

The story of Judith, though muted and played down in terms of the whole novel, is one of the most moving that Faulkner has ever written. She has in her the best of her father's traits. She is the stout-hearted little girl who witnesses without flinching scenes which force poor Henry to grow sick and vomit. She is the young woman who falls in love with a fascinating stranger, the friend of her brother, who means to marry him in spite of her father's silent opposition, and who matches her father's strength of will with a quiet strength of her own. She endures the horror of her fiancé's murder and buries his body. She refuses to commit suicide; she keeps the place going for her father's return. Years later it is Judith who sees to it that Bon's mistress has an opportunity to visit his grave, who brings Bon's child to live with her after his mother's death and, at least in Quentin's reconstruction of events, tries to get the little boy to recognize her as his aunt and to set him free, pushing him on past the barriers of color. When she fails to do so, she still tries to protect him. She nurses him when he sickens of yellow fever, and she dies with him in the epidemic. She is one of Faulkner's finest characters of endurance —and not merely through numb, bleak stoicism but also through compassion and love. Judith is doomed by misfortunes not of her making, but she is not warped and twisted by them. Her humanity survives them.

Because Henry knew what presumably Judith did not know, the secret of Bon's birth, his struggle—granted the circumstances of his breeding, education, and environment—was more difficult than Judith's. He had not merely to endure but to act, and yet any action that he could take would be cruelly painful. He was compelled to an agonizing decision. One element that rendered tragic any choice he might make is revealed in Henry's last action, his coming home to die. One might have thought that after some forty years, Henry would have stayed in Mexico or California or New York or wherever he was, but the claims of locality and family are too strong and he returns to Sutpen's Hundred.

Absalom, Absalom! is the most memorable of Faulkner's novels—and memorable in a very special way. Though even the intelligent reader may feel at times some frustration with the powerful but darkly involved story, with its patches of murkiness and its almost willful complications of plot, he will find himself haunted by individual scenes and episodes, rendered with almost compulsive force. He will probably remember vividly such a scene as Henry's confrontation of his sister Judith after four years of absence at war—the boy in his "patched and faded gray tunic," crashing into the room in which his sister stands clutching against her partially clothed nakedness the yellowed wedding dress, and shouting to her: "Now you cant marry him . . . because he's dead. . . . I killed him." Or there is Miss Rosa's recollection of the burial of Charles Bon. As she talks to Quentin she relives the scene: the "slow, maddening rasp, rasp, rasp, of the saw" and "the flat deliberate hammer blows" as Wash and another white man work at the coffin through the "slow and sunny afternoon," with Judith in her faded dress and "faded gingham sunbonnet . . . giving them directions about making it." Miss Rosa, who has never seen Bon alive and for whom he is therefore a fabulous creature, a mere dream, recalls that she "tried to take the full weight of the coffin" as they carried it down the stairs in order "to prove to myself that he was really in it."

There is the wonderful scene of Thomas Sutpen's return to Sutpen's Hundred, the iron man dismounting from his "gaunt and jaded horse," saying to Judith, "Well, daughter," and touching his bearded lips to her forehead. There follows an exchange that is as laconically resonant as any in Greek tragedy: " 'Henry's not—?' 'No. He's not here.'—'Ah. And—?' 'Yes. Henry killed him.' " With the last sentence Judith bursts into tears, but it is the only outburst of which Judith is ever guilty.

The reader will remember also the scenes of Sutpen's boyhood and young manhood—perhaps most vivid of all of them, that in which the puzzled boy is turned away from the plantation door by the liveried servant. Sometimes the haunting passage is one of mere physical description: the desolate Sutpen burial ground with the "flat slabs . . . cracked across the middle by their own weight (and vanishing into the hole where the brick coping of one vault had fallen in was a smooth faint path worn by some small animal—possum probably—by generations of some small animal since there could have been nothing to eat in the grave for a long time) though the lettering was quite legible: *Ellen Coldfield Sutpen. Born October 9, 1817. Died January 23, 1863*." One remembers also the account of something that had taken place earlier in this same graveyard, when Bon's octoroon mistress, a "magnolia-faced woman a little plumper now, a woman created of by and for darkness whom the artist Beardsley might have dressed, in a soft flowing gown designed not to infer bereavement or widowhood . . . knelt beside the grave and arranged her skirts and wept," while beside her stood her "thin delicate child" with its "smooth ivory sexless face."

There is, too, the ride out to Sutpen's Hundred in the "furnace-breathed" Mississippi night in which Quentin shares his buggy with the frail and fanatical Miss Rosa, and smells her "fusty camphor-reeking shawl" and even her "airless black cotton umbrella." On this journey, as Miss Rosa clutches to her a flashlight and a hatchet, the implements of her search, it seems to Quentin that he can hear "the single profound suspiration of the parched earth's agony rising toward the imponderable and aloof stars." Most vivid of all is the great concluding scene in which Clytie, seeing the ambulance approaching to bear Henry away, fires "the monstrous tinder-dry rotten shell" of a house, and from an upper window defies the intruders, her "tragic gnome's face beneath the clean headrag, against a red background of fire, seen for a moment between two swirls of smoke, looking down at them, perhaps not even now with triumph and no more of despair than it had ever worn, possibly even serene above the melting clapboards."

These brilliantly realized scenes reward the reader and sustain him as he struggles with the novel; but it ought to be remembered that they are given their power by the way in which the novel is structured and thus constitute a justification of that peculiar structure. . . .

Absalom, Absalom! is in many respects the most brilliantly written of all Faulkner's novels, whether one considers its writing line by line and paragraph by paragraph, or its structure, in which we are moved up from one suspended note to a higher suspended note and on up further still to an almost intolerable climax. The intensity of the book is a function of the structure. The deferred and suspended resolutions are necessary if the great scenes are to have their full vigor and significance. Admittedly, the novel is a difficult one, but the difficulty is not forced and factitious. It is the price that has to be paid by the reader for the novel's power and significance. There are actually few instances in modern fiction of a more perfect adaptation of form to matter and of an intricacy that justifies itself at every point through the significance and intensity which it makes possible.

William Faulkner: The Hero in the New World

by R. W. B. Lewis

Faulkner is in many ways the most *American* of novelists—the writer who most fully subjected a complex and painful sense of life (which for the most part he shared with his European contemporaries) to the special pressure of a home-grown Southern American imagination. Out of such a process he constructed strangely new images of experience in an odd and baffling new world. I shall want to stress that native quality and explore that new world; but both may become clearer if we begin by reminding ourselves that no American novelist in decades, perhaps none ever, has been so highly esteemed abroad—has, in fact, been so often accommodated to and naturalized within the different cultures of very different countries.

In the developing Old World view, Faulkner was seen as providing images of a world a good deal older yet: a world with the very mark and feature of oldness upon it, a world like that of the Old Testament, seen in a certain exterior perspective. The radical novelty of the world Faulkner went on to imagine is measured by the radical antiquity, something deeper than time, of the world he inhabited or could persuasively be alleged to inhabit, during the first decade or so of his literary career.

Faulkner in the Old World

What Europeans have been saying to each other about Faulkner is an important element in their more general conversation about art and experience. It is as though a sort of *pax Faulkneriana* permitted them to cross national frontiers and discuss those larger issues, a common concern with which has made the writers of the second generation a distinct group. Nevertheless, Faulkner's reputation in Europe is of course inseparable from the literary conditions and intellectual tensions of each country; and, in the absence of a detailed sketch of those conditions, any account of his reputation must be incomplete and misleading. If this is true everywhere, it is especially true in France, where the popularity of Faulkner, which began in the middle 1930s (long before it did in America), reached phenomenal proportions both of sales and of admiration by the late '40s. French readers saw in Faulkner's work ingredients that Americans were temperamentally slow to recognize or to honor. For there is a certain impressive arrogance about French criticism and French taste; they are profoundly functional and spring from a wise if sometimes exasperating ability to identify the internal dialogue of French culture at any moment with the fundamental problems of mankind. Faulkner became thus a figure in the central debate of the aging generation in France—the debate between the Catholic writers on the one hand (Mauriac, Claudel, Jammes, and Bernanos), and their "demoralizing" adversaries on the other (Gide, and then Sartre and Camus). The debate concerned the questions of existence and salvation, of the degree of rationality in the universe and the degree of man's dependence upon it. This was the context in which Faulkner rose to eminence: a context indicated by the contentious title and paradoxical content of Sartre's play *Le Diable et le Bon Dieu* (1951), Sartre's own major effort in the picaresque vein with his own ironical version—in the person of *le diable,* a Renaissance adventurer—of the picaresque saint. Faulkner over the years has managed to appeal to both sides. He was first embraced by the devil's advocates, for Faulkner's earlier fiction gave a picture of human experience so seemingly nihilistic that the nonreligious or even antireligious writers found it extraordinarily authentic. The Christ imagery of his later work is more likely to attract the followers of *le bon dieu;* though Camus, who once extolled the splendid absurdity of Faulkner's novels, has recently (1957) and successfully adapted for the stage Faulkner's quasi-religious mystery drama, *Requiem for a Nun*—an enterprise that may itself offer a clue to Camus's personal evolution.

Camus remarked in *The Rebel* that the secret of modern Europe was that it no longer loved life; and a Europe unable to do so found in the Americans and especially in Faulkner a dramatic rendering that was at once an explanation of its cosmic distaste. Like St.-Exupéry, Faulkner seemed to be crying out that he hated his epoch; for not enough was being made, in those days, of Quentin Compson's tormented iterations at the close of *Absalom, Absalom!* (1936)—"I don't hate it! I don't hate it!" Missed, too, were the implications of the character of Dilsey in *The Sound and the Fury* and the structural suggestions of *As I Lay Dying* and *Light in August*—all symptoms of a buried, furious, indestructible bias toward life. But meanwhile the role assigned to Faulkner in Europe was large and momentous: the very type of the modern artist, combining violence and metaphysics, according to André Malraux; a writer whose accomplishment was "the resurrection of myths and the renewal of tragedy"; a novelist who had found the means to convey in narrative, as Jean-Jacques Mayoux said in 1948, the unbearable pressure of time as a "quality of existence." These were the grand and terrible themes exposed in Faulkner by French observers, at a moment when he was still looked upon at home (with several distinguished exceptions) as an artless and unnerving primitive, a writer of preposterous melodrama who was devoid of a single recognizable idea.

Sartre observed in 1939 that he loved Faulkner's art but hated his metaphysics. Faulkner wrote, according to Sartre, as though man were completely without a future, possessed only of a past; but he should write *as though* man might have a future. The glance was all backward in Faulkner; and human life (Sartre added, in an excellent image that could be illustrated from almost any page of Faulkner) appeared as a road watched despairingly as it flowed away, from the rear window of a moving car. Mme. C.-E. Magny made still more of the obsessive onslaughts on the baffling retreating past in *Absalom, Absalom!* and *The Sound and the Fury*. She pointed to a view of the human condition comparable to that of portions of the Old Testament—the condition of man prior to the Incarnation of truth that made history meaningful; the condition of man groping with awful pain through his own still undecipherable history. And Mme. Magny, writing at the close of the war, underlined the relevance of that sense of experience to a generation that was itself groping its way through the inexplicable horrors of the time. Faulkner ranked high among the prophets, Mme. Magny implied, for he had uncovered in his local South and its legends the outlines of a nearly worldwide myth of enormous tragic impact.

Perceptions of this kind and enlargements upon them have not been restricted to France, though nowhere else in Europe is the mind so engrossed in ultimate and universal considerations. Another and less hectic appraisal of the defeat imputed to Faulkner's fiction was recorded as early as 1935 by the erudite Italian critic Emilio Cecchi, in a general essay on Faulkner called "The Crisis of Barbarism." Cecchi, rather anticipating Sartre, said in substance that he loved Faulkner's art but hated the culture and society and manner of living it so accurately reflected. Cecchi offered a version, too, of Mme. Magny's thesis. Almost alone among European critics at the time, Cecchi had a real grasp of American cultural history, an understanding reinforced by a visit to American that Cecchi described in a little threnody called *America Amara* (*Bitter America*). His verdict on Faulkner is one that gently indicts the American scene while praising Faulkner's picture of it: the picture of a world without an illuminated conscience—without, at least (according to Cecchi), a specifically Christian conscience, and hence prone to collapse into pagan excesses and, by consequence, self-destroying remorse. It is an appealingly Florentine verdict, benign and not impatient, deriving from a gracious and learned commitment to classical moderation in all things, including the exercise of the specifically Christian conscience.

We discover, in short, in different countries and in the views of different critics (and a more complete survey would only confirm the fact), a developed impression of Faulkner in the '30s and '40s as the supreme contemporary artist of defeat, betrayal, and death; an impression greatly honored by a Western world that felt itself defeated and dead, that was yet fighting its own past in order to get out of it and beyond, and back to the shores of life. Faulkner appealed to all those whose picture of man was the one indicated in the title and contents of a book of poems by the Swedish lyricist Erik Lindegren: *Man Without a Way,* a volume whose new Swedish idioms and rhythms owed much to the novel Lindegren was then translating: Faulkner's *Light in August.* Lindegren is perhaps the most gifted Swedish poet of his time, and *Man Without a Way* was the germinating work of an entire literary generation (known, because of the time of its flowering, as "the Fortyists"). His excitement over Faulkner's language is all the more suggestive since it was precisely Faulkner's *language*—his use of the English language, that is—that prevented Faulkner from winning much acceptance in England. The English regarded Faulkner's verbal eccentricities in somewhat the way Italians of a traditionalist temper regarded the unconventional irregularities of Silone's prose. The irregularities of James Joyce, for the English, remained conventional ones: recognizable deviations from the known center, the only center; but Faulkner's idiom, which came from no center known to them, seemed simply unforgivably bad writing. His hot Southern American Protestant rhetoric fell on deaf Anglican ears, his "ideas" seemed extravagant and intrusive, and his recurrent expression of outrage appeared dubious to a country which was to wait another decade or so before producing its own race of angry young men. But in Sweden, Erik Lindegren was unencumbered by the legacy of classical English prose; and he was driven by a native and personal demonic fury. Faulkner's prose, which Lindegren wrestled with over the months while trying to break free from his own earlier and more conventional poetic style, acted at last as an explosive liberating agent. For the prose exactly suited Lindegren's theme: the baffled wandering of the individual, spun loose from any orbit, burdened by an unsharable secret, a dreadful memory, seeking communion as a means of life but expecting only death. It is the very theme of *Light in August;* or rather, it is half of that theme. The other half went unrecognized, while the Old World was paying Faulkner its tribute as the contriver of his generation's truest myth: the myth of modern man who had lost his way.

half the theme of Light in August

"The Bear": America Transcended

If, then, as several European critics suggested, Faulkner's novels and stories through, say, *The Hamlet* (1940) possess an atmosphere not unlike the Old Testament in its most tragic and baffled moments, we can perhaps take *Go Down, Moses* (1942)—and especially its longest and richest component, "The Bear"—as Faulkner's first venture into a world of light like that following the Incarnation. Faulkner is himself our warrant for so heady an analogy, though, before pursuing it, we should also remember that "The Bear" is a story about the American South in the 1880s when the frontier was rapidly disappearing; and the vividly invoked setting is the ground of the story's being and of all that it becomes. "The Bear" is a work in the tradition of Cooper and Twain; another tale of a boy growing up and growing wiser along the border between the civilized and the still unspoiled; and it partakes, too, of that even more widespread drama of American literature, the effort of youth to mature in the face of all the obstacles our culture has erected. In "The Bear" we meet Faulkner's first full-fledged hero in the old heroic meaning of the word; and he is a young man who quite self-consciously takes up carpentering, once he has accepted his peculiar moral mission, because

> if the Nazarene had found carpentering good for the life and ends He had assumed and elected to serve, it would be all right too for Isaac McCaslin. . . .

"The Bear" is a canticle or chant relating the birth, the baptism, and the early trials of Isaac McCaslin of Yoknapatawpha County in Mississippi. We get, moreover, *an* incarnation, if not *the* Incarnation. Or better, we get a re-incarnation; and we witness an act of atonement which may conceivably flower into a redemption.

"The Bear," consequently, is a pivotal work and the key to the whole of Faulkner's fiction: though perhaps only to the whole of it. Beginning with "The Bear," and there more emphatically than anywhere else, what is positive in human nature and the moral world envelops and surrounds what is evil. The corrupting and the destructive and the desperate have their ageless being in human experience, but here they become known to us exactly in their opposition, even their subordination, to the creative and the nourishing. "The Bear" thus presents us with just the sort of dramatic clarity that has seemed otherwise denied both to American and European writers for many a long decade. The highest reaches of modern literature, in fact, have often taken the form of an ultimate duplicity, the best account of the world that honest genius has been able to construct—the poetry of unresolved dualism, with every virtue and every value rendered instantly suspect by the ironic coexistence of its forceful contrary. Those splendid discords and artful confusions are the determining marks of Faulkner's earlier fiction. And that is why "The Bear" appears as pivotal; though persons permanently at home with contradictions and who listen happily to the endless "clangor and jangle of contrary tendencies" are likely to regard it as merely old-fashioned; and to regret it, the way *Billy Budd* is sometimes regretted, as a regression to lucidity. Certainly *Requiem for a Nun* and, much more so, *A Fable*—where the moral dilemma is dissolved under the pressure of a dismayingly naked New Testament allegory—are grounds for wondering whether the pivotal achievement of "The Bear" was not artistically too costly.

There were hints of the lucidity to come in the earlier novels as well. Several of the latter have been compared to Jacobean drama, and rightly: for they seem to project worlds wherein, as in the terrible world of John Webster, what is human or decent flickers uncertainly in a darkness charged with evil violence—the violence and darkness being the norm, the known and the knowable, and the measure of such pitiful virtue as stirs hopelessly to combat them. But even there, something more ancient and enduring than the observed wickedness seems to flow through the narrative and to reaffirm itself as it flows on into the future: something that, with a wry face, we have to call life itself. In "The Bear," however, the artistic and moral balance is tipped and the former situation reversed. What we discover first, along with Ike McCaslin, and what determines his *and* our subsequent judgments, is not strident evil, but an archetypal or ideal being. We sense, too, a cluster of virtues unambiguously present from the start, as qualities to be striven for, prizes to be won—and which, taken together, comprise what we may call the honorable.

It is the honorable that permeates the wilderness, scene of the main action and home of the main actors in the drama. Old Ben, the bear, patriarch of the wilderness, embodies the virtues in some undefined and magical way; and like Old Ben, the honorable exists as an ethical reality before the story opens, "before the boy was born"—as a glimpse of immortality. This reality is independent of shifting urban moral fashions; it is an ideal prior to civilization. But it is not an uncivilized ideal; its priority is logical rather than temporal; it is prior because it is ideal, not so much older as timeless. It has nothing to do with "primitivism," or with noble savagery, or even the American Adamic dream of unspoiled original innocence in the New World—nothing except this, that in Faulkner's handling of it the honorable emerges by a dialectical transformation, a "transvaluation" of that dream and that innocence: at the instant the falsehood is exposed and the existence of evil is acknowledged.

The humanly recognizable embodiment of the honorable in "The

Bear" is an action, a repeated ritual pattern of conduct: "the yearly rendezvous . . . the yearly pageant-rite of the old bear's furious immortality," the annual duel between the skilled hunters and the shaggy, tremendous, indomitable Old Ben. The duel is enacted within a solid set of conventions and rules, older than memory and faultlessly observed on both sides; the men *hunt* all other bears in the wilderness, but with Old Ben they engage rather in a kind of ritual dance. It is by participating in this ritual that the young hero, Isaac McCaslin, is reborn and receives, as it were, a sacramental blessing. That process is the substance of the first half of the story.

"The Bear" has a plot relatively simpler than some in Faulkner's earlier writings; but here again Faulkner has played weird tricks with the temporal ordering. He has concluded his tale, for instance, with an episode that occurs at a moment earlier in time than several episodes that have preceded it in the telling. The story is divided into five sections. But if we follow the direct temporal succession of the events in the life of Isaac McCaslin—noting in parenthesis the story's arrangement of them through the successive numbered sections—we come upon this personal history:

(Sections 1, 2, 3): A boy named Ike McCaslin grows up in Mississippi in the years after the Civil War. From the time he is ten, he accompanies his cousin Cass Edmonds and several of his home town's leading citizens, every year, on bear-hunting expeditions in the untamed wilderness north of the town. Ike begins to acquire some of the skill of the older men, and with them the severe masculine virtues that the solemn game of hunting can produce. In that game, the greatest and most honored rival (not enemy or prey) is an enormous and ancient bear known as Old Ben. During the boy's sixteenth year, Old Ben is at last killed by one of the men, Boon Hogganbeck, and a mongrel dog called Lion.

(Section 5): Two years later, the boy, now eighteen, comes back once more to the wilderness to find it no longer a wilderness. The old hunting lodge is gone, the group of hunters disbanded, and lumber companies have begun to invade and transform the forest. Ike encounters Boon Hogganbeck, who is lost and nearly hysterical in the new "civilized" era.

(Section 4): Three years later, when Ike is twenty-one, he comes into his inheritance of the land and the money that have been handed down through his father (Uncle Buck) from his grandfather, Carrothers McCaslin. But Ike decides to renounce his legacy, since he has previously discovered it tainted at the source by his grandfather's misdeeds. The latter had seduced and had a child by a Negro slave, Tomasina, who was probably his own daughter as well. That combination of incest and miscegenation represents for Ike the evil condition of the South, and its betrayal of moral possibility: a version of the human legacy of evil generally, from the "original sin" at the beginning of time; but deriving, in the New World, from the corrupting effects upon both parties to it of the institution of slavery. He determines to dissociate himself from his own particular corrupt legacy; and he continues to live a simple huntsman's life in or near the forest, basing his conduct on an emulation of Jesus. He takes up carpentering and marries the daughter of his partner. He has no children.

Thus the "real-life" career of Ike McCaslin, so far as we know it from the furtive disclosures of "The Bear." But keep in mind that the incidents of his twenty-first year and of his later years are given us—as Faulkner actually wrote his narrative—*before* we learn about the return to the woods, at eighteen, in the fifth and final section. Our question is with the relation between the chronological order and artistic order of the events, and the value of Faulkner's rearrangement.

No other American writer engages his readers as mercilessly as Faulkner; and except for those who fear and resent him on quite other grounds, readers of Faulkner can and do get an immense satisfaction from that participation with him that verges on the creative. But the aim of Faulkner's deliberate deformations is not finally aesthetic; he wants the reader to participate not in a creative act but in a moral act. He wants to define a moral experience of mythological proportions and of ambiguous reality: an aim that of necessity makes heavy demands on the reader. Conrad, for example, asks no less of us when he makes his arduous way through the thickets to release his prophetic myth of modern history in *Nostromo;* nor, to name a writer even closer in feeling to Faulkner, does Virgil in his myth of Roman history. In the *Aeneid,* the last event of the poem—the duel between Aeneas and Turnus—occurs many centuries before some of the events already described: the long course of Roman history across the centuries and up to the battle of Actium, as given in the preview by Anchises in Book VI and in the pictures engraved on the shield of Aeneas in Book VIII. In the *Aeneid,* of course, the chronologically later events appear explicitly as prophecies, almost as dreams. But that, I propose, is exactly the nature of the fourth section of "The Bear," with its narrative of Ike's twenty-first and later years.

The story begins in Ike's sixteenth year, the year he is to complete his rite of initiation. Till this moment, he has grasped the importance but not the meaning of the experience.

> It seemed to him that there was a fatality in it. It seemed to him that something, he didn't know what, was beginning; had already begun. It was like the last act on a set stage. It was the beginning of the end of something, he didn't know what except that he would not grieve. He would be humble and proud that he had been found worthy to be a part of it too or even just to see it too.

"The beginning of the end of something"—an end *and* a beginning, in fact: which is why Ike has reason to be humble and proud. For the drama he is engaged in is a vast drama of death and birth: the death of Old Ben, of Sam Fathers (Ike's foster-parent and tutor), of the dog Lion, of the wilderness and the companionship Ike had known there, of an entire world; and the birth or rebirth of Isaac McCaslin as the solitary re-incarnation of those dead and the lone witness to that world and its truth. This is what Ike is disciplined to perceive, as the story returns to the great year in section three. When Old Ben dies in that section, he dies metaphorically in childbirth. He has, indeed, many features in common with the "terrible mother" of heroic mythology; and in this context, the name of Sam Fathers, Ike's spiritual guide, is intrusively significant. It requires only a twist of the tongue to convert the story's title into "The Birth."

In the fourth section we find that it was also during Ike's sixteenth year, on a December night after the last bear hunt, that he solved the riddle of his family's history. The section begins with the sentence, ominously uncapitalized: "then he was twenty-one." The defining occasion of most of it is a conversation between Ike and his cousin Cass Edmonds in the plantation commissary on the date of Ike's legal coming of age. But, while the entire span of Ike's very long life is touched upon, it is the discoveries of his sixteenth year that account for the intensity of his speech and the resoluteness of his decision to reject his inheritance. With the conversation as foreground, those discoveries pass through Ike's memory like shadows on the wall behind—shadows themselves in a ghostly conversation; for they appear as remembered entries in the commissary ledgers, written in a question-and-answer style. The entries had been made decades earlier by Ike's uncle and his father, and they had been pieced together with amazement and horror by Ike five years before the present moment. Their language has the sparse, foreshortened quality of memory:

> [Uncle Buck:] *Eunice Bought by Father in New Orleans 1807 $650. Marrid to Thucydus 1809 Drownd in Crick Cristmas Day 1832*
> [Uncle Buddy:] *June 21th 1833 Drownd herself*
> [Uncle Buck:] *23 Jun 1833 Who in hell ever heard of a niger drownding himself*
> [Uncle Buddy:] *Aug 13th 1833 Drownd herself*

The motivation for Eunice's suicide is revealed only in its impact upon Ike's oddly mythopoeic imagination. It is up to us, collaborators in the hunt, to discover that Eunice had been the mistress of the grandfather, Carrothers McCaslin (Uncle Buck's "Father"), bought by him and—when she was pregnant by him with the child Tomasina—married off to another slave, Thucydus; and that Eunice drowned herself twenty-three years later when she realized that her daughter, too, had become pregnant by Carrothers McCaslin: by her own father, by Eunice's lover. For Ike, the tragic event has the formality of legend:

> . . . he seemed to see her actually walking into the icy creek on that Christmas day six months before her daughter's and her lover's (*Her first lover's,* he thought. *Her first*) child was born, solitary, inflexible, griefless, ceremonial, in formal and succinct repudiation of grief and despair who had already had to repudiate belief and hope

Ike has a shocking revelation of the literal fact of human brotherhood: Turl, the child Tomasina bears, and Jim, the child Turl later begets, are actually Ike's cousins, and have their rights in the legacy he renounces.

The first essential link between the two large parts I have been discussing—the first three sections taken together, and the fourth as their counterweight—is the near simultaneity of the death of Old Ben and the discovery of mixed blood and incest in the McCaslin clan. The fourth section of "The Bear" is not merely the further adventures of Isaac McCaslin. The harmony of the parts may be summarized in ancient formulas: the birth into virtue, and the vision of evil. Only the person adequately initiated can have the vision at all; and only the potency of the initiation enables the reborn individual to withstand the evil when it is encountered. The action in section four (the discovery and the renunciation) is made possible by the experience that preceded it; the ritual in the wilderness *contains,* implicitly, the decision in the commissary.

This leads to a somewhat more complex view of the relationship. It is true that the fourth section is contained within the sections that have the wilderness as their setting: the containment achieved when Faulkner brings his story back to the wilderness in the fifth and final section, returning to the life of Ike before he has reached the age of decision, returning to the atmosphere and the rhythms of the hunting world. The fifth section reverts to the style—relatively straightforward, though highly orchestrated and charged with autumnal splendor—of the first, second, and third sections; picking up that style where it had been left almost sixty pages before, and so enveloping and containing the very different style in between. We may illustrate by quoting from the last lines of section four and the first of section five, breaking in anywhere on the endlessly flowing matter of section four:

> . . . and on their wedding night she had cried and he thought she was crying now at first, into the tossed and wadded pillow, the voice coming from somewhere between the pillow and the cachinnation: 'And that's all. That's all from me. If this dont get you that son you talk about, it wont be mine': lying on her side, her back to the empty rented room, laughing and laughing
>
> He went back to the camp one more time before the lumber company moved in and began to cut the timber. Major de Spain himself never saw it again.

Faulkner has even gone to the extreme, as we notice here, of employing a single quotation mark in the conversations of the fourth section: the conventional sign of the speech contained within the speech—as against the double quotation mark elsewhere. It is the sort of device peculiarly trying for those not already persuaded by Faulkner; but it is an instance of his anxiety that we should recognize the mode of existence of that phase of the whole experience.

Its *mode* of existence is as important as its content. For what we are given in the fourth section is not so much a narrative of events that have happened, as an intense, translucent vision of the future. Its appearance between the third and fifth sections—between the episodes of Ike's sixteenth and eighteenth years—allows us to suppose that it is a dream, perhaps a dream that occurred during the year between. It is a true dream, to be sure, a true prophecy, issuing securely from the gates of horn, but passing before our eyes incidents that at the moment of perception exist only in a state of possibility. The sense of something not yet realized is carried in the prose itself. We are struck by the decrease in visibility. Against an immeasurably vast setting, actions and dialogue have curiously hazy outline. Sentences spray out in all directions, almost never (within our hearing) reaching their probable periods. Everything is potential, unfinished, pushing toward a never-arrived-at completion. But the experience is not a *mere* possibility, in the sense that something quite different is equally possible. According to Faulkner, events become real not when they occur but only when they are looked back on in memory; and what Ike is mostly doing in section four is, precisely, examining his memory of certain things. The section, that is, asserts the eventual reality of its content by dreaming how it will eventually be remembered.

Beyond that, the larger implications of the dream are such that they can—or should—be presented only through a liquid mist of prophecy. To explain this we must retrench a bit and take account of the native boundaries within which Ike acts out his own backwoods drama; for the force of those larger implications are derived from Faulkner's artistic conversion of specifically American materials. Like *Moby Dick,* "The Bear" is most in tune with perennial rhythms of experience when it is most solidly American; and if we close in on the particular portion of America that provides its scene, we recognize its significant prototype in *Huckleberry Finn.* Both are narratives of boys growing up in the nineteenth century South; both record a sense of the troubled kinship between white and black, though Twain does not carry that kinship literally into the blood streams. Both suggest an ironic reversal of the conventional morality that legitimizes social injustice—though, again, Twain's humor is in charge of his outrage and prevents him from intruding lectures on social legislation and warnings to the government up north, as it protects Huck himself from a pretentious awareness of his own virtue. But the central insight Faulkner shares with Twain is one that both share with many another American writer: a sense of the fertile and highly ambiguous possibility of moral freedom in the New World. In the Mississippi wilderness of the 1880s, Faulkner has projected another image of the ethically undefined: undefined, like the river in *Huckleberry Finn,* because not yet fixed in the implicitly hypocritical conventions of civilized life. Insofar as "The Bear" is a story about death, it is about the death of the frontier world and its possibility, of the new unspoiled area where a genuine and radical moral freedom—a kind of original innocence—could again be exercised.

But to say so without fundamental qualification would be to ascribe to Faulkner a view of innocence and the New World almost exactly opposite the one finally revealed in "The Bear." It would be to forget how often Faulkner has engaged in the ritual slaughter of the animal innocent—how he has penetrated the veil of innocence to arrive at the tragic fact, performing an operation on the hopeful world of his time similar to the one Hawthorne felt impelled to perform a century ago on Emerson. A part of the history Ike McCaslin rehearses for Cass Edmonds, on his twenty-first birthday, seems to echo the cheerful story Emerson and his colleagues used to tell each other:

> He [God] made the earth first and peopled it with dumb creatures, and then He created man to be His overseer on the earth and to hold suzerainty over the earth and the animals on it in His name, not to hold for himself and his descendants inviolable title forever . . . and all the fee He asked was pity and humility and sufferance and endurance. . . . He watched it. And let me say it. Dispossessed of Eden. Dispossessed of Canaan and those who . . . devoured their ravished substance ravished in turn again and then snarled in what you call the old world's worthless twilight over the old world's gnawed bones, blasphemous in His name until He used a simple egg to discover to them a new world where a nation of people could be founded in humility and pity and sufferance and pride of one another. . . .

The identification of the New World as a divinely offered second chance for humanity after the first opportunity had been so thoroughly muffed in the Old World—the association of America with Eden—has never been more eloquently made. But Faulkner's hero is examining the myth precisely to see where it went wrong; Faulkner and Isaac McCaslin conclude that the mistake was inherent in the myth; that the New World was not ever devoid of evil, from the moment of its settling—that it was "already tainted even before any white man owned it by what Grandfather and his kind, his fathers, had brought into the new land . . . as though in the sailfuls of the old world's tainted wind which drove the ships." It was the evil of slavery, rooted in the sin of spiritual pride and the lust of possession. What Grandfather and his kind brought with them into the New World was themselves; what they brought was the nature of man.

After probing to the falsity of the myth, "The Bear" goes on, by way of atonement, to construct a new and more durable image of innocence and moral freedom: a new image of a new kind of New World. Qualities undergo a profound dialectical transformation in "The Bear"—and of a nature indicated at once in the opening sentences:

> There was a man and a dog too this time. Two beasts, counting Old Ben, the bear, and two men, counting Boon Hogganbeck, in whom some of the same blood ran which ran in Sam Fathers, even though Boon's was a plebeian strain of it and only Sam and Old Ben and the mongrel Lion were taintless and incorruptible.

The change is already apparent in the paradoxical attribution to a mongrel dog of "taintless" and "incorruptible" qualities. It is there, too, though we do not immediately know it, in the same attribution to the man, Sam Fathers, who is also a mongrel, the half-breed offspring of a Negro slave and a Chicasaw Indian. The purity transcended is, in short, a physical purity, a matter of blood, something misleadingly suggested by the physical purity of the land—a very dangerous illusion. What takes its place is a tougher kind of purity, of innocence, of moral freedom; virtues not of a historical and accidental but of an ideal and permanent kind; qualities not given but achieved, by conduct and by art, through discipline and submission. The new innocence is not other than conscience.

"The Bear" thus moves toward a "transvaluation of values" at once large and homely; and the motion is perhaps most sharply evident in the shifting use made of one key ingredient that the story shares with the whole tradition of heroic legend to which "The Bear" belongs. In that tradition, where power is always a major factor, the special character of the hero's power is often represented by a "magic weapon," and by the use made of it. We may contemplate a significant range from the great bow of Odysseus, with which he ruthlessly slays a houseful of political and domestic rivals, to, say, St. Martin of Tours telling the pagan Emperor that, "Armed only with the Cross, in the forefront of the enemy, I will fear no evil." Aeneas enters his supreme battle wearing on his shield the recorded destiny of Rome, a predestined power that makes him invulnerable to the mightiest of the Latins; and the secret source of Ahab's power is the giant harpoon baptized "not in the name of the father, but in the name of the devil." Isaac McCaslin's weapon is nothing so grandiose; but it is not much less meaningful. It is, of course, his hunter's rifle.

His first gun is too big for him, a man's weapon in a boy's hand. Then at eleven years old, the year he first encounters Old Ben, he receives his own gun, "a new breech-loader, a Christmas gift; he would own and shoot it for almost seventy years. . . ." The imagery of the gun is diffused through the story, one of its unifying motifs; an association is noted with the taintless mongrel dog, whose color is gunmetal gray. But what is important is the use Ike makes of his gun in his relation with Old Ben. The first time he meets the bear, Ike has abandoned his rifle, along with his watch and compass, to present himself in humility before the ancient patriarch: an act of communion, verging on the holy. The second time he throws his gun aside and risks his life to rescue a little fyce who was barking helplessly in the bear's path: an act of charity. That, I think, is the main symbolic movement of the narrative. It is the transmutation of power into charity.

That is what the conversion of innocence amounts to, and Faulkner's artistic conversion of the historical image of America. In it, power suffers no real loss, but undergoes a sea-change. It comes under the control of moral understanding; a kind of grace enters into it. More concretely: Ike does not give up his weapon of destruction; on the contrary, we have swift glimpses of him in his later years as the greatest hunter in Yoknapatawpha County. But he uses his power with restraint and fidelity; he uses it with conscience. Boon Hogganbeck is the vulnerably innocent man, in the inferior sense of the word, and he is last seen nearly out of his head and rabidly dismantling his own gun. Ike continues to live near and in the dwindling forest, as close as possible to the source of his moral energy: a Natty Bumppo who is also an imitator of Christ. But Ike is not intended to represent Christ in a second coming; it is only that he seems to move in a world of light—a meager light but definite enough, for instance, to read the past by (in a way Quentin Compson could not); a New World in which values are confirmed only by raising them to a higher power; not the historical and physical New World—this is precisely what is transcended—but a world so perpetually new that Ike appears to be its only living inhabitant.

The impression, we admit, is disturbing. Ike does stand for a vanished Eden and he is prepared for some purgatory to come; but he stands—insistently—alone. Living out his life in the big woods, he seems never fully to share the demoralizing and magnificant adventure of being fully human. Hence he does not share in the suffering and roguery of others, and there is thus no impulse toward companionship, toward reducing the tragic distance between man and man. History has taught him much; but it seems also to have taught him that history itself enforces a condition of solitude. His lifelong mission of atonement and of bearing witness is of necessity solitary: as though only in solitude might purity remain undamaged.

The transcendence enacted in "The Bear," to put it differently, was if anything too successful and complete. It carried Ike out of the quicksands of history, but at the same time it nearly carried him out of the company of mortal men. He has moved dangerously close to the person of the savior-god, to the person of Jesus: dangerously close, at least, for the purposes of fiction. It is worth insisting that the life of Christ is not under any circumstances a fit subject for literature: not because such a subject would be irreverent, but because within the limits of literature it would be impossible; or, what is the same thing, it would be too easy. And this is exactly why the quality of the fourth section of "The Bear"—the mode of its existence—is so uncannily appropriate to its content. It was perhaps Faulkner's most extraordinary poetic intuition to present the affinities between a human being and a divine—a Mississippi hunter and the figure of Christ—not as an actuality, but as a foggily seen prophetic possibility: something longed for and even implicit in present circumstances and character, but something that has decidedly never yet happened. "The Bear," reaching to the edge of human limits, does the most that literature may with propriety attempt to do.

William Faulkner's Reply to the Civil-Rights Program

by Edmund Wilson

William Faulkner's new novel, *Intruder in the Dust,* is the story of a Negro with white blood who refuses to behave with the submissiveness demanded of his color in the South and has developed so rigid a pride that, even when wrongfully charged with the murder of a white man, he can hardly bring himself to stoop to defend himself against the enemy of his race. The narrative deals with the adventures of the handful of people in the community (the Jefferson, Mississippi, which is the locale of most of Faulkner's fiction) who, having come to respect Lucas' independence, interest themselves in his case and exert themselves to save him from lynching. These champions include a boy of sixteen, who had once been rescued by Lucas when he had fallen through the ice; the boy's uncle, a local lawyer, who has lived abroad and has, to some degree, been able to surmount provincial prejudices; and an old lady of the best local quality, who had grown up with the accused man's dead wife in the relation of mistress and maid. All the happenings are presented from the point of view of the boy. It is his loyalty to the old Negro that leads to the discovery of evidence that the crime has been committed by someone else; and his emergence, under the stimulus of events, out of boyhood into comparative maturity is as much the subject of the book as the predicament of the Negro. The real theme is the relation between the two.

The novel has the suspense and excitement that Faulkner can nearly always create and the disturbing emotional power that he can generate at his best. The earlier Faulkner of *Sanctuary* was often accused of misanthropy and despair, but the truth is that, from *Pylon* on, at any rate, one of the most striking features of his work, and one that sets it off from that of many of his American contemporaries, has been a kind of romantic morality that allows you the thrills of melodrama without making you ashamed, as a rule, of the values which have been invoked to

Reprinted with permission from *Classics and Commercials* by Edmund Wilson (New York, 1950), pp. 460-69.

produce them. I do not sympathize with the line of criticism which deplores Faulkner's obstinate persistence in submerging himself in the mentality of the community where he was born, for his chivalry, which constitutes his morality, is a part of his Southern heritage, and it appears in Faulkner's work as a force more humane and more positive than almost anything one can find in the work of even those writers of our more mechanized societies who have set out to defend human rights. *Intruder in the Dust* is one of the most ardent demonstrations of this reconditioned Southern chivalry; and the question that arises in connection with it is not whether it paints too hopeless a picture but, on the contrary, whether it is not too positive, too optimistic—whether the author has not yielded too much to the temptations of the novelist's power to summon for innocence in difficulties the equivalent of the United States Marines.

I shall return to this aspect of *Intruder in the Dust*. In the meantime, it ought to be said that, from the point of view of the writing, this is one of the more snarled-up of Faulkner's books. It is not so bad as *The Bear*, which has pages that are almost opaque. But in his attempt to record the perceptions—the instinctive sensations and the half-formed thoughts—of his adolescent boy, in aiming at prisms of prose which will concentrate the infrared as well as the ultraviolet, he leaves these rays sometimes still invisible, and only tosses into our hands some rather clumsy and badly cut polygons. It would require a good deal of very diligent work and very nice calculation always to turn out the combinations of words that would do what Faulkner wants them to do. His energy, his image-making genius get him where he wants to go about seventy per cent of the time, but when he misses it, he lands in a mess. One cannot object in principle to any of Faulkner's practices: to his shifting his syntax in the middle of a sentence, to his stringing long sequences of clauses together with practically no syntax at all, to his inserting in parenthesis in the middle of a scene (in one case, in the middle of a sentence) a long episode that took place at some other time, to his invention of the punctuation (( )) to indicate a parenthesis within a parenthesis, or to his creation of non-dictionary words. He has, at one time or another, justified all these devices. But what is the excuse for writing "the old grunt and groan with some long familiar minor stiffness so used and accustomed as to be no longer even an ache and which if they were ever actually cured of it, they would be bereft and lost"?—a mismanagement of relatives quite common in the Faulkner of the latest books. One is willing to give the benefit of the doubt to "regurg," "abnegant," "dismatchment," "divinant," "perspicuant," until one runs into a dictionary word used out of its real meaning, as in "it's only men who burk at facts"—when one realizes that Faulkner is not merely coining but groping. It is true that his new way of writing has enabled him to render impressions more accurately than he did before: but the passages that become unintelligible on account of a confusion of pronouns or that have to be read twice for lack of proper punctuation are not really the results of an effort to express the hardly expressible, but the casualties of an indolent taste and a negligent workmanship that did not appear to the same degree in the prose—for the most part so steady and clear as well as so tense and telling—of such a novel as *Light in August*.

One finds here both the vigor of a tradition and the signs of its current decay. For the writing of Faulkner, too, has a noble and ancient lineage. Though he echoed, in his earlier novels, Hemingway and Sherwood Anderson, he belongs, really, not to their school but to the full-dress post-Flaubert group of Conrad, Joyce, and Proust, whom he has sometimes echoed since. To their kind of highly complex fiction he has brought the rich and lively resources, reappearing with amazing freshness, of English lyric verse and romantic prose (as distinguished from what we now call American). This is an advantage that the Southern writers sometimes have—a contact with the language of Shakespeare which, if they sidestep the oratorical Southern verbiage, they may get through their old-fashioned education. And Faulkner, it must be said, often succeeds as Shakespeare does—by plunging into the dramatic scene and flinging down the words and images that flow to the ends of his fingers. This book, like all his books, is full of passages that could not have been written if he had sat down and contemplated the object—as Flaubert is said to have done the cabbage garden by moonlight—instead of allowing himself to be possessed by it. Minor but admirable examples in *Intruder in the Dust* are the renderings of the impression on the white boy of the smell of a Negro cabin, with all its social implications, and of the effect of a little frame church that, though lacking a steeple and shabbily patched, speaks to him with the spirit of the Calvinism to which its Scotch-Irish congregation have erected a degenerate shrine. Though he sometimes loses his grasp of language, he has described so many things so well—got out of them so much human meaning! No other of our contemporary novelists, perhaps, can compete with him in this department—for most of the best of them were bred in a world that is based on abstract assumptions, and they cannot help sharing these; whereas, for Faulkner the Mississippian, everything that a man has made wears the aspect of the human agent, and its impact is that of a human meeting.

To be thus out of date, as a Southerner, in feeling and in language and in human relations, may prove, for a novelist, a source of strength. But the weaknesses of Faulkner, also, have their origin in the antiquated community he inhabits, for they result from his not having mastered—I speak of the design of his books as wholes, as well as of that of his sentences and paragraphs—the discipline of the Joyces, Prousts, and Conrads (though Proust had his solecisms and what the ancients called anacolutha). If you are going to do embroidery, you have to watch every stitch; if you are going to construct a machine, you have to test every part. The technique of the modern novel, with its ideal of technical efficiency, its specialization of means for ends, has grown up in the industrial age, and it has, after all, a good deal in common with the other manifestations of that age. In practicing it so far from such cities as produced the Flauberts, Joyces, and Jameses, Faulkner's provinciality stubbornly cherished and turned into an asset, inevitably tempts him to be slipshod and has apparently made it impossible for him to acquire complete expertness in an art that demands of the artist the closest attention and care.

But *Intruder in the Dust* does not come to us merely as a novel: it also involves a tract. The story is evidently supposed to take place sometime this year or last [i.e., 1949-50—Ed.], and it seems to have been partly inspired by the crisis at the time of the recent war in the relations between whites and Negroes and by the recently proposed legislation for guaranteeing Negro rights. The book contains a kind of counterblast to the anti-lynching bill and to the civil-rights plank in the Democratic platform. The author's ideas on this subject are apparently conveyed, in their explicit form, by the intellectual uncle, who, more and more as the story goes on, gives vent to long disquisitions that seem to become so "editorial" in character that it is difficult to regard them merely as a part of the presentation of the furniture of the uncle's personality. The series may be pieced together as something in the nature of a public message delivered by the author himself. This message, however, suffers from the handicap of being very obscurely expressed. Faulkner, who has shown himself a master at making every possible type of Mississippian talk in his natural idiom, has chosen to couch the uncle's conversations with the boy in a literary prose like his own at its most complicated and noncolloquial—so that it is difficult to reduce what is said to definite propositions. I shall, however, make an attempt to do so.

The point of view, then, seems to be as follows (interpolated comment by the critc):

"The people named Sambo" [the uncle's way of designating the Negroes] have survived the ordeal of slavery and they may survive the ordeal of dictatorship. The capacity for endurance of the Negro is a recurrent theme of Faulkner's, and his respect for their humble persistence is unconsciously but strikingly contrasted here with his attitude toward "the coastal spew of Europe, which this country quarantined unrootable into the rootless ephemeral cities" [as if the Italians, Greeks, Hungarians, Poles, and Czechs had not shown as much tenacity as the Negroes, and as if the Southern Negroes had not been kept alive—that is, encouraged to persist—by the people who had an interest in employing them, just as the immigrants from Europe were].

The Southerners in the United States are the only "homogeneous people." (The New Englander, in his pure and respectable form, crowded back by the coastal spew of Europe, is no longer of real importance.) "We are defending not actually our politics or beliefs or even our way of life, but simply our homogeneity, from a federal government to which, in simple desperation, the rest of this country has had to surrender voluntarily more and more of its personal and private liberty in order to continue to afford the United States." The Negro is homogeneous, too, "except that part of him which is trying to escape not even into the best of the white race but into the second best." The saving remnant of Southerners, such as the characters in the story who rescue old Lucas Beauchamp, should combine with the non-second-rate Negro—the second-rate variety being, by the author's definition, the Negro who demands "not an automobile nor flash clothes nor his picture in the paper, but a little of music (his own), a hearth, not his child but any child [back to Uncle Tom and Uncle Remus!], a God, a heaven which a man may avail himself a little of at any time without having to wait to die [oh, dem golden slippers!], a little earth for his own sweat to fall on among his own green shoots and plants [no large-scale agriculture for Sambo!]." Let the white man give the Negro his rights, and the Negro teach the white man his endurance, and "together we would dominate the United States; we would present a front not only impregnable but not even to be threatened by a mass of people who no longer have anything in common save a frantic greed for money and a basic fear of a failure of national character which they hide from one another behind a loud lipservice to a flag." [The Mississippian may have hold of something here.]

Lucas-Sambo must be defended "from the North and East and West—the outlanders who will fling him decades back not merely into injustice but into grief and agony, and violence, too, by forcing on us laws based on the idea that man's injustice to man can be abolished overnight by police." Any other course of conduct toward the Negro will risk dividing the country. Attempts on the part of the people in other sections of the United States to strengthen the hand of the Negro amount to nothing more than "a paper alliance of theorists and fanatics and private and personal avengers plus a number of others" [including a good many Negroes] against "a concorded [i.e., solid] South," which is now full of "ignorant people" from other parts of the country, "who fear the color of any skin or shape of nose save their own." Such action will force the many Southerners "who do begrieve Lucas' shameful condition and would improve it" and will eventually abolish it, to ally themselves with all those objectionable elements "with whom we have no kinship whatever, in defense of a principle [the inalienable right to keep the Negro down] which we ourselves begrieve and abhor." They will thus be forced into "the position of the German after 1933, who had no other alternative between being either a Nazi or a Jew, or the present Russian (European, too, for that matter), who hasn't even that, but must be either a Communist or dead." So the Southerners must be allowed, on their own initiative, in their own way, with no intervention by others, to grant the Negro his citizenship. Otherwise—

Otherwise, what? I have been able, I think, up to now, to make Faulkner's argument clear by quoting or paraphrasing his own words, with the addition of a little punctuation; but here I must present you with a chunk of his text without any elucidation, for I cannot be sure what it means: Otherwise "Lucas' equality" cannot "be anything more than its own prisoner inside an impregnable barricade of the direct heirs of the victory of 1861–1865 which probably did more than even John Brown to stalemate Lucas' freedom which still seems to be in check going on a hundred years after Lee surrendered." But, the other side may object: The South will never get around to doing anything for the Negro. Your policy, the South retorts, is dangerous, in any case: it will give rise to "a people divided [Faulkner thus seems to take it for granted that if Washington tries to back the Negroes, it will arouse the whole South to resistance] at a time when history is still showing us that the anteroom to dissolution is division."

But is pressure from outside worth nothing? Has it had no moral effect on the South? It seems to me that this book itself, which rejects outside interference, is a conspicuous sign that it has. The champions of Lucas Beauchamp are shown as rather reluctant, as even, at moments, resentful, in recognizing his rectitude and his dignity, but they do rally to get him cleared. It is true that you have had already, in the title story of *Go Down, Moses,* the same liberal lawyer and decent old maid working together to do the Beauchamps a kindness when their grandson has been executed for murder; but in this new book these white folks of the best old stock come to the rescue of the Negro with a zeal that I do not remember to have seen displayed by the inhabitants of Yoknapatawpha County in any other of Faulkner's books. Young Charles and his young Negro pal are transformed into Boy Scouts. Miss Habersham proves herself a dear gallant old thoroughbred. The uncle is as ironic and delightful as the uncle of the boy next door in E. Nesbit's books about the Bastable children. When this wonderful posse is on the march, they have hairbreadth escapes but get all the breaks. And, in the end, the vulgar upstarts who wanted to see Lucas lynched get into their vulgar cars and turn tail and run away. There has been nothing so exhilarating in its way since the triumphs of the Communist-led workers in the early Soviet films; one is thrilled by the same kind of emotion that one got from some of the better dramatizations of the career of Abraham Lincoln.

This is a new note to come from the South; and it may really represent something more than Faulkner's own courageous and generous spirit, some new stirring of public conscience. In the meantime, in harping on this message, I do not want to divert attention from the genius that produced the book, which sustains, like its predecessors, the polymorphous polychromatic vitality, the poetic truth to experience, of Faulkner's Balzacian chronicle of Yoknapatawpha County. Old Lucas and certain other characters have, as I say, appeared in *Go Down, Moses,* to which *Intruder in the Dust* is, indeed, more or less of a sequel, and the later adventures of Lucas are more interesting if you know his past history as recounted in the earlier volume, and understand his role in the tangle of black-and-white relationships which Faulkner has presented there. This subject of the complicated consequences of the mixture of white with Negro blood has been explored by Faulkner with remarkable intelligence and subtlety and variety of dramatic imagination; and Lucas himself, the black man who embarrasses a set of white relatives by having inherited the strongest traits of a white ancestor common to them all, is one of the author's most impressive creations. Even when the prose goes to pieces, the man and his milieu live.

Faulkner and the South Today

by Elizabeth Hardwick

There are probably very few novelists in America who have not in some depressed, sterile hour wished for Faulkner's madness. He is authentically, romantically possessed by his genius; he can lose himself not only in the act of writing but in the world his imagination has created and populated. He believes all of it, concretely, amazingly: the map of Yoknapatawpha County is not a joke. Here is a man who can take a walk in the morning and point to the spot where Wash Jones killed Sutpen or visit Compson's Mile for which Jason I swapped Ikkemotubbe a race horse. And he is so beautifully our young writers' image of the artist: he has done it by himself, in solitude, far from New York, in spite of critics, little magazines, fads, and professors—our natural genius, isolated, sure of himself, magnificently hallucinated as we feel the artist ought to be. And what a happy man he must have been, for what is there except the furious ecstasy of art's triumph over the artist's life in his extraordinary recent comments on the characters in *The Sound and the Fury*? He tells us that Candace, the heroine of a novel published in 1929, has vanished in Paris with the German occupation in 1940, that she is still beautiful and does not show her age. He's mad, of course; we remind ourselves that there is no Candace, nor a Jason, after the pages of the book are closed, to live on into a sour middle age and to sneak up the steps with his "big, plain, brazenhaired" mistress from Memphis. Still we cannot help but envy a writer so splendidly deluded; we feel an irrevocable calling to art ought to give us indifference to reality, that creative work should heal the misery of an unhappy love affair, pull us through nervous breakdowns, discount personal deficiencies, and, in that sense, most artists strive desperately for the same fantastic identification with their work and characters, the wondrous involvement with the imagination which Faulkner's little map symbolizes with an accuracy and simplicity almost beyond credulity. For it is either this or the slow, painful workings of the mind; either Faulkner's madness, large and self-sufficient, his stunning belief in his imaginary world, or something we

Reprinted with permission from "Faulkner and the South Today" by Elizabeth Hardwick. From *Partisan Review,* Vol. XV, No. 10 (October 1948), 1130-35.

secretly believe to be smaller: autobiographies, social observation, the neat situation, "the interesting but not creative."

His limitations, his overwriting and obfuscation are apparent; it is easy enough, if reckless, for Clifton Fadiman to satirize one of his most dazzling works ("One may sum up both substance and style by saying that every person in *Absalom, Absalom!* comes to no good end, and they all take a hell of a time coming even that far."), or to be really dreary about him, as Maxwell Geismar is and hint at Fascism, the great "hatred," and the threat to the body politic in Faulkner's love of the past. But his six or seven superb novels insinuate themselves, no matter, and someone is always discovering that Faulkner is our greatest living novelist and saying it with a chip on his shoulder, belligerently, as though he expected to be booted out of the room. Indeed, Faulkner's reputation is curiously incomplete, somehow not authorized and catalogued. Like a patch of thrilling and famous scenery, almost everyone admires him but no one has anything very thrilling or famous to say about him.

One does not know whether to be glad or sorry that even Faulkner, the possessed, legendary writer, could not escape forever from the real Mississippi. His novel, *Intruder in the Dust,* is astonishing: it is a tract, a polemic, even in its odd way a "novel of ideas." It is not what we expected and in it Faulkner appears as a hermit, perfect and necessary to our urban sentiments, who by chance picked up yesterday's newspaper, became annoyed with the state of the world, and ran down from the hills to make a speech in the public square. It is less than his previous work, but fascinating because of that work and because it reveals the desperation of his present condition, the possibility that his inspired madness has disintegrated, leaving him, like everyone else, hollow and uncertain with the sickness and perplexity not of the past but of the present. The sickness of *Intruder in the Dust,* the fear and despair, are intimately connected with the future of Faulkner's career, a career which demands that there be a South, not just a geographical section and an accent, but a reasonably autonomous unit, a kind of family ready, and even with a measure of geniality, to admit the existence of the people next door and to cooperate in the necessary civic responsibilities, such as the removal of garbage and the maintenance of highways, but beyond that unique and separate, not to be reproached, advised, or mourned for the goings on behind the door.

The bare situation of the novel is brilliant: an old Negro, Lucas Beauchamp, a man apart, "not arrogant, not scornful, just intractable and composed," *pretends* to be a murderer, wants to be innocently lynched, to add his own blood to the South's dishonor, as his last act of contempt for his oppressors. He is not successful because of the intense need of several white people to prevent his martyrdom, and not only in Lucas' private interest, but in their own interest as white men who already have more shame than they can bear. Lucas, or the mass Negro, has at last conquered the South by giving the white man an unendurable burden of guilt. "Lucas Beauchamp once the slave of any white man within range of whose notice he happened to come, now tyrant over the whole country's white conscience."

The brilliance of this situation is that it is not so much about the Negro as about the South's appalled recognition of its sins, its confusion before the unforgiving, alienated faces of the Negroes whose suffering has given them immense pride and dignity, the moral superiority of the victim. The Negro must be saved, Faulkner seems to be saying, so that the white man can become his moral equal, be relieved of the bondage to his terrible mistake.

Lucas' innocence is proved by a sixteen-year-old boy, Charles Mallison. The boy had been haunted for years by his feeling that he was in debt to Lucas for having, as a child, eaten part of the old man's dinner. Lucas refused money for the dinner and when the boy sent a Christmas present he was immediately repaid by a gallon jar of molasses from Lucas. By proving the Negro's innocence, the boy hopes to reassert his position again, and again he is defeated, because Lucas puts his escape from death on a business basis, insists upon paying the boy's uncle, a lawyer, two dollars for services, and thereby repudiating the equalizing gesture. The Negro is triumphant: he will not allow the white man to reduce even a penny of the incalculable debt.

Seen through the boy's eyes, this situation has great subtlety, in spite of the ludicrous improbability of some of Faulkner's inventions, which include vanishing corpses and grave-robbing scenes more suitable to Tom Sawyer and Injun Joe than to the tragic momentum suggested here. And then suddenly the novel ceases to belong to the Negro and the boy and is given over to the boy's uncle, the lawyer who also wished to save Lucas. The uncle delivers absurd, strident lectures, written with frantic bad taste (the conglomerate Negro is called Sambo) and a flippant effort in the direction of political satire. The South must "defend not Lucas nor even the union of the United States but the United States from the outlanders North, East, and West who with the highest motives and intentions (let us say) are essaying to divide it at a time when no people dare risk division by using federal laws and federal police to abolish Lucas' shameful condition . . ." and again, "I'm defending Sambo from . . . the outlanders who will fling him decades back not merely into injustice but into grief and agony and violence too by forcing on us laws based on the idea that man's injustice to man can be abolished overnight by police . . ." and, "I only say the injustice is ours, the South's. We must expiate and abolish it ourselves, alone and without help nor even (with thanks) advice."

Faulkner acknowledges the Negro's moral victory over the South, yields and desires his total civic equality ("Someday Lucas Beauchamp

. . . will vote anywhen and anywhere a while man can and send his children to the same schools anywhere the white man's children go and travel anywhere the white man does as the white man does it"), scorns as he always has the depraved Southern murderer, the Percy Grimm who killed and emasculated Joe Christmas, and whose portrait Faulkner has drawn with a passionate condemnation not achieved, to my knowledge, by any other writer.

This perception of the final emancipation of the Negro is real and historical, a fact and a victory only Stalinists and certain liberals feel compelled to underestimate. The sadistic passion these people take in disowning every triumph of the Negro in America, in predicting greater and greater injustice to him, is one of the most detestable aberrations of their minds. One can only believe they want violence in order to prove themselves right, as the deluded maniac, faced with the infuriating reason of the doctor, wishes to have a great bloody wound the next day to testify to the actual existence of his imaginary attackers. And when the Negroes are won over to the Communist Party, have they not fallen in love with their own misfortune, since at no time is there so much discussion of lynchings, humiliating segregation, such delicious examination of white deceitfulness as between Stalinists and Negroes. The one never tires of "exposing" to the other an endless chronicle of dangers past and to come, as if the Negro did not know them well enough but had to taste, touch, and fondle them over and over until both are in a frenzy of indescribable perversity.

Faulkner's best intuitions have something to do with this phenomenon and there is at least a measure of psychological truth in his understanding that a cruel, lost South is necessary to the idea of America held by certain radicals. This intuition partly informs his plea that the South be allowed to reedem itself. Unfortunately, he was not content with psychological perceptions, but had to compose a states' rights, leave-us-alone, don't-be-coming-down-here-and-telling-us-what-to-do pamphlet which falsifies and degrades his fine comprehension of the moral dilemma of the decent guilt-ridden Southerner.

I think he was compelled to this not alone by a compulsive love of the South but also by the fact that he has lost his belief in the South as a unique region; he can reaffirm that belief only by imagining a mystic separation from the North, since his will to justice does not want a South unique because of its brutality to Negroes. He must believe that the contemporary Southerner is still close to his history, still romantically doomed, unable to forget the old disgrace, a proud, driven image of the past.

> For every Southern boy fourteen years old, not once but whenever he wants it, there is the instant when it's still not yet two o'clock on that July afternoon in 1863, the brigades are in position behind the rail fence, the guns are laid and ready in the woods and the furled flags are already

loosened to break out and Pickett himself with his long oiled ringlets and his hat in one hand probably and his sword in the other looking up the hill waiting for Longstreet to give the word. . . .

But this is unimaginable; it is literary, flamboyant, historically ridiculous in terms of America today. And it is also inconceivable that the citizens of a few states are actually prepared, as Faulkner suggests, to risk their lives, their children, their futures, their wealth, or even their time in any sustained, hopeless revolt against the will of the country to which they are tied and which they need as much as anyone else. This is romantic, cowboy play-acting, the election of Talmadge, the hootings and posturings of the Dixiecrats notwithstanding. The rebel yell on the radio—an unmistakable scream of buffoonery and self-mockery. It is the end, not the beginning, the end of Faulkner's imaginary kingdom, and he is terrified by it.

The Negroes have migrated in vast numbers to the North and those who are left no longer feel tragically or gloriously fused with the destiny of the South. There are no Dilseys today, neither in the South nor in the North, neither black nor white, and Faulkner's immense, loving memorial to the Negro servant is not only a remarkable creative achievement but a contribution to social history, a painstaking study of a lost relationship which will appear, a few generations from now, as queer and archaic to the American as the role of a duenna. The white Southerner himself is ruled by the ambitions of the rest of the country, which are all he can call upon if he is to survive and manage the American present.

Faulkner has caught up with the confusion of the country today, and with bitterness he finds that it cannot be controlled and ordered or even thought about in the intimate, vitalizing way in which he knew and used the past. The language of *Intruder in the Dust* is fatefully indicative of what has happened to him and his vision. Upon a realistic, contemporary situation he has tried hopelessly, impossibly, to impose the grandiloquent cadences of *Absalom, Asalom!* and nothing could be more out of key, more jarring and defeating. The rhetoric of that gloomy marvel cannot give epic grandeur, vast passionate design to his parable of the present. Here everything is real, small, and practical. What we hear, in spite of every effort to disguise it, is not the old Faulknerian music, but the sour stutters and complaints of a writer fretting over his new, urgent, difficult material.

Regeneration for the Man

by Andrew Lytle

In [*Intruder in the Dust*] Faulkner has taken a subject, and almost it seems deliberately taken it, which the propagandists of the party line have pre-empted as theirs to have and to hold and fulminate about; or for that matter, any of the intruders upon the art of fiction who violate the Muse for pragmatic purposes, whether at the state's command, or out of private need, or through sociology's quasi-revelations. These last pretend to illuminate situation and performance, but, in effect, by meddling with the craft, obfuscate even their debased cult of good works. It is irrelevant, actually, whether Faulkner either out of irony or from some more private impulse chose what seems a current issue as subject for this novel. Such choice is beyond the artist's capacity. He does not choose his subject; his subject chooses him. And because his imagination functions in a certain way, craft against reverie, even if he deliberately sets out to make a plea to action, or to treat the accidental accidentally, he wouldn't be able to do it. The artist is simply one who cannot debase his work even when, pressed, he thinks he gives in to circumstance; certainly not after his apprenticeship is behind him. There always seem to be a few exceptions to prove the rule, but on close scrutiny I doubt if these could show more than a technical virtuosity such as magic shows.

Dickens' passionate interest in the social evils of his day and *Bleak House,* that one of his books which stirred England to reform the Courts in Chancery, together give the best example I know of the artist's inviolability. The excitement of the day and the social action *Bleak House* set afoot were residual to the central experience, the literary truth, of the novel. It happened that the injustices of the Courts in Chancery served Dickens as the complication which discovered his subject. The effect of the inertia, the circumlocutions, the mazelike ritual of the Court upon the characters, gave to its injustice the absolute quality of Fate with which man struggles but about which he can do little but realize the combinations of his character against circumstance; so that the proportion of good and evil in the nature of man is implied in all its

Reprinted with permission from *The Sewanee Review,* pp. 120-127, LVII, 1 (Winter 1949).

variety through the central drive of the action. If Dickens' concern had been with the evils of banking, say, instead of the cases in Chancery, the literary truth would have been the same. The book would merely have lacked the residual effect of reforming the banking system, which at that time the public interest had not identified with its sorrows. The artist may use anything, since whatever he uses will be absorbed by his imagination and rendered by his technical skill, and this is the artist's integrity. He will only use what his vision sees, and that according to the degree of its intensity. The surface and density of the object, illuminated in its totality, is form. Whatever failure there is is a failure of human fallibility, not of intention.

Intruder in the Dust bears comparison with *Bleak House,* with the difference that Dickens' concern is with a single institution while Faulkner deals with the complex and fundamental involvement of a whole society. The supposed murder of a white man by a Negro, a threat of lynching, and even the bill of rights, which certainly brings the material up to the moment, has all the appearance of being the author's subject; but actually this is only one aspect of it. In the first paragraph Faulkner reports sparely, tersely even, an act of violence. At high noon the sheriff has reached the jail with Lucas Beauchamp, although the entire country has known since the night before that Lucas killed a white man. The act of violence has already happened. But the pastness of it is not static. There is a continuum in the information about the spread of the news; and given the particular kind of news it is and the lapse of time between the murder and the jailing of Lucas, we are made to feel a mounting suspense which gives to the delay, as the story unfolds, a quality of mystery. This suspense and a feeling of the dark unknown is further tightened by the emphasis on time, not any hour but the hour of noon, a crucial division of time which we sense will be of importance, if for no more [reason] than that the narrow limits it suggests will contain the action. That it also will imply a symbolical reference we cannot know but later find ourselves prepared for. This introduces us to the structure. Instead of leading up to the murder as the final release to the tensions of involvement, by putting it into the past Faulkner uses the act as the compulsive force to catalyze the disparate fragments of appearance into reality, for the story is not about violence at all. It is about a sixteen-year-old boy's education in good and evil and his effort to preserve his spiritual integrity.

Charles Mallison, Jr. (he is called by name once) is not merely a sensitive boy in whom resides the consciousness of his race, although he is this, too. More particularly, he has a grief. The cause for this grief comes out of the dichotomy between the races, brought about by the long assault from the outside which has isolated Southern people and made him, along with them, overly sensitive to his racial distinction, to the extent that the integrity of his manhood has become identified with his distinction. This identification between race and manhood represents for the boy-man both Nemesis and Fate, since he is neither responsible for the imperfection of his view nor for the pattern of the action which the dead white man releases. He resists flight (washing his hands of it). His effort to escape his predicament lies in his decision to discover the truth by digging up the grave of the dead man to see what bullet killed him. He will face dangers both physical and metaphysical comprised in an undertaking beyond his capacity to perform, but in his decision he assumes the more responsibility for his humanity. The impulse behind this decision, however, is mixed. On the one hand, he hopes to wipe out the shame his manhood has suffered at the attitude of Lucas four years before the story opens (Lucas's denial of his racial pre-eminence; or so it seemed); on the other, it is to avoid the shame of lynching that attaches to any mob action, since this is another kind of emasculation both for the individual and society, as in either case the will is deprived of its function. Or, to put it another way, the individual's violation of his code of conduct and society's subversion of its laws become a kind of suicide, especially in the instance of traditional man and a homogeneous society. It is his innocence as a boy but his pride and conscience as man which in the end clarify the confused impulses and bring him into a fuller knowedge of the truth. In one sense the historic isolation of the Southern culture by a victorious and hostile force serves for the fateful drive of the story: is at once the cause for action and the clue to its meaning. By focusing it in the moral destiny of a boy, the story becomes dramatic instead of didactic—that is, a novel and not propaganda.

There is for any Southern writer of imagination an inescapable preoccupation with his native scene and especially with its historic predicament. He can no more escape it than a Renaissance painter could escape painting Her Ladyship the Virgin and the Court of Angels. He has been made to feel too sharply his uniqueness and the uniqueness of his society in the modern world. His self-consciousness does for him what blindness did for Homer. He has been forced to achieve aesthetic distance. It is this which gives to the boy protagonist in this book (a cult hero almost) the authority for his undertaking and allows him to absorb into the working out of his fate the entire complex set of relationships which represent the contradicitions, the mixed virtues and vices, even the agonies of the Southern sensibility, containing a vision at once objective and involved: the poet-prophet who defines a civilization bereft of historic destiny but which refuses the role.

It seems to me that criticism all too often attempts to isolate an author's truth by abstracting it from the context of his performance. It is the writer's nature to discover for himself his meaning by matching his knowledge of experience against his imagination. This never comes in a burst a light, but out of a gradual exploration into the dark places of the mind and heart of man. The process of writing forces the discovery; or rather, it is the discovery. What saves the writer from losing himself (the points of darkness are infinite) is his point of view. To this he may return and by this he may relate, reduce, and absorb the seemingly unrelated matters of experience until they become what to him is truth. Given the creative function, what follows is style; and style is that breath of life which makes of texture and structure, or body and bone, an organic whole. In this novel Faulkner has achieved a oneness of style and point of view which is of the first order of literary distinction. It is all effortless and so fused (which has not always been the case in his other books—he has not always removed his scaffolding) that to probe for purposes of analysis becomes a kind of bloody operation.

I shall let the point of view more or less envelop what I have to say. It lies in the close sympathy which exists between the boy and his uncle, a sympathy so intimate that at times the transference of thought does not need speech. There are many advantages to this. The novel is freed, but not entirely so, from the indistinct image the narrator-actor must present to the reader. By having two sensibilities instead of one—he would have done better had he made them more personally distinct—each is able to give to the other the grace of humanity. The boy's innocence and the uncle's maturity set up an interplay both at the center and on the periphery of the structure. Their relationship becomes strophe and antistrophe, enforcing the formal pause, defining the action as it is taking place. The center of the structure depends upon the treatment of time. A very narrow limit is set for the physical action, but the physical action, while performing at its own level, releases the flow of reverie and comment which becomes the embodiment of the intrinsic meaning. Since within this area lies the realm of truth, where all is timeless, the dual consciousness moves through past, present, and even into the future, according to the needs of the particular stage of the story's development. But for this flexibility, the continuous beat of the prose would grow monotonous—with its inversions and parentheses, and the dream-like quality of its tone (again the sense of timelessness) often threatening to make the skill of its complex delivery too apparent, which would be fatal. But always at the right moment there comes the pause, the break of dialogue—and Faulkner's dialogue surpasses itself —the added information when it is needed, or the image in a new light subtly changing the texture or the posturing of a character, as sudden as the shock of the tragic mask.

Gradually as we come to understand the achievement of the boy's education, and the achievement is manhood, we discover that the point of view has not shifted but was more inclusive than it first appeared. It is still posted firmly with the boy-uncle relationship, but it has expanded beyond the boy's discoveries, though still contingent upon them. It rests at last not upon the boy's coming into manhood, but upon manhood, or its essence: The Man. The boy set out to restore a spurious manhood (appearance), but thanks to his innocence and the guidance of his uncle reaches instead true manhood (reality). The Man is the representative of the homogeneous society. His symbol is the fire and the hearth. He maintains the right relationships between the sexes, preserving to each his natural function; guards the blood's purity; is ultimately responsible for order in his household and therefore in the state; attends to his business, does not intrude or allow intrusion. He punishes and rewards toward this end and is the trustee for the earth out of which life comes and by which it is maintained. He, not Freedom, which history has shown no man can stand, is the realizable image for society.

But in the South as it is now there are half-men, or men hamstrung out of their instinct to preserve this manhood. The uncle who understands so much is blinded by "the facts and circumstances." The sheriff, the hunter who guards the jail for five dollars as he reads the funnies, the jailkeeper who is outraged that he may lose his life for seventy-five dollars a month but will still risk it, and the old Gowrie, the father of the murdered man, are all men in Faulkner's sense, but each is circumscribed by some phase of the South's darkened image. In Miss Habersham's action the funtions of the sexes are transposed. She, an old woman, does what a man should have done, if it had to be done—digs up a grave at midnight for justice's sake. And yet she was the only one who could assist the boys. Her caste and feminine intuition both informed her beforehand of what she would find, intuition acting truly, her caste function misplaced: she, a lady peddling eggs and vegetables at the town's back doors, wearing Sears-Roebuck dresses, but thirty-dollar handmade shoes and fourteen-dollar gloves—symbols of gentility, whereas the dress was not and therefore could represent her economic status. But slavery or any like subordination is the specific image of emasculation. The South's hope for regeneration lies in its struggle to restore by itself, not from outside pressure, to that part of its population the rights of manhood of which it is deprived. Understanding of this is proof of the boy's initiation and his right to the toga virilis. But his possession is still precarious. He has not yet, as individual or symbol, established himself, because one man cannot maintain this state alone, against an environment where the spurious image is predominant and where the unrecognizable sin, the impossible sin, has been committed: fratricide. A Gowrie cannot kill a Gowrie, but one has. The fraternity of the state cannot be destroyed by internecine conflict, but it has been. Out of the South's resistance to this impossibility, which exists, has come an integrity mixed with turpitude, the misplaced functions of the sexes, a misdirected and fragmentary homogeneity.

When this is understood, Lucas's relationship to the novel grows clear. He is the basic symbol of the Southern predicament. He never actually performs as a character; that is not to say he is not characterized. He is the hone upon which all is sharpened. He is the society, both black and white, his white grandfather the founder of the plantation. He has inherited the manness (the signs of this the handmade beaver hat, which was the grandfather's, the gold toothpick, the pistol, the old frock coat) while his white cousin, the present owner, has inherited through the distaff side. Each is misplaced; each is confined by the isolation of this displacement, and will remain so, so long as Lucas says, "I aint got no friends. I pays my way."

But there is hope. The boy's uncle tells him, "Don't stop." Don't stop trying to rectify injustice or to restore the true order. It is still possible to regenerate Southern homogeneity, because of and not in spite of the sheriff, the old one-armed Gowrie, the hunter, the jailkeeper, Miss Habersham, and himself. The uncle says, "The white and the black in the South should confederate: swap him the rest of the economic and political and cultural privileges which are his right, for the reversion of his capacity to wait and endure and survive. Then we would prevail. . . ." For at this time the man will dominate again, justice be restored, and all ordered according to place and function, even to the exact degree of place and function. Then will the blood be purified of its foreign bodies.

There is one other point to make: the boy's active identity with the basic symbol. At the opening of the book on a hunting trip to the plantation he falls into a creek of icy water, in November, goes under three times and comes up to confront Lucas: the first encounter. The shock of the experience and the sight of Lucas immediately afterward (he appears almost miraculously) who does not help him, who even orders the boy's colored playmate to remove the pole, the only assistance offered (the crutch of matter), so that the boy can get out by his own effort, is a kind of baptism from which he will be forevermore changed. Even the time of year marks it, the dead season which always precedes regeneration. The boy's recognition of his involvement, in spite of his efforts to free himself, even to the temptation of flight, sends him to Lucas's cell and commits him to the central adventure of the book. Lucas's attitude toward him at the creek and in the cell emphasizes the underlying symbolism of his presence. He asks nothing of anybody, not even the boy. He is intractable, even indifferent to the inherent threat in his situation. He merely directs the boy to go dig up the grave. Even in this he is impersonal and without specific information of what he will find, so that the burden of the action is shifted to the boy as his, not Lucas's, responsibility, as baptism in the Church puts the burden of salvation upon the communicant.

This extends the point of view still further, saying in effect that in the action of the boy, or such as he and Miss Habersham, will the South's crucifixion be prevented; since it is such as they who can or will restore the true image by removing from within the initial injustice which has obscured it, at which time the threat of crucifixion, which comes out of the North, will have lost its excuse for being. This is the final enlargement of the point of view. The use of time in the action, from high noon until midnight (actually it becomes longer) is suggestive; even the three before the grave is suggestive; but quite rightly Faulkner does not belabor this. Within the needs of the action of a story the symbol to work must perform at every level as it does in this book. To do more than suggest the specific Crucifixion would weaken his narrative by introducing comparisons extraneous to his own truth, and so compromise him.

Time Frozen: *A Fable*

by V. S. Pritchett

Mr. William Faulkner has been working on this novel—if that is what it is—for the last nine years and it is, appropriately, a work of ambitious theme and dimension. It has the diffused moral glow of affirmation that writers of talent seem bound to hanker after sooner or later. In nearly all his novels he has been the regionalist and one of those who lay down the foundations of a culture. He has been called, in this respect, bardic, a worker in legend and saga, and although he has been a good deal compared with Hawthorne in American literature, he will suggest to an English critic an even greater resemblance to Scott. But there has always been an alien irritant in his talent: the contact with Europe through the Europeanized Eliot and through Joyce in literature, and through the First World War in life. The last has occasionally been explicit, as in *Soldiers' Pay* or in one or two short stories—"Turn About" is one of the best stories he has ever written. Europe is explicit also in *A Fable*.

Mr. Faulkner has always turned his subjects into history: that is to say the story has stopped, Fate has had its say, the thing is settled before it begins; we go back over it as it rots down in the compost of time. Mr. Faulkner has no sense of what things may become, instead he has the myth-maker's sense of the different ways in which experience is repetitive and over. In *A Fable* he moves from the native past of Yoknapatawpha to history on a larger scale. He goes to the Europe of 1916 which, as we know, so profoundly affected the writers of his generation. Old Kaspar sits in the sun and tells us he does not know what the war was about except that, in the end, people began to feel it must be the last war of all. Mr. Faulkner has always loved the land; he has always hated mechanical civilization and the castrated man it is thought to produce; but like Crane and Hemingway before him he is romantically curious about military *virtu* and ritual. The clash of rifle butts as the guard changes, the sounding of the *Last Post,* the pulling down of the flag, the self-mutilations of hierarchy and command, the privileged speeding of cars to headquarters, and so on, have an almost religious connotation for

Reprinted with permission from *Partisan Review,* XXI, 5 (September-October 1954), pp. 557-61.

him and are certainly marked by rhetoric and nostalgia. Mr. Faulkner is far from the same sort of thing in Vigny's *Servitude et Grandeur Militaires;* he is close to the romanticism of Crane and strikes the European as very American of its period. He describes an initiation. And there is another point to note when we consider where Mr. Faulkner's historical compulsion has taken him in this book. It is this. The tragedy of the First World War lay in the conjunction of mass slaughter with the feeling of meaninglessness. The war was felt to be an outrage committed inexplicably against each human person. This could not be said or felt of the Second World War and it cannot be said of the warlike state of the world today, for our wars are revolutionary and revolutions have meaning. They are also fought by technicians and technicians are notoriously absorbed in their work and are morally segregated and sustained by it. They may become traitors; they will never mutiny—and mutiny is Mr. Faulkner's subject. The truly symbolical figure of our time is the traitor or divided man, not the mutineer; it is Judas not Christ. *A Fable* is a fantasy natural to a past dispensation. The novel ends, with unconscious literary "placing" in the now barren ceremony at the Arc de Triomphe before the tomb of the unknown soldier. One might say that the 1914 war was the final gift of European culture to America.

It is rarely easy to disentangle the narrative of Mr. Faulkner's novels. We can simplify it however. When the book opens we are in the penultimate phase of the 1914 war. Hardly any Americans have arrived. There is a mutiny in the French army. It is a protest on the part of the ordinary human being against the terror and misery of the trenches. Why not make a simple act of will and just refuse to go on? The mutiny is seen as a rumor, a mystery which has, as it turns out, been fomented by a corporal from the Middle East who has acquired French nationality and and who has twelve secretive assistants, one of whom eventually betrays him. The story opens wonderfully with the arrival of the arrested men at Headquarters. Presently the disgraced general in command hands over his sword and the disaffected regiment is unloaded into a prison camp. They will be shot. The population is divided between its own desire for peace and its anger at the rebellion. In the meantime there is a false armistice and the Germans have been contacted. Another regiment (I believe I am right in saying one can never be sure of one's facts after reading Mr. Faulkner), setting out to emulate the doctrine of non-resistance, is shot up by its own guns. Mr. Faulkner's business is to take the situation at all levels, though not in the rule of thumb manner of realism, and to explore the conflict between the moral claims of war as an exorable but pitying institution and the anguish of man, to put man's need of hierarchy against the heart, to set Saint Paul against Christ. The crisis of the allegory lies in the interviews of the Supreme Commander with some of the prisoners, but above all with the leader. The analogy with Christian myth is covertly insinuated: the leader is, in fact, the bastard son of the once dissolute and immensely wise Supreme Commander, who is admirably drawn; he tempts the son with freedom, with the arguments of Saint Paul, but finding him obdurate, leaves him to be shot. By an odd chance he falls dead, with two others, still tied to the post of the execution yard and with a crown of barbed wire on his head. It is a crucifixion. By accident or design he is identified with the unknown soldier, a symbol of the will of man in his solitude to prevail.

Such a simplification of the theme is necessary but intolerable. Mr. Faulkner may be playing rhetorical poker with the marked cards of myth and symbol, but he is not a purveyor of melodrama. He is enriched by his vices and his idiosyncrasies as a novelist. There is the characteristic digression into the garrulous story of the stolen racehorse which can win races on three legs. There is the tale of the horse's foul-mouthed and crooked English groom, who is later seen getting the soldiers to gamble with him on their expectation of death, at a shilling a day. There is the absurd figure of the exalted Negro preacher. There are the women. These are entangled in the allegory and, with Mr. Faulkner, that means their declamatory unconscious is entangled and their pungent physical presence. The prose is written as incantation, in swelling and diminishing monologue; it is filled with purple patches, conceits, epigrams, and lapidary phrases, and those images that paralyze movement but intensify the moment. For Mr. Faulkner's aim, as an historian, is to isolate and freeze each moment of the past or to give each moment of time or experience its final own fatal judgment or epithet. The only criticism we make is the old one: that all Mr. Faulkner's moments have the same intensity.

> And that was all. Then it was sunset. As they stood in the turning flood of night, the ebb of day rang abruptly with an orderly discordant diapason of bugles, orderly because they all sounded at once, discordant because they sounded not one call, but three; the *Battre aux Champs* of the French, the *Last Post* of the English, the *Retreat* of the Americans, beginning inside the city and spreading from cantonment and depot to cantonment and depot, rising and falling within its own measured bruit as the bronze throat of orderly and regulated War proclaimed and affirmed to the end of day, clarion and sombre above the parade rite of *Mount* and *Stand Down* as the old guards, custodians of today, relinquished to tomorrow's, the six sergeants themselves appearing this time, each with his old guard or his new, the six files in ordered tramp and wheel facing each its rigid counterpart juxtaposed, the barked commands in the three different tongues ringing in the same discordant unison as the bugles, in staccato *poste* and *riposte* as the guards exchanged and the three sentries of the new ones assumed the posts. Then the sunset gun went from the old citadel, deliberate and profound, as if a single muffled drumstick had been dropped once against the inverted bowl of hollow and resonant air, the sound fading slowly and deliberately until at last, with no suture to mark its close, it was lost in the

> murmur of bunting with which the flags, bright blooms of glory myriad across the embattled continent, sank, windless again, down.

The whole conception is poetic. We shall read of "day dream's idle unexpectation." Or

> One more day I would have missed him which should have told me, warned me that what faced us was doom, not destiny, since only destiny is clumsy, inefficient, procrastinative, while doom never is.

But behind the rhetorician and the dizzy dialectician who is metaphysically wonderstruck at the way one idea, or even one word, turns into its opposite, there is another Faulkner. This is the sardonic, the "jedgmatic," the garrulous folk writer, as incurably repetitive and parenthetical as the folk. He drawls out his portraits of the soldiers, his life story of the blasphemous English groom; he drawls out the night talk in the trenches, the professional talk of the aerodrome; the nasty talk of the assassins or the burial squad and what they will do for one, or preferably, two bottles of brandy. The native Faulkner is the old pungent Faulkner and, in trying to pick his way through this consciousness and that, the reader is grateful for this survival. For what one notices is that there is no equivalent to Popeye in this book. The precise, brutal, bleeding savage pity we recall in *Soldiers' Pay* is missing—except in the murder or execution of the French Commander in the end—and this from a theme which would seem to demand all Mr. Faulkner's capacity for horror. Instead, evil is generalized by words like "anguish" and so on. The war is an atmosphere, a dark if peopled eloquence; an atmosphere that pervades like the smell of refuse and rules by some implicit yet mysterious moral and physical force of its own. There is no doubt that Mr. Faulkner's supreme gift is the creation of atmospheres of one kind or another; but we are now dealing with a writer who has moved from destructive despair, in his own work, to conscious affirmation: to that extent his world becomes more recognizable than the earlier one of idiots, sadists, and derelicts, because it is more comprehensive and humane; but it is recognizable solely on the sympathetic, engaging, and immensely ingenious level of allegory. The moral Faulkner of *A Fable* represents the sort of accomplished retreat one notices, say, in Tolstoy's *Resurrection*.

In the novels of his generation, like *Ulysses* or *Finnegan's Wake*, which have influenced Faulkner (novels which had worked back through the chaos of the mind's associations toward archetypal myth), the human representative figures, like Mr. and Mrs. Bloom for example, have been more powerful than their myth. Mr. Faulkner's are weaker. But his richness of texture is still there and, above all, there is that capacity for passion which—combining, as it does, with literary artificialities—gives him his intensity, his thwarted power, and his integrity as an artist.

I am not one to defend a novelist for being exasperating to read, or for being difficult; no amount of intellectual sophistry can make the unreadable readable and, after all, we have learned to do our best by the "difficult" writers of the last thirty years. Some private worlds are nuts that cannot be cracked except by one university on behalf of another and not on behalf of readers. But if the difficulty of Faulkner is partly the result of too much reading in an isolated society, it springs from a genuine judgment on our time. He has been a writer divided between idiosyncrasies of regional genius and a nostalgia for a contemporary means of dealing with a universal subject. The division is still apparent in the rather laden majesty of this allegory where a universal subject has been treated as the compendium of a word-drunk mind.

William Faulkner and the Problem of War: His Fable of Faith

by Norman Podhoretz

A Fable may not be William Faulkner's worst book; one would have to reread *Pylon* to make a definitive judgment, and I personally could not face the ordeal. But whether or not it is his worst, this new novel is for the most part so dull, so tortured, above all so pretentious, that it forced me back to *Red Leaves* and *Spotted Horses, Light in August* and *The Sound and the Fury,* for reassurance. Perhaps Faulkner was always as bad as this; perhaps some obsolete piety prevented us from seeing him truly. But the reassurance was there: those earlier works *are* wonderful, they *are* masterpieces. Nevertheless, they struck me as the consummation of a minor, not, as I once thought, a major talent. I found them narrower than I remembered, and what was more surprising, not in the least complex. Faulkner's prose style, perhaps, fooled us into attributing complexity to his mind. It now seems obvious, however, that he really is what he always claims to be: a simple man. His warmest admirers have usually refused to take him at his word, insisting that the pettish autobiographical remarks he has made to interviewers were a pose, the great artist's secret revenge on the impertinent intruders who came south to pester him. Yet how much more impressive, after all, and how fitting, that it should be this way!

The narrowness I am speaking of is a narrowness of range. I am not suggesting that Faulkner's work exhibits just one mode of feeling or a single quality (it is often forgotten how funny this most solemn of writers can be), but rather that he deals best with only one kind of person acting in one kind of situation. Think of his greatest achievements: the transcription of how Issetibbeha's condemned Negro slave ran from his pursuers, never resting and finally eating a nest of ants to keep himself alive; or Lena Grove walking across two states with the patience of the stupid and the saintly, expecting to find the father of her unborn child;

Reprinted by permission from "William Faulkner and the Problem of War: His Fable of Faith" by Norman Podhoretz. From *Commentary,* Vol. 18, No. 3 (September 1954), pp. 227-32.

or the picture of Quentin Compson, crazed with a sense of honor so powerful that it drives him to suicide, buying a dirty little girl soggy cakes, only to be arrested for molesting her, and laughing when he is arrested; or the description of Lion, the great yellow hunting dog, hurling himself time after time after time against a door he can never crash through and that he knows he can never crash through. These marvelous images share one overriding conception: a sense of all living things as possessed, fated, doomed—and the possessed are the simplest of creatures. They do and feel only as they must, and if they do what they must with dignity, beauty, and submission, Faulkner finds glory in their lives. "Come," his captors tell Issetibbeha's slave, "you ran well. Do not be ashamed." But the glory Faulkner attributes to the man is no different from the glory he sees in the dog—which tells us something about his view of reality.

Think also what is missing from his books. Perhaps it can be summed up by saying that as far as Yoknapatawpha is concerned, the Enlightenment might just as well have never been. The qualities of reasonableness, moderation, compromise, tolerance, sober choice—in short, the anti-apocalyptic style of life brought into the modern world by the middle class—no more exist for Faulkner than plain ordinary folks do (everyone is at least a demigod to him). To a whimsical observer, his work might almost seem a gigantic fantasy fulfilling the wish that the middle class had never been brought forth onto this earth. He doesn't even hate it accurately, as those great haters Flaubert and D. H. Lawrence did. In the very act of damning industrial, urban, middle-class man, he reveals nothing more than an abstract conception of what the type is like. Jason Compson, for example, is one of Faulkner's supreme triumphs, but he hardly represents the corrosive effects of the business ethos on a man's soul. For Jason is really another variety of the possessed creature Faulkner always writes about. There is nothing mean or diminutive—or middling, for that matter—in him, except perhaps his objectives. He has the same overwhelming compulsiveness, the same superhuman drive exhibited by his characteristic adversary, Quentin Compson—whereas the truth *is* that the middle class, if it stands for anything at all, supports the immediate exorcising of all known demons. Its great cultural triumph is precisely that it brought obsession into disrepute.

The view that takes Faulkner as a chronicler of the war between preindustrial civilization and the new world of the middle class seems to me unfounded. I cannot discover a genuine sense of history in the Yoknapatawpha series; unlike Stendhal, say, who saw a new kind of personality emerging from major historical changes and understood the drama and significance of its clash with a moribund type, Faulkner has always taken refuge from historical change in a vague sense of doom. We can speak without exaggeration of Julien Sorel's struggle with the de Moles as the nineteenth century versus the eighteenth—two different worlds quite literally meet in *The Red and the Black,* two different temperaments, two different attitudes toward the self. Jason Compson, on the other hand, is merely Quentin Compson gone wrong. And who can blame him?

Faulkner's narrowness, then, has always stemmed partly from an unwillingness or an inability either to love or to hate the world of the twentieth century enough to understand it. But it isn't contemporary reality alone that Faulkner has shied away from. The very effort to explain, to understand any living thing, seems to him sheer blasphemy. Moreover, he is utterly indifferent to subtlety and qualification. When he qualifies—and often he will do so at tiresome length—it is not with the Jamesian intent of suggesting how much the naked eye never sees. Nor does he wish to refine the gross perception and focus it on a delicate point. The fine points are a swarm of motes irritating to Faulkner's eyes; occasionally he can descend to a crude, surly tone in dismissing them as irrelevant:

> "But tell me why—No, I know why. I know the reason. I know it's true: I just want to hear you say it, hear both of us say it so I'll know it's real"—already—or still—speaking, even through the other's single vicious obscene contemptuous epithet: "You could have surrendered the horse at any time and it could have stayed alive, but that was not it: not just to keep it alive, any more than for the few thousands or the few hundred thousands that people will always be convinced you won on it"—stopping then and even waiting, or anyway watching, exultant and calm while the prisoner cursed, nor toward him nor even just at him, but him, the ex-deputy, steadily and for perhaps a full minute, with harsh and obscene unimagination, then the ex-deputy speaking again, rapid and peaceful and soothing: "All right, all right. The reason was so that it could run, keep on losing races at least, finish races at least even if it did have to run them on three legs because it was a giant and didn't need even three legs to run them on but only one with a hoof at the end to qualify as a horse."

Is it fanciful to suggest that Faulkner's sympathies are with the obscene prisoner who thinks that the young man in quest of reasons is a fool and a monster? Faulkner frequently takes a kind of mischievous delight in tantalizing us with long passages which pretend to be explanations, but whose point is that no explanations are possible. These passages almost always consist of crude metaphysical assertions written with an ineptitude even translations of Hegel rarely match. He hurls his convoluted rhetoric and clumsy thought into the air like an educated version of his own prisoner cursing those of us who ask for a reason or two now and then. In any case, the notion that nothing can be explained is a half-truth which, in my opinion, has limited Faulkner's creative range. For let us be bold and admit it: a lack of ideas is no virtue in a novelist. I do not believe that Faulkner ever had ideas. Convictions, yes, and a terrifying energy behind them, but not ideas, not the wish to understand the world, only the wish to feel deeply and to transcribe what he felt and saw. (Compare him to Dostoevsky and the difference between a demonic writer with ideas and one who has none becomes clear.) Heaven knows that what Faulkner did have was enough to make him one of the two or three first-rate writers in modern American literature. But it was not enough to make him a truly great writer.

It was also not enough to sustain his creative energy. For the paradox is that after a while the imagination of a novelist who has maintained merely an equivocal flirtation with ideas begins to flounder. At the very point when he needs more than his original enthusiasm about a subject to keep him going, he finds himself without resources. He may feel his subject as intensely as ever, but the convictions which once were enough to make him certain that it was a *significant* subject no longer appear self-evident. Eventually this loss of confidence will also affect his capacity to distinguish between emotion which refers to something outside and feeling which is created by the will to feel. (The rhetorical mode of *A Fable* seems to me evidence of Faulkner's present inability to recognize a self-generated paroxysm when he works his nerves into one.) And finally, it will betray the novelist into choosing subjects that he has no business dealing with.

The more explicitly Faulkner declares his "values"—as he has been doing lately—the more we suspect that he is terribly unsure of himself these days, unsure of the relevance of his way of looking at things. For what has the Glory celebrated in Yoknapatawpha got to do with the Korean War, that tiresome, drab, plodding, inconclusive war, from which not a single national hero emerged, a war uninspiring, nay meaningless, to the Yoknapatawpha mind, and thrilling only to children of the Enlightenment who understand its moral sublimity? What has become of Faulkner—or of us—when a speech like his Nobel Prize address affirming the nobility of man and his power to endure and to prevail despite atom bombs, falls on our ears with a sound dangerously like irrelevant cant? We do have our own kind of glory and our own kind of miraculousness, but Faulkner's vocabulary is somehow inadequate to describe them. And I think *A Fable* proves that he knows it and is trying to do something about it.

As everyone must have heard by now, the book is Faulkner's version of the Passion of Jesus Christ. It is difficult not to see in it also his attempt to bring Yoknapatawpha up to date. The allegory is superimposed upon the story of a false armistice which takes place toward the end of World War I. Faulkner portrays the war as an endless, frustrating affair which seems meaningless to those caught in it, a war so devastating to the spirit that it doesn't even provide ambitious young men with their chance for glory: a war, in fact, rather like the one we have all been living through since 1948. Into this atmosphere, Faulkner introduces his extremely shadowy Christ figure, an illiterate corporal serving in the

French army who inspires a whole regiment to mutiny. The mutiny frightens all the top brass of both sides so thoroughly that they suspend hostilities long enough to hold a conference for the purpose of forming a united front against this revolutionary move. People must never learn that they can end a war as simply as all that. But at least one man does learn. He is a former officer who has intentionally had himself degraded to the ranks and becomes a runner. When he hears of the mutiny, he experiences what can only be called a conversion, and though he has never met the corporal, he dedicates himself to spreading (among the "Gentiles") the new gospel, the secret that can transform the whole world:

> Don't you see? If all of us, the whole battalion, at least one battalion, one unit out of the whole line to start it, to lead the way—leave the rifles and grenades and all behind us in the trench: simply climb barehanded out over the parapet and through the wire and then just walk on barehanded, not with our hands up for surrender but just open to show that we had nothing to hurt, harm anyone; not running, stumbling: just walking forward like free men—just one of us, one man; suppose just one man, then multiply him by a battalion; suppose a whole battalion of us, who want nothing except just to go home and get themselves into clean clothes and work and drink a little beer in the evening and talk and then lie down and sleep and not be afraid. And maybe, just maybe that many Germans who don't want anything more too, to put his or their rifles and grenades down and climb out too with their hands empty too not for surrender but just so every man could see there is nothing in them to hurt or harm either—

That William Faulkner should be able to take such stuff not seriously but reverently, that he should see the trench mutiny as anything but a touchingly pathetic gesture of desperation! What are we to make of it?

Well, it is all done for the sake of an affirmation. Two years ago, in his Nobel Prize address, Faulkner "declined to accept the end of man." The passage in which he insisted most intensely on his faith is in *A Fable* also, spoken by the corporal's father, the Commander-in-Chief of Allied Forces in France, who acknowledges his (illegitimate) son in the act of condemning him to death:

> I don't fear man. I do better: I respect and admire him. And pride: I am ten times prouder of that immortality which he does possess than ever he of that heavenly one of his delusion. Because man and his folly will endure. They will do more. They will prevail.

Heavenly immortality, then, is a "delusion"; man's true immortality lies in his glorious career on earth. There may or may not be a God (if the corporal is Christ, are we to take the Marshal of France as God the Father?), and he may or may not have actually given his son to save the world. For all we can tell from *A Fable,* it does not matter to Faulkner. Though Faulkner is a very religious writer, his work surely constitutes a paean to Man, not to God. He has turned to the Gospels as the source of his affirmation, not because he has suddenly discovered traditional Christianity but because he rightly sees in the Gospels the greatest tribute to Man ever conceived: they tell how God became man and man became God for a brief moment, and it therefore presumably lies in man's power to become "God" again. Even today.

Yet, as far as this novel is concerned, the affirmation is empty. *A Fable* is just another one of those proofs that an artist must either accept the religious view of the universe as a literal truth or leave its myths alone. The Gospel According to Matthew is a literary masterpiece because the author saw no contradiction in the idea of a man-God. He was not disturbed by qualities in the Messiah which many modern Christians would consider a blasphemy to attribute to the Son of God. The character of Jesus, as it appears in Matthew, Mark, and Luke, is not in the least monolithic: his Godliness is conveyed mostly through his ideas, thus never deteriorating into insipid virtue, while the plentiful evidences of his humanity are unabashedly displayed: we get glimpses of his arrogance, his impatience, his playfulness, his capacity to suffer. As for Faulkner's corporal, the trouble with him is not just that he is monolithic; he simply doesn't exist. Nor does the Olympian marshal. Nor do any of the characters who take part in the religious allegory. How could they exist when Faulkner doesn't seem to believe that they ever did? Under these conditions not all the Biblical parallels in all the testaments ever compiled could give them life.

And there are parallels aplenty in *A Fable*. The corporal brings a complete biblical retinue along with him. Of the twelve men in his squad, one betrays him; he is "engaged" to a whore from Marseilles who he has said was really "a good girl"; he even has a virgin mother of sorts (his real mother had died in childbirth after having been cast off by her husband for committing adultery, so the corporal was raised by his sister who, being nine years old at his birth, could only be called his mother in a spiritual sense: I suppose). Many other analogies come to mind, including the traditional chronology of the Passion. The corporal is captured on a Wednesday, executed on a Friday, and "resurrected" on a Sunday. He is killed (at the age of thirty-three) together with two other criminals, and though he is executed by means of a firing squad, Faulkner still contrives to have him die with a crown of "thorns" around his head:

> The corporal's post may have been flawed or even rotten because . . . the plunge of the post had jammed it and its burden too into a tangled mass of old barbed wire, a strand of which had looped up and around the top of the post and the man's head as though to assoil them both in one unbroken continuation of the fall, into the anonymity of the earth.

Before he dies, however, he performs miracles. The miracle at Cana is given a particularly "modern" naturalistic interpretation, where either

Faulkner's sense of humor or his lack of reverence has got the better of his judgment. It seems that the corporal met a young American soldier who wanted to marry an orphan girl. Neither of them had any money and consequently could not prepare a wedding feast. To help them out of their predicament, the corporal walks into a crap game and calmly picks up the money lying on the floor, explaining to the soldiers (who are on the point of dealing with him as we might expect) that he needs it for one of their buddies. Miraculously, the soldiers experience a burst of sentimental enthusiasm and "adopt" the wedding, buying up all the wine in town, thus, I assume, turning water into wine. This sort of thing, embarrassingly silly as it is, can almost be compared to some of the details in D. H. Lawrence's version of Jesus' resurrection (*The Man Who Died*) which, in the monstrous reaches of its bad taste, strikes even an unbeliever as a blasphemy.

It would be dishonest to pretend that the occasional spurts of life in *A Fable* redeem the book. The story which Faulkner worked into the allegory about the wretched Cockney groom and the Negro preacher who steal a crippled race horse was written nine years ago, and though it is a good story, it certainly falls short of his best work on animals and men (for example, "The Bear"). As for the character of General Gragnon, the commander of the mutinied regiment who wants to execute all three thousand men, and would be prepared to execute a whole army for the sake of his reputation, he is Yoknapatawpha itself dressed in a French uniform. But Gragnon is buried in the allegoric mess; Faulkner never gives him the chance he deserves.

A Fable, then, is one of those disembodied, religiose affirmations that we have learned to regard as the typical literary symptom of a failure of nerve in difficult times. It can be read as a fantasy in quest of some optimistic statement on our present predicament. Faulkner offers us a "pure," primitivistic Christianity that we are meant to feel is nobler, more beautiful, somehow more effective than our worldly politics. For he can see nothing but silliness in the machinations of the political mind; his satiric chapter on the conference of the generals seems to me astonishingly simple-minded, a worthy foil to his conception of the Christian lesson for our time. We are confronted here with Faulkner's impulse to escape the complexity of a world he has no patience with, a world he cannot understand. He is saying to us: "I am tired and bored and bewildered by the way you go about things; I am sick of your conferences and your bickerings. They don't matter, they are little childish games. What matters is Love and Faith and Hope." Love of what? Faith in what? Faulkner never tells us. How could he, when he cannot realize that today as perhaps never before the question of man-and-his-destiny is inseparable from the hard, dull, wearisome details of EDCs and NATOs and Austrian Peace Treaties? Indeed, it is even possible that the committees and conferences and legalistic bickerings *are* the very question itself. The fact that this possibility is inconceivable to Faulkner may indicate that *A Fable* is something more than the usual product of social unrest.

I think this book marks conclusively, and as it were officially, the end of an era. The "modern" world of which Faulkner, Hemingway, and Dos Passos were the most penetrating interpreters, the world of the twenties and thirties whose articulate consciousness they were, froze to death in 1948. As I have suggested, Faulkner's point of view—and the same might be said of both Hemingway and Dos Passos—already has taken on that ever so slightly stilted, archaic look; the tint of brown begins to stain the photograph, the poses seem a little awkward and artificial. Even the best works of these writers, reread today, induce nostalgia rather than the exhilaration of discovery. We are living now in a limbo that is neither war nor peace, yet it has given rise to a generation not "lost" but patient, acquiescent, careful rather than reckless, submissive rather than rebellious. We will recognize fully what a new world this is only when it finds a voice of its own. Meanwhile, however, the extent to which Faulkner has lost touch with contemporary experience—the way he has been bamboozled by irrelevant religiosity, while blinding himself to the real drama of salvation being played out before his very eyes—is enough to bring home the gap between his reality and ours. In the end, *A Fable* leaves us wondering whether the time will ever come again when a writer will be able to dismiss politics in favor of the Large Considerations without sounding like a chill echo from a dead world.

Faulkner: The South, the Negro, and Time

by Robert Penn Warren

Faulkner's tale is one of the anguish of time, the tension of change. Even in *Soldiers' Pay* (1926) the theme is there, but the inner logic does not begin to emerge and find its proper images until *Sartoris* and *The Sound and the Fury.*

At first glance, *Sartoris* seems to spring from the same impulse that produced *Soldiers' Pay,* a tale of the moral maiming wrought by World War I. But in this novel there are two other dimensions. On one hand we have psychopathology related symbolically to a social situation. As a kind of mirror to the story of Bayard and Benbow, we have Narcissa, the sister with whom Horace has a crippling and morbid relationship, and who marries Bayard even though she knows "there would be peace for her only in a world where there were no men at all." She struggles to make contact with life, but fails; and therefore the obscene anonymous letters (written by a Snopes named, of course, Byron) make her, in her isolation and failure, feel "filthy," by a deep unrecognized psychological involvement.

On the other hand, as a new dimension for Faulkner, we have, set over against these doomed ones, the groups who have some sort of grasp on the world and represent some sort of continuity with life—the older people of the upper class, like old Bayard, the grandfather, and Miss Jenny (who wouldn't for a minute be bothered by anonymous letters); the yeomanry, like the MacCallums and V. K. Suratt (later Ratliff); and the Negroes, as in the scene of the Christmas dinner in the cabin, where young Bayard catches a momentary glimpse of a human communion.

In other words, though we still find the emphasis on the purely individual story, and though *Sartoris* falls into the then fashionable genre of the postwar novel in America, we can see here the beginning of

This is a revised version of an address given at the University of Mississippi, at Oxford, in April 1965. The present version is reprinted with the permission of the *Southern Review,* Vol. I, pp. 501-529, of the Louisiana State University, in which the original appeared in the Summer Issue of 1965.

Faulkner's typically "thick" conception of fiction in which history, sociology, sexual psychology, moral analysis, and the religious sense kaleidoscopically interfuse in the presentation of an image of reality. This is true even if we do not read *Sartoris* in the light of *The Unvanquished* (1938) which, in the chronology of content, gives the Civil War story of the family, and clarifies the relations of both contrast and continuity for the past and present.

If in *Sartoris* Faulkner had given rudimentary indications of the range of objective reference in which his tale of maimed modernity could be told as specifically Southern, in *The Sound and the Fury* the force is centripetal, inward. Here, in this seminal book, the characteristic Faulknerian intensity appears for the first time, achieved not by range but by concentration. The characteristic story of the tensions of time is here, but the subject of this history is the doom of a single family, and the scene of the enactment is, for all practical purposes, bounded by the four walls of the Compson house. No—it might be said that the dream is enacted, ultimately, inside the heads of the people who live inside those four walls. The objective world comes through to us, and the events of the family history, but they come through the filter of consciousness of the persons who have suffered that doom; or rather, through the special consciousness which, in each case, is, in itself—and this should be emphasized—the doom. Only Dilsey, of the main characters, is rendered objectively, and one is tempted to hazard that this objectivity is an index of her strength and fulfilment: she really exists, objectively exists.

The doom is an unfolding in time. Faulkner once said that the whole novel grew from the image of the dirty drawers of a little girl. Certainly, we see, with extraordinary clarity, how the Compson children become the adults, carrying on the traits that at first glance had seemed so casual and accidental. But the doom is also an inherited doom. The father and mother, each in a characteristic way, collaborate to doom the children. Quentin sees his mother as the source of the family ruin, the poison of its life. Mr. Compson, though a man of decent instincts, capable of affection, and able to inspire affection, has withdrawn from the world into a stoicism somewhat diluted by sentimentality and alcohol. Stoicism is a philosophy which denies freedom in the outside world and finds the locus of freedom only in the self, and so it sums up, in a way, the tortured, boxed-in subjectivity of the whole novel—a subjectivity clearly related, though in what degree it is not clear, to what Mr. Compson would self-pityingly regard as the failure and corruption of the society around him. As a stoic Mr. Compson, paraphrasing one of A. E. Housman's poems, gives this advice to his son Quentin: "We must just stay awake and see evil done for a little." The denial of the moral significance of objective action leaves Quentin with only one act to which he can attribute moral significance: suicide. We might, in fact, insist that each of the children (Benjy excepted, for obvious reasons) lives by some surrogate for the significant moral action of which they are deprived.

Though in *Sartoris* Faulkner had been objectively laying down the social and historical coordinates of his story of the South, the boxed-in world of *The Sound and the Fury* has scarcely any context in the world outside. Quentin I ventures out into the world, but takes his death with him. Caddy and Quentin II go out and carry their ruin with them. Jason, whom Faulkner regarded as his favorite "monster," is the only "sane" Compson, and the only one who manages to break out and function in the world. The only outsiders who penetrate the charmed circle are the "lovers," Dalton Ames, the unnamed man with the red necktie, and the appalling young banker Herbert.

What do these four have in common—Jason and the lovers, those who provide the nexus between the dying Compson world and, shall we say, thriving modernity? The answer is simple: their attitudes toward sex and toward money. "All bitches," Dalton Ames says of women, and his evaluation is set against Quentin's outraged and impotent idealization of Caddy's virginity—and "bitch" is echoed later by Jason with reference to Caddy's daughter Quentin II. For Ames and for Jason, sex is merely a mechanical satisfaction, meaningless because undertaken without understanding, appreciation, or love. Jason sums it all up: he wants only a good honest whore, and the only way to manage women, he says, is "to keep them guessing" and "if you can't think of any other way to surprise them, give them a bust in the jaw."

As for money, Herbert the banker is symbolically equated with Jason, to whom he has, appropriately, promised a job in the bank—appropriately because, for Jason, money is the only value, set off against all ideas of value, good or bad, that the Compsons hold. But money is an abstraction, a bleached-out sign, not a thing, and people like Jason and Herbert manipulate signs, not things, not reality.

This brings us to the question of what puts sex and money together in the making of these monsters? I do not know that Faulkner ever read Dante (though I should not be surprised if he did), but a comparison may here be relevant.[1] In the Seventh Circle Dante places those damned for crimes against nature, and among such are homosexuals and usurers, both of whom sin against the fecundity of nature. With Faulkner, for homosexual we can read "one who makes sex meaningless" and for usurer "finance capitalism"—and the sin, in both instances, is the sin against reality, the sin of abstraction, the lack of reverence for nature that permits one to manipulate and violate it. Such men are the carriers of what, for Faulkner, is "modernity," and we may remember how in our social scale we tend to put at the pinnacle of respect the man who

[1] According to Joseph Blotner (*William Faulkner's Library*), Faulkner owned the Carlyle-Wicksteed translation (Modern Library, 1932), but did not acquire it until 1938, long after the money-sex relation had been established in his work.

operates at the highest level of abstraction. The financier is at the highest level of abstraction; the manufacturer, for instance, is somewhat lower because he is involved with "things" and his hands are symbolically soiled.

And at this point, before we develop the subject, it is natural to ask what relation Faulkner's special notion of "modernity" has to our own —for we know that our age does deliver certain practical benefits and does exhibit certain moral virtues not characteristic of other ages. On this question we may refer to an essay by Norman Podhoretz,[2] who says that Faulkner does not understand the modern world, that he has entirely missed the Enlightenment, and its "qualities of reasonableness, moderation, compromise, tolerance, sober choice," and doesn't even accurately hate the middle class. It is quite proper to put Faulkner's notion of modernity over against the virtues which Podhoretz justly associates with the rise of our "enlightened" middle-class society. The triumphs of our civilization are obvious and staggering—and not all of them are at the level of technology and gadgetry. It is not idle to hope that not only physical life may be more and more enriched but that spiritual life may share the benefits of widening horizons. But every gain in life seems to carry with it a *possible* liability. The future is always open-ended, "progress" is not an automated gravy-train to the stars, and there is no written guarantee that the ethos of the middle class or of the technician (or scientist) will stand the strain of success.

This is where the question of the "relevance" of literature comes in. As a kind of short-hand, we may say that literature *may* carry a sort of built-in rebuke to the hubris of its age, and that the more powerful the drives of an age and the more successful they appear, the more powerful, radical, and complex may be the literature of "rebuke." For instance, we may cite the tragedy of Athens in the age that drove toward the debacle of Syracuse, or that of the Elizabethan period with its newly opened society of "ambition," the poetry of the English Romantics in the context of the Industrial Revolution, the work of Hawthorne and Melville in the society of the 1840s and '50s or that of Melville again, Mark Twain, and James in the Gilded Age, and of Dreiser in the age of Coolidge. Furthermore, such a "rebuke," though it may be literal and direct (as it often was, but not always, with Zola), is more apt to be "mythic" and "radical"—that is, to take a form which, because of its distance from the literal, may give a drama at once more strongly focussed than life ordinarily affords, and more deeply suggestive. As Aldous Huxley says of tragedy,[3] such a "rebuke," whether tragic or not, gives only a half-truth; it gives only one, abstracted perspective on actuality,

[2] "William Faulkner and the Problem of War: His Fable of Faith," p. 243. See also p. 16.

[3] "Tragedy and the Half Truth," *Collected Essays.* New York: Harper and Brothers, 1960, pp. 60-68.

but that may be an essential truth, a "radical" truth, not to be ignored.

It is clear that Faulkner, though he gives a scrupulously faithful report of the real world, is "mythic" in the sense used above; he is dramatizing clashes of value in a root way. But how different is this, we may ask, from a rebuke like that in *An American Tragedy,* which at first glance seems so realistic? In fact, despite its realism, it was early attacked as giving an untrue picture of America, and of life. A literalist would ask of Dreiser how many young American boys on the make murder their pregnant sweethearts to get free to marry a rich girl, and so end up befuddled in a death cell. But statistics prove little in such matters—not even on the other side of the question if Dreiser, by way of rebuttal, should give figures on non-murdering executives who wind up befuddled on the psychoanalytic couch, or locked in a death cell of "success." The real point is that Dreiser gives a mythic and root drama of the rebuke of values implicit in American society, in the worship of the "bitch goddess" Success, and in the admiration of Horatio Alger. A rebuke, we may say, to the dominant American mythology. For any society has, however deeply concealed and unspecified, a mythology of justification, and the mythology of the drama of rebuke may make us see into the inner logic of the mythology of justification: Horatio Alger would, in a pinch, drown Roberta, and in the end would be just as befuddled as Clyde Griffith was. The fruitful contrast is not between the literalness of society and the mythology of the drama of rebuke, but between the mythology of justification and that of the drama of rebuke. Let the gods struggle on the flaming battlements of Troy.

To return to Faulkner, there are other characters who share with Jason the role of the image of modernity. We find this role in Popeye (who spits in the spring, is afraid of an owl, can't drink, the impression of whose dehumanized face is characterized by "that vicious depthless quality of stamped tin"), and in Flem Snopes and Snopesism in general. These are the violators and exploiters of nature who have, in the end, only a meaningless victory—the corn-cob rape by the impotent Popeye, the marriage of Herbert to Caddy, who uses him, despises him, and deserts him, or the marriage of Flem to Eula, the earth goddess, a marriage which takes place only after she is pregnant by one of the wild boys, and which makes Flem in the end a perennial cuckold.

By some profound logic the violation of nature will, we are told, be revenged by the violators upon themselves, the act of violation entailing, in itself, the vengeance for the act. In regard to the destruction of the Big Woods, Ike McCaslin cried out at the end of "Delta Autumn": "No wonder the ruined woods I used to know don't cry for retribution. . . . The people who have destroyed it will accomplish its revenge." In other words, for all their victories, the Popeyes and Jasons and Snopeses have missed the only thing worth having: life.

To go further, if these violators and exploiters have no proper relation to nature, neither do they have a proper relation to the human community. As Jason, in his "sanity," cannot understand the sympathy and affection which bind certain members of the Compson family together (most notably Benjy and Caddie), and, hating any manifestation of such feelings, must destroy the last remnants of familial continuity, so others of his ilk are destroyers and corrupters of community; for instance, *The Hamlet* is a tale of the corruption of Frenchmen's Bend by Flem, the first stage in his long career toward the presidency of a bank. "Modernity," in this sense, is the end of that idea of community which is based on mutual recognition of human qualities and needs among its members; what may take the place of community is a mere agglomeration of individuals related by the mere mechanics of self-interest or competition—a no-society, an anti-community.

As the violators are outside of community, so they are outside of the past. In Faulkner's myth of the Snopeses, the tribe descends from bushwhackers, those who had no side in the Civil War and merely exploited it. That is, the modern Snopeses, being descended from people who had no commitment to moral reality in the past, can recognize no commitment in the present. They have, in the moral sense, no identity, no history. Popeye is anonymous[4] Jason repudiates the past, just as he repudiates family and community—for to repudiate the past is to repudiate the long story of the human effort to be human, to create, as it were, a community.

In this modern world certain of Faulkner's characters, in their aimlessness and abstraction, look back to a time when men "had the gift of living once and dying once instead of being diffused and scattered creatures drawn blindly from a grab bag and assembled"—back to a time when men were, "integer for integer," more simple and complete. Presumably the old order stood for certain values which, if we are to judge from Faulkner's work, from the considered opinions of a number of philosophers, and from accounts easily found in the daily paper, are now sadly lacking. These values entail a humanistic morality, a sense of honor and individual responsibility, a concept of community, a fruitful relation to nature.

Certainly, Faulkner's concept of tradition—specifically the Southern tradition—has nothing to do with the technicolor grandeur of the cliché of the old South. Race and social class are irrelevant to this concept, for Negroes like Lucas Beauchamp or Dilsey, and white people like Ratliff, may exemplify traditional virtues. On the negative side we see the nauseating portrayals of class pretension in Mrs. Compson and Mrs. Bland in *The Sound and the Fury,* and the broadly comic portrayal in Miss

[4] In a sense, the story of Joe Christmas may be taken as the reverse of that of the violators. Quite literally, he too has no past, does not know who he is. But this is not the story of the past-less man as violator; it is the story of the past-less man as victim, as sufferer—who also becomes a destroyer.

Sophinisba and her "Warwick" in the story "Wash." The Snopes clan, at first glance, seems to equate "modernism" with the rise of the redneck, but Jason, who is not a redneck but a Compson, is the prime villain of Yoknapatawpha.

More than one critic has said that Faulkner shies away from giving a picture of the happy traditional society of the past. But it is not so much that he shies away from picturing such a society as that he knows it never existed. What he is saying is not that it literally existed but that in a society that did exist such a vision of human possibility—such a "truth"—was cherished, and sometimes, by some individuals, acted upon. "Truth is one," says McCaslin Edmonds in "The Bear," which is a story about how young Ike McCaslin was initiated into that truth. "It doesn't change. It covers all the things which touch the heart—honor and pride and pity and justice and courage and love. Don't you see now?" Don't you see, in other words, that these are the things which affirm human worth and express human brotherhood—the things abdicated by the "loud world"?

But if the story of the past is that of an effort to create a community embodying the "truth" in which Isaac has been instructed by Sam Fathers, that effort has failed: history is always, in one perspective the record of man's failure to realize his fine ideals, of the perversion of his ideals, of the cynical use of ideals as masks for brutal and self-aggrandizing action, and at the very basis of the community created in the South there was a primary violation of the "truth"—the institution of chattel slavery. This was the "doom" of the society, and in that fact, rather than in the marshalling of any external forces against it, lay its ruin. As Mr. Coldfield, one of the several Southern emancipationists[5] in Faulkner's work, would hold in *Absalom, Absalom!,* the South had built "not on the rock of stern morality but on the shifting sands of opportunism and moral brigandage." The past described by Mr. Coldfield is not, in those works of Faulkner dealing with the post-bellum South, dead; for now the "brigandage" of slavery is merely replaced, as is said in *The Wild Palms,* by the "indelible mark of ten thousand Southern deputy sheriffs, urban and suburban—the snapped hat brim, the sadist's eyes, the slightly and unmistakably bulged coat, the air not swaggering exactly but of a formally preabsolved brutality."

In Faulkner's work we find, over and over again, this theme of the crime, the curse, for it is clear that for him the Civil War merely transferred the crime against the Negro into a new set of terms. Even in the works treating the post-bellum period, the Negro remains a central figure—one is even tempted to say *the* central figure. This centrality ap-

[5] The springs of Mr. Coldfield's attitude are rather special, differing from those of, for instance, Uncle Buck and Uncle Buddy. Mr. Coldfield's fundamental objection to slavery is that it is inefficient and not businesslike. He doesn't like Negroes. See "History and the Sense of the Tragic," by Cleanth Brooks, in this volume.

pears as early as *The Sound and the Fury* in the figure of Dilsey, the only character who embodies love, force, and fulfilled identity, and who exhibits, as Irving Howe has felicitously put it, "a sense of honor toward every person in her orbit." It is she who, after the Easter service, says: "I seed de beginnin, en now I sees de endin"—who, in other words, is the intelligence, or rather the pitying and yet judging awareness, that encompasses the saga of the Compsons.

Dilsey is central in yet another sense: the attitude of each white person to her (and, by extension, to Negroes in general) can be taken as a gauge of that person's worth. Take the contrast between Caddy's attitude toward Dilsey and that of her daughter Quentin, to whom Dilsey is "you damn old nigger." Or take Jason to whom Dilsey is "somebody in the kitchen to eat up all the grub the young ones can't tote off."

One might say, of course, that the treatment of Dilsey, even by those Compsons who are sympathetically rendered, is condescending. To go further, one might, as James Baldwin does, interpret Dilsey as merely the comforting illusion of black forgiveness which the white man must cling to; or as Irving Howe, one might see her as "historically unavailable" to us (even though a "successful" fictional figure) and, therefore, unavailable to us as a "moral archetype or model." We should grant that the novel, composed nearly forty years ago, gives the psychological data of the time and place (which is only one way of saying it is dramatically right). We may well grant, too, that Faulkner, as citizen of Lafayette County, Mississippi, may well have shared such attitudes in some degree[6] But Faulkner as the citizen of Yoknapatawpha County is not the same as the other Faulkner; once he finds that Dilsey has developed into the moral center of his novel, all sorts of attitudes and arrangements in the practical world outside the novel are called into question. Art bleeds back into life, and the blood is like the bitter, fecund, godly blood of the wounded Uranus from a drop of which, spilled into the sea, the goddess of love, according to one myth, sprang. As Ralph Ellison has said, Faulkner began with a stereotype of the Negro and ended by creating human beings. But this is true of everything else in Faulkner—as in any artist. What else can the artist begin with except the cliché, the stereotype with which society and tradition strike the wax of his mind and spirit? The artistic imagination implies, in its fullness, a moral exploration.

[6] In *Sartoris* a split of feeling appears in the treatment of the Negro characters. Undoubtedly, the tone of the treatment is sometimes conventional and condescending, not much different from a minstrel show, and it is not certain exactly what is at stake when Caspey, the son of old Simon, the coachman of old Bayard, comes back from World War I full of uppity "freedom folk," as old Simon terms it, and gets laid out by a length of stove wood in the hands of young Bayard. But in the novel there is also the episode when Bayard, after trying to scare old Simon in the car, has a sudden attack of shame; and even more significant, after the death of old Bayard, there is the redemptive Christmas dinner with the Negroes in their poverty-bit cabin.

If we turn to Joe Christmas in *Light in August* we find one of Faulkner's most brilliant and revolutionary conceptions—of character and of society. With the exception of Lena Grove, who, as a creature of instinctive and unmediated fulfillment, is set over against them, all the main characters of the novel are out of tune with nature, with community, and with time—more specifically, with the past. Byron Bunch is simply the dried-up bachelor whom life has passed by, merely by neglect, one is tempted to say. But the others are, in some deep way, maimed by life. There is an air of latent homosexuality in Hightower, Christmas, and Grimm—and how brilliantly psychology, sociology, personal fate, and symbolism are here interfused in Hightower, the romantic worshiper of the Confederate past, in Christmas the nameless orphan who has no past, and in Grimm, who tries to create a "war" to make up for the past he has missed and whose sadism, with the flash of revelation, finds its true target in the killing and castrating of Christmas. And there is Joanna Burden, like Hightower a victim of the past, whose femininity, like his masculinity, has been maimed by the past, and is perversely aroused only in the joyless violence of the rape by Christmas.

The point here about Christmas is that his alienation is merely an extension of the alienation exhibited by the other characters, a closing tragic note on the scale; his defect in humanity is, *mutatis mutandis,* an extension of their defects. Nobody knows whether or not he has Negro blood, least of all Christmas himself. If he takes himself to be a Negro, it is a role willed out of a tangle of destructive and self-destructive motives. The fact that he has some awareness of the element of will is clear enough in what he says to Joanna Burden: "If I'm not [a Negro], damned if I haven't wasted a lot of time." But the willed role is not knowledge, and without knowledge there is no "peace"—the thing for which Christmas hunts.[7] Insofar as he is a Negro, he is such by social definition and not by blood; to state it another way, Faulkner here undercuts the official history and mythology of a whole society by indicating that the "nigger" is a creation of the white man.

The same theme, in various combinations, is to appear later. *Absalom, Absalom!* is shot through with the theme. When Sutpen rejects his wife and his son Charles, he does so not because of any intrinsic qualities they possess, but because he has discovered a social definition—an "abstract" definition to which certain qualities may be imputed.[8] Again, the story of Etienne, the son of Charles Bon, at Sutpen's Hundred with his two aunts—Judith, who is white, and Clytie, who insists on being a Negro—

[7] As Faulkner put it years later: "He knew he would never know who he was, and his only salvation in order to live with himself was to repudiate mankind, to live outside the human race. And he tried to do that, but nobody would let him, the human race itself wouldn't let him." *Faulkner at the University,* p. 118.

[8] The story "Elly" in *Dr. Martino* gives a parallel situation—the tragic shock when a natural relationship is brought into contrast with the definition.

involves the same elements. When Clytie goes to New Orleans for the orphan she finds that he is elegantly dressed, but she covers his fine cloths with a denin jumper. At first he sleeps in a room with Judith and Clytie—with the "whites" and the "blacks," as it were. Later on, he peers at his face in a fragment of mirror, which he secretly keeps, to discover his "difference." By now the fine clothes which had been his "white" identity are cast-off rags. It must be recognized, of course, that fine clothes have no place in the dire poverty of Sutpen's Hundred, but the symbolic force is there in the literal circumstances, and without reference to any speculations as to whether or not Clytie or Judith had told Etienne of his origins. There is more dramatic force, as a matter of fact, if the boy is led to a deduction. But to return to this basic symbolism: Etienne in his fine clothes is white, in the clothes of Sutpen's Hundred, he is a Negro; clothes make not merely the man, but the man's race.

In *Absalom, Absalom!* there is, too, that deep scene concerning race, described by Rosa, when Clytie touches her.

> Because there is something in the touch of flesh with flesh which abrogates, cuts sharp and straight across the devious, intricate channels of decorous ordering, which enemies and lovers know because it makes them both—touch and touch of that which is the citadel of the central I-am's private own: not spirit, soul; the liquorish and unguarded mind is any one's to take in any darkened hallway of this earthly tenement. But let flesh touch flesh and watch the fall of all the eggshell shibboleths of caste and color too.

Whatever else is at stake in the episode, the final statement is clear.

In *Intruder in the Dust,* the theme of the definition of race is constantly implicit; for instance, when Lucas refuses his pay, Charles thinks: "We got to make him be a nigger first. He's got to admit he's a nigger." In "The Bear" Ike McCaslin as a man looks back upon the death of old Sam Fathers, part Indian, part Negro, and part white, thinking how Sam had been glad that it was over "because for seventy years he had had to be a negro [*n*]." But in "The Bear" the most explicit presentation of the idea of the Negro as a social creation appears in the debate between the young Ike McCaslin and his cousin McCaslin Edmonds. Ike says: "Their vices are vices aped from white men or that white men and bondage have taught them: improvidence and intemperance and evasion—not laziness: evasion: of what white men had set them to, not for their aggrandizement or even comfort but his own—"

And the cousin, McCaslin Edmonds: "All right. Go on: Promiscuity. Violence. Instability and lack of control. Inability to distinguish between mine and thine—"

Ike interrupts him: "How distinguished when for two hundred years mine did not even exist for them?" [9]

[9] As a corollary to the "nigger" as a social creation, we find the idea that the Southerner may feel that he, too, is a social creation, that his specifically Southern

If the "nigger" is a social definition, a creation of white society, what Quentin calls "a form of behavior," merely an "obverse reflection of the white people he lives among," then there is the problem of what is the reality behind the mask of such a definition. With Dilsey, the contrast becomes sharp between what the white world takes her to be and her vision in, say, the Easter service. In Joe Christmas, the key of the drama is the anguishing effort to find a personal reality; since he has only the social role—and is not even certain what his social role is—his struggle becomes somehow an image of the existential struggle of all men, an elaboration and extension that gives a scale and grandeur to the pathos of his story.

Elsewhere Faulkner deals specifically with the reality behind the Negro's social mask. For instance, in "The Bear," after the slave woman Eunice drowns herself in shock and grief, we find in the plantation ledger the entry, "Who in hell ever heard of a niger [sic] drownding him self." The human reality and the social definition are appallingly juxtaposed. And in one of the most moving stories Faulkner ever wrote, "Pantaloon in Black," we have the mad grief of the Negro Rider, who has lost his young wife, interpreted by the white world as merely brutal insensitivity, with the last irony being the brutal insensitivity of those white people who are so trapped in their stereotypes that they are incapable of the act of sympathetic imagination.[10]

The same drama of the reality behind the mask is found in the treatment of Lucas Beauchamp in the story "The Fire and the Hearth" and in the novel *Intruder in the Dust.* On one occasion in the story Faulkner specifies the shift from personal reality to social role: ". . . apparently without effort or even design Lucas became not Negro but nigger, not secret so much as impenetrable, not servile and not effacing, but enveloping himself in an aura of timeless and stupid impassivity almost like a smell." (How beautifully this is turned—"almost like a smell"; all the social echoes in that phrase!) But this is the same Lucas who, on provocation to what he regards as his honor, can go, in the story "The

---

attitudes must be accepted as a role. For instance, when Quentin goes away to Harvard he feels the obligation to be what he is expected to be, *qua* Southerner. The whole story of the ghastly Mrs. Bland and her son Gerald is a parody of this social role. All people have, of course, social roles. The question here is of the kind of awareness of the role. A person immersed in his congenial society is minimally aware of his social role; it and the personal role interpenetrate. But if tension sets in between the personal role and the social role (say between a personal notion of justice and the demands of society), then awareness increases. Or, conversely, if a Southerner goes outside the South (as Quentin goes to Harvard) the assertion of the social role becomes a way of asserting the personal role—of asserting identity.

[10] We find the same pattern in the human story of Nancy in "That Evening Sun" as set against the stereotype held by the town. In reference to her suicide attempt, for example, the jailer says that "no nigger would try to commit suicide unless he was full of cocaine"—a remark echoed with reference to Eunice, in the plantation journal of "The Bear."

Fire and the Hearth," to the bedroom of Zack Edmonds, the plantation-owner and Lucas's kinsman, for the strange duel to which they both recognize they are doomed—with the pistol flung on the bed and the two men leaning across, facing each other, gripping hands to see who can force the other's down and then grab the weapon.

Lucas and Zack Edmonds are, as I have said, kinsmen, descendants of the old Carrothers McCaslin, the founder of the line in Mississippi, with Lucas man-descended and not, as Zack is, "woman-made"; and the duel across the bed—the *bed,* mind you—is a mystic struggle of antipathy and identity of blood, which is subject to endless complexity if we try to unravel the implications, but which is, we feel, somehow right in the simple massiveness of the event. And this notion of the struggle in kinship leads to another theme in Faulkner, the rejection of the brother, the kinsman, as a symbolic representation of the crime that is the final crime against both nature and the human community. The story of old Carrothers McCaslin, "the strong and ruthless man" with "cynical foreknowledge of his own vanity and pride and strength and a contempt for all his get," is shot through with this theme, generation after generation. Old Carrothers (as Ike McCaslin learns in "The Bear") has had a child, Thomasina, by a slave named Eunice, and later, in 1833, he has a child by that Thomasina. Thomasina dies in childbirth. But already, six months before, Eunice, in shock and grief at the fact of the incest, has drowned herself. Old Carrothers instructed in his will that a thousand dollars be paid to the incestuously begot son on his twenty-first birthday, but when Ike, two generations later, discovers the fact, he sees that the legacy is an act of contempt, a repudiation: "So I reckon that was cheaper," he thinks "than saying My son to a nigger."

In the episode, already mentioned, of the duel between Lucas and Zack Edmonds, there is, in the tangle of things, an element of repudiation which comes to focus when Zack taunts Lucas: "Or maybe you aint even a woman-made McCaslin but just a nigger that's got out of hand?" The theme is more developed, in the same story, when the motherless boy Carrothers Edmonds (who has known no mother but the wife of Lucas) repudiates Henry, the son of Lucas, who has been like a brother to him. One night Carrothers lets Henry beat him to the pallet where they ordinarily sleep, and then goes calmly and coldly to get into the bed. When Henry rises and comes to get in too, he says in a voice "harsh and violent though not loud": "No!" Then for hours he lies "in a rigid fury of the grief he could not explain," caught in what Faulkner calls "the old curse of his fathers, the old haughty ancestral pride based not on any value but on an accident of geography, stemmed not from courage and honor but from wrong and shame."

At the very center of *Absalom, Absalom!* we again find this theme. It is very dangerous to read this novel, or any other of Faulkner's works, as a simple, mechanically precise allegory, and in this instance as an allegory of the rise, the crime, and the fall of the Southern establishment. But this novel, like the others, is charged with symbolic import, and a concern that intertwines with all the others is that of miscegenation—miscegenation and repudiation, for even if Bon had not come originally to visit Sutpen's Hundred hoping to get, as Shreve surmises, recognition from the unknown father, or even if Henry's motive in the end is merely to prevent incest, the powerful, massive image of the book is the killing of Charles Bon by his brother at his father's gate. Against this image of a tragic rejection, however motivated, we may set, for emphasis, the contrast of Judith's several "acceptances"; after Bon's death she invites his octoroon mistress to visit his grave at Sutpen's Hundred; later she offers to rear Bon's son and eventually dies nursing him when he has yellow fever. For another variation, Bon himself had rejected his mistress, the mother of his child, but in contrast we find that the son Etienne, white enough to "pass," clings to his "Negro-ness" in a way reminiscent of the behavior of Christmas.

The Negro of mixed blood in Faulkner's work has occasioned some peculiar comment from critics. Irving Howe, for instance, says that "The mulatto [by which he presumably means any person of mixed blood] occasions some of Faulkner's most intense, involuted and hysterical writing. As a victim, the mulatto must be shown in all his suffering, and as a reminder of the ancestral phobia must be made once or twice to suffer extravagantly."

This raises two questions. First, most of the Negroes in Faulkner—certainly those (including the problematical Christmas) who have significant roles—are of mixed blood. Waiving the fact that, even in the period treated by Faulkner, the infusion of white blood among Negroes was widespread, there remains the fact that Faulkner's theme of the rejected "brother" is at the very center of his drama and the character with mixed blood is mandatory. Second, if the "mulatto" character suffers, Faulkner can scarcely be said to be avenging *himself* because of "an inherited fear of blood mixture." The world, society—not Faulkner, the writer—"makes" the character suffer; and in those works like *Light in August,* "Pantaloon in Black," "The Fire and the Hearth," "The Bear," and *Intruder in the Dust,* where Negroes have central or important roles, what Faulkner does is to make the character transcend his sufferings *qua* Negro to emerge not as Negro but as man—man, that is, beyond complexion and ethnic considerations. It may even be said that the final story is never one of social injustice, however important that element may be, but of an existential struggle against fate, for identity, a demonstration of the human will to affirm itself. For instance, if we put the flight of the white convict on the flood in *The Wild Palms* over against the flight of the tall slave in "Red Leaves" or the flight of Christmas in *Light in August,* can it be said that complexion makes any final difference? From the social perspective of a French, Italian, or

Japanese reader, what difference does it make? They see an image of man's fate. It is "man" who suffers "extravagantly."

With the characters of mixed blood another question arises. A number of readers hold the view that when Faulkner presents characters of mixed blood who show dignity and intelligence he intends the white strain to be credited. Lucas is cited in support of this view, for he is presented as finding in the blood of the ruthless old Carrothers McCaslin a point of pride and dignity. When he goes to Zack Edmonds to demand his wife back, he says: "I'm a nigger. But I'm a man too. I'm more than just a man. The same thing [the blood of old Carrothers] made my pappy that made your grandmaw." And later in the duel with Zack it is the blood of old Carrothers that is a central fact.

Does this mean that Lucas has spiritually, if not actually, "passed," has repudiated his Negro blood? I do not think so. The key point is whether Lucas's insistence is on family rather than on race. In the same story, Faulkner is more explicit when the next Edmonds, the son of old Zach, looking into the "absolutely blank, impenetrable" face of the now old Lucas, as they talk about a still, thinks: "I am not only looking at a face older than mine . . . but at a man most of whose blood was pure ten thousand years when my own anonymous beginnings became mixed enough to produce me."

As for Sam Fathers (whose very name tells us something), he is, as Faulkner says in "The Old People," the "old dark man sired on both sides by savage kings." If McCaslin Edmonds emphasizes the blood of the Chickasaw chief Ikkemotubbe, he can also say, in the same story: "He was a wild man. When he was born, all his blood on both sides, except the little white part, knew things that had been tamed out of our blood so long ago that we have not only forgotten them, we have to live together in herds to protect ourselves from our own sources." And if Sam Fathers is, after the time of the "savage kings," an inheritor "on the one hand of the long chronicle of a people who had learned humility through suffering and learned pride through the endurance which survived the suffering," that merely makes him the appropriate teacher for the young Ike, who must learn those things in order to become fully a man. And it is Ike who, when he decides to order his life by the mystic lesson of Sam Fathers and to repudiate his inherited land, will say of the Negroes: ". . . they will endure. They are better than we are. Stronger than we are." And in the same famous passage he says: "What they got not only not from white people but not even despite white people because they had it already from the old free fathers a longer time free than us because we have never been free." And with this Ike echoes what we often find in Faulkner's work, the notion of a world that has the right relation to nature, a relation that has long since been lost through the violations and destructions of modernity—and, we may add, "white modernity."

I am not saying that we should take the word of Ike, Carrothers Edmonds, Gavin Stevens, or any other single character in Faulkner as final on this subject. We know, in fact, that Lucas regards the repudiation of the inheritance by Ike as an act of weakness, and that Faulkner later (at Virginia) implied that the withdrawal and self-purgation of Isaac are related to weakness. But characters like Ike, Stevens, and Edmonds do lie within a circumference of Faulkner's special sympathy and their utterances demand respect, for they bear relation to the context of the utterances in Faulkner's own voice or the dramatic context of his work.

For instance, Ike's view of the Civil War is, when shorn of Ike's theology, very much Faulkner's own. Slavery, the curse against "the communal anonymity of brotherhood," was in the South, and there were not enough men like Uncle Buck and Uncle Bud (two of Faulkner's Southern emancipationists who moved out of their inherited houses built by the hands of slaves); so God decreed the Civil War, decreed that the valor and skill of men like Lee and Jackson should scare the Yankees into unity, and decreed defeat, not because He wished to turn His face away from the South, but because He "still intended to save" the South, which was able to "learn nothing save through suffering." Ike, at the age of twenty-one, identifies himself with his own kind, defeated and impoverished, and not with the outside world of comfort and success.

But let us look more closely at Ike. Long after he has repudiated his patrimony to avoid any share in the inherited evil of slavery, we find a significant scene in "Delta Autumn," in which a young woman with an infant turns up when Isaac is alone in the hunting camp. He learns that the father of the child is his kinsman Roth Edmonds (of "The Fire and the Hearth"), and that the young woman is a descendant of Eunice, the slave of old Carrothers McCaslin, and has Negro blood. Roth is trying to buy her off, and so the family curse reappears in another rejection.

Another point, however, emerges here. The girl, hunting Roth, confronts Ike in his tent and flings down on his cot the money the lover had left her in place of a message. "Take it out of my tent," Ike commands her, in some complex outrage, one element of which is certainly his recognition of the fact that Roth had tried to settle such an obligation for money. We realize, however, that this act of Roth's is, in its own way, a parallel to Ike's own act, undertaken years before, when he tried to buy out of responsibility by refusing his inheritance. In his case, no more than in Roth's very different case, can the consequences of the crime be commuted by money.

But there is another stage of the scene in Ike's tent. Ike, touched by the young woman's clarity and integrity, gives her the hunting horn, his most prized possession, the symbol of the old truth he had learned from the wilderness and from Sam Fathers. But as she takes the horn, a symbol of acceptance and communion, he says, "Go back North. Marry:

a man of your own race. That's the only salvation for you. . . . We will have to wait."

To which she replies: "Old man, have you lived so long and forgotten so much that you don't remember anything you ever knew or felt or even heard about love?" Again, we have it: the consequences of the crime against love—i.e., against the "communal anonymity of brotherhood"—cannot be commuted—no more by the sentimentality of the past or a promise of the distant future than by money.

She leaves the old man lying on the cot, shaking with the horror of his vision of the wilderness ruined to make room for a world of *"usury and mortgage and bankruptcy and measureless wealth, where a breed of Chinese and African and Aryan and Jew all breed and spawn together until no man has time to say which one is which nor cares."* But out of what amounts to a racist nightmare Ike is awakened by the news that Roth has killed a deer—"nothing extra," however. By this phrase Ike knows it is not a buck but a doe that his kinsman has killed, and with this he swings from his generalized nightmare back to the other pole of his feelings, to the pathos of that particular human event: Roth, in a double sense, has killed a "doe" and has violated honor.

Before the perilously balanced resolution of the episode, Ike's bosom is a battleground for all the conflicting needs, loyalties, terrors, phobias, sympathies, loves, and hopes that revolve around the question of race. Is he to be equated with Faulkner? Clearly not—however much Faulkner may have known of such conflicts. For Faulkner stands outside Ike and criticizes him for weakness. At the same time, Faulkner presents him with sympathy, respect, and tenderness. Ike, a man of an older generation, born in 1867, is caught in his own moment of time, struggling to clear his mind and feelings, and up to that last moment he lies impotent and shaking in horror at what, *for him,* is the unresolvable issue.[11] Lying on the cot in the ruined wilderness, with "the constant and grieving rain" on the canvas of the tent, he is the image of the anguishing tale of time.

But is that image the final meaning we carry away? Does time end with an old man shuddering in horror? Some critics have said that,

[11] Ike, Faulkner says, "used 'a thousand or two thousand years' in his despair. He had seen a condition which was intolerable, which shouldn't be but it was, and he was saying in effect that this must be changed, this cannot go on, but I'm too old to do anything about it, that maybe in a thousand years somebody will be young enough and strong enough to do something about it. That was all he meant by the numbers. But I think that he saw, as everybody thinks, that a condition like that is intolerable, not so much intolerable to a man's sense of justice, but maybe intolerable to the condition, that any country has reached the point where if it is to endure, it must have no inner conflicts based on a wrong, a basic human wrong." *Faulkner at the University,* p. 46. It is well to remember, in connection with Ike's attitude, that Lincoln would have understood him perfectly, that Lincoln, though an emancipationist, was a racist, in an even stricter sense than Ike.

substantially, this is what Faulkner in the end gives us. For instance, Sartre, in a famous essay,[12] says that Faulkner's vision can be compared to that of a man in a convertible looking back; the present is represented by the points of light which flicker into vision but which become clear and hard images of objects, with "a surrealistic quality," only as they are past and immutable. The present "does not exist, it becomes." There is not, Sartre observes, even the chronological order in the past; there is the "order of the heart"—ordering by emotion and obsession. For Faulkner the "past is unfortunately never lost." Faulkner, like the mystic, who must forget something, wants to forget time. For him, the future, the dimension of choice and act, is barred. And, to paraphrase Sartre, the first task of the real historian in explaining the past (as opposed to what Faulkner allegedly does) is to inquire into the future. Sartre sums up by saying that Faulkner "uses his extraordinary art to describe a world dying of old age"—like old Ike on his cot, incapable of action. In other words, what is at stake here is Faulkner's basic conception of time.

Certainly, this conception of time—futureless time—is one held by many of the characters in Faulkner, and the tale he tells is full of frozen moments, of compulsive acts, of the doom of the past, of the pain of entrapment—those things which negate both the will and any intelligent action targeted to the future. And I feel it true that the emphasis on "doom" is much greater in Faulkner's early work than in the later. But over against the characters in Faulkner's work whose concept of time is that of the barred future we can find those who are, in fact, oriented toward the future. These two sets of characters represent, in one perspective, the two poles of the Faulknerian drama.[13]

The problem, in treating these two poles, is to avoid the temptation to take refuge in simplistic formulations. The past is, indeed, a repository of values, a pantheon, a world to which we can turn for the great images of men who were "complete," at least in contrast to Faulkner's idea of modernity, with its abstraction and loveless violation of nature and man. But, as we have seen, the past may also be the source of doom. It is not merely the source of doom in the historical and moral consequences of the evil men have wrought—specifically slavery. It is also the source of doom in a way which we rarely find indicated by students of Faulkner's work: the very awareness and reverence of the values of the past may, in a certain perspective, become the enemy of those very values. Hightower, for example: he lives in a romantic dream of the past, and in that dream he can neither deal with the present obligations of his

[12] Reprinted above, p. 87.

[13] We are here talking about the over-all import of Faulkner's work. A case might be made, however, for the notion that Faulkner, in the beginning, had something of the romantic fatalism which Sartre comments on, and that he worked from this toward his final view. The novel *Sartoris* and the character of the boy, Quentin, are both somewhat ambiguous in this respect.

church and community nor understand the nature of his religion; for his religion, too, is cut off from both human and divine reference—a secular, historical "piety," we may say, being the corrupting influence on religious piety. He is, in fact, cut off from nature too, emasculated by the dream, and the fact of his unsexing drives his wife off to Memphis to promiscuity and death. And here, in Hightower's unsexing, we find a parallel and counterpoint to the unsexing of Popeye and Flem—that is, Hightower suffers in an "abstraction" of the past, in a concept of the past as taken out of nature and the flow of time, as frozen. In Hightower's relation to Christmas there is, too, a significance: Christmas, the man of no past, and therefore of the agonized unidentifiable present, turns to Hightower and finds in his house only death. This whole situation is left shadowy, but the symbolic ordering is clear enough. But we should remark, however, that Hightower is, in the end, redeemed from his sterile obsession with the past; he is brought into contact with the normal flow of nature and reality.

Hightower, though the most complex example of a person maimed by a perverted reverence for the past, is not alone. Joanna Burden, the young Bayard (whose very name carries the irony), Drusilla, Mr. Compson, his son Quentin, Percy Grimm—they are all victims of the wrong kind of reverence for the past, and they are all, in various ways, givers of death.[14] Even Ike, who sees the crime carried by the past and who, out of the wisdom he has learned from the past through Sam Fathers, tries to expiate it, is still enough of a victim of the past to be unable to act for the future: an agony of awareness is all he is capable of at the end of "Delta Autumn."

If we take the other pole, the pole of the future, we find the same doubleness. There is a Sutpen, with his "design" (a vision of the future falsely grounded) and the ruin which he brings on himself and others. There is Flem, who, in his bushwhacker Snopesism, has no past and represents the future of cold, abstract, desexed (i.e., "unnatural," loveless) exploitation. There is Jason, who, with his hatred of the past, is oriented, like Flem, to the future of abstract, loveless exploitation. But there are others whose relation to the future is constructive. Nancy, in *Requiem for a Nun,* is concerned with the redemption of the future, as is Temple. There is the young Lucas, with the fire on his hearth, the mark of vital continuity, as well as the older Lucas of unswerving integrity. There are Chick Mallison and Gavin. There is Lena Grove, the simple, trusting, "natural" carrier of the future. There are Ratliff and Dilsey, and in their ways, Eula and Linda.

As for Dilsey, living in a world where all others are tortured by one form or another of a defective sense of time, she can say: "I've seed de

[14] Joanna, trapped in her past, to herself and Christmas; young Bayard, to his grandfather and to himself; Drusilla in offering the pistols, in "An Odor of Verbena"; Mr. Compson in grooming his son for suicide; and Quentin in the actual suicide.

first en de last." For her, time is a process, not barred on either side, but redeemed in "de blood en de ricklickshun of de Lamb." For she comes to this vision of "de beginnin" and "de endin," we may recall, just after the sermon, where she had sat "crying rigidly and quietly in the annealment and the blood of the remembered Lamb"—sitting beside Ben, who was "rapt in his sweet blue gaze," appropriately beside Ben, who is also outside the nag of time. Ratliff, too, lives in a sense of time as a vital process, observing the life around him, benign and critical, even though without Dilsey's transcendent vision of Eternity as the support and fulfillment of time.

My point is this: if Faulkner feels the past as the repository of great images of human effort and integrity, he also sees it as the source of a dynamic evil. If he is aware of the romantic pull of the past, he is also aware that submission to the romance of the past is a form of death. If he finds in modernity a violation of the dream of the "communal anonymity of brotherhood," of nature, and of honor, he does not see it merely as the barred end of history; it is also the instant in which action is possible, with a choice between action as "doom" from the past (that is, as compulsive) and action as affirmation of future possibilities. If the Flems and the Jasons drive hard to define a dehumanized future, there are the Dilseys and the Ratliffs who see the future as part of the vital human continuity. If *The Sound and the Fury* is Faulkner's *Wasteland*, it is a wasteland that, unlike Eliot's, ends in Easter. In other words, Faulkner's dialectic of time is inclusive—and painful. And is it any dishonor to him to hazard the notion that it represents a life-effort rather than an intellectual construct?

Piety is the key, one sometimes feels, to Faulkner's work. If he was capable, in the great complexity of his work, to render, without extenuation, the meanness and brutality of his society, he was also capable of piety to his place, his clan, his history, the values of his shared past—the fact of sharing of experience being, in itself, one of the values. But we may remind ourselves, too, that he saw piety as the reverence for the human capacity to struggle and endure, ultimately as reverence for the human effort for justice. In fact, struggle should be, for the writer, the very essence of his theme. The writer, as Faulkner put it in one of his talks at the University of Virginia, "believes that man can be better than he is, and that is what the writer is trying to do, is interested in—to show man as he is in conflict with his problems, with his nature, with his own heart, with his fellows, and with his environment."

In this light the piety is not for institutions and social arrangements, which are necessarily subject to the revisions of historical process, but for that "truth" that speaks to the heart. That is, to maintain a tradition with proper piety means neither to repudiate action nor to indulge in automatic, compulsive action; it means action based on a fundamental achievement of the imagination—the transliteration of values from an old context to a new, with a consequent freedom in action. As Gavin put it in *Intruder in the Dust,* "no man can cause more grief than that one clinging blindly to the views of his ancestors." But even if one should discard those views, he will, if pious, reverence those ancestors, even in their human failures. In other words, in piety itself there may be a deep tension and struggle, a struggle to convert the piety of the past into a piety of the future—a piety projected into the future.

We can read Faulkner's work as the record of such a struggle. This in two senses: it is the objective dramatization, through many situations and characters, of such a struggle; but it is also—as an artistic work always is, despite all the disguises and distortions of creation—a projection of the writer's experience. It is the work that makes Faulkner great, but we have another record of his experience in those statements he made in his role as a citizen of his native state. We know the ferocious love of place that made him hope for a solution of the South's problems by the South, and the ferocious pride of place that made him allegedly say, in an interview (*Reporter,* March 1956), that he might, in the face of outside interference, have to take a gun and shoot Negroes in the streets of Oxford. But he also wrote:

> We accept insult and contumely and the risk of violence because we will not sit quietly by and see our native land, the South, not just Mississippi, but all the South, wreck and ruin itself twice in less than a hundred years, over the Negro question.
>
> We speak now against the day when our Southern people who will resist to the last these inevitable changes in social relations, will, when they have been forced to accept what they at one time might have accepted with dignity and good-will, will say, "Why didn't someone tell me this before? Tell us this in time?" [15]

We know how much Faulkner detested self-righteousness, glibness, easy solutions, easy virtuousness, abstract formulations. We can know from his work by what a difficult, tangled, and shadowy path he came to such a statement as the one above. The weight of struggle projected into the work gives authority to such a statement. Long ago Edmund Wilson, commenting on *Intruder in the Dust,* wrote: "I do not sympathize with the line of criticism which deplores Faulkner's obstinate persistence in submerging himself in the mentality of the community where he was born, for his chivalry, which constitutes his morality, is a part of his Southern heritage, and it appears in Faulkner's work as a force more humane and more positive than almost anything one can find in the

[15] Speech made to Southern Historical Association at Memphis, November 10, 1955. Printed in *Memphis Commercial Appeal* and, in expanded form, in *Three Views of the Segregation Decisions* (Atlanta: Southern Regional Council, 1956). The lines here quoted appear in the expanded version, p. 12.

work of even those writers of our more mechanized society who have set out to defend human rights." [16]

James Joyce went forth from Ireland to forge, as he put it, in the words of his hero Stephen Dedalus, the conscience of his race, Faulkner did a more difficult thing. To forge the conscience of his race, he stayed in his native spot and, in his soul, in vice and in virtue, re-enacted the history of that race.

[16] Wilson's essay is reprinted above, p. 219.

Appendix I

Notes and Comments

Many of the most astute, seminal, or provocative ideas about the work of William Faulkner have appeared in notes or in short sections of long essays or books. I have assembled here a number of the more interesting examples of such criticism.

R.P.W.

André Malraux

Faulkner is well aware that detectives do not exist, that the police do not depend on psychology or perspicacity but rather on secret information, and that the escaping murderer is not caught by Mr. Gumshoe or Mr. Shadow, those modest thinkers of police headquarters, but by "plants" in suspicious neighborhoods. One has only to read the memoirs of police chiefs to discover that psychological penetration is not their great quality, and that a good police force is simply the one which has succeeded in organizing its army of informers most efficiently. Faulkner also knows that the gangster is first of all a dealer in alcohol. *Sanctuary* is therefore a novel with a detective-story atmosphere but without detectives, a novel of sordid gangsters who are sometimes cowardly and weak. In this way the author achieves a brutality justified by the setting, as well as the possibility, without abandoning a measure of verisimilitude, of getting credence for rape, lynching, and murder, the forms of violence which the plot imposes on the whole book.

It is probably erroneous to look for the essential part of a detective story in the plot or the hunt for the criminal. Taken by itself, the plot would be only a sort of chess game, an artistic failure. The plot is important in that it is the most efficient way of revealing an ethical or poetic fact in its greatest intensity. The worth of the plot is in what it engenders.

What does it engender in this case? An ill-assorted, powerful, and

"A Preface for Faulkner's *Sanctuary*" by André Malraux. From *La Nouvelle Revue Française* (November 1, 1933), pp. 744-747. Reprinted by permission of André Malraux and *La Nouvelle Revue Française*.

savagely personal world, sometimes one not without crudity. In Faulkner, there is no particular presentation of man, there are no values, nor, in spite of the stream-of-consciousness monologues in his early books, is there even any psychology. But there is the figure of Destiny, standing alone behind all these similar and diverse beings like Death in a hospital ward of incurables. An intense obsession crushes each of his characters, and in no case do the characters succeed in exorcising it. The obsession still hovers behind them, unchanging, summoning them instead of awaiting their summons.

Such a realm was for a long time the subject for gossip; even if American rumors did not kindly inform us that alcohol was an integral part of Faulkner's personal legend, the relationship between his universe and those of Poe and Hoffmann would be clear. The same psychological material, the same hatreds, horses, coffins, and obsessions. What differentiates Faulkner and Poe is their individual notions of the work of art. To be more exact, the work of art existed for Poe and dominated the will to express; and this is probably what most separates him from us. When the story was finished, it took on in his mind the limited and independent existence of a picture on the easel.

In the weakening of importance accorded to things, I see the principal element of transformation of our art. In painting, it is clear that a Picasso picture is ever less a canvas, and more and more the indication of a discovery, a landmark left for the passage of tormented genius; in literature, the supremacy of the novel is significant, since, of all the arts (and I am not forgetting music), the novel is the least tractable, the one in which the realm of will is most limited. One can best appreciate how much *The Brothers Karamazoff* and *Illusions perdues* dominate Dostoevsky and Balzac by reading these works after the splendid passive novels of Flaubert. The important thing is not that the author is dominated, but that for the last fifty years he has been increasingly selecting what will dominate him, that he has been arranging the resources of his art with that end in view. Certain great novels have been for their authors primarily the creation of the one thing that could engulf them. And, just as Lawrence wraps himself up in sexuality, so does Faulkner dig down into the irreparable.

A secret force, sometimes an epic one, is released in him every time he succeeds in placing one of his characters face to face with the irreparable. Perhaps his one true subject is the irreparable; perhaps for him there is no question other than that of successfully crushing man. I should not be surprised if he often thought out his scenes before imagining his characters, if the work were, in his eyes, not a story whose unfolding determined tragic situations, but contrarily that the plot was created from the dramatic opposition or crushing of unknown characters, and imagination merely served to bring forth characters for this preconceived situation. The impassioned tension, which is Faulkner's strength, stems either from enslaved powerlessness fully comprehended (the girl in the gangster's house), or from irreparable absurdity (the corn-cob rape, the burning of the inocent victim, Popeye the fugitive stupidly condemned for a crime he did not commit; in *While I Lay Dying* the farmer who treats his injured knee by encasing it in cement, the extraordinary monologue of hatred). It is, moreover, absurdity which gives to his almost comical secondary characters (the keeper of the brothel with her dogs) an intensity comparable to that of Shchedrin. I shall not suggest the name of Dickens, for even the secondary characters of Faulkner move in the aura of feeling which gives the work its worth—hatred. Here it is not a matter of the struggle against one's own set of values, of that fatalistic passion by which all the great artists, from Baudelaire to half-blind Nietzsche singing of light, express the essential part of their being; it is a question of a psychological state on which almost all tragic art depends and which has not ever been studied because aesthetics do not reveal it: fascination. Just as the opium eater does not discover his universe until he has used the drug, so does the tragic poet express his world only when he is in a particular state, so persistent that it becomes a need. The tragic poet expresses what obsesses him, not to exorcize the obsession (the obsessive object will reappear in his next work), but to change its nature: for, by expressing it with other elements, he makes the obsession enter the relative universe of things he has conceived and dominated. He does not defend himself against anguish by expressing it, but by expressing something else with it, by bringing it back into the universe. The deepest form of fascination, that of the artist, derives its strength from being both horror and the possibility of conceiving horror.

Sanctuary is the intrusion of Greek tragedy into the detective story.

Allen Tate

In the thirty-one years of our acquaintance I saw him not more than five or six times, and but for one meeting in Rome about ten years ago he seemed to me arrogant and ill-mannered in a way that I felt qualified to distinguish as peculiarly "Southern": in company he usually failed to reply when spoken to, or when he spoke there was something grandiose in the profusion with which he sprinkled his remarks with "Sir" and "Ma'ms." Years ago, when I was editing *The Sewanee Review,* I had some correspondence with him; his letters were signed "Faulkner." I wrote him that English nobility followed this practice and I never heard from him again.

I suppose the main source of my annoyance with him was his affectation of not being a writer, but a farmer; this would have been preten-

Reprinted with permission from William Faulkner: 1897-1962, *The Sewanee Review,* Vol. 71, No. 1 (Jan.-March 1963), pp. 160-164.

tious even had he been a farmer. But being a "farmer," he did not "associate" with writers—with the consequence that he was usually surrounded by third-rate writers or just plain sycophants. I never heard that he was a friend of anybody who could conceivably have been his peer.

One may leave the man to posterity, but the work must be reread now, and talked about, lest Faulkner, like other writers of immense fame in their lifetime, go into a slump. However great a writer may be, the public gets increasingly tired of him; his death seems to remove the obligation to read him. But if I had read *The Reivers,* I should be willing to say something about the work as a whole, and an essay would make some of the points that I can only suggest in this "obituary" of a man I did not like, but of a writer who since the early thirties I have thought was the greatest American novelist after Henry James: a novelist of an originality and power not equaled by his contemporaries, Hemingway and Fitzgerald.

Leaving aside the two books that I have not read, I should say that he wrote at least five masterpieces (what other American novclist wrote so many, except James?): they are *The Sound and the Fury, As I Lay Dying, Sanctuary, Light in August,* and *The Hamlet.* I know people of good judgment who would add to this list *The Wild Palms* and *Absalom, Absalom!,* books that contain some great writing but that in the end are not novels. Of the four first titles on my list, none appeared after 1932; the fifth, in 1940. *Absalom, Absalom!* and *The Wild Palms* came out in 1936 and 1939. All Faulkner's seven great books were written in a span of about eleven or twelve years. The fine long story "The Bear" was written toward the end of this period. The later books round out the picture of Yoknapatawpha County (Lafayette County, Mississippi), but nobody would know them had the earlier books not been written. William Faulkner wrote only one bad novel, *A Fable,* his version of the Grand Inquisitor, conceived in theological ignorance and placed in a setting that he had not observed. . . .

The European reader finds something uniquely American in Faulkner, and obviously no European could have written his books; the few European commentators that I have read seem to me to glorify William Faulkner in a provincial American (or Southern) vacuum. I believe that as his personality fades from view he will be recognized as one of the last great craftsmen of the art of fiction which Ford Madox Ford called the Impressionist Novel. From Stendhal through Flaubert and Joyce there is a direct line to Faulkner, and it is not a mere question of influence. Faulkner's great subject, as it was Flaubert's and Proust's, is passive suffering, the victim being destroyed either by society or by dark forces within himself. Faulkner is one of the great exemplars of the international school of fiction which for more than a century has reversed the Aristotelian doctrine that tragedy is an action, not a quality.

William Faulkner's time and place made it possible for him to extend this European tradition beyond any boundaries that were visible to novelists of New England, the Middle West, or the Far West. The Greco-Trojan myth (Northerners as the upstart Greeks, Southerners as the older, more civilized Trojans) presented Faulkner, before he had written a line, with a large semi-historical background against which even his ignorant characters, like Lena Grove or Dewey Dell Bundren, as well as the more civilized Compsons and Sartorises, could be projected in more than human dimensions. I had occasion some years ago to say in the *New Statesman* that had William Faulkner invented his myth, it could not have been as good as it turned out to be. (Sophocles was doubtless in a similarly advantageous position with respect to the Oedipean cycle.) Faulkner brought to bear upon the myth greater imaginative powers than any of his contemporaries possessed. . . .

Two secondary themes in Faulkner have obscured the critics' awareness of the great theme. These are: the white man's legacy of guilt for slavery and the rape of the land. These themes are almost obsessive, but they are not the main theme. William Faulkner was not a "segregationist." (Whether he was an "integrationist" is a different question.) But how could he not have been a segregationist when he said that he would shoot Negroes in the streets if the Federal Government interfered in Mississippi? Unless the European—or for that matter the Northern—reader understands that for Faulkner, and for thousands of other Southerners of his generation, the separatism and possible autonomy of the South came before all other "problems," he will misread Faulkner because he will not have discerned the great theme. I will repeat it in different language: the destruction of the Old South released native forces of disorder and corruption which were accelerated by the brutal exploitation of the carpetbaggers and an army of occupation; thus the old order of dignity and principle was replaced by upstarts and cynical materialists. Federal interference in the South had brought this about; and when Faulkner said he would shoot Negroes if that were necessary to keep Federal interference at bay, his response came directly out of the Greco-Trojan myth; and yet it was the response of a man who had depicted Negroes with greater understanding and compassion than any other Southern writer of his time. . . .

Graham Greene

Strip away the fake poetry [from *Absalom, Absalom!*], and you have the plot of a "blood," while Mr. Faulkner disguises the complete absence of a theme with pseudo-tragic talk of doom and fate and the furies.

"The Furies in Mississippi" by Graham Greene. From *London Mercury,* Vol. 35 (March 1937), pp. 517-518.

Alas! it is all true. Mr. Faulkner's is a talent quite easy to condemn, but there does remain over—Somthing: at the least a gift of vivid phrase heard too seldom through the Otranto thunder ("the ghost mused with shadowy docility as if it were the voice which he haunted where a more fortunate one would have had a house"; pigeons which "wheeled in short courses resembling soft fluid paint-smears on the soft summer sky"); at its best—not to be found here or in *Sartoris*—an individual blend of the romantic and the realistic which makes the gangster Popeye in *Sanctuary* so memorable a figure, a sense of spiritual evil which away from the contemporary scene becomes unconvincing and stagey. And finally we should consider whether, if the romantic costume subject is to be treated at all (if Southern gentlefolk, horsemen at night, and wistaria blossom, which do speak in certain moods like common songs to the imagination, deserve an occasional appearance), it can be treated in any other way. It can't be treated plainly, like Popeye's rape on the corn-husks of the college girl, or the crazy antique planes in *Pylon*: the artificial subject has to be carried by an artificial manner, and even at its vaguest and most resounding Mr. Faulkner's style is welcome when we consider the alternatives: *Anthony Adverse* and *Gone With the Wind.*

F. R. Leavis

It is his "technique," of course, that, together with his dealings in abnormal or subnormal mentality and his disregard of the polite taboos, has gained for him, in France as well as in America and England, his reputation as one of the most significant and peculiarly modern of writers. The technique that matters is the means of expressing a firmly realized purpose, growing out of a personal sensibility. Early in *Light in August* it should have become plain to the reader that Faulkner's "technique" is an expression of—or disguise for—an uncertainty about what he is trying to do.

There is, for instance, that Gertrude-Steinian trick: "Memory believes before knowing remembers. Believes longer than recollects, longer than knowing even wonders. Knows remembers believes" etc. Here it is incidental to a rendering (for the most part in a quite unrelated manner, and one of the best things in the book) of childhood experience. But it is sporadic, applied to various kinds of characters in various circumstances, and it is never supported by that minute intimacy in the registering of consciousness which it implies. Indeed, Faulkner is seldom for long sure of the point of view he is writing from, and will alter his focus and his notation casually, it would seem, and almost without knowing it.

This pervasive uncertainty of method goes down to a central and radical uncertainty. If what is apparently meant to be the central theme

"Dostoevsky or Dickens?" by F. R. Leavis. From *Scrutiny,* Vol. 2, No. 1 (June, 1933), pp. 91-93.

of the book, the conflict in Christmas of the white and the Negro blood, had been realized and active, we should necessarily have had somewhere and by some means an intimate and subtle rendering of his consciousness. But in spite of the technique and in spite of the digression—for it strikes us as that—back into childhood, he remains the monotonously "baleful" melodramatic villain whose mysteriousness is of so familiar a kind, depending on our having only a surface to contemplate. Faulkner, in fact, in his vision of Good and Evil is . . . at his best simple, at his worst sentimental and melodramatic. The brutal submorality of Christmas might have been significant in a Dostoevsky context and, so, interesting; but when Faulkner, rightly not trusting the job made of it by his "technique," pumps in the Significance straight-forwardly at the death of Christmas, its quality appears in the prose of this:

> Then Grimm too sprang back, flinging behind him the bloody butcher knife. "Now you'll let white women alone, even in hell," he said. But the man on the floor had not moved. He just lay there, with his eyes open and empty of everything save consciousness, and with something, a shadow, about the mouth. For a long moment he looked up at them with peaceful and unfathomable and unbearable eyes. Then his face, body, all, seemed to collapse, to fall in upon itself, and from out the slashed garments about his hips and loins the pent black blood seemed to rush like a released breath. It seemed to rush out of his pale body like the rush of sparks from a rising rocket; upon that black blast the man seemed to rise soaring into their memories for ever and ever. They are not to lose it, in whatever peaceful valleys, beside whatever placid and reassuring streams of old age, in the mirroring faces of whatever children they will contemplate old disasters and newer hopes. It will be there, musing, quiet, steadfast, not fading and not particularly threatful, but of itself alone serene, of itself alone triumphant.

Maxwell Geismar

We have noticed, then, over the mature period of Faulkner's work a curious progression. From the troubled but tender and intensely human world of *The Sound and the Fury* (looking back at this early scene now, it seems almost impossible for Faulkner to have created it), the writer has moved steadily toward the perverse and the pathological: and the denial of humanity which he uses his inversions to convey. From the touching drama of innocence, he has advanced to that of corruption. In the sequence of Faulkner's thought, the idiot Benjy Compson, who evoked in us all that was compassionate, has been replaced by the pervert Popeye, who represents all that is diseased. And we must notice the meaning of Faulkner's new phase. Faulkner is still describing the

Condensed from "The Negro and the Female" in *Writers in Crisis* (Boston: Houghton Mifflin Co., 1942), by Maxwell Geismar, pp. 167-69, 181-83.

world of childhood, but now a very different aspect of it: the world of human perversions whose precise nature is that they also are infantile emotions; they are the reflection of our early animal instincts which have been blocked and forced out of their normal channels of maturing. This is the alternate half of that realm of tender young emotions which Faulkner caught with such integrity in *The Sound and the Fury*. It is the destructive side of our primitive nature, coming so easily and richly to Faulkner, which is now being manipulated to portray a world the writer condemns. This is childhood, as it were, taking its revenge upon the maturity which had dissolved its faith. For now painting his people in these gruesome colors, seeing humanity only in terms of its aberrations, Faulkner has come, with *Light in August,* to show us the full range of his discontent: his contempt for modern maturity which displays itself so eloquently in the variety of perversions which the writer contrives for his characters. The defiance of modern society is pervasive, as we have seen, in the works of the American writers in the 1920s. But Faulkner may be seen as perhaps the supreme example of it—a hatred of life so compelling with him that there almost seems to be an inability in the writer to reach maturity itself.

We are about to trace the course of this great hatred a little further. But meanwhile we have also noticed where the crux of Faulkner's discontent has come to rest. As the series of women in *Light in August* are the factors of Joe Christmas's degeneration, we have seen how Faulkner himself has focused his anger on the feminine portraits which mark his work as a whole. We recall Cecily Saunders, the "papier-maché Virgin" of *Soldiers' Pay*. This "Virgin" turned into a vicious prostitute, the Temple Drake of *Sanctuary*. The neurasthenic Mrs. Compson of *The Sound and the Fury,* who is perhaps the most purely contemptible character in the novel. And even Caddy herself, the object of such intense devotion, on the part of Benjy and Quentin, whose sexual weakness is nevertheless the direct cause of their destruction. We remember the Belle Mitchell of *Sartoris,* whose effect, like that of Joanna Burden, was of a rich and fatal drug, "a motionless and cloying sea" in which the Faulknerian male watches himself drown. And as Faulkner has been steadily concerned in the past with these female incubae, so now, and drawn like these later women toward the black male, he will view the Negro with perhaps even greater bitterness. The Negro, who in the person of Joe Christmas has already begun to dominate Faulkner's work, whose shadow falls across not only the white writer, but in the Faulknerian view, the whole white race:

> I thought of all the children coming forever and ever into the world, white, with the black shadow already falling upon them before they drew breath. And I seemed to see the black shadow in the shape of a cross. And it seemed like the white babies were struggling, even before they drew breath, to escape from the shadow that was not only upon them but beneath them

> too, flung out like their arms were flung out, as if they were nailed to the cross. I saw all the little babies that would ever be in the world, the ones not yet even born—a long line of them with their arms spread, on the black crosses.

What, then, is the meaning of these twin Furies of the Faulknerian deep southern Waste Land, this odd, and to Faulkner quite horrifying, conjunction of the Female and the Negro? Of these symbols which he has taken to convey the entire complex of his southern revolt against modern society, and even maturity itself? In the work of Faulkner's latest period, we may at last identify this theme. . . .

Held in such reversionary superstition, moreover, to what distortions can the psyche not bring itself? What a strange inversion it is to take the Female and the Negro, who are if anything the tragic consequence, and to exhibit them, indeed to believe them as the evil cause! This turning of the logical coin is psychological prestidigitation which ends with the head becoming the tail, and all respectable sense lost! The using of the one object that is certainly not responsible for our woes as being the single creator of them (so the Fascists use the Jew)—this is an inversion all too familiar to us today in other areas, another symptom of the confused emotions of our time. What genuine ills can be ignored by this again infantile preoccupation with scapegoats (so the child blames its mother), the infatuation with chimeras, what terrible ills can be created by it. Here is a dangerous quirk of the psyche, a trick once learned never wholly forgotten, a temptation once indulged in perhaps never to be wholly denied, a trick which may end by deceiving the trickster. I have used the title of Maurice Samuel's penetrating study of the Fascist superstitions, *The Great Hatred,* to best describe Faulkner's work as a whole. For it is in the larger tradition of reversionary, neo-pagan, and neurotic discontent (from which Fascism stems) that much of Faulkner's writing must be placed—the anti-civilizational revolt which has caught so many modern mystics, the revolt rising out of modern social evils, nourished by ignorance of their true nature, and which succumbs to malice as their solution. It is not accidental that in Faulkner's novels we have watched the retrogression from the affecting era of infancy to that of infantile corruption; and that returning in *Absalom, Absalom!* to the only society he can believe in, Faulkner's affection is nevertheless thinner, and the pretension of his novel greater. Hatred, as we know, feeds upon itself, while living in the past is apt to be an attenuating process.

Yet these are dangers dormant in parts of the Faulknerian reversion rather than immediate. It would be a tragedy if the major talent of Faulkner were to yield to any such gross chicanery, or to any other smaller trickeries. But it would be unjust to claim that on the whole, really, it has. (And it is a vital fact that no major American writer has as yet succumbed, in the manner of Knut Hamsun, to the Fascist ethics, even though some of our popular entertainers have shown the signs.) If we notice the dangerous possibilities of Faulkner's position, moreover, we must remember it is still the southern world of the 1920s that the novelist rejects. It is the earlier impact of the American industrial ethics he denies, the ethics embodied so brilliantly in the Jason of *The Sound and the Fury,* whose final citadel is perhaps Mississippi, and whose last deity is Snopes. In the repudiation of our society from 1860 to 1929, Faulkner thus presents another aspect of the total cultural rejection of the American artist over this epoch. Alone among the major writers of the '20s Faulkner has remained without change, our unreconstructed rebel, like the Hightower of *Light in August* still bemused in the vision of a nobler southern past where his life began and ended. Yet to Faulkner as to Lardner, viewing the modern scene, what may have seemed like perpetuity was after all only an American adolescence. The new age, as it reached the Michigan woods of Hemingway and the metropolis of Dos Passos, may yet rout the phantoms and ghouls of Faulkner's Jefferson. The crisis and indeed the new world war may bring another glimpse of that high and impossible American destiny which for Faulkner was ended by the Civil War. A developing American maturity, this maturity that Faulkner despairs of, must at last penetrate even to Jefferson, even to the Snopeses; and may awaken in our artist that magnificent compassion which he has vouchsafed only to the children of a disintegrating aristocracy. Like his Hightower, waiting, our author may once again hear "the wild bugles, and the clashing sabres" and the thunder of martial hooves, but not dying now nor forever lost in the phantom dust. And, like Hightower, will he also find then "something to pant with, to be reaffirmed in triumph and desire with"?

Irving Howe

Now it cannot be charged against Faulkner, as John Jay Chapman did against Emerson, that a visitor from Mars would never learn from him what even the Italian opera makes clear: that there are two sexes in the world. Faulkner is all too willing to proclaim the subtle and insidious powers of women, to evoke a sense of their dizzying attractions, even to speculate, in the style of legend, on female malevolence as one of the root terrors of existence. At least as serious as Chapman's complaint against Emerson is the fact that seldom in Faulkner's work do we find a mature recognition of the possibilities in the relations between men and women—possibilities, I might specify, of fulfilled love and tragic complication. And a writer unable to summon the first of these is likely to have troubles in reaching the second.

Such splendid old ladies as Miss Rosa Millard, Aunt Jenny Du Pre

From *William Faulkner* by Irving Howe, 2nd ed. (New York: *Vintage Books,* 1962), pp. 141-144.

and Dilsey, all conspicuously beyond the age of sexual distraction, gain Faulkner's admiration. They neither threaten nor attract; they give household orders and provide intuitive wisdom; they are beyond the magical powers of sexuality. But there is hardly a young woman in Faulkner's novels—one notable exception is Linda Snopes in *The Mansion*—who does not provoke quantities of bitterness and bile; and so persistent is this distaste for the doings of "woman-flesh" that it cannot be dismissed as a vagary of either Faulkner or the characters who convey it.

Few writers have trained such ferocity on the young American bitch: Cecily the "papier-maché Virgin" of *Soldiers' Pay,* Patricia the "sexless yet somehow troubling" flapper of *Mosquitoes,* and that abomination of castrating femaleness, Temple Drake. With her "cool, predatory and discreet" eyes, Temple anticipates the kind of modern woman about whom it is hard to say which is more alarming: her coldness or her availability. At the moment she flourishes in Manhattan, but any American town with a claim to sophistication can provide examples: smoother, more "cultured" and self-contained than the Temple Drake of *Sanctuary.*[1] To have noticed and rendered her with such deadly accuracy is surely one of Faulkner's triumphs; yet she rouses currents of disturbance that cannot be understood or justified strictly in terms of the novel itself. Again and again, the thought—or sight—of her drives Faulkner to a pitch of hysteria and nausea, as if in her compulsive negation of the feminine she were also its evil apotheosis.

A similar ferocity is directed against Belle Mitchell of *Sanctuary,* the kind of woman who consciously uses her body to certify her domination over men. The same ferocity is directed against that gorgeous lump of fertility called Eula Varner in *The Hamlet,* and against those young women, like Charlotte Rittenmeyer in *The Wild Palms* and Laverne Schumann in *Pylon,* who sin not through personal malice but through the impersonal mechanics of their sex. Even Lena Grove, for all her appearance of submissiveness, digs iron claws into her man with a serene possessiveness of instinct; the affection she draws from Faulkner depends on a humorous belief that it is pointless to resist her.

Nor does Faulkner hesitate to state these feelings explicity. In *Absalom, Absalom!* Henry Bon learns that "you cant beat women anyhow and that if you are wise or dislike trouble and uproar you dont even try to"—a lesson Faulkner never tires of repeating, though always with the certainty that men, being victims of themselves, must prove incapable of learning it. Quentin Compson goes further than Bon; "women," he says "are like that . . . they have an affinity for evil." The Reverend Hightower, urging Byron Bunch not to marry Lena Grove, remarks, "No woman who has a child is ever betrayed; the husband of a mother,

[1] Faulkner realized as much when he tried to create an older version of Temple Drake in *Requiem for a Nun.*

whether he be the father or not, is already a cuckold. . . . There have been good women who were martyrs to brutes. . . . But what woman, good or bad, has ever suffered from any brute as men have suffered from good women?" And in the story "Wash" these notions are given a droll color when a hardened bachelor who has accidentally wandered into an old maid's bedroom is told he will now have to marry her: "You come into bear-country of your own free will and accord. All right; you were a grown man and you knew it was bear-country and you knew the way back out like you knew the way in and you had your chance to take it. But no. You had to crawl into the den and lay down by the bear. And whether you did or didn't know the bear was in it dont make any difference."

Exceptions to this treatment of the sexes can be found: Houston and his young wife in *The Hamlet,* like the unfortunate poor white Goodwins in *Sanctuary,* do love each other with a measure of happiness and meaning. Between Gavin Stevens and Linda Snopes in *The Mansion* there is a troubled incoherent love which at least escapes Faulkner's usual formulas. So slight a weight, however, do these exceptions carry in Faulkner's world, that they cannot set up a counterpoise to the dominant attitudes felt and expressed toward women. This inclination toward misogyny need not always be taken too literally or solemnly; the passage from "Wash" reflects the wry folk view that if people live long enough they are likely to stumble into some traps, usually those they have spent their lives avoiding. Much of Faulkner's talk about women suggests the timbre of folk humor, the sort of playful and deliberately inflated grumbling that might once have been heard on a Saturday afternoon in country stores. But so persistent a devotion to popular attitudes, in both their humorous surface and earnest core, must be related to some governing personal bias, some obscure uneasiness before these victims of "periodic filth."

Faulkner's inability to achieve moral depth in his portraiture of young women clearly indicates a major failing as a novelist. It is an instance where his reliance on the folk imagination, fruitful though it usually is, plays him false. But even as it leads to a tedious sameness and predictability of characterization, the distrust of women serves a symbolic function in the unfolding of his work. Women are the this-worldly sex, the child-bearers who chain men to possessions and embody the indestructible urge to racial survival. As the personification of the reality principle, they contrive to perpetuate the species no matter what dreams or destruction men indulge in. Faulkner's men, like Melville's, are happiest when they "get away," escaping to the woods for a few weeks of female-less companionship. His women are happiest—or, since Faulkner might say that to them happiness does not matter, they are most content—when men are subdued to their social tasks.

Leslie A. Fiedler

In the work of William Faulkner, the fear of the castrating woman and the dis-ease with sexuality present in the novels of his contemporaries, Fitzgerald and Hemingway, attain their fullest and shrillest expression. Not content with merely projecting images of the anti-virgin, he insists upon editorializing against the women he travesties in character and situation. No Jiggs and Maggie cliché of popular anti-feminism is too banal for him to use; he reminds us (again and again!) that men are helpless in the hands of their mothers, wives, and sisters; that females do not think but proceed from evidence to conclusions by paths too devious for males to follow; that they possess neither morality nor honor; that they are capable, therefore, of betrayal without qualm or quiver of guilt but also of inexplicable loyalty; that they enjoy an occasional beating at the hands of their men; that they are unforgiving and without charity to other members of their own sex; that they lose keys and other small useful articles with maddening regularity but are quite capable of finding things invisible to men; that they use their sexuality with cold calculation to achieve their inscrutable ends, etc., etc. In no other writer in the world do pejorative stereotypes of women appear with greater frequency and on more levels, from the most trivial to the most profound; had Faulkner dared treat in such terms any racial minority, his books would have been banned in every enlightened school in the country. They reflect, however, a body of prejudice so deeply ingrained in Americans that even hysterically rendered it seems too familiar to be shocking.

Until his very latest books, Faulkner has treated with respect only females, white ladies or colored women, past the menopause. The elderly maiden or widowed aunt is the sole female figure in his fiction exempt from travesty and contempt. Up to the very verge of her climacteric, woman seems to Faulkner capable of the most shameless concupiscence, like Miss Burden in *Light in August,* cowering naked in the garden of the decaying house waiting to be captured and possessed in an obscene game of hide-and-seek. Faulkner sometimes gives the impression of the village misogynist swapping yarns with the boys at the bar in order to reveal a truth about women which shocks even himself. Like old Varner in *The Hamlet,* he keeps assuring his readers that he "cheerfully and robustly and undeviatingly" declines to accept "any such theory as female chastity other than as a myth to hoodwink young husbands. . . ." But there is little robust or cheerful about his attitudes, however undeviatingly he may assert them; he is less like Varner fundamentally

From *Love and Death in the American Novel* by Leslie A. Fiedler (New York: Criterion Books, 1960), pp. 309-15.

than like Hightower, the scared and stinking refugee from life in *Light in August,* who cries out in despair that "the husband of a mother, whether he be the father or not is already a cuckold . . . what woman, has ever suffered from any brute as men have suffered from good women?"

Pubescent or nubile women, for Faulkner, fall into two classes, roughly corresponding to those of Hemingway, though for the former both are terrifying: great, sluggish, mindless daughters of peasants, whose fertility and allure are scarcely distinguishable from those of a beast in heat; and the febrile, almost fleshless but sexually insatiable daughters of the aristocracy. Not the women he observes but those he dreams inhabit Faulkner's novels, myths of masculine protest: the peasant wench as earth goddess (Lena Grove in *Light in August,* Dewy Dell in *As I Lay Dying,* Eula Varner in *The Hamlet*), or the coed as nymphomaniac Venus (Cecily of *Soldiers' Pay,* Patricia in *Mosquitoes,* Temple Drake in *Sanctuary*). Their very names tend toward allegory, "Dewy Dell," for instance, suggesting both a natural setting and woman's sex, her sex as a fact of nature, while "Temple Drake" evokes both a ruined sanctuary and the sense of an unnatural usurpation: woman become a sexual aggressor—more drake than duck.

Unlike the natural women of Hemingway, Faulkner's dewiest dells turn out to be destroyers rather than redeemers, quicksands disguised as sacred groves. In his portrayal of Lena Grove, he relents for once into something like admiration; but his Eula Varner is more typical. Faulkner begins by describing Eula, the goddess who presides over the revels of *The Hamlet* and is married off in the end to its Devil, Flem Snopes, in terms of a pagan dithyramb to Aphrodite: "Her entire appearance suggested some symbology out of the old Dionysic Times, honey in sunlight and bursting grapes, the writhen bleeding of the crushed fecundated vine beneath the hard rapacious trampling goat-hoof." What begins as a pre-Christian eulogy to the inarticulate manifestation of sheer fertility imperceptibly slips over into a puritan cry of distress and distaste before unredeemed, burgeoning life.

When Faulkner abandons mythology for more direct physical description, his uneasiness before Eula's languor and inert lusciousness is even more clearly betrayed. "She simply did not move at all of her own volition, save to and from the table and to and from bed. She was late in learning to walk. . . . She remained in it [her perambulator] long after she had grown too large to straighten her legs out. . . . She did nothing. She might as well have been a foetus." If she is a foetus, however, Eula is an almost intolerably alluring one, a foetus-vampire, as it were; for hanging sluggishly in her mother's arms, she seems, Faulkner writes, even at the age of five or six, an "indisputably female burden like a bizarre and chaperoned Sabine rape." And after she begins to walk to school, men and boys gape, whistle, and howl in the unquenchable anguish and joy of pure desire. It is an absurd conceit, hysterical, a little mad—tolerable only because Faulkner so obviously believes in it, believes in the terror of mere inert female flesh not as a fact of life but as an article of faith!

Just as his Eula figures are all motionless, quivering, mammalian softness, Faulkner's Temple figures are sheer motion, a blur of dancing legs and wind-blown hair in a speeding car: "sexless yet somehow troubling." It is the assertion of femaleness which upsets him in Eula Varner; and it is its denial which disturbs him in Temple Drake. Temple is disconcertingly almost a man, almost phallic; and, indeed, at the moment of her rape by Popeye, it is difficult to tell which one is the phallus bearer, to whom the bloody corncob really belongs. "Then I thought about being a man," Temple says later, "and as soon as I thought it, it happened. . . . It made a kind of plopping sound, like blowing a little rubber tube wrong-side outward. . . . I could feel it, and I lay right still to keep from laughing about how surprised he was going to be. . . ." In *Sanctuary,* Faulkner's revulsion from woman's betrayal of her traditionally submissive role reaches so shrill a pitch that, in simple self-defense, he has felt it necessary to disavow that novel as a pot-boiler; yet it is obviously written in earnest though at white heat, a nightmare directly transcribed. Fortunately, it is not quite convincing enough to be unbearable, though it possesses enough hallucinatory vividness to give it the baleful appeal of a Dickensian or Dostoevskian grotesque. *Sanctuary* is, on the one hand, the darkest of all Faulkner's books, a brutal protest to the quality of American life written in the pit of the Great Depression; but on the other hand, it is the dirtiest of all the dirty jokes exchanged among men only at the expense of the abdicating Anglo-Saxon Virgin.

Temple is not only a lady, but the very image of all those Fair Ladies whose fall or resistance had been the central subject of genteel literature ever since *Charlotte Temple* was published in the United States. That her name is an inversion of that of the protypical American heroine is, perhaps, only an accident, one of the more satisfactory jokes of history; and certainly Faulkner did not know that the original of Maggie Verver was Henry James's cousin Minny Temple, whose frailness, white skin, and red hair also distinguish Temple Drake. The title of his book, however, makes it clear that Faulkner is fully aware that he is dealing not with a mere change in mores but with the desecration of a cult object. Out of the "high delicate head" of Faulkner's Temple, at any rate, look eyes which are "cool, predatory and discreet," but their discretion is belied by the "bold painted mouth." She fools no one; the wife of a gangster into whose hideout she has stumbled sees immediately that though Temple, like her illustrious prototypes, is still the Girl on the Run, she no longer means to run quite fast enough to get away. And even Gowan Stevens, Temple's escort and male opposite number, is not too drunk to understand what she really wants, though drunk enough not to be able to take advantage of his knowledge. "Don't think I don't see your name where it's written on that lavatory wall!" he tells her in impotent spite. It is the final degradation; the holy name on the lavatory wall!

Before Faulkner is through, we have been compelled to watch the ex-snow maiden, the former golden girl, not only raped (which is nothing new, of course, since she was born being raped, was Clarissa before she was Maggie Verver), but begging to be had, whimpering for the consummation she had once fled in terror. Beside Temple, pleading with Red, brutal thug and stud, to satisfy her, even Daisy Buchanan seems in retrospect a quasi-lady, Brett not really a bitch at all. Western literature before the coming of Sentimentalism is rich in images of destructive women—Thaïs and Cleopatra and Lilith herself; but Temple is more than a recrudescence of that rejected orthodox archetype. She represents a lust of the nerves rather than of the flesh, a *programmatic* concupiscence entered upon as a declaration of independence, is in short a queasy male image of the flapper—the New Woman of the 1920s. What Fayaway symbolizes to Melville in *Typee* or Trudy to Hemingway in "Fathers and Sons," Red represents to Temple: sexuality detached from responsibility, impulse without mind. In Faulkner's eyes, the yearning of the male for such satisfactions is poetry, but the equal and opposite yearning of the female is horror—a desecration and a travesty. Not content to be violated, the woman becomes the violator and Faulkner responds with nausea:

> He came toward her. She did not move. Her eyes began to grow darker and darker, lifting into her skull above a half-moon of white, without a focus, with the blank rigidity of a statue's eyes. She began to say Ah-ah-ah-ah in an expiring voice, her body arching slowly backward as though forced by an exquisite torture. When he touched her she sprang like a bow, hurling herself upon him, her mouth gaped and ugly like that of a dying fish as she writhed her loins against him. . . . With her hips grinding against him, her mouth gaping in straining protrusion, bloodless, she began to speak. "Let's hurry. Anywhere. . . . Come on. What're you waiting for?" She strained her mouth toward him, dragging his head down, making a whimpering moan. . . . "Please. Please. Please. Please. You've got to. I'm on fire, I tell you."

Beyond this it is impossible to go. It is the ultimate desecration, the total denial of the archetype of the ethereal virgin, in which the Fair Maiden becomes the rapist. Not even the Marquis de Sade dreamed so utter a travesty of sentimental clichés; in fact, he depends for his effects precisely on such clichés, assumes with his readers the reluctance, the shamefaced chastity of the Pure Maiden. It is, indeed, her conviction, to which he subscribes, that the sex act itself is an assault against woman which makes sadism possible. To be sure, de Sade's Pure Maiden, Justine, possesses like the girl in the fairy tale a wicked sister, Juliette, who lives by exploiting her sex in a struggle for power; but Temple is good and wicked sister at once, Justine *as* Juliette, Hilda as Miriam. Her invention marks the final confusion of Dark Lady and Fair—or more precisely, the revelation that the blond virgin is only a mask of the insatiable brunette.

Most recently, Faulkner seems to have repented of his many blasphemies against woman and to have committed himself to redeeming one by one all his anti-virgins; but his attempts at redemption somehow do not touch the level of acceptance reached by his original travesties. In *Requiem for a Nun,* he portrays Temple as married to Gowan Stevens, who once read her name on the lavatory wall, and a mother. Insanely burning once more for a new Red, she is not permitted to abase herself again, but is redeemed by the self-sacrifice of a Negro girl, and is left at the play's end aching with a higher lust for religious belief, about to follow her husband home. In *The Town,* Faulkner carries Eula's refurbishing even further than he had Temple's, actually rewriting Eula's past history as he pretends to recapitulate it, and turning her into the very model of female courage and endurance. This time the former avatar of female corruption herself performs the act of self-sacrifice, dies to assure an honorable future for her daughter—an innocent young girl, who is left at the novel's end advancing, wide-eyed and pure, on Greenwich Village! The epitaph inscribed on Eula's grave by her impotent husband is, we are asked to believe, truer than that husband can guess or any decent citizen is prepared to grant:

EULA VARNER SNOPES
1889 1927

A Virtuous Wife is a Crown to her Husband
Her Children Rise and Call Her Blessed

And even this is not the end! In "The Long Hot Summer," a film written by Faulkner himself, Eula is de-mythicized as well as redeemed: made into the customary Hollywood image of the sexy but sincere young wife, who begins wriggling like a taken fish in the arms of her new husband, while the boys wolf-call and wail in the stifling dusk. In the end, however, she helps to win that husband from weakness to strength, returns to his arms and legitimate bliss, when he has proved himself a true son to his father and a good citizen! Eula and Temple alike fade into the stereotype of the Good Bad Girl, who in turn gives birth to the sweet young thing, and the Protestant Virgin is restored to her shrine; but it makes no difference. Faulkner's art fails him when he turns from nausea and despair to sentimentality and maudlin pity; and even the popular mind rejects his attempts at converting his achetypes into the stereotypes of market-place culture.

Clifton Fadiman

One may sum up both substance and style by saying that every person in *Absalom, Absalom!* comes to no good end, and they all take a hell of a time coming even that far. . . . Thomas Sutpen is a monomaniac, known familiarly to the other characters as The Demon. It is never quite clear what makes him so villainous, except that he has a habit of engaging in gouge-as-gouge-can fights with Negroes, and has the odd power of scaring ladies first into marrying him and then into conniption fits. However, he's the fellow you're supposed to shudder at, and if you understand Mr. Faulkner, you'll shudder. If you don't, I guess you just won't. The Demon's second wife, Ellen Coldfield, gives birth to two children, Henry and Judith, goes dotty, and dies after a while. Her younger sister, Rosa is insulted by The Demon and also goes dotty, though it takes her much longer to die. The father of Rosa and Ellen goes nuts when the Civil War arrives, nails himself up in a garret, and perseveringly starves himself to death. Now, young Henry, upon finding out that his best friend, Charles Bon, engaged to be married to his sister Judith, is (a) his half-brother and (b) part Negro, also goes dotty in a complicated way, and finally shoots Charles dead. By the end of the story Henry has been reduced to straight, simple idiocy and is kept shut up in the attic. Judith, after some years passed in a vacant-eyed trance, passes out as a result of smallpox, a death so natural as to strike a rather jarring note. There is also Clytemnestra Sutpen, daughter of Thomas Sutpen (that's dat Ole Demon Sutpen) and a Negro slave. Clytie sets fire to herself and the idiot boy Henry, and so finishes her career in a fine blaze of pyromaniacal lunacy. . . .

The Joneses furnish the nearest thing to comic relief in the book. Now, if you'll think back a few lunatics or so, you will remember Charles Bon, preserved from incest and miscegenation by Henry Sutpen's fraternal bullet. Charles had an octoroon mistress, name and mental condition unrecorded, by whom he engendered the boy Charles Etienne. Charles Etienne, realizing that he is a few thirty-seconds Negro, promptly runs amuck. He dies rather dully, of smallpox, but not before he has begotten, with the assistance of a full-blooded Negress, a son Jim. Jim is the real McCoy, a legitimate idiot. (I mean one specifically so called by Mr. Faulkner.) At the end of the book, he is the only living descendant of the accursed Sutpens, which shows you what can happen to a family once they have committed themselves to Mr. Faulkner's tender care. . . .

This cheerful little fable is filtered through the medium of a style peculiar to Mr. Faulkner. It seems peculiar to me, too. First, we have

Condensed from "Faulkner, Extra-Special, Double-Distilled" by Clifton Fadiman, pp. 78-80. From *The New Yorker,* October 31, 1936.

the Non-Stop or Life Sentence. The first two and a half pages of *Absalom, Absalom!* consist of seven sentences, composed of 123, 155, 9 (something wrong here), 146, 66, 93, and 135 words respectively. Average: 104. To penetrate Mr. Faulkner's sentences is like hacking your way through a jungle. The path closes up at once behind you, and in no time at all you find yourself entangled in a luxuriant mass of modifiers, qualifications, relative clauses, parenthetical phrases, interjected matter, recapitulations, and other indications of a Great Style. All of Mr. Faulkner's shuddery inventions pale in horrendousness before the mere notion of parsing him.

After the Life Sentence comes the Far Fetch, or Hypertrope. Very few things in the book remain themselves. Each one reminds Mr. Faulkner of something else. "Her legs hung . . . clear of the floor with that air of impotent and static rage like children's feet." See it? No? Join me at the foot of the class, where you belong.

Then we have what may be called Anti-Narrative, a set of complex devices used to keep the story from being told. Mr. Faulkner is very clever at this. He gets quite an interesting effect, for example, by tearing the Sutpen chronicle into pieces, as if a mad child were to go to work on it with a pair of shears, and then having each of the jagged divisions narrated by a different personage: the author, Rosa, Quentin, Quentin's father, Quentin's grandfather. All these people do a neat job of mixing up the time sequences, delaying climaxes, confusing the reader, and otherwise enabling Mr. Faulkner to demonstrate that as a technician he has Joyce and Proust punch-drunk. I should add that everybody talks the same language, a kind of Dixie Gongorism, very formal, allusive, cryptic. Apparently the entire population of Jefferson, Mississippi, consists of rhetoricians who would blench at the sight of a simple declarative sentence. . . .

Seriously, I do not know what to say of this book except that it seems to point to the final blowup of what was once a remarkable, if minor, talent.

Carvell Collins

Few critics are likely to think a book good because its author says it is, but many of them do not hold to this attitude in reverse when they judge *Sanctuary*. They damn it as inartistic and immoral because its author suggested it was so in the preface he wrote for the Modern Library edition of 1932, the year following the novel's shocking and remunerative first appearance. . . .

One evening in the mid-1920s Faulkner and a woman companion were

Condensed from "A Note on *Sanctuary*" by Carvell Collins. From *Harvard Advocate*, Vol. 135. No. 2 (Nov. 1951), p. 16. © (November 1951).

in a night club. A girl who at present may be identified as N. came across the room, sat down at their table, and in half an hour told them an interesting part of her autobiography. A few years later it became the core of *Sanctuary*.

N. had associated for a time with a gangster who had many of the characteristics of the gangster in the novel, the similarity later even going the odd extreme of nature's imitating art, because eight months after the book appeared the real gangster killed himself, though his method was less subtle than that used by his fictional counterpart. The real gangster was impotent and in his relations with women he was given to substitutions for his impotence. He did keep a girl for a time at a brothel in what might be called semi-privacy. And in the real, perverted rape the implement was so fantastically unnatural that compared to it the implement used by the fictional gangster in the most notorious episode of the novel seems well along the way toward normalcy. (Students of the psychology of association can be expected to make something of the fact that N. was born and reared in a village named Cobbtown.) For some years Faulkner thought on N.'s autobiography and the related events which he knew of from other sources. And during that period, according to his associates, he tried to write the story in a number of ways. . . .

But whatever the reasons for his preface . . . the point is that Faulkner did not think up a series of fictional events to startle the public gratuitously. He had brooded over specific real events for some time, with disgust for what they represented and with what might be called shocked awe for the real counterpart of Temple Drake (as Faulkner told a friend, *Sanctuary* was partly written to show that women can survive almost anything). In dealing with the startling real events Faulkner by no means exaggerated them for cheap effect—quite to the contrary, he reduced their horror, besides doing the more important work of giving them form of a high order.

Pierre Emmanuel

The powerful obscurity of genius, which is the privilege of a few great creators—no matter how lucid they may be—has been granted to Faulkner, and when I first read him, I was literally overwhelmed with a feeling of primitive evidence that made my lack of immediate understanding quite unimportant and perhaps more promising than a clear perception of the book. Faulkner's profundity does not reveal itself at the first glimpse: it has many depths of silence, unconscious energies, long-forgotten events. It contrasts with the two-dimensional space of

Permission from "Faulkner and the Sense of Sin" by Pierre Emmanuel. From *Harvard Advocate,* Vol. 135, No. 2 (Nov. 1951), p. 20.

modern psychology, even helped by the so-called discoveries of psychoanalysis; it is indeed a religious relation of Faulkner's characters with a past going far beyond their past, with a particular setting of universal myths reshaped in a family mold, so that one does not know the difference between the family taken in itself and the myths living in it and growing out of its own life. Fate as it appears in Faulkner is not a blind force but an organic reality: our different levels of responsibility in our destiny and other people's are linked together by way of permanent exchange, and yet we do not apprehend the whole of them, only the most superficial ones—our apparent responsibility being sometimes the wrong mask of our action. Contrary to the modern hero, who most of the time is uprooted and meaningless except for people of his kind, coming from nowhere and going to nowhere, Faulkner's heroes are deeply related, but their tragedy is to remain partly unconscious of it. There is always a part of the most inner world that escapes him who lives in it—and it is precisely the part which makes him live. A theologian would call that situation a state of sin; it seems to me that Faulkner is one of the rare novelists in our time for which sin is a basic and not only casual reality. Not sin *à la Mauriac,* transgression of moral laws, but original sin, human condition itself, making the sons their fathers' fathers, as Kierkegaard so admirably showed it. This explains, I think, what Faulkner does with time. The process of time as we conceive it, from past to future through present, is a mere appearance, a delusion. Real time has nothing to do with those categories: it is a simultaneous though unconscious present. Something like God's eye, and Faulkner's God is a terrible one, all the more because He is imminent and takes the figure of fate.

Eudora Welty

Faulkner's veracity and accuracy about the world around keeps the comic thread from ever being lost or fouled, but that's a simple part of the matter. The complicated and intricate thing is that his stories aren't decked out in humor, but the humor is born in them, as much their blood and bones as the passion and poetry. Put one of his stories into a single factual statement and it's pure outrage—so would life be—too terrifying, too probable, and too symbolic too, too funny to bear. There has to be the story, to bear it—wherein that statement, conjured up and implied and demonstrated, not said or the sky would fall on our heads, is yet the living source of his comedy—and a good part of that comedy's adjoining terror, of course.

From "In Yoknapatawpha" by Eudora Welty. From *Hudson Review,* Vol. 1, No. 4 (Winter 1949), p. 597.

R. W. Flint

Faulkner on home ground has a wonderfully quizzical and impassive sense of pathos. Episodes like Cash Bundren's construction of the coffin in *As I Lay Dying,* or the failure of Theophilus McCaslin in "The Bear" to make anything at all out of young Percival Brownlee, the slave, evoke a common-sense world with great verve and economy. The seething climate of Yoknapatawpha is sweetened and set in perspective. If Mr. Podhoretz were right in thinking that obsession is the *only* motor in Faulkner's people, this pathos would be quite absent. The middle class may be dead set against obsession, but it would understand itself a good deal better if it could manage to read Faulkner's best novels with some of the affection with which they were written.

Marcel Aymé

Whether it be in reading *The Sound and the Fury, Sanctuary,* or *Light in August,* it seems that we get caught in a nightmare which is now and then penetrated by a furtive and sinister glimmer of God, reflected in the murky waters of a deserted swamp. There is so much gloom, incurable misery, horror, and distress in this divine reflection, that the first reaction of any sane-minded person should be to cry, "Let us hope with all our strength that God doesn't exist, that the novelist has been mocking us, for otherwise, this is too ghastly." At least that would be the reaction of a Christian who does not relish suffering—and there are many such in France.

In this country, when a Catholic writer like François Mauriac, for instance, paints a despairing picture of human passions, it is because the characters depicted have not been visited by divine grace that the colors are dark and somber; in actual fact, God is generally absent from his works. In Faulkner's novels, on the contrary, the more brutal, cruel, bloodthirsty, lusty, and wrathful the characters are, the more tangible is the presence of God. His universe is peopled mostly with crude, sometimes monstrous, beings; describing them, we hesitate between *degenerate* and *primitive;* and yet, although plunged in the human substance of fate, Benjy and Popeye, the idiot and the puny, are possessed by a superhuman force which we would say is that of God.

From "What Price Glory?" by R. W. Flint. From *Hudson Review,* Vol. XII, No. 4 (Winter 1955), p. 604.

From "What French Readers Find in William Faulkner's Fiction," *New York Times Book Review,* December 17, 1950, p. 4.

It is strange that a man, in this case a novelist, should believe himself obliged to seek God on the lowest level, starting from the basest instincts, the most sordid dramas and unhealthy embraces, as if he were trying to concoct a visceral emulsion. Nevertheless, it is this God, who seems so at ease in struggles and fights, in drunken orgies, in blood, filth, and corn cobs, who is the veritable God of the Bible, both wrathful and vindictive.

As for a jealous God—violent and inexorable, storing up hate—Who is ever-present in the work of William Faulkner, He has few adepts here in France. In spite of the political events of the last ten years, that aspect of divinity is no longer current, and even Christians (I mean by that, practicing Christians) reject such an image quite vigorously. We are not capable, if we ever were, of understanding the sort of fury which animates William Faulkner against sin, for we accept ourselves, somewhat restlessly, for what we are. Whilst on the one hand, Faulkner's puritanism has retained a savage religiousness, French Christianity on the other hand has become merely social, thus confusing itself pathetically with one of its incidental objectives.

John Crowe Ransom

The books of this writer are unequal, and the style is less than consistently sustained. He is therefore not Ben Jonson, he is not even the indefatigable Shakespeare, he is John Webster—if we look for his equivalent among the Elizabethan writers whom he resembles in the force of his horror, as in the rightness of his sense of human goodness, as in the gift of a language which is generally adequate to the effects intended.

I would stand on the three early books which I have named as sufficient evidence of the narrative power and the detailed poetry of his creations. And since they are fictions, I suppose some of his analogues in this field need to be named. I think of Dostoevsky, and Melville, and D. H. Lawrence. Faulkner could never have done the like of *The Brothers Karamazov,* however; he may know the depths of the human soul, but he has not had the advantage of the society of his literary peers discussing the realistic novel and performing it, nor that of intellectuals with their formidable dialectic, permitting him to give to his creation so vast and controlled a spread as Dostoevsky did. He could not have done *Moby Dick,* and that is aside from the matter of whether he would quite have wished to do it; there is an encyclopedic virtuosity there, and surely at some of the great climaxes there is an academicism in the style, whereas Faulkner is not a man of great learning, and certainly his acquaintance with the academy did not adulterate the natural directness of his style. His power of language is brilliant and fitful like Lawrence's,

From "William Faulkner: An Impression" by John Crowe Ransom. From *Harvard Advocate,* Vol. 135, No. 2 (Nov. 1951), p. 17.

but he is never negative (it is not in him to labor at hateful small prose); and his positive is simple and passionate (or Elizabethan), not complicated with modern theory. I am afraid these comparisons are much too quick and crude, since they seem absurd as soon as I read them; and I think the truth must be, really, that he is not quite like any other writer whom I can think of. Perhaps they will serve to remark at least the quality of those great writers with whom, if anybody, he seems to keep company best.

I am content to say, in the last resort, that there are imperfections in his work both large and small to the extent almost of whole books sometimes, and perhaps of passages and sentences in most of the books. But his perfections are wonderful and well sustained, and without exact precedent anywhere. If he were deliberately a "perfectionist," as are some highly prepared and articulate artists, his great gift might have been paralyzed, or to some extent inhibited. To regard him is to contemplate the common human behaviors under the aspect of magnificence. And I believe we are struck with shame when we are led to think about the poverty of our own perception of life. We feel that our education, our cultural habit, has immunized us from reality, and from passion. It is for the sense that he recovers us from an immense torpor that we are so much in his debt.

Albert Camus

He [Faulkner] is, in my opinion, your greatest writer; the only one, it seems to me, whose place is in your great literary tradition of the nineteenth century, and one of the rare creators of the West. . . . *Sanctuary* and *Pylon* are masterpieces.

From a letter in the *Harvard Advocate,* Vol. 135, No. 2 (Nov. 1951), p. 21, by Albert Camus.

Appendix 2

The Genealogies

The evidence for the birth dates of Caddy and her brothers comes from various sources. In *Absalom, Absalom!* (p. 294) we learn that in January 1910 Shreve was nineteen and Quentin Compson some months older. This means that Quentin was born in 1890 and perhaps in the earlier or middle part of the year. In the appendix that Faulkner furnished for the Modern Library edition of *Absalom, Absalom!,* he says that Quentin was born in 1891, but as the appendix has a number of other errors, I prefer to follow the text of the novel.

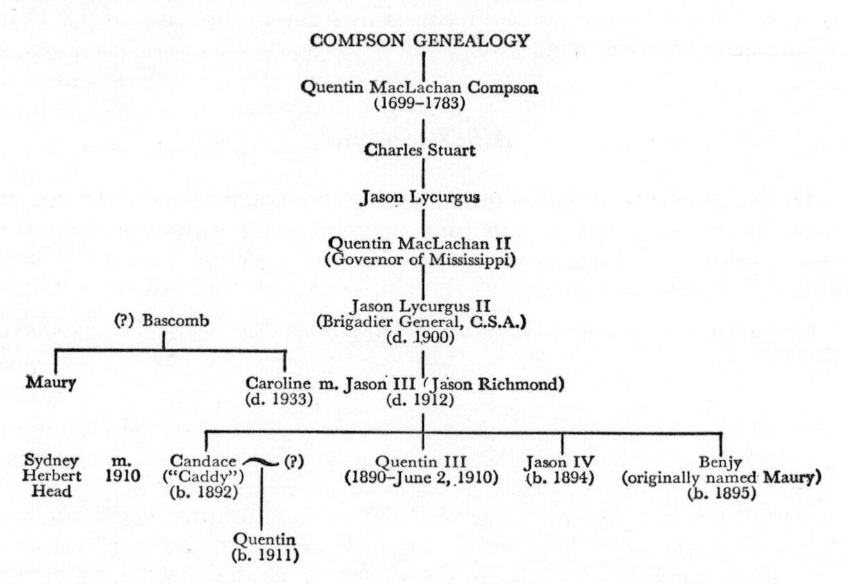

Note: The symbol ~ is used to indicate a union which resulted in an illegitimate birth.

In the story "That Evening Sun," Quentin tells us that he was the oldest: "I was nine and Caddy was seven and Jason was five" (p. 294).

Reprinted with permission from *William Faulkner: The Yoknapatawpha Country,* by Cleanth Brooks (Yale University Press, 1963).

This dating would make Caddy's birth year 1892, and the date agrees with what we are told in the appendix to the Compson genealogy. Jason, then, would have been born in about 1894, and since we are told in the Compson genealogy that Benjy was thirty-three-years old in 1928, his birth year should be 1895. It is curious that in "That Evening Sun," Benjy is never mentioned.

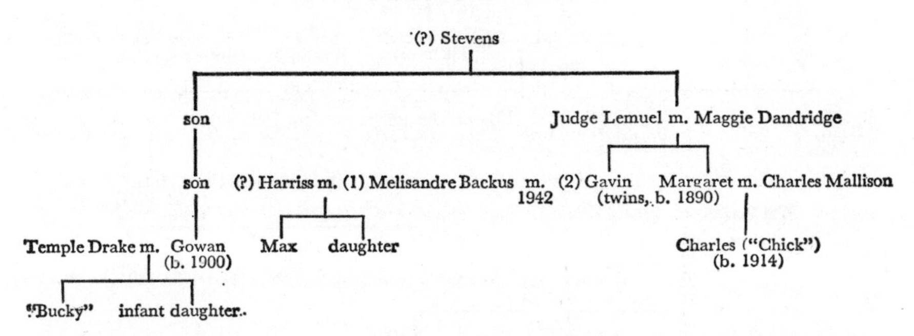

According to *Knight's Gambit,* Gavin Stevens was fifty years old in 1939, which would make his birth year 1889. But in *The Mansion* we are told that he was a year younger than Eula Varner Snopes, and *The Town* indicates that Eula was born in 1889. Accordingly, I have dated Gavin's birth as 1890.

Faulkner seems to have had two quite different notions about the age of Charles Mallison, Jr. *Knight's Gambit* and *Intruder in the Dust* point to his birth year as 1924, but in *The Town* it would seem to be 1915, and in *The Mansion,* 1914. On the genealogical chart I have put it down as 1914, in line with Faulkner's latest conception of the character. But I remind the reader that this date will apply only to the Charles that we see in the last two novels of Faulkner's trilogy.

It may be useful to set down here a brief chronology of Gavin Stevens' actions as a young man. (The dates are drawn from references in *The Mansion.*) Gavin was at Harvard in 1909. After he had returned to Jefferson he fell in love with Eula Varner Snopes. She offered herself to him in 1913. A few months later, early in the spring of 1914, Gavin went to Heidelberg. In 1915-16 he served in the American ambulance service in France as a stretcher-bearer. He returned to Jefferson in 1916, and a year later went back to France as a YMCA man. He came back to Jefferson to practice law in 1919. But it ought to be pointed out that these dates do not necessarily apply to the stories included in *Knight's Gambit,* where Gavin does not come home until 1924.

In *The Town* (p. 3) it is made plain that Chick Mallison and Gowan Stevens are second cousins, and this is the relationship that I have depicted on the genealogical chart; but in *Requiem for a Nun* (p. 127) Gavin Stevens says that Gowan is his nephew.

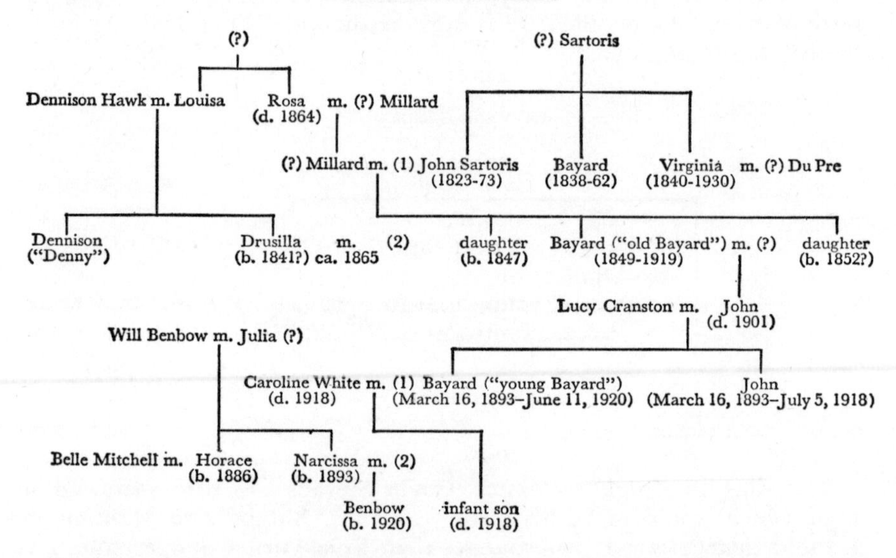

In *Sartoris* (p. 375) Colonel John Sartoris dies in 1876; in *Requiem for a Nun* (p. 238) in 1878. In *The Unvanquished* his death occurs when his son Bayard is twenty-four-years old, and therefore took place in 1873 or 1874, depending upon whether Bayard was born in 1849 or 1850.

The problem of old Bayard's age is not easy to settle. The several inconsistent references to it in *The Unvanquished* are as follows: on page 5 of *The Unvanquished* we are told that Bayard was twelve when Vicksburg fell—that is, in July 1863. On page 216 of *The Unvanquished* we are told that he was fifteen just before Christmas of 1864. On page 253 we are told that four years after his father remarried, he was twenty. All the indications are that Colonel John Sartoris married Drusilla very shortly after the war had ended, in 1865, which would make Bayard twenty-years old in 1869. Bayard was twenty-four when he was recalled in October on the occasion of his father's death. The second, third, and fourth of these references would suggest that Bayard was born in 1849, but the first of them points to a later date. If Bayard is right in saying that he was twelve-years old in July of 1863, he had to be born in 1850, and possibly was born as late as 1851. (Had Faulkner forgotten that Vicksburg fell in 1863?) In view of three other references that point to the year 1849, one is inclined to say that this was when Bayard was born.

Yet it must be pointed out that on page 271 of *The Unvanquished* we are told that Aunt Jenny came to Mississippi on a cold January day "six years ago." The year, if we are to trust *Sartoris,* was 1869. This would point to the year of Colonel Sartoris' death as 1875 or possibly 1874. On this reckoning Bayard's birth year goes up to 1850 again. The truth of the matter is that one cannot construct a chronology which will make all the references consistent with each other. Faulkner was careless or perhaps simply did not attach very much importance to exact dates—though he *was* carefully exact in indicating the day of the month and the year of the deaths of the twins John and Bayard, and Bayard's first wife, Caroline. It is not really of great consequence whether the climactic event in *The Unvanquished* took place in 1873, 1874, or, as *Sartoris* has it, 1876, or even, as in *Requiem for a Nun,* 1878. In the interests of simplicity I have decided to set down Bayard's birth date as 1849 and so adjust all the other dates keyed to it. But the reader is warned to give or take a year or two for all of them.

In "There Was a Queen" young Bayard is said to have died at the age of twenty-six rather than at twenty-seven, as indicated in the genealogical chart.

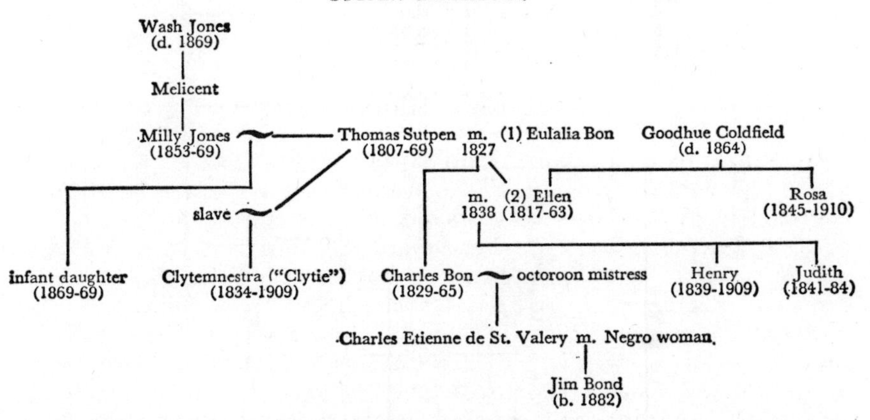

The daughter of old Lucius Quintus Carothers McCaslin and sister of Theophilus and Amodeus is not named in any of Faulkner's novels or stories, but she is called "Mary" in a manuscript genealogy in Faulkner's hand. See James B. Meriwether, *The Literary Career of William Faulkner* (Princeton: Princeton University Library, 1961), p. 31.

When Faulkner came to write *The Reivers,* he connected the Priest family with the McCaslins. He also related Ned McCaslin and Bobo Beauchamp to the McCaslins. Ned, we are told on pages 30-31, was born in the McCaslin back yard in 1860. The legend—"which had no firmer supporter than Ned himself"—was that "his mother had been the natural daughter of old Lucius Quintus Carothers himself and a Negro slave."

McCASLIN GENEALOGY

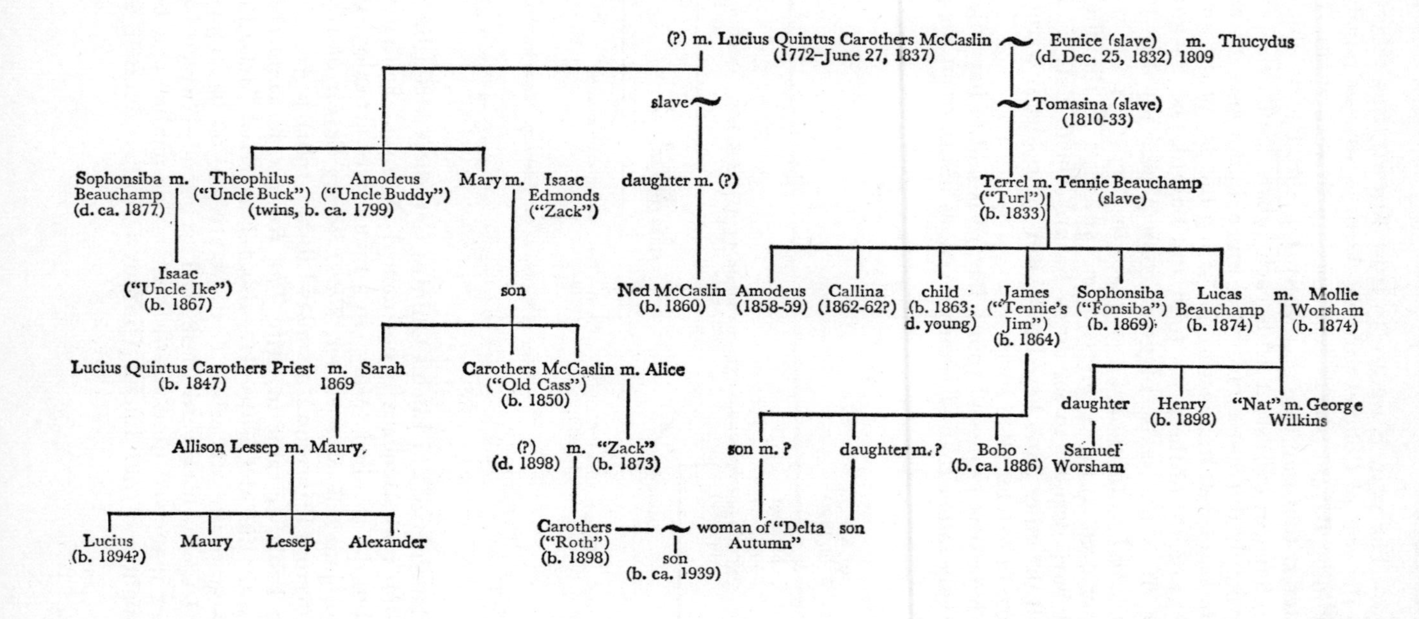

SNOPES GENEALOGY

"... they were just Snopeses, like colonies of rats or termites are just rats and termites" (*The Town*, p. 40).

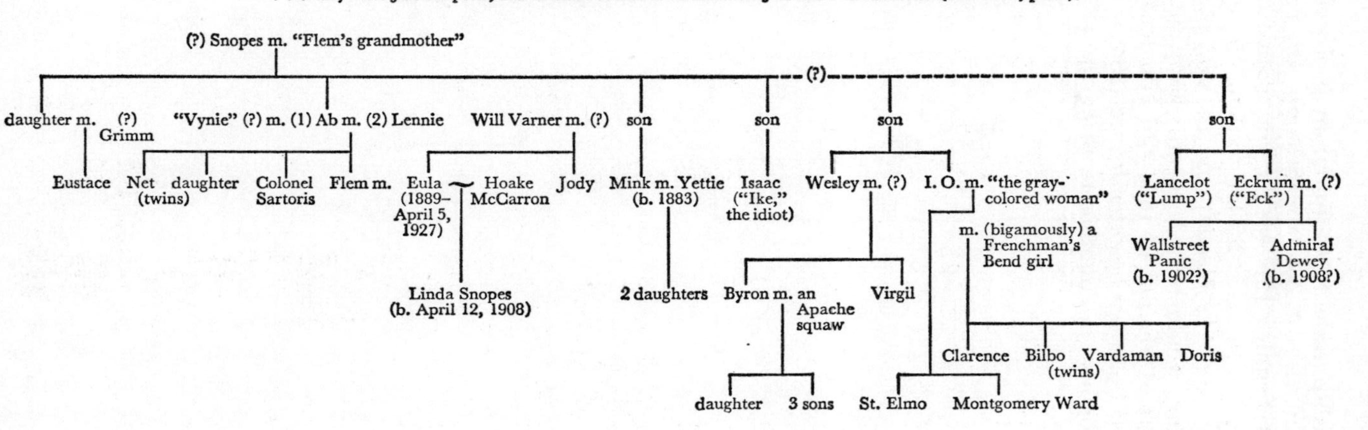

Ned's relationship to the McCaslin family is obviously an afterthought. So also is the ancestry of Bobo Beauchamp. On p. 22 of *The Reivers* we are told that Tennie's Jim was the grandfather of Bobo Beauchamp, but "grandfather" must be a slip for "father." In 1905 Bobo must have been at least 20 (see *The Reivers,* pp. 13, 229), but in 1905 Tennie's Jim, if still living, would have been only forty-one. Incidentally, since Tennie's Jim left Mississippi in 1885 and apparently never came back, one supposes that Bobo was begotten before 1885; in any case, he was left in Mississippi for his grandmother to bring up (*The Reivers,* p. 229).

Appendix 3

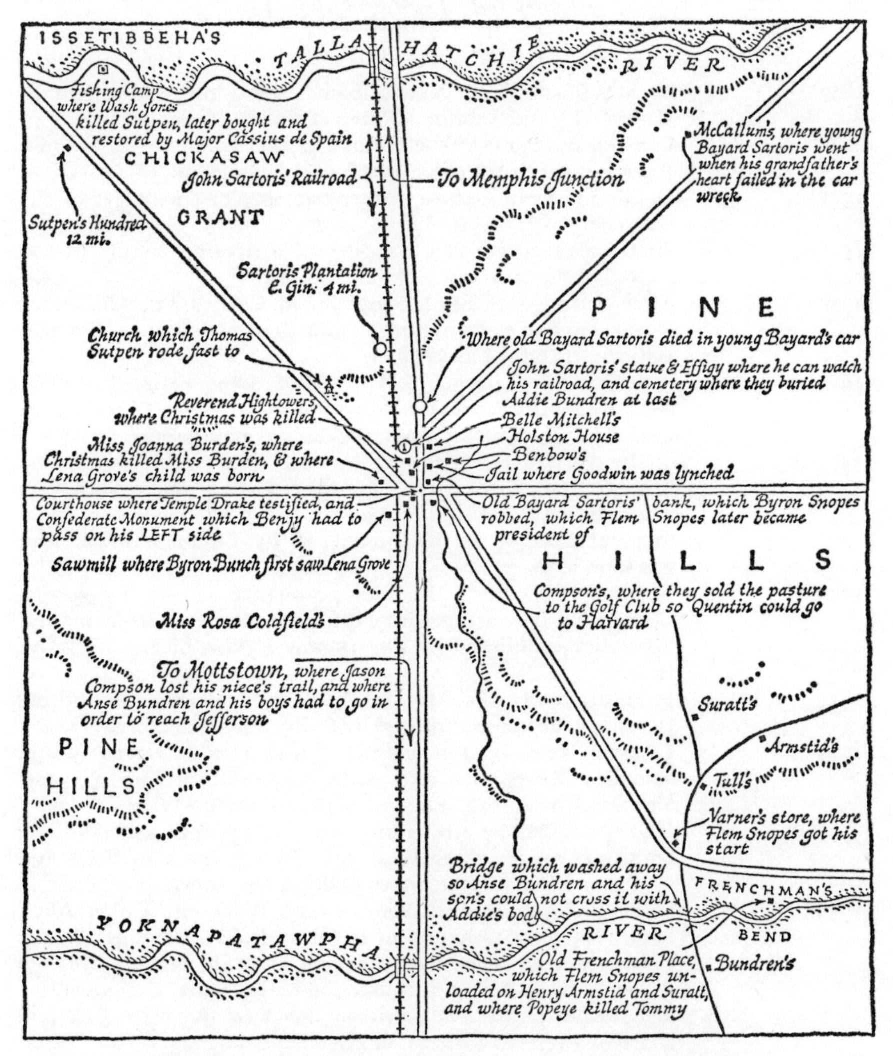

JEFFERSON, YOKNAPATAWHA COUNTY, MISSISSIPPI

Area, 2400 square miles. Population: Whites, 6,298; Negroes, 9,313.
William Faulkner, sole owner and proprietor.

(From *Absalom, Absalom!*, New York, Modern Library, Random House, 1951. By permission of the publisher.)

Chronology of Important Dates

1897	Born September 25, New Albany, Mississippi, oldest son of Murry C. and Maud Butler Falkner; great-grandson of Colonel William Cuthbert Falkner, the prototype of Colonel John Sartoris of *Sartoris* and *The Unvanquished.*
1902	Family moves to Oxford; father later business manager of the University of Mississippi.
1916-17	First published work, a drawing of a dancing couple in the annual of the University of Mississippi.
1918	After marriage of Estelle Oldham to Cornell Franklin, joins Royal Air Force; training as cadet pilot at Toronto, Canada. Returns to Oxford, December.
1919	First published poem, "L'Apres-Midi d'une Faune," in *The New Republic,* August 6. First published story, "Landing in Luck," in *The Mississippian,* the campus newspaper.
1919-20	Student at University. Begins work on "The Marble Faun."
1920	Resigns from University, November. Goes to New York City where he stays with Stark Young; clerks in Doubleday Bookshop, at Lord & Taylors, managed by Elizabeth Prall, who was soon to marry Sherwood Anderson.
1921	Returns to Oxford. Becomes postmaster at the University. Continuing friendship with Phil Stone. Becomes scout master.
1922	First poem published in *The Double Dealer,* of New Orleans, June.
1924	Publication of *The Marble Faun,* by Four Seas Publishing Company, Boston, subsidized by Phil Stone, December.
1925	Lives in New Orleans, associated with *Double Dealer* group, including Roard Bradford, Lyle Saxon, Oliver LaFarge, and Sherwood Anderson. Flies with barnstormers. Writes *Soldiers' Pay,* sponsored by Anderson. Sails for Europe, with William Spratling, on freighter West *Ivis,* July 7. Stays in Paris and works on "Elmer." Returns to Oxford, December.
1926	*Soldiers' Pay* published, February 25. Work on "Father Abraham," apparently chapter of novel to deal with Snopes family. Publication of *Sherwood Anderson & Other Famous Creoles,* drawings by Spratling, introduction by Faulkner, December.
1927	*Mosquitoes* published, April 30. *Flags in the Dust* (later, in shortened version *Sartoris*) finished September 29.
1928	*The Sound and the Fury* finished in New York, October. Refused by Harcourt Brace.
1929	*The Sound and the Fury* accepted by Jonathan Cape and Harrison Smith, January. *Sartoris* published, January 31. Marriage to Estelle Oldham, June 20. Honeymoon at Pascagoula, Mississippi; correction of proofs of *The Sound and the Fury.* Settles in Oxford. Begins *As I Lay Dying* while working night-

shift in power plant of University. *The Sound and the Fury* published October 7, with good critical reception but poor sale.

1930 Begins sale of accumulated stories. Buys Rowan Oak. *As I Lay Dying* published, October 6. Begins hunting again.

1931 *Sanctuary,* revised version, published, February 9. Change in reputation in America—sadism, violence, decadence. *These Thirteen* published, September 21. Publication of stories and Maurice Coindreau's essay in *La Nouvelle Revue Française* begins reputation in France. Stay in New York City.

1932 *Light in August* finished in Oxford, February 19. First Hollywood stay with MGM begins May 10. *Light in August* published, October 6.

1933 *A Green Bough* published, April 20. *Today We Live,* moving picture based on Faulkner's story "Turnabout," with scenario by him, released April 28. *Story of Temple Drake* released May 12. Birth of Jill, June 24. Purchase of first plane.

1934 Flight to New Orleans for dedication of Shushan Airport, February. Background for *Pylon. Dr. Martino* published, April 16.

1935 *Pylon* published, March 25. Brother Dean Swift killed in Faulkner's Waco, barnstorming, November 10. Return to Hollywood. Work on *Absalom, Absalom!*

1936 *Absalom, Absalom!* published, October 26.

1938 *The Unvanquished* published, February 15. Purchases farm.

1939 *The Wild Palms* published, January 19. Elected to National Institute of Arts and Letters.

1940 *The Hamlet* published, April 1.

1942 Return to Hollywood on long contract with poor terms. Screen credits for Hemingway's *To Have and to Have Not* and Raymond Chandler's *The Big Sleep. Go Down, Moses* published, May 11.

1946 Publication of *The Portable Faulkner,* edited by Malcolm Cowley, April 29.

1948 Work on *A Fable* suspended, *Intruder in the Dust* begun, January. *Intruder* published, September 27. Better sale than any previous book (18,000 copies). Elected to American Academy of Arts and Letters.

1949 *Knight's Gambit* published, November 27.

1950 *Collected Stories* published, August 2. Howell's Medal for Fiction, of The American Academy, May. Nobel Prize announced, November.

1951 National Book Award for *Collected Stories,* March. *Requiem for a Nun* published, September 27. Legion of Honor, October.

1953 Commencement Address at Pine Manor College; Jill's graduation.

1954 International Writers' Conference, Sao Paulo, Brazil. *A Fable* published, August 2. Marriage of Jill, August 21.

1955 National Book Award for *A Fable,* March; Pulitzer Prize, May.

	Series of letters on segregation to Memphis *Commercial Appeal.* First production of play *Requiem for a Nun,* in Zurich. State Department tour, Seminar at Nagano. Speech at Meeting of Southern Historical Association, on integration. *The Big Woods* published, October 14.
1956	Articles in *Life, Harpers, Ebony* on integration. *Requiem for a Nun* produced in Paris, September.
1957	Begins term as Writer in Residence at the University of Virginia. State Department trip to Greece. Receives Silber Medal of Athens Academy. Greek production of *Requiem for a Nun. The Town* published, May 1.
1958	Second period at University of Virginia, February to June.
1959	*The Mansion* published, November.
1961	State Department visit to Venezuela, April.
1962	Visit to West Point, April. Refusal of invitation to White House. *The Reivers* published, June 4. Died July 6, at Oxford. Buried July 8.
1963	*The Reivers* awarded the Pulitzer Prize.

Notes on Editor and Contributors

ROBERT PENN WARREN, the editor of this volume, teaches at Yale University. Poet, novelist, and critic, his latest books include *Wilderness, Flood, Who Speaks For The Negro?* and *Selected Poems: New and Old.*

MALCOLM COWLEY, author and editor, has written many works on American writers, including *Exile's Return, After the Genteel Tradition, The Literary Situation.*

CONRAD AIKEN, poet, critic, and novelist, has collected some of his literary criticism in *Reviewer's A B C.*

WARREN BECK teaches at Lawrence College. In addition to his study of Faulkner, *Man in Motion,* he has published many novels and short stories.

CLAUDE-EDMONDE MAGNY has written several studies on modern literature, including *L'Age du Roman Américain, Les Sandales d'Empédocle,* and *Arthur Rimbaud.*

GÜNTER BLÖCKER, journalist and critic, is the author of *Heinrich von Kleist, Kritisches Lesebuch,* and *Die Neuen Wirklichkeiten.*

JEAN POUILLON, philosopher and critic, is the author of *Temps et Roman.*

JEAN-PAUL SARTRE, philosopher and man of letters, is the author of several books of literary criticism, the most recent of which is *Saint Genet.*

MICHAEL MILLGATE teaches at the University of York, Ontario. In addition to *The Achievement of William Faulkner,* he has written on Tennyson and Fitzgerald.

LAWRANCE THOMPSON teaches at Princeton University. Among his studies of American Literature are *Fire and Ice: The Art and Thought of Robert Frost, Melville's Quarrel with God,* and *William Faulkner.*

OLGA W. VICKERY is the co-editor of *William Faulkner: Three Decades of Criticism,* in addition to her own study of Faulkner. She teaches at Purdue University.

LAWRENCE S. KUBIE, neurologist and psychiatrist, is the author of several books on psychoanalysis and psychology.

ALFRED KAZIN, critic, is the author of *On Native Grounds, A Walker in the City,* and *Contemporaries,* among other books.

JOHN L. LONGLEY, JR. teaches at the University of Virginia, and is the author of *The Tragic Mask: A Study of Faulkner's Heroes.*

HYATT H. WAGGONER has written several studies of American literature, including *William Faulkner, The Heel of Elohim,* and *Hawthorne.* He teaches at Brown University.

CLEANTH BROOKS teaches at Yale. Among his many studies are *Modern Poetry and the Tradition, The Well Wrought Urn, The Hidden God,* and *William Faulkner: The Yoknapatawpha Country.*

R. W. B. LEWIS has written on American and European literature in *The American Adam, The Picaresque Saint,* and *Trials of the Word.* He also teaches at Yale.

EDMUND WILSON, man of letters, has written many volumes of literary criticism, including *Axel's Castle, The Wound and the Bow, The Triple Thinkers,* and *Patriotic Gore.*

ELIZABETH HARDWICK, novelist and essayist, has collected some of her criticism in *A View of My Own.*

ANDREW LYTLE, novelist, teaches at the University of the South.

V. S. PRITCHETT, novelist, journalist and critic, has included some of his fiction criticism in *The Living Novel.*

NORMAN PODHORETZ is the author of *Doings and Undoings: The Fifties and After in American Writing.* He is the editor of the magazine *Commentary.*

Notes on Contributors of Notes and Comments

ANDRÉ MALRAUX, novelist, art critic, and Minister of Cultural Affairs in the government of De Gaulle.

ALLEN TATE, critic, poet, and novelist, teaches at the University of Minnesota. His volumes of criticism include *On the Limits of Poetry, The Man of Letters in the Modern World,* and *Collected Essays.*

GRAHAM GREENE, novelist and playwright, has also written on English literature in *The Lost Childhood.*

F. R. LEAVIS taught at Cambridge until his retirement a few years ago. His critical works include *Revaluation: Tradition and Development in English Poetry, The Great Tradition,* and *D. H. Lawrence, Novelist.*

MAXWELL GEISMAR, critic and historian of the novel, has written *Writers in Crisis, The Last of the Provincials, Rebels and Ancestors,* and *Henry James and the Jacobites.*

IRVING HOWE, critic and historian, teaches English at Hunter College. He is the author of *Sherwood Anderson, William Faulkner: A Critical Study, Politics and The Novel,* and *A World More Attractive.*

LESLIE FIEDLER, novelist and critic, is the author of *Love and Death in the American Novel, No! In Thunder,* and *Waiting for the End.* He teaches at the University of Buffalo.

CLIFTON FADIMAN's criticism appears in *Party of One, Any Number Can Play,* and *Enter Conversing.*

CARVELL COLLINS has edited much of Faulkner's early writing and is co-author of *Literature in the Modern World.* He teaches at Massachusetts Institute of Technology.

PIERRE EMMANUEL, French poet and essayist, has most recently published *Evangélaire.*

EUDORA WELTY, the novelist and short story writer, has also written many essays on writers and writing.

JOHN CROWE RANSOM, poet and critic, taught until his retirement at Kenyon College. Among his works of criticism are *The World's Body* and *The New Criticism.*

ALBERT CAMUS, French novelist, playwright, and philosopher.

Selected Bibliography

Interviews

Cynthia Grenier, "An Interview with William Faulkner—September 1955," *Accent* v. 16 (Summer 1956), pp. 167-177.

Frederick L. Gwynn and Joseph L. Blotner (eds.), *Faulkner in the University* (Charlottesville: University of Virginia Press, 1959).

Robert A. Jeliffe (ed), *Faulkner at Nagano* (Tokyo: Kenkyusha Ltd., 1956).

Jean Stein, "William Faulkner," *Paris Review* v. 4 (Spring, 1956).

Faulkner numbers of periodicals:

English Institute Essays 1952 (New York: Columbia University Press, 1954).

The Harvard Advocate (William Faulkner Issue) v. 135 (November, 1951).

La Revue des Lettres Modernes (William Faulkner: Configuration Critique II) v. 5 (Winter, 1958-59).

Modern Fiction Studies (William Faulkner Special Number) v. 2 (Autumn, 1956).

Critical books on Faulkner, and general studies containing essays on Faulkner

Warren Beck, *Man in Motion: Faulkner's Trilogy* (Madison: University of Wisconsin Press, 1961).

Cleanth Brooks, *William Faulkner: The Yoknapatawpha Country* (New Haven: Yale University Press, 1963).

Richard Chase, *The American Novel and Its Tradition* (Garden City: Doubleday Anchor Books, 1957).

Malcolm Cowley, *The Portable Faulkner* (New York: Viking Press, 1946).

——— *The Faulkner-Cowley File* (New York: Viking Press, 1966).

Leslie Fiedler, *Love and Death in the American Novel,* second edition revised (New York: Stein and Day, 1966).

Maxwell Geismar, *Writers in Crisis, The American Novel Between Two Wars* (Boston: Houghton Mifflin, 1942).

Frederick J. Hoffmann and Olga W. Vickery (eds.), *William Faulkner: Two Decades of Criticism* (East Lansing: Michigan State University Press, 1951).

————, *William Faulkner: Three Decades of Criticism* (East Lansing: Michigan State University Press, 1960).

Irving Howe, *William Faulkner, A Critical Study,* second edition, revised and expanded (New York: Vintage Books, 1962).

Alfred Kazin, *On Native Grounds* (New York: Harcourt Brace, 1942).

John Longley, Jr., *The Tragic Mask: A Study of Faulkner's Heroes* (Chapel Hill: University of North Carolina Press, 1963).

Claude-Edmonde Magny, *L'Age du Roman Américain* (Paris: Editions du Seuil, 1948).

Michael Millgate, *The Achievement of William Faulkner* (New York: Random House, 1965).

William Van O'Connor, *The Tangled Fire of William Faulkner* (Minneapolis: University of Minnesota Press, 1954).

Sean O'Faolain, *The Vanishing Hero: Studies in Novelists of the Twenties* (Boston: Little, Brown, 1956).

Jean Pouillon, *Temps et Roman* (Paris: Gallimard, 1946).

Jean-Paul Sartre, *Literary Essays* (New York: Philosophical Library, 1957).

Lawrance Thompson, *William Faulkner* (New York: Barnes and Noble, 1963).

Olga W. Vickery, *The Novels of William Faulkner: A Critical Interpretation* (Baton Rouge: Louisiana State University Press, 1959).

H. H. Waggoner, *William Faulkner: From Jefferson to the World* (Lexington: University of Kentucky Press, 1959).